GOING PUBLIC

Transformations in Higher Education: The Scholarship of Engagement

GOING PUBLIC

CIVIC AND COMMUNITY ENGAGEMENT

EDITED BY

Hiram E. Fitzgerald and Judy Primavera

Michigan State University Press • *East Lansing*

Michigan State University Press
East Lansing, Michigan 48823-5245

Printed and bound in the United States of America.

19 18 17 16 15 14 13   1 2 3 4 5 6 7 8 9 10

LIBRARY OF CONGRESS CATALOGING-IN-PUBLICATION DATA

Going public : civic and community engagement / edited by Hiram E. Fitzgerald
and Judy Primavera.
            pages cm
Includes bibliographical references and index.
ISBN 978-1-60917-379-1 (ebook)—ISBN 978-1-61186-089-4 (cloth : alk.paper)
1. Service learning—United States. 2. Civics—Study and teaching (Higher)—United States.
3. Education, Higher—Social aspects—United States. 4. Community and college—United States.
I. Fitzgerald, Hiram E. II. Primavera, Judy.
            LC221.G65   2013
            361.3'7—dc23

                                                    2012046614

Book design by Aptara
Cover design by Charlie Sharp, Sharp Des!gns, Lansing, MI

Visit Michigan State University Press at www.msupress.org

We dedicate this volume to two individuals who each in his own way had a profound influence on what has become known as service learning and community-based research, respectively. In so doing, their influence has directly and indirectly affected thousands of students, shaped disciplines, and made a difference in the lives of everyday folk.

John S. Duley

John Duley, now in his ninth decade and still serving, is known affectionately by colleagues across the United States as the "grandfather of service learning." While serving at Michigan State University (MSU) as professor and campus minister, Reverend Duley was instrumental in the development and implementation of the Student Tutorial Education Project (STEP), a program that utilized MSU students and faculty at summer tutorial programs at Rust College in Holly Springs, Mississippi. In the 1970s he strove to incorporate service learning into MSU's curriculum and helped create the National Society for Experiential Education.

Seymour B. Sarason (1919–2010)

Seymour Sarason is often called the "father of community psychology." His work abounds with many of the central tenets of what we now call the scholarship of engagement. Starting in the early 1960s, Sarason called for a shift in our focus in solving social problems from the individual to the community and a change in the faculty role from expert to collaborator. He urged faculty and students to leave campus and work in community settings, especially schools, to find workable solutions to community problems by developing meaningful relationships with community partners based on mutual respect, resource exchange, and a psychological sense of community.

Contents

PART 1

Scholarship-Focused Civic Engagement and Service Learning

Introduction

Hiram E. Fitzgerald and Judy Primavera

The founding of Campus Compact in 1985 was intended to connect students to the "civic purposes of higher education." Whether Campus Compact sparked higher education's efforts to reconnect with society will be debated by historians, but it seems that Campus Compact stoked more than kindling when it encouraged higher education to develop students' citizenships skills by providing them with opportunities to work as volunteers in community contexts. Shortly after Campus Compact was founded, Ernest Boyer (1990) was challenging higher education to extend "scholarship" beyond its discovery mission to include teaching and application as well. The notion of the civic was being extended to involve faculty and administrators as well as students in discussion about the public purposes of education.

Scholarship of Engagement

By 1996 Boyer was calling for higher education to embrace the scholarship of engagement, the New England Resource Center had established the first national award for community engagement, the Kellogg Commission on the Future of State and Land Grant Universities had completed the first of many meetings encouraging higher education to return to the principles upon which the democratization of public higher education was based (Kellogg Commission, 1999), and Glassick, Huber, and Maeroff (1997) had offered a clear prescription for assessing faculty work that penetrated to the core of scholarly life rather than deferring to the ease of counting scholarly products produced for personal or disciplinary consumption, not for the public good. Moreover, they argued that scholarship should be characterized by clear goals, adequate preparation, appropriate methods, significant results, effective

3

presentation, and reflective critique regardless of whether such work reflected the scholarships of discovery, integration, application, or teaching.

The Kellogg Commission reports focused on reinvigorating the student experience; improving student access; enhancing partnerships with the public; addressing the role of public universities in a learning society; attending to the culture of the campus; and renewing the partnership of the public university with the society it serves. Public support of higher education was being bound to public expectations that the "public's universities" would become more directly engaged in the transformation of society across the broad disciplinary domains that define higher education. The final report of the commission called on public universities to "renew their covenant" with society by refocusing their scholarship agenda to place students first and to elevate the status of teaching and service within institutional mission and faculty rewards. This call to a covenant relationship moved the conversation beyond student experiences to include faculty life and work as well as institutional mission.

Community Engagement

Few can question the impact that prophets of change such as Boyer, Lynton, and the Kellogg Commission have had on higher education during the past 25 years. When Boyer published his treatise, there were no public psychologists, public sociologists, or public anthropologists. There are today! Few universities recognized faculty for their public scholarship or community partnerships. Nearly all do so today! There was no call from the National Institutes of Health to translate science findings to practice, and the National Science Foundation did not require grant writers to address the potential societal impact of their proposed research. Both are explicit aspects of grant requirements today. Handbooks have been published (Fitzgerald, Burack, & Seifer, 2010) and how-to primers have been published (Beere, Vootruba, & Wells, 2011). Indeed, Boyer most likely did not anticipate the worldwide response to his call for higher education to reconsider the breath of its mission. But if we judge from the list of organizations in table 1, the question whether higher education was ready to commit to community engagement (Burkardt, Holland, Percy, & Zimpher, 2004) seems to have been answered with a resounding "yes."

The Kellogg Commission challenged higher education to engage with communities. From the commission's perspective, engagement embraces two-way or systemic relationships between higher education and community. Institutions were asked to challenge their faculty and students to move beyond "outreach" and "service" and to become engaged with their communities (Kellogg Commission, 2000, p. 22), regardless of whether community was defined from a sociological perspective (a group that is united by at least one common characteristic, geography, shared interests or values, etc.) or a systems perspective (a group sharing distinct characteristics or interrelationships, such as gender, kinship, tribal, schools, transportation, faith, etc.) (Center for Disease Control, 2012). The commission fell short, however, of offering an explicit definition of engagement from a scholarly perspective.

Although numerous definitions of engagement have been offered (Glass & Fitzgerald, 2010), all seem to embrace three core qualities: scholarship, alignment across the mission,

Table 1. History of the Development of Organizations Focused on Civic and Community Engagement

Higher Education Networks: Focus on Civic and Community Engagement

Campus Compact	1985
New England Resource Center for Higher Education	1988
Coalition of Urban and Metropolitan Universities	1990
Corporation for National and Community Service	1993
HBCU Faculty Development Network	1994
Community Campus Partnerships for Health	1996
Rede Unitraballio	1996
Outreach Scholarship Conference (now, Engagement Scholarship Consortium)	1999
Living Knowledge: The International Science Shop Network	1999
Imagining America: Artists and Scholars in Public Life	1999
Universidad Construye Pais	2001
Australian Universities Community Engagement Alliance (AUCEA)	2002
New Eurasia Foundation Community-University Network	2004
Canadian Alliance for Community Service Learning	2005
El Centro Latinoamericano de Aprendizaje y Servicio Solidario	2005
The Talloires Network	2005
The Research University Civic Engagement Network (TRUCAN)	2005
International Association for Research on Service Learning and Community Engagement	2006
Higher Education Network for Community Engagement	2006
The Coalition of Urban Serving Universities	2007
Association of Commonwealth Universities (ACU) Extension Network	2008
Campus Engage (network for the promotion of civic engagement in Irish higher education)	2008
Community Based Research Canada	2008
Global Alliance on Community Engaged Research	2008
Ma'an Arab University Alliance for Civic Engagement	2008
The National Co-ordinating Centre for Public Engagement in Higher Education	2008
Transformative Regional Engagement Networks	2008
REDIVU (Ibero-American Volunteer Network for Social Inclusion)	2010
South African Higher Education Community Engagement Forum	2010

Secondary Focus on Civic and Community Engagement

Association of Public and Land Grant Universities (formerly, NASULGC)	1887
Association of American Colleges and Universities	1915
International Association of Universities (IAU)	1950
National Association of Universities and Higher Education Institutions	1950
Association of Columbian Universities (ASCUN)	1957
American Association of State Colleges and Universities	1961
Association of African Universities (AAU)	1967
Global University Network for Innovation (GUNI)	1999
PASCAL International Observatory	2002

SOURCE: Adapted from Watson et al. 2011.

and reciprocity of mutual benefit. Scholarly engagement means that the scholarships of discovery, application, and integration can be applied to the formation of university-community partnerships (models for bringing universities and communities together, or models of systems change) and the outcomes produced as a result of the partnership (the spread of discipline-generated, evidence-based practices in communities) (Glass & Fitzgerald, 2010).

Engagement as alignment means that opportunities for community engagement are present in every component of the institutional mission: teaching, research, and service. In this sense, engagement becomes a central component of the institution's mission (Council on Engagement & Outreach, 2011), fully aligned with other mission emphases. Engagement as mutually beneficial stresses the two-way, systemic relationship necessary for the cocreation of solutions to societal problems, sustainability of demonstrated outcomes, and generation of the scholarly products necessary for faculty to succeed in the academy.

Engagement partnerships contribute to an institution's civic mission by connecting students and faculty with public partners to create knowledge that is of value to both scholars and society, and to demonstrate workable solutions to community-defined problems. Key to the partnership is the recognition that knowledge is not the sole province of the academy; it also resides within the community (Barker, 2004), and it is the melding of these two sources of knowledge that can generate sustainable and evidence-based change (Fitzgerald, Allen, & Roberts, 2010; Peters, 2010). The three core qualities of engagement were emphasized in the Big Ten's Committee on Institutional Cooperation's Committee of Engagement draft report (Fitzgerald, Smith, Book, Rodin, & the CIC Committee on Engagement, 2005), which defined engagement as "the partnership of university knowledge and resources with those of the public and provide sectors to (1) enrich scholarship, research and creative activities; (2) enhance curriculum, teaching, and learning; (3) prepare educated, engaged citizens; (4) strengthen democratic values and civic responsibilities; (5) address critical societal issues; and (6) contribute to the public good" (p. 4).

Engagement scholarship is oriented toward problem solving, recognizes that the observer is always an implicit part of the observation, understands that change is ever present, is antithetical to positivist epistemologies (Fisher, 2006), and instead embraces epistemologies historically linked to dialectics (and all of its contemporary systems models) and pragmatism (and its emphasis on problem solving) (Baker, 2004). As a result it embraces a broad range of methods that span the qualitative-quantitative continuum and adheres to a set of principles that guide community-based research (CBR) and its various iterations (community action research, CAR; community-based participatory research, CBPR; tribal participatory research, TPR). These principles include, at the very least, those offered by Hall (1975, pp. 28–30) nearly four decades ago, but which continue to have relevance today:

1. Research methods have ideological implications.
2. A research process should be of some immediate and direct benefit to a community and not merely the basis for an academic paper.
3. A research process should involve the community or population in the entire research project from the formulation of the problem to the discussion of how to seek solutions and the interpretations of the findings.
4. If the goal of the research is to change an environment, then the research team should be composed of representatives of the elements in the situation that have a bearing on the change.
5. The research process should be seen as part of a total educational experience that serves to establish community needs and increases awareness and commitment within the community.

6. The research process should be viewed as a dialectic process, a dialogue over time and not as a static picture from one point in time.

7. The object of the research process, like the object of the educational process, should be the liberation of human creative potential and the mobilization of human resources for the solution of social problems.

To this we add that scholarly publication of new effective models of partnership development, evidence-based systems change models, and evaluation outcomes from tested preventive-intervention programs provides the "mutual benefit" for faculty involved in engagement scholarship and supplements the civic purpose of public scholarship. As Peters (2005) emphasizes, "Engagement is a scholarly activity that draws upon both academic and local knowledge and expertise in ways that facilitate and/or produce significant learning and discovery aimed at addressing a wide range of 'real-world' problems and issues" (p. 3).

Civic Engagement

The first part of *Going Public* focuses on issues directly related to civic engagement, and although there is clearly a public purpose to engagement scholarship, there is no clear definition of civic engagement. So pervasive is the pool of individual definitions that Adler and Goggin (2005) were moved to ask the question, "What do we mean by 'civic engagement'?" They concluded that the majority of extant definitions could be squeezed into one of four categories, focusing on civic engagement as, respectively, community service (voluntary work in communities), collective action (groups working to achieve some kind of community change), political involvement (perhaps the purist form of civic action via stress on active citizens in public life), and social change (an explicit focus on changing some aspect of society). Parsing through all of the possible definitions, Adler and Goggin suggest that "civic" engagement describes how an active citizen participates in the life of a community in order to improve conditions for others or to help shape the community's future" (p. 241). When participation and shaping are done in the context of a university-community partnership, the foundation has been made for effective engagement scholarship.

Establishing engagement scholarship as a central component of an institutional mission requires administrators, faculty, students, staff, and community partners to achieve consensus on what engagement means for their work, educational experiences, and institutional investments. Numerous authors have made the point that if engagement scholarship is to become a core aspect of an institution's teaching, research, and service mission, it is essential to have faculty buy-in. Achieving such buy-in is rife with challenge (Silka, 1999). As Cynthia Jackson-Elmoore points out in the first chapter of this book, "The Challenges of Scholarship," a key aspect of faculty buy-in is to have the scholarships of teaching, application, and integration seriously considered within the portfolio of work that any faculty member submits as evidence for promotion and tenure. Use of such portfolios requires serious discussion about institutional and disciplinary definitions of scholarship, the types of scholarly publications that count for promotion and tenure review, and the overall criteria used to evaluate faculty performance (Stanton, 2008).

7

In their contribution, Jackson-Elmoore, Wawrzynski, Colbry, and Boucher-Niemi provide case examples of the blended forms of scholarship provided by mentored student involvement in community research, opportunities that not only bring students into the university's research enterprise, but provide them with case examples of how to apply classroom and disciplinary knowledge to societal problems. Students who are involved in service learning or are part of faculty-guided research also are exposed to ethical issues related to the protection of research participants, use of ethical research designs, and a host of civic and ethical practices related to working with diverse communities. But most importantly, they are challenged to critically reflect on their engagement experience in much the same way that faculty are challenged. Moreover, challenge here goes beyond self-reflective process; it embraces the kind of scholarship implicit in autoethnographic stories created through critical reflections about their community engagement work (Fear, Rosaen, Bawden, & Foster-Fishman, 2006). As Fear and colleagues put it, "The learning to which we refer is a critical, self-interrogating, embedded process, where learners (acting both as individuals and collectives), consciously pursue the nature and consequences of their knowledge at and across different levels of cognitive processing" (p. 230). Such reflections can become the autoethnographic stories that describe life-changing experiences, or meaningful shifts in the nature of one's career pathway (Peters, 2010). In their contribution to this book, a professor (Stewart) and a director of service learning and civic engagement (Casey) comment on events that transformed Professor Stewart's traditional undergraduate lecture-style classroom environment into one that stressed critical reflection, active learning, and student involvement in service-learning and civic engagement experiences.

Classroom service-learning experiences as well as non-classroom-based service learning comprise much of what occurs to support student-focused civic engagement for residential students. Increasingly, however, many degree programs are being offered online for students from widely dispersed geographic locations. This is particularly true for many adult learners enrolled in professional degree programs, such as social work and nursing. In "Intersecting Civic Engagement with Distance Education," Block and Lindeke describe their Model for Civic Engagement Teaching/Learning Activities, a five-step model for engaging distance learners in local community engagement activities. They provide case examples of unsuccessful and successful projects and highlight the important ingredients for maximizing success, not the least of which is use of learning contracts to clarify objectives and expected outcomes.

Successful community collaborative work requires many communication skills, not the least of which is the ability to engage in deliberative discourse focused on development of a shared vision for partnership outcomes, clarity of shared responsibility for partnership development, and shared resources necessary to achieve the mutual gains expected through partnership. These require commitment to deliberative democracy, the ability for multiple perspectives to achieve consensus through civil dialogue and the ability to focus on change that will benefit the common good. Historically, the disciplines that comprise the humanities have provided the backdrop for civil discourse, debate, and consensus building, and the various philosophical approaches to epistemology, ontology, and ethics, all of which are of paramount importance to discourse about engagement as a public good. But have the humanities been at the forefront of the civic engagement movement, or did they abdicate their role, shifting responsibility to the social and behavioral sciences? In his contribution,

David Cooper argues that the humanities did the latter. One result is that the emphasis of civic engagement became focused on projects and program outcomes, rather than critical self-reflection, including a self-identity as a member of democratic society with an ethical, if not practical, obligation to be a participant in civil society. He argues that by reemphasizing deliberative democracy, oral tradition, narrative, and a method he labels "participatory photography," the humanities can provide the tools that individuals need to participate in civic process and civil discussion about even the most difficult topics.

In the next chapter, Cooper and Fretz describe their efforts to engage students in deliberative discussions through involvement in two important public issues of the day. Teaching separate courses, they selected one common text, arranged joint meetings of their classes for half of the scheduled class sessions, and conducted two National Issues Forums on critical societal issues (public schools, community violence), each of which included invitations to individuals from the community to participate in the dialogue. Each instructor also conducted small group meetings called Study Circles, in order to provide greater opportunities for students to participate in the deliberative process.

Do service-learning experiences actually instill a sense of civic engagement and public purpose in students? Or, as Eyler and Giles (1999) queried, "How much learning occurs in service learning? Although there is a body of literature in support of the outcomes that service learning was designed to produce, it is rare to find stories that trace life course pathways retrospectively to a distant past in ways that provide a link between a late adolescent experience in service learning and one's subsequent life's work. Peters (2010) has captured some of these connections through narratives provided by faculty members at Cornell. But a celebratory event in 2007 provided a unique opportunity for Reverend John Duley to explore this question with a group of former Michigan State University students who participated in one of the most profound social movements in U.S. history.

From 1965 to 1968 students and faculty from Michigan State University participated in a service-learning project at Rust College, Mississippi. One of the co-organizers of the Student Tutorial Education Project (STEP) was Robert Green, then an assistant professor in the College of Education at Michigan State. The other organizer was Reverend John S. Duley, a professor and campus minister at Michigan State University. Thirty-nine years after the STEP service-learning experience, the university hosted a reunion of the STEP program participants. It was at this event that Reverend Duley had the opportunity to interview 12 of the STEP students and to capture their reflections on the impact of their involvement in STEP. In the final chapter in part 1, their narratives provide resounding confirmation of the premise that service learning not only can have a life-course impact, but can ingrain a deep sense of civic purpose that truly can be described as transformational (Boyte, 2004).

References

Adler, R. P., & Goggin, J. (2005). What do we mean by "civic engagement"? *Journal of Transformative Education, 3*, 236–253.

Baker, D. (2004). The scholarship of engagement: A taxonomy of five emerging practices. *Journal of Higher Education Outreach and Engagement, 9*, 123–137.

Beere, C. A., Votruba, J. C., & Wells, G. W. (2011). *Becoming an engaged campus: A practical guide for institutionalizing public engagement.* San Francisco: Jossey-Bass.

Boyer, E. L. (1990). *Scholarship reconsidered: Priorities of the professoriate.* Princeton, NJ: Carnegie Foundation for the Advancement of Teaching.

Boyer, E. L. (1996). The scholarship of engagement. *Journal of Public Service and Outreach, 1,* 11–20.

Boyte, H. E. (2004). *Going public: Academics and public life.* Dayton, OH: Kettering Foundation.

Burkardt, M. M., Holland, B., Percy, S. L., & Zimpher, N. (2004). Is higher education ready to commit to community engagement? A wingspread statement. Milwaukee: University of Wisconsin-Milwaukee.

Center for Disease Control. (2011). Community engagement: Definitions and organizing concepts from the literature. Retrieved February 5, 2012, from http://www.ced.gov/phppo/pce/part1.hlm.

Council on Engagement and Outreach. (2012). White paper: Centrality of engagement in higher education. Available from fitzger9@msu.edu, chair of CEO work group.

Eyler, J., & Giles, D. (1999). *Where's the learning in service-learning?* San Francisco: Jossey-Bass.

Fear, F., Rosaen, C. L., Bawden, R. J., & Foster-Fishman, P. (2006). *Coming to critical engagement: An autoethnographic exploration.* Lanham, MD: University Press of America.

Fisher, F. (2006). Environmental expertise and civic ecology: Linking the university and its metropolitan communities. In A. C. Nelson, B. L. Allen, & D. L. Tranger (Eds.), *Toward a resilient metropolis: The role of state and land grant universities in the 21st century* (pp. 83–101). Alexandria: Metropolitan Institute at Virginia Tech.

Fitzgerald, H. E., Allen, A., & Roberts, P. (2010). Campus-community partnerships: Perspectives on engaged research. In H. E. Fitzgerald, C. Burack, & S. D. Seifer (Eds.), *Handbook of engaged scholarship: Contemporary landscapes, future directions,* vol. 2, *Community-campus partnerships* (pp. 5–28). East Lansing: Michigan State University Press.

Fitzgerald, H. E., Burack, C., & Seifer, S. D. (Eds.). (2010). *Handbook of engaged scholarship: Contemporary landscapes, future directions.* Vol. 1, *Institutional change.* East Lansing: Michigan State University Press.

Fitzgerald, H. E., Smith, P., Book, P., Rodin, K., & the CIC Committee on Engagement. (2005). Draft CIC report: Resource guide and recommendations for defining and benchmarking engagement. February. Champaign, IL: Committee on Institutional Cooperation.

Glass, C. R., & Fitzgerald, H. E. (2010). Engaged scholarship: Historical roots, contemporary challenges. In H. E. Fitzgerald, C. Burack, & S. D. Seifer (Eds.), *Handbook on engaged scholarship: Contemporary landscapes, future directions,* vol. 1, *Institutional change* (pp. 9–24). East Lansing: Michigan State University Press.

Glassick, C. E., Huber, M. T., & Maeroff, G. I. (1997). *Scholarship assessed: Evaluation of the professoriate.* San Francisco: Jossey-Bass.

Hall, B. (1975). Participatory research: An approach for change. *International Journal for Adult Education, 2,* 24–32.

Kellogg Commission. (1999). *Returning to our roots: The engaged institution. Third report.* Washington, DC: National Association of State Universities and Land Grant Colleges

Kellogg Commission. (2000). *Renewing the covenant: Learning, discovery, and engagement in a new age and different world.* Washington, DC: National Association of State Universities and Land Grant Colleges.

Peters, S. J. (2005). Introduction and overview. In S. J. Peters, N. R. Jordan, M. Adamek, & T. R. Alter (Eds.), *Engaging campus and community: The practice of public scholarship in the state and land-grant university system* (pp. 1–37). Dayton, OH: Kettering Foundation.

Peters, S. J. (2010). *Democracy and higher education: Traditions and stories of civic engagement.* East Lansing: Michigan State University Press.

Silka, L. (1999). Paradoxes of partnerships: Reflections on university-community collaborations. *Politics and Society, 7,* 335–359.

Stanton, T. K. (2008). New times demand new scholarship: Opportunities and challenges for civic engagement—opportunities and challenges. Los Angeles: University of California. Retrieved from http://www.compact.org/initiatives/civic-engagement-at-reserch-universities/trucen-intr/.

Watson, D., Hollister, R. M., Stroud, S. E., & Babcock, E. (2011). *The engaged university: International perspectives on civic engagement.* New York: Routledge.

The Challenges of Scholarship

Cynthia Jackson-Elmoore

What is scholarship? Or perhaps the question really is: what is valued scholarship? Academic achievement for faculty and increasingly graduate and undergraduate students is typically measured in terms of scholarship. However, there continues to be a lack of clarity and consistency in defining and assessing scholarship on university campuses worldwide. Many people have a good sense of the term; others will tell you that they know it when they see it. However, this does not speak to the various forms of scholarship that persist. At the most basic level, scholarship is defined in dictionaries as knowledge that results from or is the product of study and research in a particular discipline or profession. This definition in and of itself does little to help faculty and their universities make consistent determinations of what activities rightfully count as scholarship.

In an attempt to actualize the concept, several scholars and universities offer their own interpretations and definitions of scholarship. For example, Weiser & Houglum (1998, p. 1) assert that scholarship is "creative intellectual work that is validated by peers and communicated—including creative artistry and the discovery, integration and development of knowledge." Another definition posits that scholarship is "outcomes, insights, creations, and products arising from activities and creative processes that utilize the methods of inquiry and accumulated knowledge" (Outeach and Engagement, University of Conneticut, 2010, p. 1). Similarly, it is asserted that "the essence of scholarship is the thoughtful discovery, transmission, and application of knowledge, including creative activities, that is based in the ideas and methods of recognized disciplines, professions, and interdisciplinary fields" (Glass, Doberneck & Schweitzer, 2010, p. 3). It is generally accepted that scholarly work has at least three common properties: (1) new knowledge or new interpretation, use, or application of existing knowledge; (2) evidence or documentation of accomplishment; and (3) a process of providing or sharing knowledge (Southern Polytechnic State University, 2010). However it is defined, scholarship is a critical activity in the life of a university, its faculty, and students.

Elsewhere in this volume are examples of the range and diversity of scholarship that can and should be celebrated. As a collectivity, the chapters highlight the importance and benefits of being and going public with scholarship, whatever form it takes. This chapter explores some of the challenges of scholarship given varying conceptions of what exactly scholarship is and how faculty get credit for their scholarly activities. It begins with a discussion of different types of scholarship and how scholars and universities worldwide wrestle with acknowledging scholarship in its various forms. The chapter continues with alternative perspectives for thinking about scholarship and acknowledges obstacles that inhibit a more comprehensive perspective on and approach to scholarship on many campuses. It concludes with a discussion of the commonalities among forms of scholarship, highlighting the range, variety, and yet consistency across the work that faculty and students do every day. Of particular note in this chapter is a consideration of the scholarship of teaching and scholarship of application as means to undertake community engagement, an activity that spans across all forms of scholarship.[1]

What Do We Mean When We Call Ourselves Scholars?

Boyer (1990) claims in *Scholarship Reconsidered: Priorities of the Professoriate* that there is more than one way to understand the scholarly endeavor; he identifies four modes of scholarship: discovery, integration, teaching, and application (figure 1). The scholarship of discovery involves generating new knowledge and theories; while the scholarship of integration draws on multiple disciplines and methodologies to place new knowledge in a larger and broader context, spanning disciplinary boundaries. The scholarship of teaching is concerned with transmitting and translating knowledge to learners and understanding how this translation occurs. Finally, the scholarship of application involves communication and interaction between the researcher and a practitioner or community. It is the translation of research into practice; and in the process both research and practice are informed,

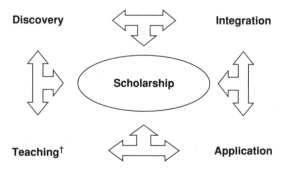

FIGURE 1 Scholarship and the Cycle* of Knowledge Acquisition and Transmission
* This is a dynamic and non-hierarchial relationship
† This is often referred to as the scholarship of teaching and learning (SoTL) given the inherent links between teaching and learning.
SOURCE: Adapted from Boyer (1990) and McGrath (2006).

Dimensions of scholarship*	Components of academic activity		
	Research	Teaching	Service
Discovery			
Integration			
Teaching			
Application			

Primary focus

Secondary focus

Tertiary focus

FIGURE 2 The Academic Endeavor and Dimensions of Scholarship
* These dimensions are based on Boyer's (1990) conceptualization of forms of scholarship. Scholars note that community engagement can and should occur in each of these aspects of research.
SOURCE: Adapted from Potter et al. (2009, p. 9, Figure 2).

invigorated, and enhanced. Boyer (1996) also discusses the scholarship of engagement, whereby faculty at a university consciously and deliberately interact with external constituencies. Specifically, Boyer (1996, pp. 19–20) asserts that "the scholarship of engagement means connecting the rich resources of the university to our most pressing social, civic, and to our teachers, and to our cities. . . . ethical problems, to our children, to our schools." It is the essence of going public with all aspects of research—discovery, integration, teaching and application (Provost's Committee on University Outreach, 1993; Barker, 2004; Sandmann, 2006). As such, the scholarship of engagement is a mechanism for meaningful, sustained involvement in civic and community matters; it carries an inherent opportunity and obligation for collaboration and partnerships with a myriad of stakeholders.

Boyer's (1990, 1996) conceptions of scholarship are typically mapped onto traditional academic themes of research, teaching and service (figure 2), where the scholarship of discovery is the primary emphasis of research and the scholarship of teaching is often linked directly and exclusively to teaching. The scholarship of application is typically linked to service functions, with the scholarship of integration crossing all three functions. However, this mapping in and of itself makes value statements about what forms of scholarship matter, how much, and at what point in the careers of faculty. As Weiser (1996) notes, "A university's values are most clearly described by its promotion and tenure policies, and by the criteria used to evaluate faculty performance" (para. 2). Similarly, the Boyer Commission (1998, p. 7) notes, "Every research university can point with pride to the able teachers within its ranks, but it is in research grants, books, articles, papers, and citations that every university defines its true worth." Similarly, what often goes unstated in this generic mapping to research, teaching, and service categorizations is the reality that one of the inherent strengths of the scholarship of engagement is realized when community engagement is embedded in all components of scholarly endeavors.

Figure 3 provides a visual representation of the commonly accepted connections between traditional academic themes and forms of scholarship.[2] It is important to note that the figure does not demonstrate the relative distribution of time and weighting of value assigned by departments and institutions to any one of these scholarly activities. If it did, on many occasions, depending on the type of university, knowledge application would be dwarfed by the generation and transmission of knowledge. There would also be instances where research (i.e., knowledge generation) might occupy a larger portion of time and value than teaching

15

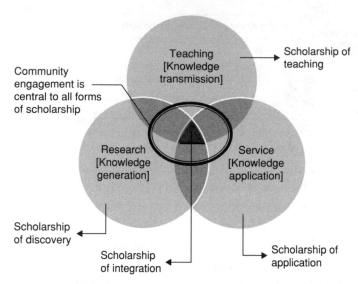

FIGURE 3 Association between Academic Themes and Forms of Scholarship

(i.e., knowledge transmission), when it comes to faculty reward systems. Even within the same institution, the relative size of any one sphere of activity may vary by discipline or profession. Similarly, the relative importance of any one form of scholarship may also vary for a given faculty member over the course of one's career and possibly on an annual basis. For some faculty, it may come down to a choice of one form of scholarship over another; while other faculty may find themselves balancing across the range of scholarship, though not necessarily at the same time. For those that do endeavor to undertake multiple forms of scholarship, it may seem less like a balancing act (figure 4) and more like juggling an ever changing set of expectations and priorities.

There is little doubt where academe weighs in on this issue. An overwhelming emphasis is placed on the scholarship of discovery, that is, original, basic research that creates new knowledge and is published in refereed journals or other venues highly valued by the disciplines (Gaston, 1971; Mensah, 1982; Adams, 2003; O'Meara, 2005; Braxton, Luckey, & Helland, 2006; Defleur, 2007; Seeger, 2009). Similarly, to the extent that it advances knowledge and contributes to disciplinary discussions, the scholarship of integration receives wide-ranging acceptance. However, in this quest to create new knowledge for the sake of knowledge, it is

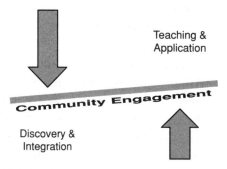

FIGURE 4 The Balancing Act of Scholarship

possible to overlook or undervalue other activities that could legitimately be called scholarship. Or, perhaps more accurately, some faculty may choose to set aside certain activities—the scholarship of teaching and the scholarship of application—for fear that they are inappropriate or out of place; and hence may adversely affect tenure and promotion decisions (Fairweather, 1996; Boyer Commission, 1998; Taylor, 1999; Nora et al., 2000; Lynch, Sheard, Carbone, & Collins, 2002; Jaeger & Thornton, 2006).

Each type of scholarship presents its own set of challenges and opportunities. For example questions as to which journals are more highly regarded within a given discipline or profession and thus essential to tenure and promotion have to be carefully negotiated. Yet in many instances this matter may never be explicitly discussed, let alone documented for individual faculty, disciplinary/professional subfields, or at the departmental level. Obtaining the necessary resources to successfully engage in the scholarship of discovery can also be a challenge, one that can leave faculty seeking a delicate balance of time and focus between writing grant proposals and producing the manuscripts or creative works necessary to establish oneself as relevant, let alone significant in the field. The very nature of the scholarship of integration may raise concerns about the time and effort needed to successfully navigate multiple disciplines, methods, and the diversity of intellectual perspectives and individuals that may be brought together to address key issues and contribute broadly to the existing knowledge base and societal advancement as a whole. These are interesting and important issues to consider; indeed discussions of community engagement with regard to the scholarships of discovery and integration abound (e.g., Fitzgerald, Burack, & Seifer, 2010). This chapter focuses on the scholarship of teaching and the scholarship of application and the rich opportunities for community engagement as part of one's scholarly pursuits.

What does it mean in the life of faculty to give credence to Boyer's (1990) understanding of the scholarship of teaching and application, or to more broadly embrace the scholarship of engagement? Individual faculty may struggle with an array of questions, including wondering how engaged teaching might impact their research agenda or how their scholarly work with and in communities will be viewed by disciplinary colleagues. Underpinning these and other issues is a concern for the likelihood of success at one's university and the ability to not just survive, but thrive in one's career. Several resources have emerged to help faculty confront the challenges of having their scholarly community engagement recognized and rewarded (e.g., Calleson, Kauper-Brown, & Seifer, 2005; Stanton & Howard, 2009). Similarly, it continues to be important for faculty to find support networks that value and celebrate their work, keeping in mind that these networks may be outside the department, discipline, college, or even university in which faculty are situated.

One might also consider what it would take for higher education to accept and respect the scholarship of teaching and the scholarship of application such that this work is more highly valued in tenure and promotion cases. Key insights are gained by examining the Research Assessment Exercise (RAE), an assessment of university research activities that is a key factor in university ranking and funding in the UK. The 2008 guidelines for assessing research activity at universities in Great Britain and Northern Ireland include very specific language about how the scholarship of teaching and the scholarship of application or practice are to be evaluated and valued relative to the scholarship of discovery (table 1).[3] Such

Table 1. Assessment of the Scholarship of Teaching and Learning and Applied Research in the UK

	Teaching and learning	Applied research
Generic statement	"Research is encouraged where it meets the definition of research for the RAE."[*]	"Treat on an equal footing excellence in research across the spectrum of applied research, practice-based and basic/strategic research, wherever that research is conducted. Panel criteria encompass a range of indicators of excellence that are sufficiently broad to enable them to recognise the distinctive characteristics of applied research and practice-based research, and to ensure that they apply their quality benchmarks equitably."

Disciplinary-Based Examples[†]

	Teaching and learning	Applied research
Politics and international studies	"Teaching materials and subject-related pedagogy … will be treated in the same way as textbooks. Higher education pedagogic research will be judged by the standards applied to all forms of research output."	"Judge the quality of applied and commissioned research according to the same standards of originality and rigour as for all other forms of output, while recognising that its significance may relate particularly to its relevance to policy and/or practice."
Sociology	"Teaching materials and textbooks will be considered only in so far as they embody research as specified in the RAE definition of research."[*]	"Applied research and practice-based research activity … may include action research and participatory research … [and is assessed] against the same indicators of excellence as other forms of research, i.e., in relation to its originality, significance and rigour." There is a recognition that this research will have an impact on "the policy-making or user community"
Business and management studies	"Teaching materials or non-text output … where they contain original research … will be assessed in the same way as other work. … HE (higher education) pedagogic research into the teaching and learning of business and management studies … will be assessed in the same way as other work."	"Research that is applied, policy-based or practice-based … will be assessed on the same basis as all other work submitted."
History Philosophy	"Where there is a visible contribution to research, the following forms of scholarly outputs will be evaluated: teaching materials where these contain a significant research element … textbooks which incorporate considerable personal research or substantially advance the subject area"	"The sub-panel recognises the importance of considering all types of research … a scholarly exhibition or television programme or museum-based or gallery-based activity might be submitted as a research output."

	Teaching and learning	Applied research
Epidemiology and public health	"Teaching materials that embody research outcomes will be admissible but, as noted above, in all cases departments should ensure that the work complies with the RAE definition of research."[*]	"Applied research and practice-based research, which will be considered equally with other forms of research and will be judged according to the way in which it has advanced a field and/or changed its practice."
Biological sciences	The statements do not speak directly to teaching; however there is language that provides an avenue for making a case for SoTL: in the case of "items other than scientific papers" a case can be made for "how the output embodies original research."	"Full recognition will be given to applied research and practice-based research … which is directly relevant to the needs of the public and voluntary sectors, commerce and industry. Departments should ensure that such work is innovative and that it adheres to the RAE definition of research."[*]
Preclinical, human biological sciences		
Agriculture, veterinary, and food science		"All forms of research output will be treated equivalently and will be taken to represent the range of activity within the submission (e.g., curiosity-driven, applied and practice-based)."

SOURCE: Research Assessment Exercise (2006).

[*]"Research' for the purpose of the RAE is to be understood as original investigation undertaken in order to gain knowledge and understanding. It includes work of direct relevance to the needs of commerce, industry, and to the public and voluntary sectors; scholarship; the invention and generation of ideas, images, performances, artefacts including design, where these lead to new or substantially improved insights; and the use of existing knowledge in experimental development to produce new or substantially improved materials, devices, products and processes, including design and construction. It excludes routine testing and routine analysis of materials, components and processes such as for the maintenance of national standards, as distinct from the development of new analytical techniques. It also excludes the development of teaching materials that do not embody original research. (*Note:* Scholarship is defined as the creation, development and maintenance of the intellectual infrastructure of subjects and disciplines, in forms such as dictionaries, scholarly editions, catalogues and contributions to major research databases" (Research Assessment Exercise 2006, annex 3).

*Disciplines are grouped together if the statements on SoTL and applied research are similar.

an approach helps the scholarship of teaching and learning and the scholarship of application gain and maintain equal status with disciplinary/professional research that is often assessed as the scholarship of discovery and heralded as the epitome of scholarship. Yet there remain opportunities to be even more explicit about how each of these forms of scholarship is connected to community engagement. The work of the Community-Campus Partnerships for Health, the Clearinghouse and National Review Board for the Scholarship of Engagement, and Imagining America's Tenure Team Initiative (TTI) can go a long way toward bridging the gulf between current, emerging, and future perspectives on the appropriate valuation of different forms of scholarship and the centrality of community engagement (e.g., Driscoll & Sandmann, 2001; Jordan, 2007; Goettel & Haft, 2010).

There is global recognition of the relevance and saliency of discussing the scholarship of teaching and application relative to tenure and promotion decisions (e.g., Ramsden, Margetson, Martin, & Clarke, 1995; Healey, 2000; Trigwell, Martin, Benjamin, & Prosser, 2000; Canadian Health Services Research Foundation, 2006; Levinson, Rothman, & Phillipson, 2006). As evidenced in the literature, discussions regarding a broadening consideration of scholarship and the implications for faculty rewards are under way in the UK, Europe,

Australia, and Canada, among other places. Similar conversations are also occurring in the United States (e.g., Diamond, 1994; Fiddler, McGury, Marienau, Rogers, & Scheideman, 1996; Glassick, Huber, & Maeroff, 1997; Krahenbuhl, 1998; Driscoll & Lynton, 1999; Rice, 2002; Ellison & Eatman, 2008).[4] Martin and colleagues (1999) maintain that there are three interrelated components of the scholarship of teaching; given this complexity, it is important that institutions develop mechanisms to support, recognize, and advance these efforts. In particular, the scholarship of teaching requires thoughtful and considerable reflection on one's own teaching practices and the impact on student learning, active engagement with the peer-reviewed literature on teaching and learning, and intentional efforts to communicate and disseminate information on the theory and practice of teaching (within and across disciplines). Holland (1997) identifies several characteristics of institutional efforts to support and advance the scholarship of application. Specifically, Holland asserts that the scholarship of application is fully incorporated into an institutional structure when, among other things, (1) community-based research and teaching are key criteria in hiring and tenure and promotion evaluations; (2) community-based research and service learning are high priorities for faculty; and (3) students are involved in community-based research and curriculum-based service learning.

Beyond stating what is encompassed in these forms of scholarship or the need for institutional support, it is equally important to have a metric for assessing these forms of scholarship in order to include them in tenure and promotion decisions should an institution choose to do so. Toward that end, Glassick, Huber, and Maeroff (1997) posit six criteria that are key to assessing any and all types of scholarship: clear goals, adequate preparation, appropriate methods, significant results, effective presentation, and reflective critique. In addition, Glassick and colleagues (1997) suggest that there are six basic stages involved in scholarship:

1. Reviewing the literature
2. Defining measurable objectives
3. Choosing appropriate methods and analysis
4. Challenging your assumptions
5. Reflecting critically
6. Communicating results

Building on this and other work, Hofmeyer, Newton, and Scott (2007) provide a concise overview of criteria and associated questions for assessing the various forms of scholarship. These and similar efforts are key to continuing the dialogue on scholarship and faculty reward systems. It is equally important that due consideration be given to artistic and creative endeavors in discussion about the forms and corresponding values of scholarship.

While not as wide-reaching and systematic as the RAE approach noted above, there are U.S.-based efforts to raise the level of awareness and acceptance of various modes of scholarship (e.g., Glassick, Huber, & Maeroff, 1997; Weiser & Houglum, 1998; Nora et al., 2000; Popovich & Abel, 2002; Wise, Retzleff, & Reilly, 2002; Potter-Witter, Beede, Kaplowitz, & Whalon, 2003; Jordan, 2010).[5] A Strengths, Weaknesses, Opportunities, and Threats (SWOT) analysis of scholarship conducted as part of a strategic planning process at one U.S. university identifies an opportunity to define the role of the scholarship of teaching and learning as it relates to tenure and promotion decisions (Taylor et al., 2007). The 2007–2010 strategic plan also calls for this same university to "seize scholarship opportunities within service learning, industry and community partnerships" (Schlegel & Associates 2007, p. 2). Many argue that whatever form it takes, scholarship and associated scholarly activities need to contain some amount of originality and be subject to some extent of external review or evaluation. Acknowledging that there are various forms of scholarship, another U.S. university notes that "what qualifies an activity as scholarship is that it be deeply informed by the most recent knowledge in the field, that the knowledge is skillfully interpreted and deployed, and that the activity is carried out with intelligent openness to new information, debate, and criticism" (Glass, Doberneck, & Schweitzer, 2010, p. 3). Table 2 highlights examples of evaluative criteria under consideration at various U.S. universities.

Despite efforts under way worldwide, there remains much work to be done to adequately reflect the scholarship of teaching and the scholarship of application into the overall university framework, particularly as it relates to tenure and promotion decisions (Schweitzer, 2000; Boshier, 2009). Take, for example, the field of public health:

> Many SPHs [schools of public health] have revised their faculty promotion and tenure guidelines to recognize practice-based scholarship. [The Council on Education for Public Health] CEPH has added and revised accreditation criteria to emphasize practice activities in community-based research, experiential learning, and faculty credentials. . . . Nevertheless, much remains to be done to reinforce practice-based scholarship's equal footing with traditional theory-based scholarship in the public health field. (Potter et al., 2009, p. 2)

McDowell's (2001) work suggests that the scholarship of teaching and the scholarship of application may often be overlooked, discounted, or flat out ignored in tenure and promotion decisions because evaluating these forms of scholarship is more difficult that counting (e.g., number of publications or grants), as is typically done for research (i.e., work recognized under the scholarship of discovery). Indeed, evaluation standards and agreement on the value of the scholarship of teaching and scholarship of application relative to the scholarship of discovery remain elusive (Ward, 2003; O'Meara, 2005; 2010; Jordan, 2010). Similarly, it is quite possible that graduate school training and subsequent faculty socialization processes may work against an institution's ability to encourage faculty to engage in multiple forms of scholarship (Braxton, Luckey, & Helland, 2002; O'Meara, 2005). Cognizant of this potentiality, Austin and McDaniels (2006) assert that doctoral education has the opportunity and responsibility to be strategic in the training and socialization of future faculty who are able to work across the various domains of scholarship. This suggests a need to be more assertive and intentional in efforts to shift the culture and climate toward the acceptance of various forms of scholarship and to be intentional about pursuing opportunities for community engagement (e.g., Doberneck, Brown, & Allen, 2010; Jordan, 2010; O'Meara, 2010). Indeed, a careful review of the criteria highlighted in table 2 reveals the need to underscore the importance of embedding community engagement in all aspects of scholarly activity (Provost's Committee on University Outreach, 1993):

> Outreach (engagement) is a form of scholarship that cuts across teaching, research, and service. It involves generating, transmitting, applying, and preserving knowledge for the direct benefit of external audiences in ways that are consistent with university and unit missions.

Table 2. Definitions and Examples of Alternative Criteria for Assessing Scholarship

Type of scholarship	Definition/example from U.S. universities

Discovery	• Activities that extend the stock of human knowledge through the collection of new information with a goal to confront the unknown with dedication to free inquiry, disciplined investigation, and the pursuit of knowledge for its own sake. It includes, but is not limited to, basic or original research.[*]
	  o The Scholarship of Artistic Endeavor: scholarly activities directly related to the creative process and artistic creations, especially in music, the fine, or applied arts
	• The pursuit of original knowledge and creativity. Includes original and creative work in software development and in the literary, visual, and performing arts. Evidence of achievement includes publication of original contributions to knowledge:[†]
	  o Refereed journals or books
	  o Refereed conference papers
	  o Refereed creative or artistic works
	    □ Exhibitions, performances, compositions, recordings, designs, or software of an innovative nature and recognized international standard.

Integration	• Activities that are primarily interdisciplinary or interpretive in nature. The goal is to better understand existing knowledge by making connections across disciplines, illuminating data in a revealing manner; drawing together isolated factors, or placing known information into broader contexts. It synthesizes, interprets, and connects the findings in a way that brings new meaning to facts.[*]
	• Original contributions that make connections between disciplines, create new contexts for viewing knowledge, or establish new models. Beyond simply collecting or cataloging information and knowledge from various disciplines, contributions must[†]
	  o Reflect original insight
	  o Put apparently unrelated facts into perspective
	  o Place specialized knowledge into a larger context

Teaching and learning	• Activities directly related to pedagogical practices that seek to improve the teaching and advising of students through discovery, evaluation, and transmission of information about the learning process.[*]
	• Activities with intellectual merit that contribute to teaching and learning, or the understanding of teaching and learning.[†]
	  o Creating original instructional materials
	  o Developing original curricula
	  o Incorporating new knowledge or new technology into existing courses
	  o Evaluating the effectiveness of pedagogical procedures
	  o Examining ethical and/or societal issues in the course context in an original manner

Application	• Activities that relate knowledge in one's field to society. Engagement with the community:[*]
	  o Using social problems as the agenda for scholarly investigation
	  o Drawing upon existing knowledge for the purpose of crafting solutions to social problems
	  o Making information or ideas accessible to the public
	
	• Contributions with intellectual merit outside the teaching role—including consultancies—that demonstrate the ability either to enrich knowledge and skills or to apply knowledge and skills in a particular situation.[†]
	  o Productive consultancies with outside groups resulting in innovative practical outcomes
	  o Acceptance by the profession of resources or techniques developed
	  o Major original performances or exhibitions where appropriate

SOURCES: [*]Center for Faculty Excellence (2009); [†]Southern Polytechnic State University (2010).

Reconsidering Scholarship

Even with a push to reconsider definitions of scholarship, old models persist (Young, 2006). Research is valued most and often measured by the number of grants (submitted and awarded), peer-reviewed publications, graduate students, and national or international recognition one obtains (Jaeger & Thornton, 2006). Teaching is primarily measured by the number of courses taught and ratings on student evaluations; its value is still suspect. In addition, evaluations of teaching are locked into traditional modes in many disciplines. Little or no peer review occurs. There is a need, both internal and external to academia, to improve how teaching is viewed, delivered, and assessed. The concept of a scholarship of teaching provides a vehicle to do this (e.g., Rice, 1992; Shulman, 1993; Schön, 1995; Andresen & Webb, 2000). The scholarship of teaching is an approach to raising the visibility and relative importance of teaching to a new level. It provides a mechanism by which faculty can achieve the following:

- Think about and reflect on excellence in teaching
- Discuss practice and philosophy with one another
- Develop new approaches and try them out
- Present results to colleagues in a way that can be evaluated for excellence rather than just recorded as "done"
- Improve student learning by situating the results of one's own work in existing literature

In many settings, outreach, engagement, and community-based research—all terms used to describe some form of applied research—is considered 'service' along with committee work and extension activities.[6] It is valued in much the same way 'citizenship' grades were valued in K-12 report cards from past decades. Like teaching, there is a need to change how people think about the work that faculty and students do with, for, and in communities. The scholarship of application provides one such mechanism for community connectivity and enhancing the value of making scholarship public because it provides opportunities to do the following:

- Identify new research questions
- Gain nuanced or new understandings of existing research questions
- Disseminate new research findings broadly
- Gain access to new funding sources, especially those that award grants to partnerships between agencies/organizations and communities
- Build community access to resources
- Facilitate community and institutional capacity building
- Generate and exchange knowledge between the community and university
- Learn what it takes for a community to become self-sufficient and self-sustaining
- Develop positive feelings in our communities toward the university
- Place academe in society as a genuine partner

The scholarship of application also enables researchers to make and sustain meaningful connections with funders who are looking to carry out civic-minded missions and/or requiring justifications for their investments (Shapiro & Coleman, 2000).

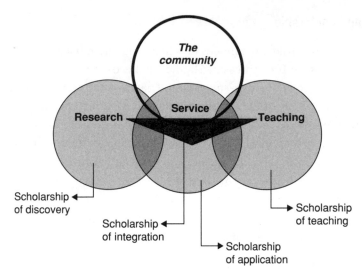

FIGURE 5 Intersectionality of the Broader Community with a University's Research, Teaching and Service Mission

There are many mechanisms for applying knowledge. Community engagement is just one of them, but a key one for sure, especially since it allows scholars to engage in and with communities to advance learning and problem solving for all involved (Ellison & Eatman, 2008). It is not, however, simply relegated to what might traditionally be considered application. Community engagement can and should happen within and across the various forms of scholarship. The intersections between research, teaching, and service, as well as the ways in which they connect to and with the community, are highlighted in figure 5. There is little doubt that research and related activities within the broader community can inform teaching and that faculty can become adept at navigating across these functions. The Boyer Commission (1998, p. 16) aptly notes that "in a research university, students should be taught by those who discover, create, and apply, as well as transmit, insights about subjects in which the teacher is expert." In short, students are advantaged when they are exposed to teacher-scholars, dedicated individuals and a community of scholars who pursue all forms of scholarship, discovery, integration, teaching, and application.

Overcoming the Obstacles, Taking On the Challenges

Progress is slow but sure. Campuses are changing and faculty are thinking about their teaching in new ways. Much of this activity is occurring because of the support and momentum offered by some of the early programs developed to foster teaching excellence. Examples include the Lilly Teaching Fellows program and the Carnegie Academy for the Scholarship of Teaching and Learning (CASTL) forums and resources. Just as programs in teaching excellence have fueled interest in and development of the scholarship of teaching, national organizations and forums have fostered a growth in appreciation for the scholarship of application and its development. For example, the New England Research Center for Higher Education (NERCHE) has a history of providing grants to faculty who work with community partners to investigate an issue of concern to the local partner. The start of the twenty-first century was marked by several efforts to convene individuals committed to impacting communities with and through their scholarship.[7] Since that time the national commitment to community engagement has expanded considerably. Examples include the Association of Public and Land-Grant Universities' Council on Engagement and Outreach, the Higher Education Network for Community Engagement (HENCE), Imagining America's efforts to advance community-university partnerships on behalf of the civic and public purposes of the arts, humanities, and design, the Research University Civic Engagement Network (TRUCEN), Community-Campus Partnerships for Health (CCPH), and the Outreach Scholarship Partnership and its associated National Outreach Scholarship Conference (e.g., Burns, 2010; Goettel & Haft, 2010; Sandmann & Weerts, 2010). Similarly, scholars in a number of disciplines and professions (e.g., sociology, psychology, anthropology, health, business, and engineering) acknowledge the importance of community engagement.

While there are advances in the scholarship of teaching and the scholarship of application, these movements also experience some obvious obstacles. They range from agreeing on a definition of scholarship and even a definition of terms (i.e., engagement, outreach, service), to finding the time and interest to successfully conduct these activities. Many faculty may be concerned about building credentials in a new area of expertise. They may wonder how someone trained in the sciences or arts and letters can claim to have deep understanding in the scholarship of teaching when that is supposedly the bailiwick of education departments. It is necessary to overcome such inertia in order to move forward. Most faculty members and other higher education decision makers still accept the scholarship of discovery as a key and possibly the only true marker of scholarship. Thus many of the ways to evaluate one's work still favor research in the scholarship-of-discovery sense, though this is changing, campus by campus.

The outcomes of the scholarship of teaching and the scholarship of application may not always be journal publications (McDowell, 2001; Braxton, Luckey, & Helland, 2002). Other likely products include innovative teaching materials, seminars and workshops, reports for local organizations, policy briefs, community newsletters, congressional testimony, technical reports, and public reforms (Pellino, Blackburn, & Boberg, 1984; Sundre, 1992). It is important to remember that the outcomes of the scholarship of discovery are not always journal publications either, a point that is often lost or forgotten in the debate. Indeed, the aforementioned venues are equally applicable to products generated under the scholarship of discovery or integration. The question then becomes, what is the place of these varied products in higher education? Should higher education only value refereed publications in the category of scholarship? Must the other types of products that might result from these types of scholarship be categorized as instructional activity or professional service (Lynton, 1995)? Or should higher education be open to a broader definition of scholarship so that this work can be assessed for the tenure candidate in the category of scholarship also? Should the weight and consideration that is given to the various categories be reconfigured, putting teaching and service/outreach on a more equal footing with the traditional notion of scholarship (i.e., discovery)? There's no easy or clear-cut answer. Nor should there be; rather, it is a matter of creating a space for the discussions to happen and removing hindrances for those who may desire to pursue alternative strategies and mechanisms of scholarship. One form of scholarship should not replace the other, instead, it is interesting to consider how the various forms of scholarship can and do coexist together to create an overall greater good for students, faculty, institutions, and ultimately society.

As the scholarship of teaching and scholarship of application movements continue to advance, it is important that careful consideration continue to be given to issues of measurement and assessment. This raises several key questions, which, though beyond the scope of this chapter, are worth noting. How will faculty and institutions identify and generate a set of benchmarks for both immediate and long-term impacts of the work that faculty (and their students) do? How can these activities be used to generate internal and external resources, to improve student learning, and to enhance faculty career development? What is the impact of the scholarship of teaching and application on the people and programs served? What is the evidence that the activities can be sustained or that the knowledge generated has value and will be used? The importance of developing best-practice models and sound measures of success cannot be underestimated or overstated.

Conclusions

So what does it mean to be a scholar? Bruns and colleagues (2002–2003, p. 4) argue that "to be a scholar is to integrate our work (teaching, research, and service), engage with those outside the academy, and synthesize what we learn into our other works." The connection to the scholarship of teaching and application is important for faculty, staff, administrators, students, communities, and everyone else involved in and affected by the education process. Faculty and administrators across the disciplines and professions need to understand how and why these activities are part of scholarship. There is a need for a common language for demonstrating what faculty do in and across disciplines, especially as it relates to workload and responsibilities. There is an opportunity to make sense of the myriad of scholarship that gets done and to prepare and train faculty to work in community settings. Developing a greater sense of and respect for the interconnections between application, teaching, discovery, and integration is just as important for faculty as it is for administrators because a broader understanding and definition of scholarship sets the tone for decisions regarding rewards and responsibilities. For instance, a reassessment of scholarship could translate into different workload policies defined by units and acknowledged elsewhere within the university system.

By engaging more fully at all levels of scholarship, institutions may enhance their ability to achieve a variety of missions. For example, the scholarship of application provides an opportunity to satisfy institutional goals that require community involvement and provide a means for institutional resource development. Similarly, connecting application and teaching to discovery and integration activities provides opportunities to enhance student learning, promote civic responsibility, and provide cocurricular learning experiences that prepare students for future careers and as citizens. Regardless of the form it takes, scholarship requires the following:

- Thoughtful reflection
- Careful review of extant knowledge

- Data collection
- Systematic analysis
- Open, public discussion of ideas, philosophies, theories, and practices
- Development of new ideas, approaches, and methodologies (i.e., knowledge generation)
- Peer review
- Public presentations/publications of outcomes

Individual faculty can help their disciplines to value the scholarship of teaching and the scholarship of application by publishing the products of these endeavors in highly respected journals. In essence, play the new game by the old rules. Few can dispute that quality publications count, though not all count equally. Furthermore, it is well past the time to urge higher education institutions to broaden their understandings of scholarship to include these forms in their conceptualization, even if their products are not accepted in highly respected journals. Higher education institutions can also be encouraged to value other kinds of products that may result from teaching and application—reports, documents, etc., for community groups—even if these institutions don't want to call this work "scholarship." Indeed, one might challenge any attempts to outright and a priori assert that teaching and application endeavors are not scholarship.

Institutions willing to adopt a broader perspective on scholarship provide advantages to many groups, including faculty, students, and the community. These points may resonate with scholars and practitioners who are committed to conducting research on community issues and problems. From this perspective, there is little doubt that there exists the need to advance a scholarship of application. The call is just as important for those individuals who care about student learning and work to constantly improve teaching within higher education. These enhancements can be accomplished in part through the kind of reflection, writing, and public sharing that the scholarship of teaching encourages. Working together to advance these parallel movements will go a long way toward redefining the work that scholars do and creating continuous learning environments for students, faculty, and communities. It is important to note that not all faculty are expected to buy into either the scholarship of teaching or the scholarship of application and hence incorporate these activities into their portfolio of experiences. Rather, the point being asserted is that it is time for a wider range of work to be accepted and valued as legitimate, scholarly activity. That means that those who choose to engage in this work—the scholarship of teaching and the scholarship of application—will be valued and their products measured and assessed based on commonly agreed-upon metrics.

Notes

1. *The Handbook of Engaged Scholarship: Contemporary Landscapes, Future Directions* provides an interesting discussion of community engagement and the scholarships of discovery, integration, teaching, and application (Fitzgerald, Burack, & Seifer, 2010). It is an excellent starting point to consult for current thinking on these broader discussions.
2. See Krahenbuhl (1998) for a fulsome discussion and visual representations of the complexity of relationships between the generation, transmission, and application of knowledge, as well as relative weightings of each activity.

3. Consistent criteria for evaluating the scholarship of teaching and the scholarship of application are necessary, though not sufficient, steps in leveling the playing field across dimensions of scholarship within the academy.

4. O'Meara (2010) highlights the value of considering a vast array of faculty rewards, acknowledging that tenure and promotion is not all that matters in the daily life of faculty and there are many faculty who are not in tenure-track positions.

5. For example, in line with the Boyer model of scholarship, the College of Education and Allied Professions at West Carolina University provides minigrant program to help faculty "move service activities to scholarly engagement" (Western Carolina University, 2010, p. 1).

6. "Community-based research" is one of several terms that is used in the literature to describe "research-oriented activity that meets scholarly objectives while contributing to the welfare of the community" (Wade & Demb 2009, p. 7). Other terms include "outreach scholarship" and "action-based research."

7. For example, the 2002 national conference of the American Association of Higher Education was devoted entirely to the scholarship of engagement. That same year, the University of Pennsylvania and the University of Michigan partnered to convene a conference for teams of higher education faculty and administrators to work together with their community collaborators to strategize on methods to further advance community-based research initiatives. Similar efforts have continued to be pursued throughout the United States and the world.

References

Adams, J. (2003). Assessing faculty performance for merit: An academic accomplishment index. *Journalism & Mass Communication Educator, 58*(3), 240–250.

Andresen, L. W., & Webb, C. A. (2000). *Discovering the scholarship of teaching.* Richmond: University of Western Sydney Hawkesbury.

Austin, A. E., & McDaniels, M. (2006). Using doctoral education to prepare faculty to work within Boyer's four domains of scholarship. *New Directions for Institutional Research, 129*, 51–65.

Barker, D. (2004). The scholarship of engagement: A taxonomy of five emerging practices. *Journal of Higher Education Outreach and Engagement, 9*(2), 123–137.

Boshier, R. (2009). Why is the scholarship of teaching and learning such a hard sell? *Higher Education Research & Development, 28*(1), 1–15.

Boyer Commission. (1998). *Reinventing undergraduate education: A blueprint for America's research universities.* Boyer Commission on Educating Undergraduates in the Research University. Princeton, NJ: Carnegie Foundation for the Advancement of Teaching.

Boyer, E. L. (1990). *Scholarship reconsidered: Priorities for the professoriate.* Princeton, NJ: Carnegie Foundation for the Advancement of Teaching.

Boyer, E. L. (1996). The scholarship of engagement. *Journal of Public Service and Outreach, 1*(1), 11–20.

Braxton, J. M., Luckey, W., & Helland, P. A. (2002). Institutionalizing a broader view of scholarship through Boyer's four domains. *ASHE-ERIC Higher Education Report, 29*(2).

Braxton, J. M., Luckey, W., & Helland, P. A. (2006). Ideal and actual value patterns toward domains of scholarship in three types of colleges and universities. *New Directions for Institutional Research, 129*, 67–76.

Bruns, K., Conklin, N., Wright, M., Hoover, D., Brace, B., Wise, G., ... Childers, J. (2002–2003). Scholarship: The key to creating change through outreach. *Journal of Higher Education Outreach and Engagement, 8*(1), 3–11.

Burns, K. S. (2010). Small partnership leads into national outreach conference. In H. E. Fitzgerald, C. Burack, & S. D. Seifer (Eds.), *Handbook of engaged scholarship: Contemporary landscapes, future directions*, vol. 2, *Community-campus partnerships* (pp. 349–359). East Lansing: Michigan State University Press.

Calleson, D., Kauper-Brown, J., & Seifer, S. D. (2005). Community-engaged scholarship toolkit. Seattle: Community-Campus Partnerships for Health. Retrieved September 20, 2012, from http://www.communityengagedscholarship.info.

Canadian Health Services Research Foundation. (2006). The creative professional activity dossier. *Recognition* (1).

Center for Faculty Excellence. (2009). Types of scholarship at Ithaca College: Spring Faculty Development Conference. Retrieved March 26, 2010, from http://www.ithaca.edu/cfe/docs/09Events/springconf09program.pdf.

Defleur, M. L. (2007). Raising the question: What is tenure and how do I get it? *Communication Education, 56*(1), 106–112.

Diamond, R. M. (1994). The tough task of reforming the faculty-rewards system. *Chronicle of Higher Education, 40*(May), B1–B3.

Doberneck, D. M., Brown, R. E., & Allen, A. A. (2010). Professional development for emerging engaged scholars. In H. E. Fitzgerald, C. Burack, & S. D. Seifer (Eds.), *Handbook of engaged scholarship: Contemporary landscapes, future directions*, vol. 1, *Institutional change* (pp. 391–409). East Lansing: Michigan State University Press.

Driscoll, A., & Lynton, E. A. (1999). Making outreach visible: A guide to documenting professional service and outreach. Washington, DC: American Association for Higher Education.

Driscoll, A., & Sandmann, L. R. (2001). From maverick to mainstream. *Journal of Higher Education Outreach and Engagement 6*(2), 9–19.

Ellison, J., & Eatman, T. K. (2008). *Scholarship in public: Knowledge creation and tenure policy in the engaged university: A resource on promotion and tenure in the arts, humanities, and design*. Syracuse, NY: Syracuse University.

Fairweather, J. S. (1996). *Faculty work and the public trust: Restoring the value of teaching and public service in american academic life*. Needham Heights, MA: Allyn and Bacon.

Fiddler, M., McGury, S., Marienau, C., Rogers, R., & Scheideman, W. (1996). Broadening the scope of scholarship: A suggested framework. *Innovative Higher Education, 8*(2), 127–139.

Fitzgerald, H. E., Burack, C., & Seifer, S. D. (Eds.). (2010). *Handbook of engaged scholarship: Contemporary landscapes, future directions*. 2 vols. East Lansing: Michigan State University Press.

Gaston, J. (1971). Secretiveness and competition for priority of discovery in physics. *Minerva, 9*, 472–492.

Glass, C. R., Doberneck, D. M., & Schweitzer, J. H. (2010) Summary of the 2001 revisions to the reappointment, promotion, and tenure form at Michigan State University: Expanding the definition of scholarship to include engagement. *Engagement Exchange 1*(January). East Lansing: Michigan State University, National Collaborative for the Study of University Engagement. Retrieved September 20, 2012, from http://www.ncsue.msu.edu/files/EngagementExchange_No.1_Jan2010.pdf.

Glassick, C. E., Huber, M. T., & Maeroff, G. I. (1997). *Scholarship assessed:Evaluation of the professoriate.* San Francisco: Jossey-Bass.

Goettel, R., & Haft, J. (2010). Imagining America: Engaged scholarship for the arts, humanities, and design. In H. E. Fitzgerald, C. Burack, & S. D. Seifer (Eds.), *Handbook of engaged scholarship: Contemporary landscapes, future directions,* vol. 2, *Community-campus partnerships* (pp. 361–372). East Lansing: Michigan State University Press.

Healey, M. (2000). Developing the scholarship of teaching in higher education: A discipline-based approach. *Higher Education Research and Development, 19*(2), 169–189.

Hofmeyer, A., Newton, M., & Scott, C. (2007). Valuing the scholarship of integration and the scholarship of application in the academy for health sciences scholars: Recommended methods. *Health Research Policy and Systems, 5*(5). Retrieved September 20, 2012, from http://www.health-policy-systems.com/content/pdf/1478-4505-5-5.pdf.

Holland, B. A. (1997). Analyzing institutional commitment to service. *Michigan Journal of Community Service Learning, 4,* 30–41.

Jaeger, A. J., & Thornton, C. H. (2006). Neither honor nor compensation: Faculty and public service. *Educational Policy, 20,* 345–366.

Jordan, C. M. (Ed.). (2007). Community-engaged scholarship review, promotion & tenure package. Peer Review Workgroup, Community-Engaged Scholarship for Health Collaborative. Seattle, WA: Community-Campus Partnerships for Health.

Jordan, C. M. (2010). Redefining peer review and products of engaged scholarship. In H. E. Fitzgerald, C. Burack, & S. D. Seifer (Eds.), *Handbook of engaged scholarship: Contemporary landscapes, future directions,* vol. 1, *Institutional change* (pp. 295–305). East Lansing: Michigan State University Press.

Krahenbuhl, G. S. (1998). Faculty work: Integrating responsibilities and institutional needs. *Change, 30*(6), 18–25.

Levinson, W., Rothman, A. I., & Phillipson, E. (2006). Creative professional activity: An additional platform for promotion of faculty. *Academic Medicine, 81*(6), 568–570.

Lynch, J., Sheard, J., Carbone, A., & Collins, F. (2002). The scholarship of teaching: Risky business in ICT education. Paper presented at the conference of the Australian Association of Research in Education. Retrieved December 3, 2009, from http://www.aare.edu.au/02pap/lyn02030.htm.

Lynton, E. A. (1995). *Making the case for professional service.* Washington, DC: American Association for Higher Education.

Martin, E., Benjamin, J., Prosser, M., & Trigwell, K. (1999). Scholarship of teaching: A study of the approaches of academic staff. In C. Rust (Ed.), *Improving student learning: Improving student learning outcomes* (pp. 326–331). Oxford: Oxford Centre for Staff Learning and Development.

McDowell, G. R. (2001). *Land-grant universities and extension into the 21st century: Renegotiating or abandoning a social contract.* Ames, IA: Iowa State University Press.

McGrath, D. (2006) The scholarship of application. *Journal of Extension* 44, 2FEA8.

Mensah, L. L. (1982). Academic espionage: Dysfunctional aspects of the publish or perish ethic. *Journal of Advanced Nursing, 7*(6), 577–580.

Nora, L. M., Pomeroy, C., Curry Jr., T. E., Hill, N. S., Tibbs, P. A., & Wilson, E. A. (2000). Revising appointment, promotion, and tenure procedures to incorporate an expanded definition of scholarship: The University of Kentucky College of Medicine experience. *Academic Medicine, 75*(9), 913–924.

O'Meara, K. A. (2005). Principles of good practice: Encouraging multiple forms of scholarship in policy and practice. In K. A. O'Meara and R. E. Rice (Eds.), *Faculty priorities reconsidered: Encouraging multiple forms of scholarship* (pp. 290–302). San Francisco: Jossey-Bass.

O'Meara, K. A. (2010). Rewarding multiple forms of scholarship: Promotion and tenure. In H. E. Fitzgerald, C. Burack, & S. D. Seifer (Eds.), *Handbook of engaged scholarship: Contemporary landscapes, future directions*, vol. 1, *Institutional change* (pp. 271–293). East Lansing: Michigan State University Press.

Outreach and Engagement, University of Conneticut. (2010). A sample of definitions of scholarship and engagement. Retrieved March 26, 2010, from outreach.uconn.edu/info/definitions.doc.

Pellino, G. R., Blackburn, R. T., & Boberg, A. L. (1984). The dimensions of academic scholarship: Faculty and administrator views. *Research in Higher Education, 20*, 103–115.

Popovich, N. G., & Abel, S. R. (2002). The need for a broadened definition of faculty scholarship and creativity. *American Journal of Pharmaceutical Education, 66*(Spring): 59–65.

Potter-Witter, K., Beede, D. K., Kaplowitz, M. D., & Whalon, M. E. (2003). Final report: Ad hoc committee on the definition of scholarship (to the college advisory council). Retrieved December 3, 2009, from http://www.canr.msu.edu/canrhome/files/documents/canr_promotion_and_tenure_guidelines_2008–09.pdf.

Potter, M. A., Burdine, J., Olson, D., Silver, G. B., Smith, L. U., Villanueva, A. M., & Wright, K. (2009). Demonstrating excellence in the scholarship of practice-based service for public health. ASPH Special Edition. *Public Health Reports*, July–August. Retrieved September 20, 2012, from http://www.asph.org/UserFiles/FINAL-SPBS.pdf.

Provost's Committee on University Outreach. (1993). *University outreach at michigan state university: Extending knowledge to serve society.* East Lansing: Michigan State University.

Ramsden, P., Margetson, D., Martin, E., & Clarke, S. (1995). *Recognising and rewarding good teaching in Australian higher education.* Committee for the Advancement of University Teaching. Final report. Australian Government Publishing Service.

Research Assessment Exercise. (2006). RAE 2008 panel criteria and working methods. RAE 01/2006. Retrieved November 19, 2009, from http://www.rae.ac.uk/pubs/2006/01/.

Rice, R. E. (1992). Towards a broader conception of scholarship: The American context. In T. G. Whiston & R. L. Geiger (Eds.), *Research and higher education: The United Kingdom and the United States* (pp. 117–129). Buckingham: SRHE and Open University Press.

Rice, R. E. (2002). Beyond scholarship reconsidered: Toward an enlarged vision of the scholarly work of faculty members. *New Directions for Teaching and Learning, 90*(Summer), 7–17.

Sandmann, L. R. (2006). Scholarship as architecture: Framing and enhancing community engagement. *Journal of Physical Therapy Education, 20*(3), 80–84.

Sandmann, L. R., & Weerts, D. J. (2010). Hence: A federation to advance community engagement across higher education. In H. E. Fitzgerald, C. Burack, & S. D. Seifer (Eds.), *Handbook of engaged scholarship: Contemporary landscapes, future directions*, vol. 2, *Community-campus partnerships* (pp. 381–391). East Lansing: Michigan State University Press.

Schlegel & Associates. (2007). Strategic plan: 2007–2010 objectives. N. Falmouth, MA: UMass Dartmouth Strategic Planning Workshop.

Schön, D. A. (1995). Knowing-in-action: The new scholarship requires a new epistemology. *Change*, November–December, 27–34.

Schweitzer, L. (2000). Adoption and failure of the "Boyer model" at the University of Louisville. *Academic Medicine, 75*(9): 925–929.

Seeger, M. (2009). Does communication research make a difference: Reconsidering the impact of our work. *Communication Monographs, 76*(1), 12–19.

Shapiro, E. D., & Coleman, D. L. (2000). The scholarship of application. *Academic Medicine, 75*(9), 895–898.

Shulman, L. S. (1993). Teaching as community property. *Change,* November–December, 6–7.

Southern Polytechnic State University. (2010). Criteria for scholarship. Retrieved March 26, 2010, from http://www.spsu.edu/aa/criteriascholar.htm.

Stanton, T. K., & Howard, J. P. (2009). Research University Engaged Scholarship Toolkit. Boston: Campus Compact. Retrieved September 20, 2012, from http://www.compact.org/initiatives/civic-engagement-at-research-universities/trucen-overview/.

Sundre, D. L. (1992). The specification of the content domain of faculty scholarship. *Research in Higher Education, 33,* 297–315.

Taylor, M., Zanella-Litke, J., Hegedus, S., Peacock, E., Braha, D., Buck, J., … Altabet, M. (2007). Scholarship: Swot analysis. *SWOT 6 Report: Community of Scholars Is Established.* North Dartmouth: University of Massachusetts Dartmouth.

Taylor, P. G. (1999). Linking developmental-cycles to career progress: Recognising and rewarding ICT-enriched teaching. Paper presented at the Sixth International ALT-C Conference, University of Bristol.

Trigwell, K., Martin, E., Benjamin, J., & Prosser, M. (2000). Scholarship of teaching: A model. *Higher Education Research & Development, 19*(2), 155–168.

Wade, A., & Demb, A. (2009). A conceptual model to explore faculty community engagement. *Michigan Journal of Community Service Learning* (Spring), 5–16.

Ward, K. (2003). Faculty service roles and the scholarship of engagement. *ASHE Higher Education Report, 29*(5).

Weiser, C. J. (1996). The value system of a university—rethinking scholarship. Retrieved December 3, 2009, from http://www.adec.edu/clemson/papers/weiser.html.

Weiser, C. J., & Houglum, L. (1998). Scholarship unbound for the 21st century. *Journal of Extension, 36,* n.p.

Western Carolina University. (2010). Scholarship of application mini-grants. Retrieved February 11, 2010, from http://www.wcu.edu/12890.asp.

Wise, G., Retzleff, D., & Reilly, K. (2002). Adapting scholarship reconsidered and scholarship assessed to evaluate University of Wisconsin–Extension outreach faculty for tenure and promotion. *Journal of Higher Education Outreach and Engagement, 7*(3), 5–17.

Young, P. (2006). Out of balance: Lecturers' perceptions of differential status and rewards in relation to teaching and research. *Teaching in Higher Education, 11*(2), 191–202.

Undergraduate Research: Blending the Scholarship of Discovery, Teaching, Application, and Integration

Cynthia Jackson-Elmoore, Korine Steinke Wawrzynski,
Katy Luchini Colbry, and Juliette C. Daniels

I gained a really specific set of skills and deepened my understanding of a lot of concepts. . . . I feel like I have had a unique educational experience.

—Second-year professorial assistant

Traditionally, academic research has focused on discovery—uncovering new knowledge, finding new ways to solve problems, or using new data to revise and clarify previous understanding. In a seminal discussion of the professoriate, Boyer describes this process of discovery as "the commitment to knowledge for its own sake, to freedom of inquiry and to following, in a disciplined fashion, an investigation wherever it may lead" (Boyer, 1990, p. 17). Although discovery is an essential component of research, Boyer also expands the definition of scholarship to include integration, application, and teaching. Boyer's scholarship of integration focuses on drawing connections between different data and across different disciplines and on investigating how new knowledge complements and extends existing understanding. While discovery and integration may take place primarily within the research community, the scholarship of application requires that researchers engage the community at large and find ways to apply new discoveries to solve societal problems. Similarly, the scholarship of teaching focuses on actively engaging students in understanding and transforming knowledge and assisting them in developing skills for life-long learning.

By embracing Boyer's (1990) call to blend the scholarship of discovery with integration, application, and teaching, traditional research can be extended to engage and transform the community.[1] Previous chapters discussed ways that civic engagement and service learning can bridge the gap between academia and the community. This chapter examines how participating in research encourages undergraduate students to apply what they learn in the

33

classroom to real-life situations and helps students understand how research connects to society. Although research endeavors, particularly in academia, have overwhelmingly focused on discovery rather than practical applications or civic engagement,[2] this chapter describes the potential of undergraduate research experiences to help students integrate the scholarship of discovery, integration, application, and teaching by applying classroom knowledge to research problems and making connections between research and broader social concerns. This chapter provides a broad overview and context for undergraduate research experiences. Later chapters will explore specific examples of community engagement and practical applications of academic research.

The chapter focuses on the experiences of a set of undergraduates who engaged in research at Michigan State University (MSU) during the 2008–2009 academic year. It begins by discussing why undergraduate research is important, then presents the study methodology and discusses the value of discovery and teaching in and through undergraduate research. Specifically, the chapter highlights instances where students are able to apply classroom and laboratory knowledge to real-world problems and in the process gain an understanding of and appreciation for the contributions of research to society. It also underscores the importance of intentionally developing mentored undergraduate research experiences that are rich in opportunities for community engagement. The chapter concludes with a discussion of the value and benefits of undergraduate research and suggestions for what remains to be done in encouraging and assessing undergraduate research experiences.

Why Undergraduate Research?

Undergraduate research is an interactive process that engages students with faculty and their scholarship (Dotterer, 2002) and effectively combines research and teaching. Undergraduate research is also one component of inquiry-based learning, which engages students in hands-on activities like teaching, research, and knowledge acquisition and production (Boyer, 1990; Keeling, 2004). There is some debate about what constitutes an undergraduate research experience, particularly when trying to distinguish between inquiry-based learning experiences and research activities that lead to novel discoveries. The Council on Undergraduate Research defines research as "an inquiry or investigation conducted by an undergraduate student that makes an original intellectual or creative contribution to the discipline" (n.d., para. 2). Others posit that undergraduate research does not require an original contribution; rather, students benefit by learning research techniques, being exposed to academic culture, and developing cognitive skills (Kremer & Bringle, 1990; Seymour, Hunter, Laursen, & Deantoni, 2004). Participating on a research team is also valuable, as students learn how individual efforts can contribute to a larger research project. One faculty mentor of undergraduate researchers explains the distinctions between inquiry-based learning and research this way:

> If you follow a question and discover something that is new to you but already known to the scholarly community, what you are doing is inquiry-based learning. If you follow a question and discover something that is new to you *and* new to the scholarly community, it's research. Research is the subset of inquiry that is *new to the scholarly community*.[3]

Undergraduate research and creative activities take multiple forms depending on the academic discipline; examples include laboratory-based or agricultural experimentation, musical composition, creating art, developing materials, historical analysis, and working with primary source materials in a library or museum (Kinkead, 2003). Research experiences, defined broadly to include creative works and activities, usually share several key characteristics (Kinkead, 2003; Hunter, Laursen, & Seymour, 2007; Hu, Scheuch, Schwartz, Gayles, & Li, 2008):

- Mentoring by a faculty member, post-doctoral scholar, or advanced graduate student
- Developing a research idea (independently or stemming from the mentor's work)
- Formulating an initial proposal to outline the student's plan of action
- Training in necessary research methodologies
- Collecting and analyzing data
- Creating a final product (e.g., written or oral)
- Presenting results (e.g., meeting, conference, symposium, etc.)

Of course, the degree to which undergraduate researchers experience these characteristics varies based on students' skills, maturity, year in school, and the length of the research project. For example, students adept at learning research techniques may gain new responsibilities more rapidly than students who need a semester of training. Similarly, students who work on a project for multiple semesters are more likely to participate in a range of activities (e.g., data analysis and interpretation, writing, and dissemination of results) than are students involved for shorter periods of time. While specific characteristics vary, the undergraduate research experience is more than just an independent study—it is a deep educational experience that requires students to invest time and effort into their work on a regular basis (Kuh, 2008).

Although participating in a research experience requires an investment from students and faculty mentors alike, there are numerous benefits for all involved. Students participating in undergraduate research develop academic, personal, and cognitive skills, such as deeper understanding of a subject area; enhanced ability to collect, analyze, and interpret data; development of critical thinking abilities; and improved writing skills. Research experiences can also help undergraduates develop important lifelong abilities, such as organization, self-confidence, improved speaking skills, and learning to both work independently and collaborate with a team (Bauer & Bennett, 2003; Hunter et al., 2007; Kardash, 2000; Lopatto, 2004a; Seymour et al., 2004). Students involved in research are also more likely to persist in school and complete degrees (Astin, 1993; Nagda, Gregerman, Jonides, von Hippel, & Lerner, 1998; Pascarella & Terenzini, 2005). In particular, students from underrepresented populations demonstrate increased retention rates by participating in a research experience (Hurtado, Cabrera, Lin, Arellano, & Espinosa, 2008; Nagda et al., 1998).[4] Additionally, undergraduate research provides opportunities for students to apply classroom learning in hands-on environments (Karukstis, 2005) and can help students clarify plans for graduate school or careers (Bauer & Bennett, 2003; Hathaway, Nagda, & Gregerman, 2002; Hunter et al., 2007; Hurtado et al., 2008; Lopatto, 2007).

Participating in an undergraduate research experience may also help students understand how research impacts society. Paul (2006) asserts that undergraduate education should help foster civic awareness in students and help them to understand how the knowledge and skills that they gain in college can give them the ability to make a difference in society. Schneider (2008) pushes the issue further by stating that a college degree is meaningful "when it represents forms of learning that are both valued by society and empowering to the individual" (p. 2). These points echo Boyer's (1990) observation in *Scholarship Reconsidered* of the nexus that should exist between higher education and society: "If the nation's colleges and universities cannot help students to see beyond themselves and better understand the interdependent nature of our world, each new generation's capacity to live responsibility will be dangerously diminished" (p. 77).

Accordingly, the Association of American Colleges and Universities calls for a new framework for education that can prepare graduates for the realities of the twenty-first century (AAC&U, 2007). Institutions have an obligation to acknowledge the increased interdependence and interconnectivity between higher education and society (Boyer, 1990) and design learning environments that foster deep learning experiences. The AAC&U (2007) describes educational practices, such as undergraduate research, as deep learning experiences because they utilize a variety of active learning methods that challenge, connect, and educate—and can have a profound impact on students. Kuh (2008) observes:

> Such an undergraduate experience deepens learning and brings one's values and beliefs into awareness; it helps students develop the ability to take the measure of events and actions and put them into perspective. As a result, students better understand themselves in relation to others and the larger world, and they acquire the intellectual tools and ethical grounding to act with confidence for the betterment of the human condition. (p. 17)

Undergraduate research experiences are a type of experiential learning that allows students to test-drive the knowledge and skills gained in the classroom in very real settings where they can witness the impact of their work. Undergraduate research can also have a broader impact on society by exposing students to the transformative nature of research and creative activities and by encouraging students to make connections between their scholarship and the larger community—with the goal of developing a habit of civic engagement that can be sustained throughout their careers.

The Setting: Study Population and Methodology

Extant research clearly notes that participating in undergraduate research has the potential to help students apply classroom knowledge to real-life situations and to increase students' understanding of how research impacts society. The current analysis examines these claims for 288 undergraduate students who participated in an undergraduate research or creative activity experience at a large public university during the 2008–2009 school year. The student participants are drawn from three different undergraduate research programs at Michigan State University: (1) a university-wide undergraduate research initiative; (2) the professorial assistantship program; and (3) the Honors College research seminar. While the first program is open to all undergraduates at MSU, the professorial assistantship and research seminars are tailored to academically talented, high-achieving students in the University's Honors College. The professorial assistantship program provides research opportunities to first- and second-year students who rank in approximately the top 1% of incoming first-year students, based on standardized test scores. The Honors College research seminars provide course-based research opportunities to students in their first or second year of college.[5]

During the 2008–2009 academic year, 691 students participated in one of these three research programs. A web-based Undergraduate Research Survey was administered in April 2009 to students who participated in research experiences during the fall and spring semesters, and the same survey was also administered in July 2009 to participants in a summer research experience in engineering that was a subprogram of the university-wide research initiative. Participation in the survey was voluntary, and students did not receive any compensation, reward, or incentive for their participation. The survey was approved by the Michigan State University Institutional Review Board and administered by the University's undergraduate research office. The overall response rate was 42%, with 293 students completing some or all of the survey. After eliminating four duplicates and one invalid survey response, 288 cases remained in the sample.

The Undergraduate Research Survey was designed primarily to assess learning outcomes and student perceptions of their research experiences at the University. The 40-question survey covers three broad areas: (1) the structure of students' research experiences (e.g., compensation, hours worked, training received, frequency of mentor meetings); (2) the impact of the research experience on students' learning (e.g., how participating in an undergraduate research experience impacted their knowledge, academic skills, and abilities) (Lopatto, 2004b); and (3) the outcomes of participating in such a learning experience (e.g., applying classroom knowledge to a practical setting, understanding how research contributes to society, affirmation of career choice). Demographic data was obtained through self-reporting and institutional records.

This chapter discusses how intentionality in undergraduate research experiences can enable young scholars to make connections to the broader society. It is based on an assessment of students' agreement with two statements: (1) participating in undergraduate research enabled me to take what I have learned in class and apply it to a practical setting (the APPLYPR variable); and (2) participating in undergraduate research enabled me to understand how research contributes to society (the SOCIETY variable). Students were asked to respond to these statements using a five-point Likert scale where 1 represented "strongly disagree" and 5 represented "strongly agree." Students' responses as to whether or not they agreed with each statement were examined in relation to several other factors: how frequently students met with their research mentor(s); students' assessments of the usefulness of these mentoring opportunities; and student demographics (e.g., gender, race/ethnicity, year in school, etc.). SPSS 17 was used for basic quantitative analyses (e.g., descriptive statistics, frequencies, difference of means tests, cross-tabulations, ANOVA) and NVivo 7 was used to analyze open-ended responses to the survey questions. The reactions and experiences quoted in this chapter reflect those of students from a wide spectrum of majors (e.g., English, journalism, human biology, pre-vet, mathematics, chemistry, psychology, anthropology, business, and engineering).

The average GPA of the students responding to the Undergraduate Research Survey was 3.71 (SD = 0.29), and approximately 58% of respondents were female. More than two-thirds of the students were in their first two years of college (i.e., 37% first-year students, 35% sophomores, 14% juniors, 13% seniors, 1% lifelong education students). The racial/ethnic distribution of the sample was 87% Caucasian, 0.7% Black/African American, 2.8% Hispanic, 0.4% American Indian/Alaskan Native, 5.6% Asian/Pacific Islander; race/ethnicity information was not available for 3.6% of the students responding to the survey. Approximately 76% of the respondents were members of the Honors College, a university-wide program designed to give high-achieving students opportunities to craft personalized degree programs, engage in undergraduate research and international experiences, and demonstrate leadership on campus and in the community.[6]

The Value of Discovery and Teaching in and through Undergraduate Research

When students described the most positive aspects of their undergraduate research experience, several telltale themes emerged, including the benefits of the following:

- Being able to make an impact and connect with others and society
- Working with a research mentor and/or research team
- Gaining insight into their choice of major/career
- Developing or enhancing research skills and experiences
- Developing or enhancing their personal skill set
- Being able to participate in a project culminating in presentations and publications
- Being exposed to an interesting research topic
- Being compensated

More than half of the students who responded to the survey (51.5%) indicated that their most important reason for becoming involved in research was to gain practical experience. It appears that the rewards and outcomes of their research experiences met their expectations, at least with regard to having some practical utility.

The benefits of engaging in undergraduate research went beyond the perceptions of enhanced personal and professional skills. A second-year student participating in an Honors research seminar wrote, "I learned how to write a coherent blog entry and make a persuasive political argument. I also became a more avid and discerning consumer of the news." This is one of several instances where the undergraduate research experiences allowed the students to grow as informed and engaged citizen scholars. The overall impact of their research experiences become even clearer when the students reflected on what they have gained personally, other than compensation via class credits or an actual stipend. Several students noted that the most positive aspects of their research experience were that it:

helped me learn to work independently

helped me to strengthen my leadership and organizational skills

[encouraged me] to share my thoughts and opinions

taught me to be well rounded and to use my resources to find answers

Table 1. Examples of Impact of Undergraduate Research (percent)

Undergraduate research experiences	Students' agreement with statement		
	Agree	Undecided	Disagree
Enable undergraduates to apply classroom knowledge to a practical setting (APPLYPR)	75.8	11.8	12.5
Help undergraduates to understand how research contributes to society (SOCIETY)	75.6	13.1	11.2

NOTE: Numbers do not total to 100 because of rounding.

These are important life skills and are essential in working to make knowledge public, relevant, available, and applicable to society as a whole.

The survey research also revealed that students were appreciative of the opportunity to go beyond themselves and make connections to the larger community. As reflected in table 1, over 75% of the students responding to the survey agreed that participating in undergraduate research helped them apply classroom knowledge to practical settings (APPLYPR) and understand how research contributes to society (SOCIETY). The discussion that follows examines these impacts with respect to differences between students and the nature of their research experiences. Given the interest in encouraging students to engage with the community in a myriad of ways (e.g., Fretz & Longo, 2010; Ramaley, 2010; Reich & Nelson, 2010; Springer & Casey, 2010), it is useful to consider how undergraduate research helps to achieve this goal.

Applying Classroom/Laboratory Knowledge to Real-World Problems

The data for the current study clearly indicated that students valued the opportunity to apply what they learned through coursework to more complex, real-life scenarios. A second-year student participating in an Honors research seminar noted that "[the most positive aspect of my research experience was the] opportunity to apply what I learned in the class into research and also gaining new insight on a research field other than my major." This sentiment was echoed by many of the students. Interestingly, the students who had an opportunity for mentoring were more likely to report that their undergraduate research experience enabled them to apply classroom knowledge to practical situations than were those who were not mentored (table 2). The magnitude of the differences in the means was moderate (mean difference = 1.52, 95% CI: 0.78 to 2.26, $\eta^2 = 0.06$).[7] Although each of the students in this study had at least one faculty member engaged in the project, they did not all meet and interact meaningfully with that faculty member or other research team members. Thus, in this study the opportunity to meet with research mentors made a significant difference in students' ability to apply classroom knowledge to practical settings. This indicated that intentionality in mentoring relationships was an important component in helping students think about their learning more broadly.

The ability to apply classroom learning to real-world situations was impacted by both the frequency and the nature of mentoring interactions (Steinke Wawrzynski, Jackson-Elmoore, Boucher-Niemi, & Luchini Colbry, 2010). The more frequently that students and research mentors met, the more likely students were to be able to apply what they learned in class to practical situations. Meeting just once a month as opposed to meeting more infrequently or never meeting made all the difference between a student being able to apply classroom learning more broadly or not; however, more frequent meetings did not significantly increase students' ability to use classroom lessons in real-world applications (ANOVA: $F(2,241) = 9.19$, $p < .05$). Students were also more likely to report that they could apply what they learned in class to practical settings if they perceived the meetings with their research mentor to be of value (ANOVA: $F(4,238) = 10.96$, $p < .05$). This suggests that what occurs in the student-research mentor meetings can be impactful enough to enable students to bridge the gap between classroom learning and practical applications.

There were no statistically significant differences based on year in school (or class level), gender, or race/ethnicity[8] in this group of students' perception of their ability to apply classroom knowledge to practical settings because of having engaged in undergraduate research. The data did suggest, however, that undergraduate research may have been particularly valuable for students who may not typically have had opportunities to make meaning out of their classroom learning experiences (see table 2). For instance, students who were not members of the Honors College reported stronger agreement with the idea that undergraduate research helped them apply classroom knowledge in practical settings than did students in the Honors College; however, the effect size is small ($\eta^2 = 0.03$, mean difference $= -0.38$). Similarly, students who did not participate in one of the specialized research programs (professorial assistant or Honors research seminar) were more likely to agree that undergraduate research helped them apply classroom knowledge in practical settings than were students who did participate in one of the special research opportunities.[9] The effect size in this case is small to moderate ($\eta^2 = 0.05$, mean difference $= -0.45$). To the extent that these experiences are valid for larger sets of students, it suggests that providing opportunities for a range of undergraduates to conduct research is a critical component of higher education. Furthermore, it demonstrates the potential of undergraduate research to help students make meaningful connections between academics and societal issues.

Understanding and Appreciating the Contribution of Research to Society

One of the goals of any high-quality, high-impact educational experience is to help students see how what they learn and do contributes to and impacts society. Undergraduate research experiences present such an opportunity, both directly and indirectly. Some of the students in the current study were involved in community-based research where they could immediately see how research makes a difference in the lives of others. Other students did not have this direct experience, but in both cases students were able to observe connections between research and society at large:

> I felt like I was really contributing to society for the first time. It [engaging in undergraduate research] helped me to see how the scientific community relates to the business and public; how everything is really connected; and I was connected to it. (First-year professorial assistant)

> [My undergraduate research experience] gave me a better understanding of how our research affects the community and how appreciative members of the community are for it. This was especially true for my research because it dealt with a cancer prevention program. (First-year honors research seminar participant)

Table 2. Ability to Apply Classroom Learning to Practical Settings and Enhanced Understanding of How Research Contributes to Society Based on Student Characteristics

Student Characteristics	Apply classroom learning			Understand research's societal contribution		
	Mean	SD	T-statistic[†]	Mean	SD	T-statistic[†]
Student has						
Mentoring opportunity	4.02	0.90	4.04*	4.05	0.83	5.46*
No mentoring opportunity	2.50	1.23		2.17	0.98	
Member of the Honors College						
HC	3.89	0.94	−2.58*	3.95	0.90	−1.76
Non-HC	4.27	0.90		4.20	0.83	
Participant in two year early career research program						
Professorial Assistant	3.91	0.96	1.73	3.85	0.95	−0.57
Non-Professorial Assistant	3.64	0.88		3.94	0.84	
Participant in yearlong research seminar						
RSP	3.68	0.87	−1.14	3.95	0.88	0.63
Non-RSP	3.90	0.96		3.85	0.96	
Participant in either specialized experience[‡]						
PA/RSP	3.83	0.94	−3.74*	3.89	0.91	−2.69*
Non-PA/RSP	4.28	0.87		4.20	0.79	
Class level[§]						
Underclassmen	3.92	0.83	−0.82	3.99	0.86	−0.08
Upperclassmen	4.01	1.01		4.00	0.90	
Gender						
Women	3.97	0.94	0.22	4.01	0.93	−0.30
Men	4.00	0.93		3.98	0.80	
Race/ethnicity						
Caucasian	3.97	0.92	−0.14	3.99	0.90	−5.15
Students of color	4.00	0.90		4.09	0.79	

[†]Based on independent samples *t*-test, assuming equal variance.

[‡]Comparing students who are professorial assistants or participants in the yearlong research seminar to all other student researchers.

[§]Freshmen and sophomores are categorized as underclassmen; juniors and seniors as upperclassmen.

*Significant at the 0.01 level.

Certainly, some faculty—and by default, their student research assistants—pursue work that is community-based and/or translational in nature. For example, one student created linguistically and culturally appropriate health care brochures, a website, and a video to increase awareness of and access to health care services in the Metro Detroit area for immigrant families from Asia and the Pacific Islands. Another student examined policy mechanisms that will allow Michigan schools to benefit from producing renewable energy; while another group of students investigated the amount of phantom energy lost in residence hall rooms across the MSU campus. Students involved in these types of research projects had direct opportunities to see how research contributes to society.

Several of the Honors research seminars were also designed to encourage community interaction: examining theoretical and popular debates about the efficacy of vaccinations for school-aged children and corresponding policy implications; exploring issues related to breast cancer awareness and prevention among African American women; or researching and blogging about the presidential election process. Another seminar taught undergraduates to use a scanning electron microscope for scientific observation and analysis, and then brought K-12 students to the MSU campus and had the undergraduates teach the visitors how to use the equipment, thereby fostering science knowledge and excitement in future generations. Still another seminar encouraged students to research and implement strategies to enhance the MSU Museum experience for sight-impaired visitors. These types of research experiences intentionally challenge students to engage with the community, and as a result help students see how research connects to society.

These are all examples of intentionality in the design of the research experience, whereby students were given an opportunity to understand the connections between research and society as a whole. Key in all of this was the mentorship relationship. Not surprisingly, there was a significant difference in the students' ability to understand how research contributes to society based on whether or not they had a mentoring opportunity. Students with a mentoring opportunity were substantially more likely to understand how research contributes to society than were students with limited or no mentoring opportunity (see table 2). The magnitude of the differences in the means was moderate to large (mean difference = 1.88, 95% CI: 1.20 to 2.25, $\eta^2 = 0.11$); indicating that mentoring helped students advance their understanding of the societal importance and relevance of research.

The more often students interacted with mentors within a month; the more students were likely to understand how research contributes to society (ANOVA: $F(2,240) = 19.80$, $p < .05$). Students were also more likely to report being able to understand how research contributes to society if they found the meetings with their research meetings to be of use (ANOVA: $F(4, 237) = 12.14$, $p < .05$). Frequent and useful meetings provide an opportunity for students and mentors to discuss the implications of the research and its relative contribution and value to society. Understanding how research contributes to society as a result of participating in undergraduate research was not impacted by year in school (or class level), gender, or race/ethnicity in this group of students. However, the students who were more likely to report that their undergraduate research experience helped them understand how research contributes to society were students who had not participated in one of the specialized research experiences geared toward students in the Honors College (see table 2). It may be that by having an opportunity to engage in deeper level learning—that may not have otherwise been provided—this set of students was able to make connections between research and its impact on society.

Pulling It All Together: The Value and Benefits of Integration

Without a doubt, participating in community-based research is a powerful way to help undergraduates make connections between their scholarship and society at large. It is useful, however, to consider other mechanisms for helping students appreciate community engagement and understand the relevance of research outcomes to society when it is not possible or likely that they will engage in community-based research. More specifically, *mentoring* is one way that students participating in undergraduate research can begin to appreciate how and why addressing community issues is important. Undergraduate research experiences can also provide opportunities for students to *transmit and apply knowledge* in ways that enhance their conceptual understanding or address a local, regional, national, or global challenge (Provost's Committee on University Outreach, 1993).[10] Granted, not all students will be exposed to community-based research, nor will all students be engaged to the point of actively translating research findings into practice. However, undergraduate research opportunities can provide an opportunity for students to develop a deeper understanding of how research contributes to society and understand how education can enhance or improve society.

The quantitative data indicated that students participating in this study who did not have specialized research experiences were more likely to report that they were able to apply the knowledge and skills they acquired in the classroom to practical settings and understand how research contributes to society as a result of their undergraduate research experience. Similarly, students who were not members of the Honors College were more likely to report that their undergraduate research experience helped them to understand how research contributes to society. These findings emphasize the important role of faculty mentors who help students move beyond the classroom or laboratory and connect their campus experiences to a larger community.

It is reasonable to expect that the high-functioning, high-achieving students in the Honors College may be predisposed to apply classroom learning to other settings and to understand the impact of research on society. Interestingly, a review of the qualitative data from the open-ended survey responses indicated that—for this sample—only Honors College students participating in specialized research experiences for first- and second-year students were able to clearly articulate what they learned through undergraduate research. This is not to suggest that these are the only students capable of developing and articulating a nuanced understanding of the broader impact of their undergraduate research experience. However, it is a reflection of this particular group of participants—and perhaps of the intentional design of the professorial assistant program and Honors research seminars. Indeed, the very nature of the Honors College at Michigan State University affords students multiple opportunities to interact with faculty in and out of class, and to think deeply about their educational experiences. Thus, students in the Honors College have access to built-in mentorship experiences and are encouraged to think critically at the level necessary to go beyond self and make connections to the world around oneself.

The Office of the Associate Provost for Undergraduate Education has created research and mentorship opportunities for undergraduates throughout the university, regardless of major, year in school, or college affiliation. Such an approach is crucial, since as Kuh's (2008) research demonstrates, these types of engaged learning opportunities benefit all students— not just high-achieving students. In particular, they help students with lower standardized test scores coming out of high school "catch up" with their peers. Undergraduate research experiences provide opportunities for a broad spectrum of students to apply classroom learning to more complex and practical settings, and help students understand the nexus between higher education and society.

This study demonstrates that students believe that undergraduate research is valuable to them. One key outcome is that undergraduate research helps students to see how their work contributes to society. This is particularly the case when there is a committed mentor working with students. It is clear from student commentary that having a mentoring opportunity yields manifest benefits, including an enhanced ability for students to demonstrate critical thinking and to clearly and carefully articulate their experiences. Therefore, to the extent that undergraduate research works to help students apply classroom knowledge to practical settings and understand how research contributes to society, it is important that these mentoring opportunities be plentiful and substantial. After all, the overall goal of undergraduate research experiences should be both to advance knowledge and to facilitate the development of scholars and professionals who can make positive, meaningful, and sustainable contributions to society.

Where Do We Go from Here?

Several interesting observations can be made from the data that are tied to both the nature of faculty interaction with students and the qualities of the students themselves. First, mentorship has a tremendous impact on a student's ability both to apply classroom knowledge to a practical setting and to understand how research contributes to society. Thus mentoring is one mechanism by which students can be encouraged to engage with the community and make their research relevant and applicable to society. Accordingly, faculty mentors can intentionally design learning opportunities that enable and encourage student researchers to consider how their work may impact others beyond the scope of their projects. While novice student researchers may not perceive how their work connects to society at large, it is important for mentors to communicate that research does not end when a project is finished or when a student graduates.

Knowledge is not as valuable if contained in a vacuum; rather, scholars are trained to disseminate new knowledge and newly discovered applications. Research mentors can initiate conversations that ask thought-provoking questions: How does this work fit into a broader scheme? Does it contribute to the greater body of knowledge of a respective field? How can it be applied? How can it be used to the benefit of others? Research mentors can and should provide students with tools to begin thinking about potential applications and discuss how to make those connections between research and society at large. These types of conversations appear to happen during many mentoring opportunities in this study—and students appreciate the guidance—but educators need to be more aware of this potential outcome and intentionally create occasions for this type of learning to occur.

A related area to consider is how these deep learning experiences[11] should affect and fit into the overall undergraduate curriculum in colleges and universities. Having the opportunity to internalize and apply their learning excites students and engages them more deeply in their studies. It also helps students make connections to the world outside of the academy that may be obvious to faculty and administrators—but not necessarily to students balancing classes, work, and extracurricular commitments. The current study, as well others (Hunter et al., 2007; Kuh, 2008; Lopatto, 2004a, 2007; Seymour et al., 2004), demonstrates the tremendous impact that undergraduate research can have on undergraduates' learning and achievement. Yet these innovative learning opportunities are only available to a small portion of undergraduates (Schneider, 2008), so how can colleges and universities offer more structured opportunities for undergraduate research and other deep learning experiences?

One way to begin to change the curriculum is to educate faculty and administrators on the value of these engaged learning experiences. The more that faculty members advocate for and invest in undergraduate research, the more likely it is that students will participate. Kuh, Chen, and Nelson Laird (2007) observe that undergraduate research is not a by-product of faculty working on research; rather faculty must take an interest in and promote undergraduate research in order to engage students in their work. Convincing faculty of the benefits of offering this type of learning activity is one step toward modifying the curriculum at colleges and universities. Another approach lies with the administration, as senior administrators and department chairs facilitate discussions on how to institutionalize deep learning opportunities for undergraduates in order to maximize the number of students engaged in these types of learning experiences.

Undergraduate research experiences also afford students opportunities to experience the relationship between academic discovery, integration, and application. Undergraduate research experiences socialize novice researchers into their future profession and help students develop the skills, abilities, habits, and perspective essential to success in the discipline. In particular, community-based undergraduate research experiences socialize students as emerging research professionals and public scholars, allowing them the opportunity to fully appreciate how empirical inquiry can impact the society in which they live (Paul, 2006). Not only does this intentional approach encourage a meaningful educational experience at the undergraduate level, it also sets the stage for a generation of researchers fully aware of the impact of academic inquiry on society as a whole. Undergraduate research experiences create a space for students to consider their role in advancing knowledge and benefiting society, and exposing undergraduates to the impact of research on their community, now and in the future, can be a transformational learning moment.

Engaged learning opportunities like undergraduate research can also help institutions of higher education bolster their public perceptions. In a time when budgets are continuously shrinking and public criticism continuously increases, institutions—both large and small—need to be cognizant of how external constituents (e.g., parents, legislators, future employers of graduates) view the products of our higher education system. Land-grant institutions, in particular, hold a special responsibility to contribute to the communities that surround them. Institutions have to combat the idea that education is only a personal benefit, instead demonstrating that their graduates and the university community contribute to and are engaged in society at local, regional, national, and international levels (Boyer, 1996).

Society relies on the educational system to produce high-quality, competitive graduates capable of leading their communities into the future. Accordingly, institutions of higher education have an obligation to provide opportunities that will help prepare

45

students for the challenges of the twenty-first century. Indeed, employers expect graduates to have these nuanced skills and abilities (Peter D. Hart Research Associates, 2006), and students need a variety of hands-on experiences to solidify connections and concepts in order to observe how their learning fits into the world around them and to understand how they can contribute. Undergraduate research and other hands-on learning experiences represent one piece to this curricular challenge, and is a component that can engage students and faculty in academic endeavors while improving society's perspective on the value of higher education. The role of mentoring in helping to achieve these goals cannot be overstated: It is essential.

Notes

1. Embedding community engagement in all aspects of research is the most reliable way to ensure that there are meaningful and sustained exchanges between the broader community and the academic realm.
2. There are certainly exceptions to the idea of exclusive focus on discovery over practical application (e.g., engineering, business, public administration).
3. Michael Velbel, professor of geography, Michigan State University, personal communication.
4. Hurtado et al.'s (2008) study of how underrepresented students of color experience science also reveals that this population of undergraduates faces additional challenges related to being involved in research programs specifically targeted for students of color, feel pressured to prove their academic abilities due to negative perceptions of their race, and have difficulties establishing a credible science identity. Despite these concerns, it is clear that students, regardless of race or gender, benefit in multiple dimensions by engaging in a research experience during their college experience.
5. A professorial assistantship is a two-year program in which high-achieving students in their first and second years of college at Michigan State University are assigned to a research mentor. The students can change mentors between years one and two if they so choose and can do an assistantship in any area of interest; it is not restricted to a student's preferred major. The Honors College research seminars are a yearlong research experience in which a small group of students work with faculty members to both learn about and engage in research. The seminar participants are expected to prepare a research presentation as part of their experience.
6. In addition, 60% of the survey respondents had participated in either a professorial assistantship or an Honors research seminar.
7. The effect size is measured by eta^2 (η^2); η^2 values < 0.01 denote a small effect, $\eta^2 < 0.06$ a moderate effect and $\eta^2 < 0.14$ a large effect (Pallant, 2007).
8. This sample is fairly homogenous and thus may be masking in racial/ethnic differences. It would be interesting to see if differences would emerge in a more diverse sample.
9. It is possible to be a member of the Honors College who participates in research but is not a professorial assistant or participant in an Honors research seminar.
10. Community-based research experiences that involve undergraduates are an example of an opportunity that goes a step further by serving a particular need in the community (Paul 2006) while providing real-world applications of an academic discipline that helps to illustrate the relevance of the subject and its practical applications (Karukstis, 2005).

11. The AAC&U highlights the following teaching and learning practices as deep learning opportunities: First-year seminars and experiences, common intellectual experiences, learning communities, writing-intensive courses, collaborative assignments and projects, diversity/global learning, service learning and community-based learning, internships, and capstone courses and projects.

References

Association of American Colleges and Universities (AAC&U). (2007). *College learning for the new global century.* Washington, DC: Association of American Colleges and Universities.

Astin, A. (1993). *What matters in college? Four critical years revisited.* San Francisco: Jossey-Bass.

Bauer, K. W., & Bennett, J. S. (2003). Alumni perceptions used to assess undergraduate research experience. *Journal of Higher Education, 74*(2), 210–230.

Boyer, E. L. (1990). *Scholarship reconsidered: Priorities for the professoriate.* Princeton, NJ: Carnegie Foundation for the Advancement of Teaching.

Boyer, E. L. (1996). The Scholarship of Engagement. *Journal of Public Service and Outreach, 1*(1), 11–20.

Boyer Commission. (1998). *Reinventing undergraduate education: A blueprint for America's research universities.* Princeton, NJ: Carnegie Foundation for the Advancement of Teaching.

Council on Undergraduate Research. (n.d.). Frequently asked questions. Retrieved from http://www.cur.org/about_cur/frequently_asked_questions_/#2.

Dotterer, R. L. (2002). Student-faculty collaborations, undergraduate research, and collaboration as an administrative model. In Kenneth J. Zahorski (Ed.), *Scholarship in the Postmodern Era: New Venues, New Values, New Visions,* New Directions for Teaching and Learning (90), 81–89.

Fretz, E. J., & Longo, N. V. (2010). Students co-creating an engaged academy. In H. E. Fitzgerald, C. Burack, & S. D. Seifer (Eds.), *Handbook of engaged scholarship: Contemporary landscapes, future directions*, vol. 1, *Institutional change* (pp. 313–329). East Lansing: Michigan State University Press.

Hathaway, R. S., Nagda, B. A., & Gregerman, S. R. (2002). The relationship of undergraduate research participation to graduate and professional education pursuit: An empirical study. *Journal of College Student Development, 43*(5), 614–631.

Hu, S., Scheuch, K. R., Schwartz, R., Gayles, J. G., & Li, S. (2008). Reinventing undergraduate education: Engaging college students in research and creative activities. Special issue of *ASHE Higher Education Report, 33*(4). Hoboken, NJ: Wiley Periodicals.

Hunter, A.-B., Laursen, S. L., & Seymour, E. (2007). Becoming a scientist: The role of undergraduate research in students' cognitive, personal, and professional development. *Science Education, 91*(1), 36–74.

Hurtado, S., Cabrera, N. L., Lin, M. H., Arellano, L., & Espinosa, L. L. (2008). Diversifying science: Underrepresented student experiences in structured research programs. *Research in Higher Education, 50*(2), 189–214.

Jaccard, J., Becker, M. A., & Wood, G. (1984). Pairwise multiple comparision procedures: A review. *Psychological Bulletin, 96*(3), 589–596.

Kardash, C. M. (2000). Evaluation of an undergraduate research experience: Perceptions of undergraduate interns and their faculty mentors. *Journal of Educational Psychology, 92*(1), 191–201.

Karukstis, K. (2005). Community-based research: A new paradigm for undergraduate research in the sciences. *Journal of Chemical Education, 82*(1), 15–16.

Karukstis, K. (2007). The impact of undergraduate research on America's global competitiveness. *Journal of Chemical Education, 84*(6), 912–914.

Keeling, R. P. (Ed.). (2004). *Learning reconsidered: A campus-wide focus on the student experience.* Washington, DC: National Association of Student Personnel Administrators and the American College Personnel Association.

Kinkead, J. (2003). Learning through inquiry: An overview of undergraduate research. In Joyce Kinkead (Ed.), *Valuing and supporting undergraduate research*, New Directions for Teaching and Learning (93), 5–17.

Kremer, J. F., & Bringle, R. G. (1990). The effects of an intensive research experience on the careers of talented undergraduates. *Journal of Research and Development in Education, 24*(1), 1–5.

Kuh, G. D. (1996). Guiding principles for creating seamless learning environments for undergraduates. *Journal of College Student Development, 37*, 135–148.

Kuh, G. D. (2008). *High-impact educational practices: What they are, who has access to them, and why they matter.* Washington, DC: Association of American Colleges and Universities.

Kuh, G. D., Chen, D., & Nelson Laird, T. F. (2007). Why teacher-scholars matter: Some insights from FSSE and NSSE. *Liberal Education, 93*(4), 40–45.

Lopatto, D. (2004a). Survey of undergraduate research experiences (SURE): First findings. *Cell Biology Education, 3*(4), 270–277.

Lopatto, D. (2004b). What undergraduate research can tell us on research on learning. Retrieved August 24, 2009, from http://www.pkal.org/documents/Vol4WhatUndergradResearchCanTellUs.cfm.

Lopatto, D. (2007). Undergraduate research experiences support science career decisions and active learning. *Life Sciences Education, 6*(4), 297–306.

Nagda, B. A., Gregerman, S. R., Jonides, J., von Hippel, W., & Lerner, J. S. (1998). Undergraduate student-faculty research partnerships affect student retention. *Review of Higher Education, 22*(1), 55–72.

Osborn, J. M., & Karukstis, K. K. (2009). The benefits of undergraduate research, scholarship, and creative activity. In M. K. Boyd & J. L. Weseman (Eds.), *Broadening participation on undergraduate research: Fostering excellence and enhancing the impact* (pp. 41–53). Washington, DC: Council on Undergraduate Research.

Pallant, J. (2007). *SPSS Survival Manual* (3rd ed.). New York: McGraw Hill Open University Press.

Pascarella, E. T., & Terenzini, P. T. (2005). *How college affects students*, vol. 2, *A third decade of research.* San Francisco: Jossey-Bass.

Paul, E. L. (2006). Community-based research as scientific and civic pedagogy. *Peer Review, 8*(1), 12–15.

Peter D. Hart Research Associates Inc. (2006). How should colleges prepare students to succeed in today's global economy? Retrieved September, 2009, from www.aacu.org/leap/public_opinion_research.cfm.

Provost's Committee on University Outreach (1993). *University outreach at Michigan State University: Extending knowledge to serve society.* East Lansing: Michigan State University Press.

Ramaley, J. A. (2010). Students as scholars: Integrating research, education, and professional practice. In H. E. Fitzgerald, C. Burack & S. D. Seifer (Eds.), *Handbook of engaged scholarship: Contemporary landscapes, future directions*, vol. 1, *Institutional change* (pp. 353–368). East Lansing: Michigan State University Press.

Reich, J. N., & Nelson, P. D. (2010). Engaged scholarship: Perspectives from psychology. In H. E. Fitzgerald, C. Burack, & S. D. Seifer (Eds.), *Handbook of engaged scholarship: Contemporary landscapes, future directions*, vol. 2, *Community-campus partnerships* (pp. 131–147). East Lansing: Michigan State University Press.

Russell, S. H. (2006). Evaluation of NSF support for undergraduate research opportunities: Draft synthesis report executive summary. NSF Contract Number GS-10F-0554N. Arlington, VA.

Schneider, C. G. (2008). Introduction. In G. D. Kuh (Ed.), *High-impact educational practices: What they are, who has access to them, and why they matter* (pp. 1–9). Washington, DC: Association of American Colleges and Universities.

Seymour, E., Hunter, A.-B., Laursen, S., & Deantoni, T. (2004). Establishing the benefits of research experiences for undergraduates in the sciences: First findings from a three-year study. Center to Advance Research and Teaching in the Social Sciences.

Springer, N. C., & Casey, K. M. (2010). From "preflection" to reflection: Building quality practices in academic service-learning. In H. E. Fitzgerald, C. Burack & S. D. Seifer (Eds.), *Handbook of engaged scholarship: Contemporary landscapes, future directions*, vol. 2, *Community-campus partnerships* (pp. 29–49). East Lansing: Michigan State University Press.

Steinke Wawrzynski, K., Jackson-Elmoore, C., Boucher-Niemi, J., & Luchini Colbry, K. (2010). The impact of mentoring on students' broader understandings of undergraduate research. Poster presented at the AAC&U Conference on Creativity, Inquiry, and Discovery: Undergraduate Research in and across the Disciplines, Durham, NC, November 11–13.

From Passive Transfer of Knowledge to Active Engaged Learning: A Reflection and Commentary

Cyrus Stewart and Karen McKnight Casey

This chapter offers one professor's personal reflection on almost 20 years of service learning methods and experience in the context of general education courses at Michigan State University, followed by a response regarding the future of civic engagement and service learning by the director of Michigan State University's Center for Service-Learning and Civic Engagement.

One Professor's Reflection

Cyrus Stewart

The following provides my personal reflection on almost 20 years of service-learning experience in the context of general education courses I teach at Michigan State University. It is ironic that I have not done what I require my students to do, namely, keep a "critical incident journal" that I could now draw upon, because the moment for reflection is now.

In the early years of my teaching experience, when students asked if there was any additional work that they could do to improve their grades, the only option that I found acceptable at that time was to tell them to dig deeper into some of the concepts, processes, and applications of the course content for an extra-credit paper. I was never satisfied with this option, for, in my experience, the papers that resulted often seemed to be very superficial and the time required to do them was taken away from studying, which resulted in lower grades. I became, therefore, quite unwilling to provide what I considered to be a dysfunctional option. That changed when the possibility of providing a service-learning experience became available.

My background includes years of undergraduate instruction in psychology, graduate education in sociology, research involvement in practical social issues, clinical experience as a marriage and family counselor, and practice as a licensed clinical social worker, as well as being a member of Michigan State University's social science general education faculty. These experiences primed me for the kind of experience that service learning offers. Regardless of one's area of specialization, theoretical inclinations, or pedagogical style, students' active participation in service-learning opportunities helps them acquire critical thinking skills, retain knowledge, and apply that knowledge in real-life situations. In order to retain and apply knowledge, students must develop strategies that enhance their personal connection to its meaning and relevance.

Service Learning: Benefits to Community and Self

Service learning has proven to be a great way to deal with the vague dissatisfaction with the experiential restrictions students face in a classroom environment. Just as my own horizons were opened dramatically by my active participation in the clinical treatment of individuals and families, my students have benefited from community-based engagement experiences. Over time, as I became aware of how academic concerns sometimes seem to have only questionable relevance to the world beyond the classroom, I became increasingly committed to providing students with illustrations of the direct application and usefulness of course materials to their everyday life. I moved away from providing instruction as a passive transfer of known information to the active exchange between learner and teacher and the pursuit of knowledge for the solution of contemporary social issues (Palmer, 1998; Tanner & Tanner, 1980).

In applying one's knowledge and experience in critical inquiry, the focus is on whether the information is of practical utility in the solution of problems. Such critical engagement in concrete practice develops an awareness of the applicability of knowledge. If we perceive and reflect with a discerning eye on what we do, the realistic consequences of our actions will guide future practice. I asked myself: "Could I integrate the problem-focused nature of my general education offerings with experiences external to the university such that personal reflection combined with social action could produce a caring self and a collaborative critical consciousness of social justice?" In other words, could I place my students in circumstances that they were not accustomed to and, thereby, enable them to experience both themselves and the "other" in the context of difference? (Rhoads, 1997). My answer to both of these questions was an unequivocal yes.

It has, therefore, been my goal these many years to help ensure that, through university-community integration, students are able to apply what they are learning in class to actual external situations. In being given the opportunity to be of service to communities with self-defined needs, students are afforded the possibility of experiencing how what they are learning might actually create an impact in the real world. Additionally, through reciprocal interactions with diverse others, students are encouraged to see themselves through another's eyes and develop a compassionate self based on an ethic of caring. The relevance of education is also clear, and learning is actively and experientially grounded.

Active Reflection in Service Learning

Recognizing the role of external engagement in the development of a caring self and a social consciousness is the foundation of service learning. When rehearsing behaviors and active engagement are combined with self-reflection, community service becomes service learning. The reflection component is not simply a free association. Rather, it is a structured processing of experience that connects self-awareness and insight with academic content to produce a critical consciousness where neither is privileged. Service learning stands at the intersection between academic instruction and education for reality-based practice or experience. It is the point where learning becomes education for practical use. Education and practice, in the context of real people and their problems, require the resolution of three interrelated problems: (1) the "disciplinary purity" of the student engaged in service; (2) self-determination among those privileged; and (3) paternalism directed toward the receiver of preset notions of what the problems are and what solutions are most workable. Frequently, the problems defined and the solutions offered are not what the community has seen as most relevant or important.

Interaction and Sustainable Solutions

Effective problem definition and the development of appropriate solutions require a coincidence of interest between the parties involved. This becomes quite obvious when the helpers listen to problems as experienced by, and possible solutions from, those being assisted. Moreover, if our desire is to develop and maintain sustainable solutions, it is necessary to design interventions consistent with the cultural ideologies, economic and political resources, and dynamics of interaction and personality styles of those who deal with the issues on a daily basis. Such self-determination places an emphasis on the multiplicity of problem identification, decision making, and cultural/personal compatibility. The only reliable and sustainable resolutions are those that are designed and implemented by those directly involved. Roles of "helping" and "helped" are in continual flux as resources for problem solutions are not a stable component of either role. It is the connection of practical experience resulting from community service, together with academic knowledge, that is the jewel of service learning. Not only can a student be of service to the community; the community can also enable the student to realistically and critically examine the usefulness of academic learning.

From "I" and "They" to "We"

Many of our students are more experienced with community service than are the faculty. I have been continually amazed, given the stereotypic assumptions about the self-centeredness and job preparation foci of contemporary students, how many students have already experienced community service as they enter our classes and are eager to continue volunteering in some manner.

For some, though, the original motivation to volunteer their time from quite hectic schedules is to obtain the additional "points" that can be earned from service-learning experiences. However, while these students may initially be only interested in the extra points, it does not take long for such external rewards to recede in favor of internal gratification. Students often become increasingly attached to the young people with whom they are working. Teaching children their multiplication tables, helping them with spelling lists or the geographic identification of the states, quickly yields to a greater emotional and personal caring. They begin to accept the role of "my MSU friend." A self based on an ethic of compassion and caring is developed as students extend themselves to assist others and, in this process, discover significant and unrecognized aspects of themselves.

Thus, what may have started as an individualistic concern for self and class success turns into a concern for others. While this giving to another may be dismissed as "the privileged providing charitable contributions to those less fortunate," the focus soon changes from "I" and "they" to "we." Many students have indicated that whatever may have been received by those they worked with and assisted seems incomparable to the feelings of personal contribution, accountability, and responsibility that the students found in themselves.

Vignette 1: A Sense of Responsibility

It was near the end of the semester, when the responsibilities for service-learning participation were almost over, that "Mary" had an experience that illustrates the growing sense of personal commitment and voluntary engagement typical of the latter stages of service learning. The weather was inclement and Mary had overslept and would not be able to catch her bus to the service-learning site. It was also the final week of her responsibilities, and no one would have blamed Mary if she had called her site placement and told them that she was unable to make it. No one, that is, except Mary herself. She related how guilty she would have felt if she had not been there for her student, for he always looked forward to being with his "MSU friend." Their relationship, combined with her commitment, would not allow her to sidestep her responsibility. She resolved the situation quite simply. Since she did not have a car at her disposal and no one she knew had one that she could borrow, she called a local taxi company and paid the fare to her site with her own money. Rather than feeling put upon, Mary felt that she had done nothing special—she was simply meeting her responsibility to another person and responding to some quite significant aspects of herself. She could not have imagined doing anything else.

Learning through Doing

Many of our students originally approach the service-learning opportunity with a background of experience in community service. While faculty may distinguish between these two types of service, most of our students do not. Students may complain about the lack of seeming relevance of their courses. However, the discerning of relevance is facilitated by their active participation in venues where their course material is not only conceptually relevant but is being directly applied. Many students have acknowledged that it is much easier to remember and apply their learning when they have had the chance to "experience it for themselves" through doing.

Some Impacts of Service Learning on Self-Awareness

This process of discerning relevance and applying learning to actual problems in real-life situations has many indirect and unanticipated effects. For a select minority of the students, service learning has been anticipatory of their future occupations. Many have reflected on how these experiences confirmed and solidified their choice of academic majors and intended professions. Such critical reflections provide an opportunity to assess the drawbacks and benefits they see displayed in their supervisor's approach to various circumstances. While their perspectives might change with further experience, they often discover that they already have a base for future decision making.

Another indirect and unanticipated consequence is that the service-learning experience either reinforces or produces a desire for further involvement in volunteering. The students want to see for themselves if what they have done has had any meaningful impact. While academic discussions of social problems may emphasize a rather abstract or generalized view of communities and the world beyond, most of our service-learning students take a more specific and individual approach. As a result of their service-learning experiences they are faced with the reality that their actions do have an impact. While the effect may be small compared to impacts on communities and nations, it is of great significance to those directly affected.

Impact of Service Learning on Teaching and Pedagogy

The service-learning experience has crystallized many students' awareness of the relevance and applicability of class material to the real world. From this instructor's perspective, this is the most concrete advantage of active student participation outside the classroom. When confined by the classroom walls and the limitations of the university, students and faculty alike have a tendency to see the fruits of their instruction and consequent learning to be correspondingly limited. Active learning styles most certainly are of great aid to student learning and retention, but it is only when active learning is integrated into service-learning methodologies that true education results. Questions are asked that have no easy or immediate answers. The excitement of discovery felt by both student and teacher is what is meant by the joy of learning (Palmer, 1998).

But perhaps nothing is more enjoyable than acquiring sensitivity to and learning about unrecognized aspects of oneself. This excitement can be intensified when that which was previously unknown becomes accepted as part of oneself. The integrity (Carter, 1996) of the self is established by the acceptance of morality and the recognition that, whether rewarded or chastised, one acts on the basis of one's moral consciousness. As a direct result of service learning activities, students acquire confirmation of cherished attributes about themselves. More importantly, they gain access to knowledge about who they are that had lain dormant before their engagement in service.

Vignette 2: Seeing through Others' Eyes
During a Michigan State University study-away program at the University of Hawaii, three MSU students came to understand how critical their involvement had been. The circumstance

was a service-learning placement with the Chinese Community Center in downtown Honolulu. MSU students were helping recent immigrants prepare for their citizenship exams. Not only were the students facilitating the development of English language competency, but they were helping their partners increase their understanding of American society and its political institutions.

One might anticipate that these experiences would reinforce the MSU students' awareness and commitment to the American ideology. However, one of the Chinese students overheard their tutors expressing frustration and impatience with some problems of American society that were current at the time. In an animated exchange, the MSU students were treated to a personal history of their Chinese student and the difficulties encountered in his long journey to America. What was most interesting was the rapt attention of the MSU students as they began to see their country through the eyes and experience of another. They were told, in no uncertain terms, the value of their birthright to United States citizenship and that they should never take it for granted. The MSU students were sobered by these emotional comments from a man who had experienced tremendous challenges in order to become an American. They recognized the value of what they had provided this man and the reciprocal gift of wisdom that he had given them.

Importance of Diversity

One recurrent theme that surfaces in student self-reflections is a recognition of the importance of diversity, not only in their personal lives but also in the structure and conduct of society. Many describe their experiences in their families and home communities as being quite homogeneous; their schools and churches lacked diversity. The inevitable consequence was that their perspectives, goals, and expectations remained largely unchallenged. Family and friendship networks, likewise, produced homogeneous experiences. The result was that they didn't perceive or appreciate the ways in which their own opportunities, decisions, and moralities were restricted.

In these situations, the students develop the kinds of stereotypes that, while not based on hostilities, certainly do impede any reaching out to encounter the changes in perception of self and others that can occur when encountering difference. Service learning provides these students with the chance to confront their impressions of others with a critical consciousness and a discerning analysis of their validity and their impact on self. The general result is recognizing personal change in the direction of greater tolerance of diversity, based on the development of enhanced compassion and caring.

Vignette 3: Reciprocal Relationships
The student was from an up-scale suburb surrounding a large metropolitan area and described his situation as "privileged." Having seldom, if ever, been in significant material or emotional need, he was both surprised and excited to discover what he could give of himself via the service-learning experience. His family had not been bashful when it came to giving charitable contributions, but this service learning was something different. Here he was able to give of himself in a nonprivileged encounter and experience the personal impact that he could

have on another—a significant self-revelation, most certainly, but emotionally secondary to a related experience that happened during the last week of his participation. He was invited to dinner by his learning partner's family.

Recognizing the financial restrictions that the learning partner's family must have been under, he was quite hesitant to accept the kind invitation. However, he also recognized the impact that a polite refusal could have on his partner and his family. Realizing how giving, while motivated by the most well-intentioned motives to give assistance to those in need, could continue to cast him in a superior position, he felt obliged to accept the family's offer. He described the dinner, which was meager in comparison to what he was used to, in the most glowing terms, never having had a sandwich that "tasted so good." The brightest strand in this tapestry was the experience of being able to receive benefit from those he had benefited. A truly mutual and reciprocal relationship had been experienced, where the roles of "giving" and "receiving" alternated.

In addition to an increased tolerance of diversity based on the development of a sense of attachment, involvement, and caring, students also experience a stronger sense of morality, which sometimes leads to change. Many students who recognize the impact they are having on their learning partners become increasingly cognizant of the modeling role they are providing. This mentoring often becomes more comprehensive in scope, not being confined to the situation of the service-learning encounter. The students become increasingly aware of what they have learned from their learning partners and the virtues of becoming committed to something larger than oneself. Their reflections often enumerate the benefits and changes experienced as a result of connection, something not always experienced in a world of individuality.

An increased awareness of and commitment to societal virtues (e.g., equality, freedom, justice, and responsibility) become, for some, a rallying cry not only for self but also for the wider community and society. The students' increasing concern with social policy and activism, both locally and beyond, is expressed in their expanded personal horizons, application and retention of course material, extension of its relevance to recurrent and contemporary social problems, and confidence in their critical thinking and judgment. They start to recognize the potentially beneficial changes in their community and nation that they could be a part of.

Many enter the service-learning program with the feeling that, as individuals, they can do little to significantly impact things and create change. However, the experience of reciprocal impact on their learning partners and themselves plants the seeds of increased community and societal activism. In addition to their plans to continue to volunteer service to others, many have planned to return to their home community institutions, to actively pursue personal changes in their community involvement, and to enhance the civic engagement of others.

Future of Civic Engagement and Service Learning

I wonder what the future holds for civic engagement. If those who have passed through my courses are any indication, future students will benefit in innumerable ways in terms of their compassion and sensitivity and their capacities and skills. They will develop a commitment to future volunteering in their communities through the recognition that a single individual can have a substantial impact, the constructive consequences of which can only be imagined and hoped for. And while they may not carry forward their desires for change personally, they may offer substantial support and encouragement to those who enthusiastically pursue social change and justice through activism.

I wonder what the future holds for service learning. After all these years, I am even more committed to the inclusion and central role of service learning in the general education offerings at Michigan State University. Such experiences most certainly underscore the relevance of our course materials and facilitate student retention and application. More important, however, is the impact that the experience has on our students. If the goal of general education is to expose students to recurrent and significant social issues and to develop the critical consciousness necessary to be an active and responsible participant in a democratic society (Tanner & Tanner, 1980), then general education cannot be effectively taught unless service learning is a central and integrated component of the class experience. It will create knowledge where only passive learning had previously taken place. It will make instructors into true teachers. And this active partnership between teachers and students will enable them to pursue questions with no known answers as their inquiry breaks the boundaries between the "known" and the "contemporarily improbable" in the pursuit of wisdom.

Response to the Future of Civic Engagement and Service Learning

Karen McKnight Casey

In his reflection Professor Cyrus Stewart (hereafter "Cy") ponders, "I wonder what the future holds for civic engagement" and "I wonder what the future holds for service learning." These thoughts can be framed as questions, "What is the future of civic engagement?" and "What is the future of service learning? These are questions that this director of service learning and civic engagement for the pioneer land-grant and a major research-intensive university committed to engagement seeks to answer. Although short in length, the questions are long in terms of considerations to address.

Acknowledging That the Past Informs the Present—and the Future

It is this author's belief that projections of the future of civic engagement and service learning cannot be made until the past, the histories, are examined. There is no denying that civic engagement and service learning are pervasive in today's cultures of education and community practice. An Internet search of the term "civic engagement" netted a response of 5,690,000 hits(retrieved August 2011). Narrowing the search to include "higher education," the yield was 1,090,000. Results in searching "service-learning"/"service learning" also yielded responses in the millions, 4,540,000, and 2,180,000 with "higher education" added as the qualifier. Books and articles on both pedagogy and practice abound. Organizations such as Campus Compact; associations, for instance, the International Association on Research in Service-Learning and Community Engagement; and government offices, for example, the Corporation for National and Community Service-Learn and Serve, exist to support this endeavor. Yet this pervasiveness in the culture of education was not instantaneous. It was built over decades. The origins inform the current work and provide significant views to the future. To assist in setting the context and this author's viewpoints, although Cy raises the question regarding the future of civic engagement before that of service learning, this author will explore service learning first and, at times in the discussion, intertwine the two. The histories cited are not meant to be exhaustive, but pertinent.

In *Service-Learning: A Movement's Pioneers Reflect on Its Origins, Practice and Future*, Stanton, Giles, and Cruz note that the earliest definition of service learning recorded appeared in publications of the Southern Regional Educational Board in 1969, "the accomplishment of tasks that meet genuine human need in combination with conscious educational growth" (Stanton, Giles, & Cruz 1999, p. 2). Although not formally defined until the late 1960s, service learning was expressly noted and seen in student-faculty-community projects and endeavors in the mid-1960s, as evidenced by the 1965 "Manpower for Development" project, the first to be termed "service-learning," in conjunction with the Oak Ridge Institute of Nuclear Studies–University Relations Division, Tennessee Valley Authority and University of Tennessee (Stanton, Giles, & Cruz, 1999), and the Michigan State University Student Tutorial Education Project (STEP) with Rust College in Mississippi (see the chapter by Duley and Springer in this volume). These and multiple other projects involving the intersections of concern, community need, student action, and faculty and staff support (Stanton, Giles, & Cruz 1999) were born from convictions pervasive in the turbulent civil rights and anti–Vietnam War eras of the 1960s and early 1970s. While defined as service learning, these university-community interactions, with students at the core, were in many cases what today would be called civic engagement, that is, "individual and collective actions designed to identify and address issues of public concern" (American Psychological Association, 2012; see also Zukin, Keeter, Andolina, Jenkins, & Dell Carpini, 2006).

Civic engagement "includes a wide range of work undertaken alone or in concert with others to effect change" (Zukin, et al. 2006, p. 7). Service learning can be civic engagement if it includes a civic dimension, an issues-oriented examination leading to the action (American Psychological Association, 2012), but not all service learning is civic engagement. Key components of civic engagement in the contexts of today's definitions include exploration of underlying/prevailing social issues, the context of "self" in the equation in a way that stresses and strengthens reciprocity with community, and a service orientation, but not exclusively, as additional components, such as action research, community dialogue, and advocacy can be integrated (Casey 2009). The earliest projects defined as service learning, although different from one another in scope and design, combined responses to current social issues and concerns, with community interaction and institutionally supported student action targeted at remedy and change. Student learning was key, at times less in the academic or curricular sense than in the students' need to know the issues, challenges, and tactics in order to build process, begin to enact solutions and help to lay groundwork for change. Social justice, education's service to society, or democratic education, in some form, was embedded in early work. Relationships between service and social change, the purpose of education in a democracy, and education as serving society were examined and debated.

These conditions occurred whether the institution was a liberal arts college, a research university, a professional school, or a community college (Stanton, Giles, & Cruz, 1999). Thus, the roots of service learning had definite civic dimensions. Service learning in its beginnings, in fact, also was civic engagement.

In early service learning, the work involved student learning and the involvement of faculty and staff, but was not always related to a specific academic course. In Robert Sigmon's pivotal statement in *Synergist*, "Service-learning programs are distinguished from other approaches to experiential education by their intention to equally benefit the provider and the recipient of the service as well as to ensure equal focus on both the service being provided and the learning that is occurring" (1979, p. 10), the context is that of "service-learning programs." Institutions like Michigan State University have considered academic/course-imbedded, curricular service learning and civic engagement linked to a particular area of study or academic major, but not a particular course within the discipline (Center for Service-Learning and Civic Engagement, 2009), and cocurricular service learning and civic engagement as authentic and viable practices in the field as long as the essentials of the Preparation, Action, Reflection, Evaluation (PARE) model of service learning (Jacoby, 2002; Ayers & Lavin, 2003) are practiced and an issues-oriented approach is provided. However, numerous other institutions and related organizations currently define service learning only as academic/course-connected service, "course-based, credit-bearing educational experience that allows students to (*a*) participate in an organized service activity that meets identified community needs and (*b*) reflect on the service activity in such a way as to gain further understanding of course content, a broader appreciation of the discipline, and an enhanced sense of civic responsibility" (Bringle & Hatcher 1995, p. 112). Curricular service learning is most often not defined as a unique form, and the "cocurricular" is seen simply as community service and possibly civic engagement, depending on the definition used or viewpoint of civic engagement taken.

The issues-oriented focus and response to community conditions helped to make the college/university involvement with external communities reciprocal and mutually beneficial by nature, if anything favoring the needs of the community over the institution. Some colleges and universities held on to or adopted these premises over time. Others did not, in later years coming instead to adopt a model of service learning that linked student learning to community interactions focused on service and incorporated sound pedagogy, but without the issues-focused education, emphasis on reciprocity, and attention to social justice and democratic action. This drift occurred in the 1980s and 1990s and was a departure not only from the projects and definitions of the 1960s, but also from Robert Sigmon's pivotal definition from the late 1970s in which service in and with the community is weighted equally with learning outcomes for students (Sigmon 1979). It is understandable, in part, that the need for academic rigor in the then emerging field and practice of service learning, as well as the emergence of service learning as a teaching pedagogy, led to the to a separation of the academic/course-connected service learning from the curricular, non-course-related (as defined by Michigan State University) aspects and the cocurricular pieces. This separation, although the most widely accepted definition, does include civic responsibility (Bringle and Hatcher 1995), in many instances also allowing for a decoupling of the civic from the practice of service. In addition, from the observations of this author, the balance of reciprocity often shifted from that of community, students, and the institution as equals, and tipped toward the benefits to students, investment in low-risk endeavors, and the ease of administration on the part of the institution.

In the view of service learning as separate from civic engagement, service learning can indeed occur when the PARE model is followed. For example, there are many instances where pre-education/teaching majors serve in local, urban elementary school classrooms to learn firsthand what is like to serve in a city-school setting. Satisfactory, if not quality, service-learning experiences can be facilitated as long as the students prepare for the experience via class readings and service-learning orientations; serve consistently in the setting jointly agreed upon among the faculty, students, and the schoolteacher or administrator, for example, facilitate one third-grade reading group weekly; and reflect meaningfully on the experience, while the processes and placements are evaluated jointly by the faculty, students, and supervising teachers. The service-learning experience would become a civic engagement opportunity if the same service opportunity, that is, facilitating the third-grade reading group, occurred with preparation that included (1) exploration via readings and research as to why urban schools have higher needs for supplemental services and are more likely to request college/university tutors; (2) conversations with the classroom teachers to discuss challenges faced, for example, the highly transient nature of the child population enrolled; and (3) reflection incorporating questions related to whether or not students perceived that the situations in the school were likely to change (to include why/why not), and encouraged students to think about their potential roles and responsibilities related to schools and education in their respective home communities post graduation.

Dependent on one's views, the service-learning-only experience, as distinguished from the civic engagement-based opportunity, was not necessarily a less valuable experience for the student and for the elementary school. The former met curricular objectives, certainly a necessary component of academic/course-connected service learning. This model of service learning was reinforced by a rise in volumes dedicated to embedding service learning in disciplines through academic service learning. Edward Zlotkowski made a case for grounding service learning in the disciplines in order to increase rigor and bolster legitimacy (Zlotkowski 1995). This was followed by his groundbreaking series Service-Learning in the Disciplines (1997–2006), which indeed provided much-needed quality models and examples of incorporating service learning into a range of fields and related courses, and addressed questions related to applicability to a range of disciplines and to rigor. These works, while necessary for the advancement of service learning as teaching pedagogy, inadvertently may well have added to separation of service from civic.

Removing the concepts of civic education and responsibility from service learning in some instances is seen as safer for the institution. In the example given above for service learning, no one would question an institution's role in preparing quality teachers, but may do so if students choose to appear at local school board meetings to ask questions of their own or contact legislators regarding policy. Indeed many early practitioners of service learning resigned from, were ushered out of, or were fired outright from their positions because the civic nature of their work was seen as "political" and threatening to the status quo of the institution (Stanton, Giles, and Cruz 1999). Whether the reason for the shift was a change from the view of true reciprocity to that of "students first," the view that teaching pedagogy cannot be seen as rigorous in certain disciplines if it is also civic, expediency in terms of administration and facilitation, or an institution's need for a perceived "safe environment," there simply was a shift in the history of service learning such that some institutions decoupled service learning from civic engagement. Although there has been a strong reemergence nationally of reciprocity, not only in service learning but in institutional work with and within communities, the decoupling has persisted in pockets in the writer's own institution, as well as nationwide.

The separation of service learning from civic engagement was not instantaneous, nor was it absolute. At the first college and university presidents' meeting in 1985 of Campus Compact, an international coalition (with a membership of more than 1,100 college/university presidents) committed to "educate college students to become active citizens who are well-equipped to develop creative solutions to society's most pressing issues" (Campus Compact 2011a), cofounder Frank Newman, then president of the Education Commission of the States, stated, "The most important thing an institution does is not to prepare a student for a career, but for a life as a citizen" (Campus Compact 2012b). In 1990, Ernest Boyer urged colleges and universities to reexamine missions, the roles of faculty, and the use of their talent, and stated, "We proceed with the conviction that if a nation's higher learning institutions are to meet today's urgent academic and social mandates, their missions must be carefully redefined and the meaning of scholarship creatively reconsidered" (Boyer 1990, p. 13).

The mid-1990s continued to see some institutions articulate a view of service learning for students, at least on an institutional level, to include service in achieving public good and social and civic responsibility (Edens 1994, cited in Keith, Perkins, Greer, Casey, & Ferrari, 1998). In 2001, the American Society for Higher Education (ASHE) hosted the symposium, "Broadening the Carnegie Classifications' Attention to Mission: Incorporating Public Service," in which Barbara Holland defined civic engagement as "a specific conception of faculty service that connects the intellectual resources of the institution to public issues such as community, social, cultural, human and economic development" (Holland 2001). If one looks at this view of civic engagement along with, for example, the Michigan State University definition of outreach and engagement, that is, "scholarship that cuts across teaching, research and service" (Provost's Committee on University Outreach 1993, p. 1), to include engaged teaching, of which service learning is one form, the connection to and consistency of service learning in the context of civic, community, and reciprocal work remains. Campus Compact has continued to champion the civic missions of institutions, faculty, and students on the national, now international, level, yet this has not always been the case in the state affiliates, where the work in some cases has been reflective of, and reactive to, the majority of the institutions involved, funding sources, affiliated constituencies other than institutions of higher education, and the like, which can indeed lack a civically based agenda, and not necessarily be indicative of the national agenda. Related to specific faculty practice, it is clear that some institutions, as evidenced by Cy's reflection earlier in this chapter, have kept the connection between service learning and civic engagement. The reality is that countless other examples could be provided where the separation, deliberate or otherwise, has occurred.

Where Are We Now? An Overview of Recent and Current Trends and Practice

In the late 1990s Campus Compact introduced the "Service-Learning Pyramid," in which whole-institution buy-in of service learning as civically engaged work is critical: In this model, "service-learning and other practices of engagement are aligned with institutional mission," and the "campus is experimenting with other ways to deepen the impact of civic education through initiatives on and off campus to increase student, faculty, institutional, and community capacities for 'public work' in a diverse democracy." This formulation helped reinvigorate the idea that service learning is linked to democratic values and action, although many campus were and remain in early stages of implementation (Campus Compact, 2011a). The Pyramid was followed by the Compact's "Indicators of Engagement," in which articulation of the civic mission of the college/institution, coupled with implementation of the mission via scholarship and practice across the institution, was viewed as key (Campus Compact, 2005).

In 2005 the Carnegie Foundation piloted its Elective Classification on Community Engagement. Fourteen institutions of varying types participated in the pilot, with the first round of elective classifications being awarded in 2006. The original construct allowed colleges and universities to apply to Carnegie to be classified in the areas of curricular engagement, community partnerships, or both (Carnegie Foundation, 2011). For the first time colleges and universities could apply to Carnegie, rather than classifications being assigned, and the volume and types of curricular and institutional engagement with communities became the benchmarking standards, rather than an institution's size and range and types of programs offered. Although determining what to measure and count as curricular engagement and community partnerships came with challenges (Church, 2001), the desire of colleges and universities to achieve classification under the umbrella "community engagement" was evidenced by the number of institutions that sought the classification once the application process extended beyond the pilot stage. A total of 196 institutions were awarded the elective classification as a result of the 2006 and 2008 application periods. An additional 115 received the designation in 2010. Not all institutions that applied were awarded the designation, making it a selective process. In 2010 Carnegie revised criteria so that the separate categories of curricular engagement, community partnerships, or both were eliminated and a single classification of community engagement was awarded (Carnegie Foundation, 2011).

The work of the Carnegie Foundation related to community engagement, and the Compact's Indicators of Engagement project came on the heels of the efforts of the Kellogg Commission on the Future of State and Land-Grant Universities and the corresponding "Returning to Our Roots" and other related reports. State institutions were encouraged to examine their own roots and reimagine their visions in the context of the twenty-first century. University-community partnerships, service learning and learned values of informed citizenship, a related sense of responsibility in and with community, community-based learning, and engaged, public scholarship all were seen as necessary to the viability, validity and value of state institutions (Association of State and Land-Grant Colleges, 2011). Further solidification of service learning, curricular engagement, and engaged scholarship with external communities occurred with the incorporation of such endeavors as that of the

63

regional accreditation bodies including evidence of community engagement as a criterion for accreditation, beginning with the Higher Learning Commission–North Central Association of Colleges and Schools in 2005 (Higher Learning Commission, 2007).

Coinciding with national trends focused on mutually beneficial and reciprocal service learning, true engagement partnership with external communities, and emphasis on the civic mission of higher education, arose new and renewed emphasis on research and rigor in the fields of service learning, engaged scholarship, and the scholarship of engagement. As examples, the Kellogg Foundation, Campus Compact, and others supported of the International Service-Learning Research Conference, 2001–2005. The conference obtained enough of a following to become the International Association for Research on Service-Learning and Community Engagement (IARSLCE) in 2007, and is now housed in the Center for Public Service, Tulane University (IARSLCE, 2011). Initiated by Tufts University and endorsed by Campus Compact, TRUCEN (The Research University Civic Engagement Network) was formed in 2006 to bring together a group of campus administrators responsible for community-engaged work on "very high, research-intensive" (Carnegie) campuses, public and private, to discuss and strategize the work in research-intensive environments (Campus Compact 2011c). These and other similar endeavors, initiatives, and associations have helped to reemphasize the need for institutions of higher education to examine and rededicate their missions, to connect to external communities in ways that are reciprocal, responsive, and evidenced-based, and which view the university as citizen and include faculty and students in the work.

The Future of Service Learning and Civic Engagement: What Needs to Happen?

Recent and current trends point to a recoupling of service learning and civic engagement, despite a plethora of definitions of civic engagement that are not always congruous. What is clear is a resurgence of and commitment to the missions of higher education to engage with communities in support of the public good, for faculty to view their scholarship in ways that include work in and with communities, local and beyond, and to educate students to become current and future citizen-scholars. How do colleges and universities sustain the momentum so that current philosophies, pedagogies, scholarship, and practice do not fall victim to changing national and international landscapes and future, potentially divergent, trends, but capture the momentum and build upon it?

To sustain and build on institutional, faculty, and student commitment to civically based missions of colleges and universities, institutions, faculty, and entities that support their work must not shy away from the word "civic" but embrace it. "Civic" does not have to be seen as partisan politics or examining politically based issues, or a countercultural method of dealing with social issues presenting threats to local power structures or the status quo, but instead a core construct of citizen involvement in a democratic society, to include service. Certainly terms such as "community engagement," "university-community partnerships," "community-based education," and others are viable and valuable components of the overall construct, and each institution needs to define what is meaningful for itself. If, however, higher education is going to honestly educate students to become viable, productive, proactively critical, contributing, and truly engaged members of society, on campus and beyond, current and future, the term "civic engagement" needs to be embraced. Doing so will not cause civic engagement to be a "sign of the times" at risk when the nation and world move into different times, as with the early activist stance of service learning, but instead an honored tradition, high-stakes expectation, and ongoing way of being.

Building a consensus as to a definition of civic engagement across higher education is one aspect that needs to happen. This is no easy charge to be sure. The one or two most widely applied definitions of service learning currently in use took years to craft, as previously noted, and there has been mission drift in terms of little attention to civic responsibility in some practices. Colleges and universities have tailored the practice, if not the definition itself, to meet institutional-specific needs. Yet there is currently little argument as to what one means by service learning, given the widely accepted definitions. The importance and relevance of definition is also evidenced more recently in understanding faculty engagement with community, where the most widely cited definitions view such engagement as scholarship. How scholarship is perceived and counted at institutions varies, but a baseline can be referenced as the terminology becomes more embedded in institutional discussions and cultures. What is civic engagement? Is it institutional? Institution wide? Is it faculty focused? Student focused? Academic? Cocurricular? A combination? What are its core philosophies and components? While defining civic engagement nationally will take time and thoughtful consideration, and institutions will adapt according to their own needs, a strong and consistent definition, agreed upon across higher education constituencies, will be significant in strengthening service learning's agenda and longevity. In this author's opinion, consideration of the Dell Carpini (American Psychological Association, 2012) and Zukin and colleagues (2006) definitions is critical.

Too few colleges and universities are educating students to understand that it is not enough to simply help in the soup kitchens; instead students need to understand why soup kitchens exist and why socially just policies and programs must be enacted to proactively and effectively lead to their demise (Colby, Ehrlich, Beaumont, Stephens, & Shulman, 2010). Disciplinary rigor in the pedagogy can be maintained while educating for civic engagement and responsibility (Battistoni, 2003). As an example, for their semester project a team of students in a senior capstone course in mechanical engineering worked with a mobility-challenged child from a low-income family to design an adaptive cycle, as the child is unable to ride a standard bicycle. The faculty for the course and university service learning practitioner met with a local special education program in advance of the course to ascertain the need for the project and to determine the recipient client. The academic department and the faculty secured outside, corporate funding for materials. During the semester, the university students met with the child (client), the parents, and school-based occupational and physical therapists to gather input prior to designing the apparatus and to test their design and product prior to completion. The students applied knowledge and skills learned in their engineering curricula in order to design and fabricate the cycle. They provided the cycle to a child who would otherwise not obtain one. Their preparation, process, challenges, successes during implementation, and feelings about the experience were shared with an audience of peers, faculty, school partners, the corporate sponsor, and the family during their final class presentation. Attending faculty, peers, community partners, and the family provided feedback, and the course faculty provided assessment via grading. The cycle was fully operational and of benefit to the client. Preparation, successful action, reflection, and evaluation were attained, making for quality service learning.

Suppose, however, the same students had been asked to "preflect" on how current and prevailing norms make the ability to ride and acquire a bicycle the "mainstream" practice for children, how this norm makes any specialized cycle highly costly, and, therefore, too costly for a lower-income family, subsequently further marginalizing a child who already is distanced from his or her peers, and to explore how it must feel for a child to be "out of the mainstream" simply by being unable to ride a two-wheel bike. In that case, the university students would have been able to begin the process of civic engagement. The preparation could have included readings on social stratification related to mobility-related disability, limitations in government and insurance programs in providing what are considered nonessential mobility devices, and the reflection tied not only to process, success, challenges, and feelings, but understanding of the ways in which the project addressed the issues of norms and marginalization, thus integrating civic engagement throughout. Discipline-based pedagogy and rigor related to service learning would not have been compromised, but rather enhanced, underscoring Newman's premise and this author's stance that pedagogy and practice need to reintegrate the two.

In his section of this chapter Cy writes about the importance of exposure to and understanding of diversity within the context of service learning and civic engagement. This response echoes its importance. For true reciprocity to occur, understanding of the other becomes critical. The importance of the understanding of diversity related to disability is provided in the example of service learning pivoted into civic engagement above. Such exposure and understanding comes into play in a myriad of settings related to ethnicity, country of origin, social-economic status, sexual orientation, family structure, and more. Cy's writings and vignettes speak to his awareness and also his abilities to interact with his students to help move their views from "me" and "them" to "us" in a way that is reciprocal and respectful. Not all faculty have this ability, and some may shy away from discussions that are germane to the situation. In addition, they may reinforce, intentionally or unintentionally, a "missionary" view of service that many students have when they begin their service and engagement with community. Some tensions in the work are inherent (Stewart & Webster, 2011), and direct or indirect reinforcement of worldviews that are based in uniformed, preconceived notions may be detrimental in promoting and internalizing civic engagement and responsibility. In these instances, "preflection" and preparation of faculty and staff is as critical as it is with students.

The call to reintegrate civic engagement with service learning is not simply rooted in an administrative or institutional perspective. It is echoed in the voices of students. The Michigan State University Center for Service-Learning and Civic Engagement (CSLCE) surveys a cross-range and representative subset of academic and curricular service-learning students at the end of each semester. One of the questions asks students to rank their motivations for engaging. The Spring Semester 2010 responses to this question ($n = 372$) illustrate that students are motivated to serve first to fulfill responsibilities of citizenship, followed, in rank order, by the need/desire to fulfill course requirements, the desire to learn more about

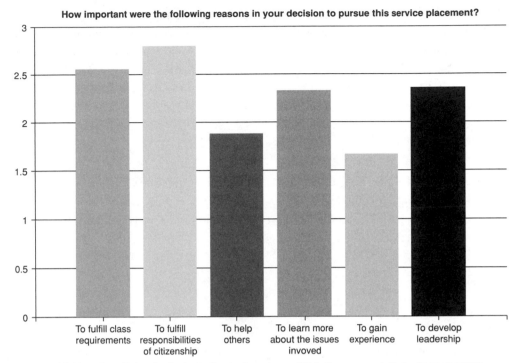

How important were the following reasons in your decision to pursue this service placement?

Michigan State University Center for Service Learning and Civic Enagagement, Spring Semester 2010, Responses in ranked order. H = 372

FIGURE 1

the issues involved, to develop leadership, and to help others. Engaging in service learning in order to gain experience was the least motivating factor.

Conclusion

This writer sees civic engagement as embedded in institutional mission, incorporating institution-wide commitment and practice, engaging those in the college and university with community where it is pragmatic and wise to do so and where service learning becomes an integral component. In recent and current trends of engaged campuses and engaged scholarship, in Dell Carpini's and Zukin's definitions of civic engagement, in Westheimer and Kahne's views of the three levels of citizenship—"personally responsible citizen," "participatory citizen," and "justice oriented citizen" (Westheimer & Kahne, 2004)—and in the views of this author, the future of service learning is integrally linked to that of civic engagement. For service learning to remain viable in its academic and curricular forms, it has to exhibit its relevancy beyond pedagogy that enhances learning related to curricula and critical thinking and builds skills. Yes, service learning, when well executed, has been proven to increase student learning and retention, and, yes, service learning needs to contribute in this manner to be relevant to and succeed in academe. However, other forms of teaching engagement and student engagement can do the same, often in a less resource- and labor-intensive model. The characterizing of service learning as significant to the institution's civic mission is essential. Essential to this engagement are reciprocal, mutually beneficial relationships with community; focus on the issues that led to the community's request for student and faculty involvement; process, service, and engagement that contribute to the public good; incorporation of dialogue that helps lead to a respect for diversity; and intentional education for students that such work is critical to becoming productive citizens. Frank Newman's words from 1985 echo and remain true: "The most important thing an institution does is not to prepare a student for a career, but for a life as a citizen."

Note

The authors would like to thank Linda Chapel Jackson and Catherine Gibson, Michigan State University Outreach and Engagement, for their editing expertise, and Lisa Sarno and Nicole C. Springer, MSU Center for Service-Learning and Civic Engagement, for their assistance with the literature review.

References

American Psychological Association. (2012). Civic engagement. Retrieved September 21, 2012, from http://www.apa.org/education/undergrad/civic-engagement.aspx.

Association of State and Land-Grant Colleges. (2011). Kellogg Commission on the Future of State and Land-Grant Universities. Retrieved September 21, 2012, from http://www.aplu.org/page.aspx?pid=305.

Ayers, J., & Lavin, J. (2003). Preparation, action, reflection. Retrieved September 21, 2012, from http://www.marylandpublicschools.org/MSDE/programs/servicelearning/PARDIA.htm.

Battistoni, R. (2003). *Civic engagement across the curriculum: A resource book for service-learning faculty in all disciplines.* Boston: Campus Compact.

Boyer, E. L. (1990) *Scholarship reconsidered: Priorities of the professoriate.* Princeton, NJ: Carnegie Foundation for the Advancement of Teaching.

Bringle, R., & Hatcher, J. (1995). A service-learning curriculum for faculty. *Michigan Journal of Community Service-learning, 12,* 112–122.

Carnegie Foundation for the Advancement of Teaching. (2011). Carnegie selects colleges and universities for 2010 community engagement classification. Retrieved September 21, 2012, from http://www.carnegiefoundation.org/newsroom/press-releases/carnegie-selects-colleges-and-universities-2010-community-engagement-classification.

Carter, S. L. (1996). *Integrity.* New York: Harper Perennial.

Campus Compact. (2005). Indicators of Engagement. Retrieved September 21, 2012, from http://www.compact.org/resources/service-learning-resources/indicators-of-engagement-project/campus-compactaacc-campus-engagement-survey/3520/.

Campus Compact. (2011a). About us. Retrieved May 2011 from http://www.compact.org/about/.

Campus Compact. (2011b). Newman Civic Fellows Award. Retrieved May 2011 from http://www.compact.org/initiatives/campus-compact-awards-programs/the-frank-newman-leadership-award/.

Campus Compact. (2011c). The Research University Civic Engagement Network (TRUCEN). Retrieved September 21, 2012, from http://www.compact.org/resources/the-research-university-civic-engagement-network-trucen/4951/.

Campus Compact. (2012a). Building the Service-Learning Pyramid. Retrieved September 21, 2012, from http://www.compact.org/resorces/faculty-resources/building-theservice-learning-pyramid-2/3463/.

Campus Compact. (2012b). Quotes to use. Retrieved September 21, 2012, from http://www.compact.org/resources-for-presidents/quotes-to-use/.

Casey, K. M. (2009). Service-learning & student civic engagement: Journeys toward discovery, contribution & civic responsibility. NAPSA—Student Affairs Administrators in Higher Education Membership Call, national Webinar. Retrieved April 2011 from http://outreach.msu.edu/documents/MSU-NAPSA_May09-KMC.pdf.

Center for Service-Learning and Civic Engagement, Michigan State University. (2009). Fact sheet. Retrieved September 21, 2012, from http://outreach.msu.edu/documents/flyers/CSLCEflyer_Oct09.pdf.

Church, R. L. (2001). Counting public service: Can we make meaningful comparisons within and among institutions. Presentation to the ASHE symposium Broadening the Carnegie Classifications' Attention to Mission: Incorporating Public Service, November 18.

Colby, A., Ehrlich, T., Beaumont, E., Stephens, J., & Shulman, L. S. (2010). *Educating citizens: Preparing America's undergraduates for lives of moral and civic responsibility.* San Francisco: John Wiley.

Corporation for National and Community Service. (2012). Learn and Serve America. Retrieved September 21, 2012, from http://www.nationalservice.gov/about/programs/learnandserve.asp.

Edens, M. (1994). Community-linked learning: The role of the service-learning center. Unpublished manuscript. East Lansing: Michigan State University Service-Learning Center.

Higher Learning Commission, North Central Association of Colleges and Schools. (2007). Chapter 3, Criterion 5. Retrieved June 2011 from http://www.ncahigherlearningcommission.org/download/Overview07.pdf.

Holland, B. A. (2001). Measuring the role of civic engagement in campus missions: Key concepts and challenges. Presentation to the ASHE symposium Broadening the Carnegie Classifications' Attention to Mission: Incorporating Public Service, November 18.

International Association for Research on Service-Learning and Community Engagement (IARSLCE) (2011). Contact us. Retrieved September 21, 2012, from http://www.researchslce.org.

Jacoby, B. (2002). PARE model. Retrieved September 21, 2012, from http://www.evergreen.loyola.edu/rcrews/www/sl/archives/oct02/msg00067.html.

Keith, J. G., Perkins, D. F., Greer, J. C., Casey, K. M., & Ferrari, T. M. (1998). The Young Spartan Program: A bridge between the ivory tower and the community. In R. M. Lerner and L. A. K. Simon (Eds.), *University collaborations for the 21st century: Outreach scholarship for youth and families.* New York: Garland.

Palmer, P. J. (1998). *The courage to teach: Exploring the inner landscape of a teacher's life.* San Francisco: Jossey-Bass.

Provost's Committee on University Outreach. (1993). *University outreach at Michigan State University: Extending knowledge to serve society.* East Lansing: Michigan State University

Rhoads, R. A. (1997). *Community service and higher learning: Explorations of the caring self.* Albany: State University of New York Press.

Sigmon, R. (1979). Service-learning: Three principles, *Synergist,* Spring, 9–11.

Springer, N. C., & Casey, K. M. (2010). From "preflection" to reflection: Building quality practices in academic service-learning. In H. E. Fitzgerald, C. Burack, and S. D. Seifer (Eds.), *Handbook of engaged scholarship: Contemporary landscapes, future directions*, vol. 2, *Community-campus partnerships* (pp. 29–49). East Lansing: Michigan State University Press.

Stanton, T. K., Giles, D. E. Jr., & Cruz, N. I. (1999). *Service-learning: A movement's pioneers reflect on its origins, practice, and future.* San Francisco: Jossey-Bass.

Stewart, T., & Webster, N. (2011). *Exploring cultural dynamics and tensions within service-learning.* Charlotte, NC: Information Age Publishing.

Tanner, D., & Tanner, L. (1980). *Curriculum development: Theory into practice.* 3rd ed. Englewood Cliffs, NJ: Merrill.

Westheimer, J., & Kahne, J. (2004). What kind of citizen? The politics of educating for democracy, *American Educational Research Journal, 41*(2), 237–269.

Zlotkowski, E. (1995). Does service-learning have a future? *Michigan Journal of Community Service-learning, 2*(Fall), 123–133.

Zlotkowski, E. (1997–2006). Service-learning in the Disciplines 21 vols. American Association of Higher Education and Accreditation (formerly American Association of Higher Education).

Zukin, C., Keeter, S., Andolina, M., Jenkins, K., & Dell Carpini, M. X. (2006). *A new engagement? Political participation, civic life, and the changing American citizen.* New York: Oxford University Press.

Intersecting Civic Engagement with Distance Education

Derryl Block and Linda Lindeke

This chapter examines opportunities and challenges of integrating community-based research and civic engagement in higher education programs where students are distant from faculty and campus. Such programs often rely on technology-enhanced teaching/learning delivered through the Internet or interactive television. Building relationships between faculty, students, and communities involves special opportunities and challenges when interactions are mediated by technology and parties are geographically dispersed. Examples of successful and less than successful integration of community-based scholarship and civic engagement in distance education programs are explored.

Nursing education has been an early adopter of distance education delivery methods. In these programs, faculty members are distant from learners and their communities of interest. The authors have experience using technology-enhanced teaching/learning modalities to integrate community-based scholarship and civic engagement into distance-education undergraduate and graduate nursing programs.

Nursing Education

There are many educational routes for professional nursing in the United States. Students can choose to prepare for registered nurse (RN) licensure by attending associate degree nursing programs in community or technical colleges, diploma programs in hospitals, baccalaureate nursing degree programs in universities, and even entry-level graduate degree programs if they have degrees in other fields and desire to add the RN credential. After successfully completing an entry-level program or a specified portion of a graduate program, nursing students are granted permission to take a licensing exam. Nurses who pass the registered nurse licensing exam can use the registered nurse title.

Advanced education includes masters and doctoral nursing programs that prepare for advanced practice nursing roles of nurse practitioner, clinical nurse specialist, nurse anesthetist, and nurse midwife as well as other advanced roles such as nurse administrator, public health nurse, and nurse informaticist. Doctoral programs in nursing include research focused PhD programs as well as newly developed doctor of nursing practice (DNP) programs.

There is an urgent need for health care improvement involving access, quality/safety, efficiency, and accountability (Institute of Medicine, 2001, 2011). In order for nurses to be active in health care improvement for individuals, families, communities, and populations, they need to be actively engaged in their communities at all points in the prelicensure and postlicensure education.

Community-Based Education

Many students in nursing programs are adult learners. Adult learners often have multiple roles and responsibilities and typically enter their higher education programs already having deep community connections (Cragg, Andrusyszyn, & Fraser, 2005). Utilizing those connections is meaningful to learners and can result in the educational process genuinely contributing to the community. There can be powerful synergy when the papers and projects from courses serve a purpose beyond attaining the degree or credential. Learners are often retained in their communities with new employment opportunities and contacts as a result of their experiences during their education. Their education can be more meaningful because their learning is based on life experiences and community collaboration.

Distance Education

In order to increase accessibility for students who are place- or time-bound because of job, family, and/or community responsibilities, many entry-level and advanced nursing education programs are available through distance education. For example, the University of Kansas has long used technology-enhanced distance education modalities to deliver nursing programs throughout that rural state (Connor, Warren, & Weaver, 2007). The University of Colorado also delivers nursing education in numerous western states though many programs and projects (Stanton et al., 2005). Distance education allows nurses in rural areas, nurses on active military service, and nurses working variable shifts to continue their education within their own communities or worksites.

Though not specific to distance education, participatory action research (PAR) is a widely used civic engagement teaching/learning activity. PAR has a long history and is highly promoted by scholars, communities, and funding entities (Lewin, 1946; Montero, 2000). PAR promotes direct participation of the entities being studied and ongoing input by communities though dynamic community/researcher collaboration from the earliest stages of the research process. The goal of PAR is to produce solutions to societal issues that are significant and timely. Paulo Freire brought PAR to the forefront as a strategy that is credible and ethical as well as effective (Freire, 2000; Freire & Horton, 1990). Foundationally, Freire promoted connecting educators to the daily lives of learners and communities to promote pedagogy that is specifically linked to students' social and political realities. Civic engagement is a derivative of Freire's philosophy of pedagogy.

Development of distance education programs in nursing has been aided by grants from foundations and government to support technology and programs that make nursing education accessible to distance students. In some cases, there has been a gradual integration of technology into nursing education distance learning, and in other cases, programs have utilized technology to change to distance modalities all at once. Blended models are also common in nursing education with a mixture of face-to-face and distance education courses (often called "hybrid courses") that mix face-to-face and distance modalities.

There is a plethora of research evaluating distance education and distance education in nursing (Avery, Cohen, & Walker, 2008; Bata-Jones, & Avery, 2004). Distance education has been found to be at least as good if not superior to traditional classroom-based education (Western Cooperative for Educational Telecommunications, 2009). Specifically, distance education in nursing has proven to be effective in allowing nursing students to attain degrees and credentials while maintaining their home lives and employment.

In order to facilitate active learning, many distance education nursing programs utilize techniques such as discussion forums, simulations, gaming, and case studies. The authors find that meaningful community-based assignments incorporating civic engagement are also important teaching-learning strategies. Table 1 includes examples of community-based assignments that have been used by the authors.

Table 1. Examples of Successful Distance Teaching/Learning Civic Engagement Projects

Collaborating with a community to encourage a restaurant association to adopt nonsmoking areas in restaurants

Assessing the availability of public transportation routes from poor neighborhoods to health facilities and working with community groups to modify bus routes

Assessing products in neighborhood grocery stores in underprivileged areas to determine the availability of items such as fresh produce and low-fat milk; doing a price comparison of the grocery stores in low-income neighborhoods compared to other urban/suburban neighborhoods

Helping a free clinic set up an appointment system to improve access to clinic facilities for clients from disadvantaged backgrounds

Assessing adequacy of services for the elderly in a specific community to encourage advocacy for specific needed services

Planning, implementing, and evaluating an "Internet café" in a long-term care facility to help residents stay in touch with family members by staffing it with volunteers

Implementing and evaluating a policy for emergency treatment for anaphylactic reactions within a large school district in collaboration with administration, health services, teaching staff, parents, and students

Convincing county commissioners of the need to increase staffing levels of school nurses within a school district

Working in a rural poor state with the local Head Start program on early childhood nutrition to prevent obesity by working with staff, parents, and children in an interactive way and tracking menus

Advocating for allowing breast-feeding in designated and suitable public spaces (i.e., allowing a mother and baby to breast-feed in an unused dressing room in a department store)

Working with a community to have a law passed to enforce families' use of child safety seats in automobiles

The learning activities listed in table 1 are within the mainstream of teaching/learning in health and social service professional education. Conducting these learning activities when faculty and students are geographically distant obviously presents challenges. For example, distant students may find themselves without entrée to community agencies. Without a faculty member physically present, students may be negatively received by the site because of exaggerated demands on field site personnel. Conversely, well-meaning community agencies may make inappropriate demands or requests of students that do not match the student's learning objectives or competencies.

Civic Engagement and Distance Education

Distance education is commonly used for increasing knowledge, developing roles, and enhancing careers. However, pairing distance education delivery methods with intentional civic engagement, while evident in courses and curricula, is rarely explicitly described. A literature review shows that the intersection of civic engagement and distance education has not been a major topic of pedagogical research.

Civic engagement is defined as "working to make a difference in the civic life of our communities and developing the combination of knowledge, skills, values and motivation to make that difference. It means promoting the quality of life in a community" (Ehrlich, 2000, p. vi). Ehrlich's emphasis on knowledge, skills, values, and motivations supports the strong synchrony of civic engagement and active learning. Within the discipline of nursing, "community" is broadly defined and includes health care professionals, families, and others who are involved in improving the health of a group of individuals. Thus civic engagement teaching/learning activities may focus on a community-dwelling group or population, a group of staff members, or a particular part of an agency. Civic engagement of students can directly or indirectly affect a larger community.

Civic engagement teaching/learning activities may reduce the potential for students to feel isolated when engaged in online learning because they are connecting their learning to the real concerns and needs of their own communities. Students may receive feedback from community members about their ideas and projects, thus increasing the relevance of the learning activities as well as students' capacity to integrate feedback into their scholarly products.

Feminist theorists have critiqued the rigidity and social isolation of online learning. For instance, Nipper (1989) considered that distance education delivery methods favor educated learners and ignore social aspects of teaching/learning. However, web-based distance education has often evolved to be less rigid and include multiple types of social interaction (Blumenstyk, 1997). In a similar vein, Dreyfus (2001) criticized distance learning because of its tendency to result in social isolation of learners who primarily interact with their computers in a private physical space. Civic engagement teaching/learning activities have the potential to refute Dreyfus's concerns that distance learning removes learners from their environments and reduces the learning experience to passionless screen time that does not that result in behavior change.

Steps in Civic Engagement Teaching/Learning

Civic engagement teaching/learning activities can be brief or time-extended, focused or broad in scope. Regardless, certain steps are necessary to ensure successful student learning and benefit for the community. The Lindeke/Block model (figure 1) is one way of describing the steps involved in civic engagement teaching/learning whether in face-to-face or distance-learning situations. The steps in the model involve fostering trust among student, faculty, and community agencies. Steps 1 through 4 are essential for all civic engagement teaching/learning activities. Step 1 involves careful planning and examination of the assignment. The assignment should be appropriate for the ability level of the student, the time

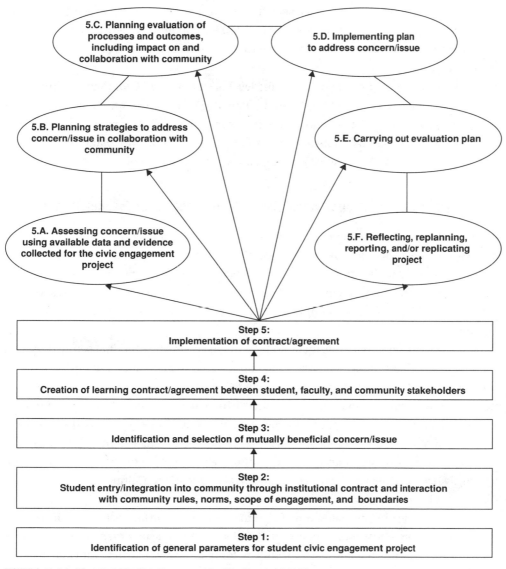

FIGURE 1 Lindeke/Block Model for Civic Engagement Teaching/Learning Activities

frame, and the setting. In step 2, the student is matched with the project site based on faculty knowledge of the community and past student successes. This step involves a mutual introduction of the student to the community and vice versa. A general institutional contract or memorandum of agreement (MOA) must be signed that outlines the legal issues from both the educational institution's and the community agency's perspectives. The institutional contract or MOA must be followed by thorough orientation to ensure that the student understands the community agency's rules, norms, and boundaries, and that the scope of the community engagement is appropriate.

The next step, step 3, involves identifying and selecting a focus of mutual concern for the student learning activities. The faculty member helps the student and the community select this focus through dialogue, participatory negotiation, and consensus-building.

Step 4 consists of the creation of a specific learning contract or otherwise explicit agreement between the student, the faculty member, and the community. Here as well, the faculty member brokers agreement and ensures that roles, responsibilities, and timelines are clearly described.

Steps 5A through F are dependent on the level of student, length of time, and the scope of the civic engagement teaching/learning activity. For instance, an assignment might involve only assessment (5A), or only planning an evaluation (5C). Alternately an assignment might involve multiple phases such as assessment (5A), planning (5B), planning evaluation (5C), implementation (5D), evaluation (5E), and/or replanning (5F).

Face-to-Face versus Distance Modalities in Civic Engagement Teaching/Learning

Table 2 differentiates the faculty role in the Lindeke/Block model when implemented in face-to-face versus distance modalities. Identifying the general parameters of the project (step 1) is identical in face-to-face and distance teaching/learning modalities. Working with students in both modalities requires trust that they will carry out activities in a responsible way and significant faculty monitoring of student activities and student-community relationship.

Step 2 (described as relationship building through general institutional contracting, and interaction with community rules, norms, scope of engagement, and boundaries) requires more effort on the part of student and faculty when done at a distance. Faculty members may have little prior information and no direct experience with the selected communities. It is necessary to work with students to identify appropriate project sites based on available information and student exploration. Likewise, arranging a general contract or memorandum of agreement between academic institutions and community entities that have not previously been partners may involve significant time and effort. Culture, policies, and legal issues must be taken into account.

Step 3, identification and selection of a mutual concern/issue for the focus of the activity, also requires more effort on the part of the student and the faculty member in a distance modality. It is typically not feasible for faculty to form direct relationships with distant community agencies. Therefore, those crucial relationships are often mediated via the students, sometimes with less than optimum outcomes (see case 1).

Table 2. Civic Engagement Teaching/Learning: Faculty Role in Face-to-Face versus Distance Modalities

Steps in carrying out civic engagement teaching/learning	Faculty role when employing face-to-face modalities	Faculty role when employing distance modalities
1. Identification of general parameters for student civic engagement project	Clearly articulate assignment instructions	Clearly articulate assignment instructions
2. Student entry/ integration into community through institutional contract and interaction with rules, norms, scope of engagement, and boundaries	Match student with a project site based on faculty's knowledge of community and past students' successes. Arrange institutional contract or memoranda of agreement (MOA) with selected site	Work with student to identify appropriate project sites based on available information and student's exploration of community. Discuss site pros and cons to select best available site that matches assignment criteria and student locale based on student input. Arrange institutional contract or MOA with selected site, being sure to factor in typical time lag for new site development; consider geographic factors as well as possible issues (i.e., community culture, differences in policies, legal issues, boards of nursing licensure rules)
3. Identification and selection of mutual concern/issue	Use dialogue, participatory negotiation and consensus-building to select concern/issue beneficial to community and suitable for student learning in the context of project.	Use dialogue, participatory negotiation, and consensus-building to select concern/issue beneficial to community and suitable for student learning in the context of project. It is typically not feasible for faculty to form direct relationship with distant community.
4. Creation of learning contract/agreement between student, faculty, and community stakeholders	Create agreement between faculty, student, and community that explicitly describes each partner's roles and responsibilities; create timeline for project completion	Create agreement between faculty, student and community that explicitly describes each partner's roles and responsibilities; create timeline for project completion
5A. Assessing concern/issue using available data and evidence collected for the civic engagement project	Assist student to identify existing data (published or unpublished reports, peer review articles) or to collect data through surveys, interviews, focus groups, etc., making use of *faculty's and students'* network of community colleagues	Assist student to identify existing data (published or unpublished reports, peer review articles) or to collect data through surveys, interviews, focus groups, etc., making use of *student's* network of community colleagues

Steps in carrying out civic engagement teaching/learning	Faculty role when employing face-to-face modalities	Faculty role when employing distance modalities
5B. Planning strategies to address concern/ issue in collaboration with community	Assist student to plan strategies and collaborate with community site representative/advocate, with *direct* faculty oversight and involvement	Assist student to plan strategies and collaborate with community site representative/advocate, with *little or only indirect* faculty oversight and involvement
5C. Planning evaluation of processes and outcomes, including impact on and collaboration with community	Assist student to plan to evaluate processes, outcomes, impact on community, and effectiveness of collaboration with the selected civic engagement environment, doing so with *direct* faculty oversight and involvement	Assist student to plan to evaluate processes, outcomes, impact on community, and effectiveness of collaboration with the selected civic engagement environment, doing so with *little or indirect* faculty oversight and involvement
5D. Implementing plan to address concern/issue	Act as resource for student who is typically independent and does not require faculty oversight	Act as resource for student who is typically independent and does not require faculty oversight
5E. Carrying out evaluation plan	Act as resource for student who is typically independent and does not require faculty oversight	Act as resource for student who is typically independent and does not require faculty oversight
5F. Reflecting, replanning, reporting, and/or replicating project	Act as resource for student who is typically independent and does not require faculty oversight	Act as resource for student who is typically independent and does not require faculty oversight

Step 4, creation of a student-specific learning contract or agreement between the student, faculty, and community stakeholders is similar in face-to-face and distance modalities. Likewise there are typically no differences in steps 5A through 5F by modality. Here, as in the previous steps, direct faculty knowledge about the community may be lacking in distance modalities.

Using the Model with Distance Teaching/Learning

The following case examples of four nursing student projects show how the Lindeke/Block Model for Civic Engagement Teaching/Learning Activities can be implemented in distance based teaching/learning. Table 1 contains other examples of successful projects.

Case 1: An Unsuccessful Student Project

A graduate student living in a state distant from the educational institution developed a project for a major civic engagement assignment. After the assignment parameters were clarified (step 1), a community clinic gave verbal agreement to allow the student to plan and implement a blood pressure screening project for high-risk clients. The faculty member did not have a direct relationship with the agency. Unfortunately, the formal institutional contract (step 2) was never signed. Additionally, although the student learning contract (step 4) was developed, the community partner did not fully agree to the specifics of the student learning activities. There was a delay before the faculty member and the student realized that they had not received full buy-in from the community partner. The student worked extensively on the project, including planning the actual intervention. Unfortunately, the student had to abandon the project when the agency withdrew its support and decided to concentrate on other priorities. The student subsequently carried out a successful project with another community entity and learned a lot about the importance of extensive community participation and formal contracting. However, the potential for student learning experiences with that community entity was diminished because of this experience.

Case 2: A Successful Student Project

A civic engagement project involving a group of graduate nursing students and a large teaching hospital progressed well through steps 5A, 5B, and 5C with students and hospital distant from the faculty member. At the time of implementing the project (step 5D), the students were unable to communicate the impact of the project to the agency's satisfaction. The faculty member intervened by telephone conference call with the agency representative and the students. The telephone conversation built agency trust and provided pertinent information about the project. The agency representative clarified concerns that the intervention would have unintended consequences. The students addressed those concerns, and the project was very successful. Though the faculty did not visit the agency at any time, this case demonstrated that even at a distance, direct communication between community entities and faculty members may be necessary for community engagement.

Case 3: A Successful Student Project

A student worked with American Indian tribal leaders to promote physical activity and appropriate weight in their community. Collaborating with public health nurses, health educators, teachers, and a community coalition, the student linked with an athletic shoe company's outreach campaign for the project. Athletic shoes especially designed for Native Americans were sold by the company to the community at a very discounted price. Building on the community enthusiasm for these specially designed, culturally branded shoes, the student helped initiate a walking club and also promoted a basketball initiative. Further, the opportunity of getting low-cost athletic shoes was also targeted to adults as an incentive for being screened for diabetes and cardiovascular risk factors. The student was a participant observer in a strong goal-focused and culturally competent community collaboration. Success was based on sequentially following the steps of the model. Steps 5E and 5F were not part of this student's learning contract.

Case 4: A Successful Student Project

Based on anecdotal information about oral health status, baccalaureate nursing students distant from their faculty member worked with a school nurse and a dental hygienist in a rural area to assess first- and third-graders' dental hygiene, fluoride exposure, and presence of tooth decay. Data were presented to health department staff for follow-up. Students then planned and implemented health education sessions for children and parents of both grades. Home activities were developed, and each participating child was given dental hygiene products. Project data were used by the health department in grant writing. Again, success was based on carefully following the steps of the model.

Conclusion

Civic engagement is a powerful pedagogy that stays true to Freire's emphasis on educators' social responsibility to link students to community social and political realities. Community-based assignments are important in order to build students' skills in interacting with communities, a key component of nursing as well as other disciplines. The Lindeke/Block Model for Civic Engagement Teaching/Learning Activities (figure 1) provides a stepwise process that fosters trust and enhances the likelihood of successful community engagement and rich learning outcomes. The intentional pairing of civic engagement and distance education has great potential to produce skilled learners whose careers and communities are enhanced by the relevance of their scholarship. Educators have a powerful tool for creating courses and curricula that are meaningful to learners and that can result in genuine contributions to learners' communities.

References

Avery, M. D., Cohen, B. A., & Walker, J. D. (2008). Evaluation of an online graduate nursing curriculum: Examining standards of quality. *International Journal of Nursing Education Scholarship, 5*(1), article 44.

Bata-Jones, B., & Avery, M. D. (2004). Teaching pharmacology to graduate nursing students: Evaluation and comparison of web-based and face-to-face methods. *Journal of Nursing Education, 43*(4), 185–189.

Blumenstyk, G. (1997). A feminist scholar questions how women fare in distance education. *Chronicle of Higher Education*, October 31. Retrieved September 21, 2012, from http://chronicle.com/article/A-Feminist-Scholar-Questions/98026/.

Connor, H., Warren, J., & Weaver, C. (2007). HIT plants SEEDS in healthcare education. *Nursing Administration Quarterly, 31*, 129–131.

Cragg, C. E., Andrusyszyn, M., & Fraser, J. (2005). Sources of support for women taking professional programs by distance education. *Journal of Distance Education, 20*(1), 21–38.

Dreyfus, H. (2001). *Thinking in action.* New York: Routledge.

Ehrlich, T. (2000). *Civic responsibility and higher education.* Westport CT: Oryx Press.

Freire, P. (2000). *Pedagogy of the Oppressed.* 30th anniversary ed. New York: Continuum.

Freire, P., & Horton, M. (1990). *We make the road by walking: Conversations on education and social change.* Philadelphia: Temple University Press.

Institute of Medicine. (2001). *Crossing the quality chasm: A new health system for the 21st century.* Washington, DC: National Academies Press.

Institute of Medicine. (2011). *Future of nursing: Leading change, advancing health.* Washington, DC: National Academies Press.

Lewin, K. (1946). Action research and minority problems. *Journal of Social Issues, 2*(4), 34–46.

Montero, M. (2000). Participation in participatory action research. *Annual Review of Critical Psychology, 2*, 131–143.

Nipper, S. (1989). Third generation distance learning and computer conferencing. In R. Mason and A. Kaye (Eds.), *Mindweave: Communications, computers and distance education* (pp. 63–73). Oxford: Pergamon Press.

Stanton, M., Crow, C., Morrison, R., Skiba, D., Monroe, T., Nix, G., and Gooner, V. (2005). Web-based graduate education in rural nursing case management. *Online Journal of Rural Nursing and Health Care, 5*, 53–63.

Western Cooperative for Educational Telecommunications. (2009). No significant difference phenomenon. Retrieved September 21, 2012, from http://www.nosignificantdifference.org/.

Can Civic Engagement Rescue the Humanities?

David D. Cooper

The relationship between the civic engagement movement and the contemporary humanities reminds me of a Nora Ephron movie like *Sleepless in Seattle* or *You've Got Mail*. Typically, the movie begins with two single, upwardly mobile characters who face a growing void in their otherwise successful lives. Serendipity steers them to each other. Circumstance or plain dumb luck often intrudes and keeps them apart. The plot becomes a study of their romantic, often heroic, and sometimes comic journey to find each other. Just before the movie fades to the credits, they finally meet and either walk away together hand in hand, followed by a golden retriever, or drive off in a Volvo.

The kitschy cinematic analogy may not be as farfetched as it seems when assessing the renewed commitment on the part of colleges and universities to become more responsible institutional citizens and the struggle within the humanities to shake a two-decade-long identity crisis. In fact, the story of two people seeking to complete each other through a longed-for relationship fits the thrust of my argument perfectly: the civic engagement movement needs the humanities, and the humanities need civic engagement. They belong to each other. But circumstances, professional pressures, career demands, chronic cutbacks, and institutional inertia, among other frustrations, stand in their way. I am not equipped to predict the outcome of this courtship, nor do I propose to become a matchmaker. I would like to explore, however, some of the subplots and backstories that make the relationship between civic engagement and the humanities a portrait in missed opportunities, hopeful reconciliations, and, who knows, maybe even consummation.

Those backstories, for the most part, involve complex ambivalences and politically charged perceptions that hamper the contemporary humanities from meaningful participation in democratic renewal. At the same time, those ambivalences and perceptions, I hope to show, hint at just how important the humanities can be to cultivating the essential arts of citizenship and democracy.

I should note that common theoretical, political, social, and critical alignments are shared by many, if not most, humanities fields today. As such, I often blur lines between the cultural disciplines and address the "humanities" collectively. In particular, I focus on a brand of cultural criticism—generally referred to by the deceptively generic label "cultural studies"—that cuts across and through traditional departments as well as new academic subfields like gender studies, global studies, border studies, and queer studies. With its emphasis on poststructural theory, cultural production, and radical social critique, cultural studies as a critical project capitalizes on what Stuart Hall calls "the enormously productive metaphor of hegemony" (1992, p. 279) that has dominated scholarship and criticism for the past 20 years. This fascination with social space as a predatory arena along with the general "cultural turn," as some put it (Sterns 2004), have made the contemporary humanities, in effect, a cross-disciplinary project.

The Humanities under Siege

Have core humanities disciplines and subdisciplines gathered under the umbrella of "cultural studies" earned a legitimate place at the institutional table where civic engagement and social responsibility are subjects of so much spirited conversation? The answer is a reluctant no. And a qualified yes.

Ever since the late 1980s the humanities have been perceived, as Frank Rhodes, former president of Cornell University, observed, as devoted "to areas of high abstraction . . . while the larger issues of the world and humankind's place in it elude them" (Fisk 1988, p. B12). The widespread perception of the humanities' irrelevance to the public interest was set in motion by a tsunami of highly critical and politically charged reports, beginning with a scathing 1988 National Endowment for the Humanities white paper that blasted literary studies and theory, in particular, for preferring mind-numbing mental aerobics over fundamental questions of human purpose and moral meaning. The NEH broadside was accompanied by a volley of widely read and reviewed books whose apocalyptic titles alone speak to the siege mentality weathered by academic humanists during the late 1980s and the 1990s: *The Closing of the American Mind, Killing the Spirit, The Last Intellectuals, Literature Lost, Bonfire of the Humanities,* to name just a few. Meanwhile, American college students started voting with their feet. While undergraduates stampeded into business majors, the number of degrees awarded in the humanities began to plummet. In the mid-1970s, for every student majoring in English, for example, five of her peers were pursuing degrees in business management. By 1994, that ratio sank to one out of 20. In a 1989 NEH report, then-chair Lynne Cheney warned: "You have students going to college who don't know what the humanities are and who may never find out." A few years later, Christopher Lasch, addressing fellow academics generally and zeroing in on the humanities professoriate in particular, scolded the "new [academic] elite," as he calls them in *The Revolt of the Elites and the Betrayal of Democracy,* for living "in a little world of their own, far removed from the everyday concerns of ordinary men and women" (1995, p. 176) and speaking an incomprehensible jargon that completely subverts any "attempt to communicate with a broader audience, either as teachers or as writers" (p. 178).

It comes as no surprise, then, that the humanities haven't played much of an active or, indeed, welcomed role in the national dialogue about the public roles of colleges and universities begun in earnest in the mid-1990s when "the engaged campus" and "institutional citizenship" became stock phrases in the lexicon of higher education. Humanists are only sparsely represented, for example, in one of the most ambitious national endeavors to recover the public voice of higher education in America. The Kellogg Forum on Higher Education for the Public Good, headquartered at the University of Michigan, sponsored four "Leadership Dialogues" in 2002 aimed at bringing together 150 prominent faculty and academic leaders committed to the academy's central role in nurturing education for liberty, democracy, and citizenship. The roster of participants reads like a who's who of university and foundation-based civic engagement heavyweights. While that roster includes a small number of academically trained humanists who have risen to positions of leadership in academic administration, very few practicing humanities faculty have taken part in the dialogues. The ratio, for example, of humanists to social scientists is roughly 1:17. The numbers themselves may mean very little. But in light of the visionary moral language that energizes the Forum's mission, one has to question the missing-in-action status of the humanities and arts professoriate. The Forum architects speak of a "new covenant" between higher education and society, a sacred trust that permeates the history, the culture, the values, as well as the research, teaching, and outreach practices of the academy. "Only if colleges and universities become clearer about their shared roles in service to American society," the Forum leaders write, "can they hope to maintain integrity and focus in a changing world" (2002, p. 4). "Covenant," "culture," "values," "integrity," "heritage" . . . this is the turf of the cultural disciplines, the venue of their best teaching practices, their finest contributions to intellectual and public culture, and their most enduring scholarship. Yet the relative silence of humanities faculty, artists, and writers in the Kellogg forums strikes me, paradoxically and painfully, as deafening. It points to a deep irony in the disciplinary culture that comprises the contemporary civic engagement movement.

This may not be such bad news at all. The awakening of social and natural science disciplines to their obligations and roles in what Ernest Boyer viewed as "the urgent new realities both within the university and beyond" (1997, p. 3) is cause for celebration and hope. Engaging those new realities is a healthy sign of ethical vitality as biologists and psychologists join their colleagues in higher education administration to examine the civic and democratic purposes of curricula, the potential of a more socially responsive and publicly intelligible scholarship, and the value of forming collaborative partnerships and conducting community-based teaching and research at their colleges and universities.

There seems to me nonetheless an inescapable paradox in the disciplinary culture that comprises and drives the agenda of the current civic engagement movement: namely, a moral language rooted in the rhetorical traditions of the humanities has been co-opted by social science at a time when the critical language of the contemporary humanities disciplines—literary studies is an obvious example—has adopted a decidedly social science cast and tone. Contemporary humanists, it would seem, have gladly surrendered a moral discourse shaped by twentieth-century liberalism to social scientists eager to renew their civic mission and recover their roles, first articulated by social progressives like John Dewey and Jane Addams in the 1920s, as advocates of the public good. At the same time, the humanities, once dedicated to the weighty proposition that students must think deeply about the moral and ethical issues of their own lives in order to become more enlightened and active citizens, have assumed the guise as well as the critical discourse of the social sciences through a preoccupation with such things as theories of social control, power, commodification, and identity politics. This inversion of roles has also made the object and aim of postmodern scholarship the mirror opposite of public scholarship. The public scholar asks, "How can the practices, methods, and conventions of my disciplinary scholarship yield knowledge that contributes to public problem solving and public creation?" The strategy of postmodernism, on the other hand, is to wrench us from what one critic called the "charted and organized familiarity of the totalized world," "to generate rather than to purge pity and terror; to disintegrate, to atomize rather than to create a community" (Spanos 1992, p. 81).

The Perfect Calm

Three forces or "fronts" are at work in the contemporary humanities that have simultaneously lined up to form a "perfect calm," marooning academic insight and critical intellect worlds apart from the agitations of democratic culture and the felt public sphere. In addition to a migration into the social sciences discussed above, those forces also include the triumph of high theory and a widespread and uncritical skepticism over civic culture as a broken project of the Enlightenment, another fracture in the aging bulwark of liberal humanism.

It is no profound insight to point out that high theory has supplanted affective praxis—the felt impacts of moral commitment on our actual practices of living and learning together—as the gold standard of political relevance in the contemporary humanities. When invited to speak at a MLA Presidential Forum on scholarship and commitment, celebrated French sociologist Pierre Bourdieu offered the audience little by way of exalting the possibilities of engaged teaching and scholarship as important cultural work in the public interest. In fact, he urged higher levels of detachment from the gritty spade work of community activism, preferring instead the intellectual project of "critical reflexivity" as "the absolute prerequisite of any political action by intellectuals." He exhorted literary scholars to "engage in a permanent critique of all the abuses of power and authority that are committed in the name of intellectual authority" (2000, p. 41). Unfortunately, what Bourdieu offered as a prerequisite has become instead a substitute for public work as cultural studies scholars "interrogate" power and politics at ever higher altitudes of stratospheric abstraction and specialization. As Maria Farland has argued, "Rather than reexamining . . . disciplinary or professional affiliations to consider in what sense their work might engage questions and concerns that are public in nature, [academic professionals] have continued in the mode of specialization. . . . [I]ntellectuals remain largely disconnected from the very public which captivates them, insulated within the specialized languages and frameworks of their disciplinary knowledge" (1996, p. 56). For the contemporary literature classroom, one upshot is that the lived and affective impact of moral questions that might otherwise bear directly on such important matters as the dynamics of social class and the history of gender oppression get sacrificed to the clinical purity of theory and the increasingly "complex relationship[s] between power . . . and exploitation," as Stuart Hall explains, "that Marxism as a theoretical project put on [our] agenda" (1992, p. 279).

Let me give a brief ground-level illustration of what I mean. I recently took part in an external department review at another university. I sat in on some writing and literature classes. In one Introductory Lit section, students were immersed in a very sophisticated skein of ideas about fiction and theories of social control, about characters and the social construction of identities, and about the power dynamics of social class that were playing out in plotlines. I made a careful review of the syllabus (it was elegant) and assignments (they were thoughtful and articulate). But I also came away surprised, even a little astonished, that while students were parsing important ideas about racial or gender oppression they were never invited or challenged by their professor to become intellectually, publicly, or socially engaged in those issues as they are lived out and suffered through in their own lives and local community.

Widespread skepticism throughout the humanities over foundational constructions like "civil society" or the "public good" comes at a time of deep moral ache among an American public for shared democratic truths. In a speech to the National Civic League's 100th National Conference, Daniel Yankelovich reported, well before the galvanizing events of 9/11, that American public opinion continues to reflect a widespread desire "to reconcile new social mores with American core values," including "a sense of community, neighborliness, hope, [and] optimism" (1994, p. 15). That sentiment was confirmed by several national surveys. They showed that the fraying of social integuments worried a majority of Americans who are eager to conciliate individual and group differences in the interest of dispelling what many perceive as a malaise that had settled over the public sphere. In one survey, 80% of respondents agreed that more emphasis should be put on community-building even if it meant compromising the pursuit of self-interest and individualism Americans have always cherished (Putnam 2000, p. 25).

Whether these public sentiments and concerns are credible or perhaps exaggerated is not at issue here. What concerns me is the stark disconnect between a public perception of civic malaise and the life and mind of the contemporary humanities. Trained in the rigorous critical skepticism of postmodern theories of power and social predation, for example, many cultural studies academics downplay reports of social or moral decline and fall as "declensionist narratives" that tend to obscure hegemonic practices lurking in the shadows of social and rhetorical fictions like the "breakdown of community" or the "decline of civic virtue." While average Americans aspire to strengthen community bonds, academic humanists have taken a sharp left turn into a critique of *difference* and the ubiquitous struggle for power they perceive as the engine of human history. Asked in an interview to explain who struggles against whom, Michel Foucault replied with a degree of absolutism unusual among postmodern social theoreticians that "it's all against all. We all fight each other. And there is always within each of us something that fights something else" (1980, p. 115).

This fascination with the will to power as the moral pulse of the individual as well as the genetic code of the body politic has not driven a scholarship, as one might otherwise expect, that would make academic postmoderns very good partners in the civic engagement movement. I am thinking of a public scholarship that meets a threshold laid down by land-grant historian Scott Peters: "how a scholar's work of constructing and communicating knowledge might contribute to community-building, to public problem solving, to public creation, and to the process of coming to public judgment on what ought to be done . . . to address important public issues and problems" (2001, p. 32). Liberation from constraining notions of "public," "common knowledge," and "shared truths" comes at a cost tallied by Richard Rorty who called into question the hard inward turn of humanities scholarship and postmodernism's "spectatorial approach" to the public arena. "To step into the intellectual world which [postmodernists] inhabit," Rorty warns, "is to move out of a world in which citizens of a democracy can join forces to resist sadism and selfishness into a Gothic world in which democratic politics has become a farce" (1998, pp. 95–96).

Rorty organizes his brutal critique of contemporary humanities scholarship around two related points. First, citing Fredric Jameson's canonical *Postmodernism, or The Cultural Logic of Late Capitalism* as an example, Rorty complains that, like the lion's share of scholarship in new hybrid fields like cultural studies spawned by celebrity intellectuals like Foucault and Jameson, *Postmodernism* "operates on a level of abstraction too high to encourage any particular political initiative" (1998, p. 78). Second, while ostensibly concerned with important matters of political relevance like discrimination and oppression of minorities, the split between "spectatorship and agency," Rorty observes, renders "futile [any] attempts to philosophize one's way into political relevance. . . . Disengagement from practice produces theoretical hallucinations" (p. 95). Never before has the critical rhetoric of the humanities been more politically inflected and ideologically supercharged. Never before has its intellectual world been more devoid of commitment to the commonweal, to civic activism, and to democracy as social praxis. Call it what you will—deep irony, paradox, a split between spectatorship and agency, hypocrisy, or identity crisis—the predicament of the humanities is obvious and inescapable. New culture critics can brilliantly deconstruct politics and power out of just about every text and every "artifact" of "cultural production." Meanwhile, they have very little to communicate to the larger public. They form a professoriate, as Alan Wolfe puts it simply, "that has forgotten its public obligations" (p. 38).

From "The Other" to *One Another*

One way to reawaken the public purposes of the contemporary humanities is to reframe our teaching and scholarship as ethical practices that supplement, maybe even complement, cultural studies' critique of the politics of liberalism. I understand "ethical practice" as bound up in a pragmatic question: "How am I obligated?" The humanities disciplines, in my view, have neglected that question of moral praxis for the past couple of decades in favor of a brand of high theory more concerned with matters of power, authority, identity, and the limits of individual agency. There is a real difference, however, between radical theories of social transformation, class liberation, identity politics, and cultural production currently much in fashion in today's critical marketplace and the hard labor of democracy. That neglect of application and inattention to praxis—the bulwarks of ethical pedagogy and democratic change—is what prompts Rorty to complain about the arid material cranked out by an unself-critical and self-referential theory industry out of touch with human needs and interests.

Besides, the ideological and political agitation and the proletarian sympathies of so much academic cultural analysis are empty posturings without an activist component. This is why some humanities faculty were drawn to the alternatives we found in community-based teaching practices and the service-learning movement in the 1990s. There we met peers, senior colleagues, and mentors (in my case the Reverend John Duley and, later, Robert Coles)—many of whom were tempered and tested by the civil rights and experiential learning movements of the 1960s (Stanton, Giles, & Cruz, 1999)—with calluses on their hands and solid track records of public work in communities and neighborhoods outside the privileged, safe havens of their campus seminars.

Our students, to be sure, can benefit greatly from the political perspectives and critical insights introduced by contemporary cultural studies. Students need to know, for example, how to see through glib ideologies of common sense that cloak the trappings of abusive power and the maintenance of the political status quo. The problem, however, is that students might be overwhelmed by the ubiquitous metaphor of hegemony and led to the unfortunate conclusion that powerlessness is a virtue or that individual efficacy and agency are nothing more than socially constructed ideas used to enforce a discredited ideology. For me, the most important question for a socially engaged literature and writing curriculum is not *how* to recognize or even reclaim historically excluded groups and discourses but *what* enables diverse voices, once reclaimed, to find legitimate courses of public action that are consistent with what is valuable to the community as a whole—and not to shirk the language of consensus-building out of fealty to postmodernism's dislike of foundations and its insistence that narratives of wholeness are insidious cartoons of privilege and hegemony. This calls on us to shift the ethical center of gravity in our teaching and scholarship from "The Other" to *one another*. The communities—rhetorical and *real*—where our students live their lives and many of the actual rhetorical and ethical situations in which they find themselves as writers and citizens call on them to search for common ground, act through compromise, make decisions among imperfect and incomplete choices, and search for ways to achieve and maintain social cohesion, inclusion, and harmony.

Humanities as Cultural Work in the Public Interest

I do sense an awakening, maybe even a genuine soul-searching, in the academy and especially among humanists spurred by our loss of public purpose and relevance and the recognition that the vast majority of hyperspecialized humanities scholarship is completely unintelligible to a literate public. Concerted efforts are under way to shore up the declining cultural capital of the humanities. Nationally, for example, the consortium Imagining America is leading the way with exciting programs of renewal aimed at arts and humanities teaching, scholarship, and performance as cultural work in the public interest. Julie Ellison, founding president of Imagining America, acknowledges that there are important differences among today's humanities professoriate in our subfields and areas of specialization, in cultural agendas and professional status, and in the diverse communities and locations where we conduct our work. "But there is also startling agreement on what content is interesting," she reminds us, and "what aesthetic and thematic strands are most promising, what complexity is worth capturing. This, it seems to me, is the basis for 'educated hope' about public scholarship" (2008, p. 467).

At its 2004 national convention, the outgoing president of the Modern Language Association—the poster child for out-of-touch academics—organized several well-attended forums on the future of the humanities. Much frank discussion took place around the contemporary humanities' neglect of public purpose and responsibility and loss of credibility and respect in the eyes of the public. Other national organizations have devoted similar energies to repositioning the humanities into closer contact with problems and issues that confront the public today, including a book on the place of the humanities in democratic life published by the Kettering Foundation, an AAU report on reinvigorating the humanities, and a series of national leadership dialogues convened by the American Council of Learned Societies, the latter two groups not particularly known for their civic activism and agitation for public engagement.

In another chapter in this book my colleague Eric Fretz and I write about the Service Learning Writing Project at Michigan State University as one example of rejuvenating the humanities classroom with an active pedagogy based on deliberative democracy. I close here with a brief companion profile as a case study of engaged scholarship and creative activity. While based on my own unique experience, the broader challenges I face as a humanities scholar/teacher may nonetheless feel familiar to my colleagues across the cultural disciplines, irrespective of their institutional settings: namely, the challenges of balancing, coordinating, and integrating a self-satisfying research agenda, an active teaching life, creativity, and a strong commitment to public purpose.

In my case, this balancing act has been made more urgent recently by an irresistible urge to renew a long-standing interest in photography, both as a practicing photo essayist in my spare time and as a scholar of public culture with a side interest in the documentary arts. How could I legitimately reposition documentary photography—something I had pursued as an avocation for 40 years—into an academic vocation consistent with my appointment, something that would pass rigorous peer review while satisfying the demands of research, teaching, and service to my university and community?

Since I could not "compete" with established photographers in my college's Studio Art Department or photojournalism colleagues in the School of Journalism, the key in my case has been to repurpose photography into a sufficiently specialized topic of investigation and engaged scholarship. After much research, soul-searching, and churn, I finally settled on a practice of citizen empowerment and deliberative decision-making called "PhotoVoice." Used for several years internationally as a way of bringing grassroots communities and neighborhoods into the public policymaking arena, PhotoVoice puts cameras into the hands of ordinary citizens, often groups at the social margins with no experience in photography and little, if any, influence in the public sphere. After simple instruction in camera use and picture-taking techniques, citizen-photographers take pictures that reflect their unique perspectives and vantage points on issues facing their communities. With the help of trained facilitators, PhotoVoice participants come together and use their photographs as prompts for discussion, reflection, and problem-solving. They always exhibit their best photographs in public venues in order to engage local leaders in insightful conversations about their photographs and what light they shed on matters of community concern.

One of the first things I did was set up actual PhotoVoice projects through partnerships with local schools, neighborhood associations, and community centers. I also adapted PhotoVoice techniques to active learning practices in my classes. Fortunately, I was able to arrange a course assignment in a new Residential College in the Arts and Humanities at Michigan State University that stresses connections between student civic engagement and creativity activity. In one case, my students in a photo essay workshop designed and facilitated a PhotoVoice experience for a small group of visiting dignitaries from the West African country of Mali, including everything from an orientation workshop and guided reflection sessions to a public exhibit at the end. Another project brought together dorm students and residents living in nearby neighborhoods to explore, through photographs, persistent myths and misperceptions about campus/community tensions. As a result of my involvement in and coordination of these PhotoVoice projects, I came to view photography as an important democratic art form, a wonderful medium for storytelling, and a powerful teaching and learning tool. As an experienced journal editor, I took on an assignment as photo essay editor for a journal of literary nonfiction looking to beef up its photography section. I also accepted an invitation from an out-of-state colleague to contribute a chapter on narrative photography to a book she was editing on creative writing as social action. I received, in addition, two grants to shoot, process, draft, and design for exhibit three original photo essays of my own, two of which were published as chapbooks through a partnership I have with Michigan Campus Compact.

PhotoVoice has become, in effect, a legitimate slipstream for my engaged faculty work and creative interests. It enables me to enhance my involvement with communities and publics. At the same time it is a dynamic active learning resource for classroom use. Participatory photography energizes my research agenda by focusing my scholarship onto visual narrative and public documentary arts. It gives me a platform for publication and connects me to a network of like-minded colleagues and new community partners. In the bargain, it scratches my creative itch as a practicing photographer.

These criteria and impacts have been sufficient for modest but successful peer review. In my case, they are also necessary for a life.

References

Bourdieu, P. (2000). For a scholarship with commitment. *Profession 2000* (pp. 40–45). New York: Modern Language Association.

Boyer, E. (1997). *Scholarship reconsidered: Priorities of the professoriate.* San Francisco: Jossey-Bass.

Ellison, J. (2008). The humanities and the public soul. *Antipode, 40*(3), 463–71.

Farland, M. (1996). Academic professionalism and the new public mindedness. *Higher Education Exchange*, 51–57.

Fisk, E. B. (1988). *New York Times*, October 5, B12.

Foucault, M. (1980). *Power/knowledge: Selected interviews and other writings, 1972–1977.* C. Gordon (Ed.). Brighton: Harvester Press, 1980.

Hall, S. (1992). Cultural studies and its theoretical legacies. In L. Grossberg, C. Nelson, & P. Treichler (Eds.), *Cultural studies* (pp, 272–294). New York: Routledge.

Kellogg Forum on Higher Education for the Public Good. (2002). Mission, goals, strategies, and intended impact. In Leadership Dialogues Series 2002, participant binder. Ann Arbor, MI: Kellogg Forum on Higher Education for the Public Good.

Lasch, C. (1995*). The revolt of the elites and the betrayal of democracy.* New York: Norton.

Peters, S. (2001). The civic mission question in land grant education. *Higher Education Exchange*, 25–37.

Putnam, R. (2000). *Bowling alone: The collapse and revival of American community.* New York: Simon and Schuster.

Rorty, R. (1998). *Achieving our country.* Cambridge: Harvard University Press.

Spanos, W. (1992). The detective and the boundary: Some notes on the postmodern literary imagination. In P. Waugh (Ed.), *Postmodernism: A Reader* (pp. 78–86). New York: Edward Arnold.

Stanton, T., Giles, D., & Cruz, N. (1999). *Service-Learning: A Movement's Pioneers Reflect on Its Origins, Practice, and Future.* San Francisco: Jossey-Bass.

Sterns, P. N. (2004). Teaching culture. *Liberal Education, 90*(3), 6–15.

Wolfe, A. (1997). The promise and the flaws of public scholarship. *Higher Education Exchange*, 37–57.

Yankelovich, D. (1994). Three destructive trends: Can they be reversed? Presentation to the National Civic League's 100th National Conference, Philadelphia, November 11.

Service Learning through Public Work and Public Deliberation

David D. Cooper and Eric Fretz

During the spring semester of 2002, we both taught integrated classes in the Writing, Rhetoric and American Cultures (WRAC) program at Michigan State University. That course is described at length below. This experience turned out to be a watershed teaching experience for each of us. Cooper was a veteran of service-learning pedagogy at that time, and Fretz, through Cooper's mentoring, was just beginning to experiment with the pedagogy. Now, a decade later, we are taking this opportunity to reflect on how these teaching experiences shaped our subsequent thinking and practice and to chart the progress of the service-learning movement toward practices of public work and public deliberation. Our motivation for revisiting the classroom experience is to tell the story of how we used a teaching experience to craft the public nature of our careers as higher education professionals as well as to tell the larger story of how the service-learning movement is developing.

At that time, we were both teaching in the Writing, Rhetoric and American Cultures department at Michigan State University, a department that serves the first-year writing needs of the 40,000 students at that land-grant, research-based institution.

One of the reasons Fretz agreed to teach the course that Cooper proposed was because of an experience he had in the classroom immediately after the September 11 terrorist attacks. Fretz was wondering how the attacks were being handled in college classrooms, so he polled his students one day to discover what they had to say. The results were sobering. Of the 70 students who responded to the questions, 68 said they were interested in taking a week to discuss the war. Two said they didn't care. Here's the surprising part: only five students reported that the issue of the war and the bombings were being discussed in their other classes. Sixty-five students reported that the war was not being discussed in their classes. Nearly all of those 65 students were confused and angry about the silence in their classrooms. Here are a few excerpts:

> In all my other classes we haven't been talking about it [the war] at all, like we're ignoring or avoiding the situation. It's understandable with some teachers if that's how they feel. But, they show that they don't care, so we then in turn won't either.
>
> We have not even brought the subject up in any of my classes. My days just go on like any other.
>
> None of my other professors have even brought up the topic of this past month's events other than to say, "I assume you all have seen the news, but we really need to concentrate on the topic of this class." I was outraged and left the class.
>
> All my other classes are continuing on like this isn't even happening.

Young adults can figure out what's important to the adults in their lives, and implicitly or explicitly, they pattern their own values and ways of living around adult models. If higher education professionals are not establishing a groundwork of civic action in our classrooms, how will students learn to participate in the life of a democracy? Where will they learn the required civic skills of deliberation, negotiation, participation? If faculty members by and large believed that their own disciplinary inquiries were more important than the national trauma that was at hand, what did that say about the kind of intellectual narcissism of the academy and, moreover, what kind of a message was it sending about public-ness and pub-lic culture to our students? (Fish, 2008; Butin, 2005; Colby, Beaumont, Ehrlich, & Corngold, 2007). And while it seems daunting, almost insurmountable, we saw the civic engagement movement as a counterforce to the trends of commercialism, consumerism, and self-involvement that were sweeping higher education.

The emerging service-learning literature at that time was arguing that faculty members and higher education institutions had a responsibility to help students develop a set of dem-ocratic skills, exercise their public voices, and acquire a public work ethic (Boyte & Farr, 1997; Battistoni, 2002). Boyte and Farr argued that "substantial civic education through service . . . requires that young people be thought of as productive actors, citizens in the present, not citizens in the making, who have serious public work to do" (1997, p. 7). In 2004, Boyte went on to define public work as "sustained effort by a mix of people who solve public problems or create goods, material or cultural, of general benefit" (p. 5). There was a growing sense at the time that service-learning courses should do more than simply get students out in the community. In addition to paying more attention to the *learning* of service learning (Eyler & Giles, 1999) practitioners were trying to figure out how to engage students in meaningful community experiences and activate the skills, knowledge, and capacities of community members as well as students. Practitioners and advocates were arguing that service-learning experiences should animate students' imagination to do public work and to accept the responsibility of active citizenship, which includes learning to identify and solve community problems through negotiation and participation, finding ways to be involved in the public life of communities, and understanding that democracy depends on civic life (Campus Compact, 1999, 2002).

Our Class: How We Practiced Democracy in the Classroom

In an effort to engage these new ideas in the service-learning movement, we designed a course to help push service learning into new directions of civic engagement, deliberative classroom practices, and public work. We were excited by the trends taking place in the service-learning movement, and we looked for ways to be a part of new learning initiatives.

Through this course, we wanted to provide students opportunities to study techniques of deliberation and practice public dialogue and public problem solving. We wanted to encourage student participation in the public sphere through active participation in class discussions and public forums as well as through direct involvement in public work and community service. As Cooper wrote in his syllabus, "Our goals throughout the course will be to deepen our awareness of important public issues and concerns, to build our problem-solving capabilities and to strengthen and improve public life in our community." In order to accomplish these goals, we planned a course where students engaged in traditional community service, organized a public forum from soup to nuts, and facilitated study circles on controversial topics.

Inputs/Learning Strategies, Pedagogy, and Methods

We taught separate but related issues for each of our courses. Cooper was interested in exploring issues and problems of the American public educational system through a Public Life in America class; he ordered books and designed his course to reflect those interests. Fretz had been teaching the Race and Ethnicity course with discussion-based pedagogies and methods, and he wanted to see how an injection of service learning into this class would affect student learning and help students develop habits of civic engagement. As a result, Fretz chose texts and designed the course to reflect his interest in American race and ethnic questions. We each designed our own syllabus, although there was a good deal of overlap in required texts, learning strategies, and goals. In an effort to create some intellectual commonalities between the two classes, we chose Jonathan Kozol's *Savage Inequalities* as one text that both classes could read in common. Over the course of the semester we met as a large group (both classes together) about half of the time and broke off into our separate classes the other half of the class periods.

Our class consisted of three experiential learning components that we instituted in order to connect to the academic issues of the course, foster a learning community, and practice democratic skills of deliberation, collaboration, and participation. The first component involved setting up a fairly traditional service experience for the students, and the next two components involved requiring the students to organize a National Issues Forum on Youth Violence and then moderate study circles.

Service Learning

Traditional service learning, where students work with local community-based organizations, was an important part of our curriculum. During the semester before we offered our service-learning course, we searched for local community organizations that were willing to

95

provide service experiences for our students. We looked for organizations engaged in activities that would suit the intellectual work of our classroom, and we found a match with a Neighborhood Network Center in Lansing. The purpose of the Network Centers is to provide services and support for families and children in some of Lansing's economically disadvantaged areas. The intellectual issues of race and education would converge in these kinds of service experiences.

Over the course of the semester, students worked two to four hours in the Network Centers and performed a variety of tasks including tutoring elementary and GED students, working with Girl Scouts troops, and initiating food and clothes drives for the centers. They reflected on their service experiences in critical incident journals that we regularly discussed during class time and used to connect their service experience with the academic issues of the class.

National Issues Forum: The Public Use of Reason

In an effort to extend the work of the service-learning classroom and to help our students develop habits of civic engagement, we included in the class the preparation and organization of two National Issues Forums (NIF). The first, a mock forum on public schools and how to make them more effective, simply gave the students a taste for the deliberative process of public forums. The second, a full-fledged public forum, tackled the subject of youth violence and how to stop the trend.

National Issues Forums are structured public deliberations about a controversial social topic. Content and information for the forums are available through issue booklets prepared by Public Agenda and the Kettering Foundation. Each issue booklet explains the issue and then provides a series of solutions to the problem.

The public forums provide opportunities for students, community members, public policymakers, legislators, and community leaders to meet together and discuss a range of solutions to specific community problems. The NIF website describes the forums as "a way for citizens to exchange ideas and experiences with one another, and make more thoughtful and informed decisions." The two-hour forums are moderated by a NIF-trained moderator who leads the audience through an organized discussion of the problem at hand and possible solutions to the problem.

The NIF was important to us because it helped students and community participants develop what James Bohman (1996) calls, "self-governing capacities" that include "understanding, imagining, valuing, desiring, storytelling and the use of rhetoric and argumentation" (p. 7). Acquiring these "self-governing capabilities" provides students with experience to effect change in our democracy. Through the public forum process, students learned how to engage in the public life of their communities, understand multiple perspectives relating to complex problems, work out solutions to community problems, develop critical thinking skills, and engage with course work in a meaningful way.

For our text, we used a Kettering Foundation–sponsored national issues booklet, *Violent Kids: How Can We Change the Trend?* The booklet is a slim volume that succinctly defines the problem of youth violence and then provides three alternatives to stopping the problem. After students read the booklet and spent time in class discussing, researching, and writing about the problem of youth violence, they began organizing the public forum, a four-week, project-oriented endeavor where students broke into work groups and accomplished necessary duties in the organization of the forum. Among other things, students (1) set up a timetable for forum planning, (2) met with community partners and invited potential forum participants, (3) wrote press releases, letters to editors, and designed posters announcing the event, (4) assisted NIF moderators, (5) managed the logistics of the forum, (6) organized electronic communication systems for the group to communicate and (7) researched and summarized relevant source materials on the topic. Students archived their forum activities on line.

Study Circles

At the end of the semester, we committed four weeks to the organization and implementation of student-led study circles about youth and race issues. A study circle is a group of 8–10 people who come together to discuss an important or controversial topic. They provide an environment where ordinary citizens can exercise their public voices, and practice the democratic skills of deliberation and negotiation. Study circles also serve as agents of community action and problem solving through dialogue because they provide opportunities for ordinary citizens to get involved in the public life of their communities. While expert views are important, study circles give ordinary people opportunities to converse, find common perspectives, and tease out differences over issues that are important to their lives. Study circle topics include, among other things, race, education, crime and violence, immigration, youth issues, building strong neighborhoods, and urban sprawl.

We held a total of eight one-hour study circle discussions over the course of two weeks. Study circle resource booklets provide a structured format that helps members identify the problem at hand, consider its implications, and provide possible solutions. Through their facilitation of a youth issues study circle guide, Cooper's class engaged the group in dialogue about contemporary youth problems and how they can be resolved. Fretz's class used the race relations guide to initiate conversations on racial identities, participants' experiences with race, and the roots and solutions to these problems.

Facilitating a study circle was a way for students to exercise their public voices and practice the art of deliberation, something they were not necessarily able to do in the NIF forum. Study circles are smaller and more intimate than the NIF public forums, so they consequently give students more opportunities to actively engage in and moderate public discussions. Since moderation and facilitation of difficult issues are critical skills for an effective deliberative process, we required each student in our class to moderate one study circle discussion. The study circle booklets consider group moderation an art, and they provide facilitators with opportunities to practice habits of critical listening, asking leading questions, generating and sustaining discussions, staying neutral, and leading groups toward consensus. In order to impress upon our students the importance of moderating a discussion and setting a framework for a deliberative discussion, we spent an entire class period talking about what qualities that make a good moderator and practicing moderating a small discussion. (For more information on study circles, see Everyday Democracy 2008.)

Creating an Organic Learning Community through Committee Work and Deliberative Evaluation

In an effort to enter into a learning partnership where students actually performed some of the public work of the classroom, we included student committees in the design and implementation of class assignments. Our goal was to create a learning community where students participated in the organization and development of learning strategies in the class. To that end, we involved students in as much of the day-to-day class activities and curricular planning as we could. At the beginning of the semester, we chose the books, set up relationships with community-based service organizations, and wrote the syllabus. After that, we set things up so the students could share in the work of the classroom.

Typically, we would confer in our offices before class and make a list of long- and short-term tasks and responsibilities that needed to be performed. In class, we would set up working committees where the students would engage in the public work of the class. This dynamic had the effect of extending the kind of learning that went on in our classroom. Students discussed, imagined, and worked with each other to accomplish classroom tasks that had tangible products. They designed assignments, edited each other's papers, coauthored letters and discussion guides, authored web pages, and conducted research. Our classroom quickly became a working environment and was frequently a buzz of activity.

We engaged in several intentional tasks to cultivate students as partners in the work of the classroom, such as involving students in the process of writing and designing assignments and engaging students in a dialogue about grading and evaluation. Bringing students into the realm of decision making was a challenging process. We needed to learn to give up a good deal of control in the classroom, and the students found themselves struggling with the responsibility of actively participating in the organization of the class. At the beginning of the semester, when we would break off with small groups of students to design writing and presentation assignments, they tended to act sheepish and confused. They were not used to making decisions about how class was run, and the newfound authority made them uneasy. As the example below will illustrate, students became used to taking control and comfortable working with us to develop assignments and perform the "work" of the classroom as the semester wore on. We discovered that working with students in this capacity takes a great deal of time and patience. It's much easier to close the office door, sit in front of the computer, and design a writing or reading assignment.

During the first few weeks of the semester, Fretz's class read and discussed an *Opposing Viewpoints* text on race relations, and Cooper's class read and discussed an *Opposing Viewpoints* text on education. Both classes read Jonathan Kozol's *Savage Inequalities*. We agreed that each class should make a presentation about their reading and discussion to the other class. We asked for volunteers to join us in the process of designing the presentation assignment. A few days later, Fretz met with a group of students, and they spent about two hours discussing the ingredients of a good presentation and drafting the assignment. After some initial confusion and shyness, the committee produced a more thoughtful and interesting presentation than Fretz could have ever done on his own. The Assignment Committee broke our class into four working groups and assigned a controversial topic on race to each group.

Topics included affirmative action, diversity and multiculturalism, segregation, and racial profiling. Each group was responsible for developing a 30-minute presentation that introduced and dramatized the controversy, used class texts to educate the audience on the nature of the debate, and initiated a class discussion. The assignment committee typed the assignment and sent it electronically to the rest of the class and followed that up with a brief explanation and question-and-answer session in class.

Evaluation and grading practices tend to be exercised in private, behind closed doors—hardly the ingredients of a democratic process! One of the most effective ways to show students that deliberation is taken seriously in your classroom is to open up grading and evaluation practices to deliberation. An example from our class will serve as an illustration.

Throughout the organization of the NIF forum, students wrote editorials and press releases announcing the event, performed extensive research on the topic of youth violence, composed invitation letters to community partners, legislators, and public officials, designed discussion guides, and worked out logistics (including seating arrangements and microphone placement) for the forum. We set up a Portfolio Committee to archive and organize all this material, and the forum portfolio, then, became our way of evaluating the public work students performed in the organization of the forum.

At the beginning of the forum preparation, we discussed, as a group, possible evaluation procedures. The students agreed that the final portfolio project would serve as a major class assignment (worth about 15% of their grade), and that we would evaluate the final portfolio project and give each student a common grade. After we collected the final portfolio, Cooper and Fretz each wrote a detailed (six pages, single spaced) evaluation that analyzed and evaluated the forum as it was archived in the portfolio. Our standards here were rigorous, and we used the document as a way to evaluate students for their learning rather than their service—one of the "best practices" of service-learning pedagogy. We emailed our evaluation to each student and invited them to respond to our evaluation in writing. We were slightly disappointed by the number of responses—only 10 out of 50 students took us up on our offer and, unsurprisingly, each of the 10 used effective argumentation skills to petition for a higher grade. On the last day of class, we held our final public forum, this time to deliberate the final grade of the portfolio project (see Cooper 2008 for more detail on this process).

Motivating Ideas and Practices: Deliberative Democracy

In 2002, we believed that deliberative democracy had an important role to play in higher education. We found the theoretical and the historical foundations of this work compelling, and we sought ways to bring these theories and practices to our students.

Jürgen Habermas (1989) offered a useful critical theory of public deliberation. For Habermas, a robust democracy is contingent upon the existence of a public sphere where citizens can participate in civic life and debate controversial public issues. Bohman (1996) defined public deliberation as a "cooperative activity "where individuals with competing opinions use the art of dialogue to resolve controversial problems (p. 2). Bohman explained that a nation is as democratic as it practices deliberation; in other words, deliberation is a way to measure the value and effectiveness of a particular democratic order. A strong and reasoned public sphere needed informed, active citizens who could act on public judgment rather than public opinion. Daniel Yankelovich (1999) defines public judgment as an enlightened opinion that is arrived at through dialogue, engagement, and the consideration of multiple perspectives (p. 5). For Yankelovich, the "struggle for the soul of America" is being fought between the forces of the market economy and the promise of a civil society. The market side argues that new directions in technology and a spreading global economy will foster democratic cultures worldwide. The civic vision of America is rooted in a belief that the best way to promote democracy is to encourage public deliberation of controversial issues, foster strong families and communities, and help promote citizens' civic, rather than professional, identities. Finally, we found useful James Fishkin's (1995) explanation of deliberation as a way to engage citizens in local and federal issues: "The public can best speak for itself when it can gather together in some way to hear the arguments on the various sides of an issue and then, after face to face discussion, come to a collective decision" (p. 4). Deliberative democracies involve ordinary citizens in the public discourse and decision making of local and federal issues—it uses the opinions and judgments of experts without simply defaulting to what Bohman (1996) calls "strategic rationality" (p. 5).

Nevertheless, there are legitimate and important critiques of the deliberative process. As we write, for instance, a national health care debate has turned acrimonious as legislators are being violently confronted by 'ordinary' citizens in 'town hall' meetings ostensibly designed to provide open forums on how to solve the health care crisis. Given these recent events, it is easy to go along with critics of deliberative democracy who explain that cultural pluralism, social complexity, and deep economic inequalities preclude deliberative democracy from being an effective means of conducting public policy and solving public problems. The nation, they argue, has become too heterogeneous, too complex, and too fragmented for citizens to effectively deliberate about public issues. Moreover, deliberation never happens on a level playing field—the voices of individuals with more education, income, organization, and power will inevitably ring louder than citizens with less privilege (Bohman, 1996, p. 3; Fraser, 1992, pp. 109–142). Jane Mansbridge explains some of the pitfalls of deliberation when she argues that "the transformation of 'I' into 'we' brought about through political deliberation can easily mask subtle forms of control. Even the language people use as they reason together usually favors one way of seeing things and discourages others. Subordinate groups sometimes cannot find the right voice or words to express their thoughts, and when they do, they discover they are not heard" (as cited in Fraser 1992, p. 119).

We considered these arguments and counterarguments as we were teaching the class and we continue to grapple with them today. Despite the critiques, though, and realizing that our scope of influence and power is limited, we come down on the side that in a nation as pluralistic, diverse, and open as the United States, democratic deliberation can be seen as an effective way to mend a balkanized nation.

We take a capacious view of civic discourse, one that breaks down the convenient yet somewhat misleading distinctions we tend to enforce between civil behavior in the public sphere and the inevitable and welcomed agitations of civic exchange and churn in a healthy democracy. Our work with deliberative and public work practices in the classroom have left us wary and critically questioning of the way the mass media, in particular, tends to conflate civil behavior and civic speech in an otherwise understandable effort to truncate complex exchanges over public policy issues. The civic engagement movement tends to treat guidelines for civil behavior—show respect for others, use a civil tone of voice, be courteous, weigh different points of view equally—as interchangeable with practices of civic dialogue: for example, making tough choices over controversial issues that people care passionately about, aggressively countering misinformation, recognizing that divisions exist within communities and not glossing over them, and respecting that consensus-making brings felt personal sacrifices to some citizens.

One of the things we have grown to admire about the NIF style of public deliberation and its adaptability to the humanities classroom is the way it respects and elevates personal experience in the calculus of public problem solving. Personal stories in the public sphere can be powerful boosts to public creation and action. Asking participants how a particular issue impacts them personally or what personal experiences have shaped their perspectives on an issue—these are absolutely crucial foundations for deliberation and for public work. This reciprocity between what people care about deeply and passionately and the hard work of hammering out the political will it takes to get people acting together is the greatest asset and the most daunting challenge of deliberative learning.

While experimenting with deliberative democracy and public work in the classroom, Cooper also edited a journal of literary nonfiction—*Fourth Genre: Explorations in Nonfiction*—that kept him in touch with good writing and the vitality of contemporary narrative. Reading literally thousands of essays submitted to the journal during that period reminded him daily that a writer's unique voice and the palpable sense of his or her unique presence in a piece of writing are essential hallmarks of the contemporary essay. He found it interesting that NIF-style public forums are another discursive arena where story, voice, and personal presence matter. In this sense, *narrative* connected his work as a literary editor and his experiments in public conversation and deliberation in the undergraduate classroom. In skillfully moderated forums, the power of personal stories—of people using their lived experience as a primary way of engaging social or political issues—is often a more fertile source of conviction and persuasion than formal modes or skills of rhetorical training and debate or perfectly framed choices. How many of us haven't been moved to new perspectives or had our fixed convictions on an issue derailed by a powerful story of personal experience shared by a forum participant? The same thing happens in a good essay.

A deliberative democracy strives for a shared vision that gets beyond individual and group interests, not by sacrificing them, but by incorporating competing visions and ideas into a consensual sphere. Public deliberation is not an effort to create a forced consensus and ignore cultural, ethnic, racial, and religious differences. Rather, deliberation is a tool to acknowledge difference and attempt to build dialogue and understanding through discussion, storytelling, and explanation. Through the development of what Fraser (1992) calls "subaltern counter publics," marginalized groups (e.g., blacks, gays, students, fast-food workers) can organize to develop strong, public voices that can become a part of the public sphere. Creating spaces for citizens to discuss and dialogue is one of the best ways to recognize differences and use them as a way to create a shared vision of how we want our communities to operate and what we choose to value and support. Pluralism and diversity do not have to separate us and turn the nation into fragmented interests rooted in race, ethnicity, class, and gender. We may celebrate different holidays, speak different languages, hold different political and religious beliefs, and still work together to weave a strong democratic fabric. As John Dewey notes, democracy may be the only thing we have in common.

What We Went On to Do and What We Continue to Learn

We began this essay by noting that the service-learning course we taught in 2002 was designed to reflect and extend what we saw as promising trends in the service-learning movement, namely public deliberation and public work. Since then, both of us have continued to craft our teaching and writing life by continuing the pedagogical practices we experimented with in the 2002 course at MSU. Additionally, we have watched and participated as the service-learning movement has embraced ideas and practices of public work and public deliberation (Boyte, 2004; Peters, Jordan, Adamek, & Alter, 2005; Colby et al., 2007; Harriger & McMillan, 2007; Dedrick, Grattan, & Dienstfrey, 2008; Barker & Brown, 2009). We will close this essay with a brief discussion about developments in the field of service learning as they relate to public work and public deliberation.

Civic Professionalism

One of the things we learned from the course we taught in 2002 is that the way we taught our classes shaped our roles as faculty members. Specifically, this shared teaching experience in 2002 made us realize that these kinds of classrooms demand an open, democratic, and participatory set of teaching practices. In *The Courage to Teach*, Palmer (1998) reflects on his teacher training and notes, "Like most professionals, I was taught to occupy space, not open it: after all, we are the ones who know, so we have an obligation to tell others all about it" (p. 132). Before we understood that teaching is public work, we believed our responsibility in the classroom was, in Palmer's words, "to occupy space," or to *perform* intelligence by demonstrating mastery of the material, preparing an organized class period, and a skillfully articulating complex ideas.

Since that time, a good deal of work on reshaping faculty roles within the contexts of the civic engagement movement has developed (Boyte 2004; Matthews 2005; Ward 2005; Rice and O'Meara 2005; Harriger and McMillan 2007; Colby et al., 2007). We have benefited from all of this work, and we have been especially inspired by the recent work of Albert Dzur, who provides a framework and a context outside of higher education for us to continue to rethink our roles in higher education. In *Democratic Professionalism* (2008) Dzur examines recent innovations in the fields of public journalism, restorative justice, and bioethics as a way to encourage other "helping" professions to develop a culture of professional practice that shares tasks and responsibilities with laypeople in order to bring lay people into problem-solving relationships. Dzur sees a "democratic significance" stirring within many professions. He views the professions as places where public life and public culture can be nurtured and facilitated. In his own words, democratic professionals

> are concerned about the effects of their expertise on the lay public's ability to make self-confident choices both inside and outside a particular professional domain. . . . [They] recognize that they may know only part of what is important in reaching a decision about a treatment plan, a service,

or a public policy that relates to their domain. Above all, they seek to open their professional domain to other voices, other experiences. (p. 104)

For Dzur, democratic professionals are facilitators of public knowledge. They seek out common interests that link professional inquiry and local knowledge, and they work to develop systems of communication and knowledge production that involve laypeople in the solution of public problems. Democratic professionals "refuse to 'dominate discussion'" and are capable of "stepping back and allowing laypeople the chance to take up responsibilities" (p. 41).

When we taught our class in 2002, we did not have Dzur's framework, and we often wondered about our teaching practices would be received by our colleagues or even if we were doing the right thing for our students. Now, however, we have benefited from the reexamination of faculty work that has been accomplished by scholars across the disciplines, and it seems that the pedagogical risks we took in 2002 are part of larger cultural questions about how professionals (not just in higher education) do their work.

Students as Colleagues

One of the lessons we took from our teaching experience in 2002 was that to engage in public work in higher education means including students and their interests in the work and life of the classroom. In an organic classroom like ours, teaching in the traditional sense of disseminating knowledge and downloading information into students gets transformed into a collaborative process where professors and students work toward a common goal. To really take the idea of teaching liberty seriously, the professor has to turn the objectivist, positivistic classroom into a working environment. No small task! John Dewey articulates this idea in *Democracy and Education* (when he calls for a distinction between education and training. Dewey likens "training" to the work that horses do for their masters. Horses, Dewey notes are trained to perform actions, but since they have no interest in the work they perform, they remain aloof and disconnected. Educating means, in Dewey's words, making students "partner[s] in a shared activity" (p. 15).

Recent trends in the field suggest that our emphasis on including students in the work of the academy is on the right track. In 2001, a group of 33 students met in Racine, Wisconsin, for the Wingspread Summit on Student Civic Engagement. They discussed their experiences with political and civic engagement and subsequently published *The New Student Politics* (Campus Compact, 2002), a document that articulates student civic engagement as "a form of alternative politics" (p. vi). *The New Student Politics* is an important document because it began the process of returning civic engagement development in higher education back to the voices and the experiences of students (see also Shor, 1996; Cooper, 2004; Zlotkowski, Longo, & Williams, 2006; Fretz & Longo, 2010). Following the publication of this document, Campus Compact sponsored the Raise Your Voice Campaign, which was followed up in 2006 with *Students as Colleagues,* a volume of case studies written by students that examines how students are playing active roles in the production of knowledge in higher education, especially as it relates to civic engagement. This is all to say that over the last decade, college students have extended themselves into the service-learning/civic engagement equation and have made significant contributions to the field. As Kiesa and colleagues (2007) discovered, there is every reason to believe that the next generation of college students, the Millennials, will continue to participate in community life and think and act in public ways.

Politics and Public Work

Finally, since 2002, the service-learning movement has gradually taken on some of the practices of public work that Boyte has articulated and that we practiced in our 2002 class. Perhaps the best example of this is evident in a 2008 colloquium that was sponsored by the New England Research Center for Higher Education and the Kettering Foundation. The purpose of the colloquium—an invitational event made up of 33 academic leaders—was to "critically examin[e] the state of civic engagement in higher education." The main assumption of the colloquium's organizers was that the civic engagement movement was adrift, even stalled, and the organizers called leaders together to address this issue and make recommendations for reigniting the movement. Colloquium proceedings and recommendations were published in "Democratic Engagement White Paper" (Saltmarsh, Hartley, & Clayton, 2009), which argues that in order to move forward, the civic engagement movement will need to focus on democracy and politics. "Democratic processes and purposes," the authors argue, "reorient civic engagement to what we are calling 'democratic engagement—engagement that has significant implications for transforming higher education such that democratic values are part of the leadership of administrators, the scholarly work of faculty, the educational work of staff, and the leadership development and learning outcomes of students" (p. 6). The authors go on to state that "the measure of the democratic processes and purpose of engagement is demonstrated by a capacity to learn in the company of others and not to rely solely on the expertise of the academy." The white paper critiques the apolitical nature of the civic engagement movement, and it recommends that the movement find ways to teach students the "political dimensions of their activities" and to take seriously "questions of power" (p. 8).

Summary

In closing, we find ourselves reflecting on the transformation possible, for students and faculty alike, when we engage in public deliberation in the classroom. Transformation springs from the meeting of pedagogy and practice in often unexpected ways. Organizing public forums, facilitating service-learning experiences, practicing deliberative strategies, and designing assignments with students put us in a new position in the classroom. No longer the "sage on the stage," we gradually became facilitators and, in many ways, colearners with our students. In addition to learning new ways to teach and to "be" in the classroom, we were also participating with our students as we all worked together to organize the public forum and the study circles. No longer directing from the sidelines, or articulating abstractions behind a podium, we were doing work right alongside our students. In many ways, we became servants to them. We fetched envelopes and department letterhead, provided campus contacts to facilitate logistics for the forum, arranged for the use of printers and fax machines, and offered access to our office phones and computers. It is not always a comfortable position. This is a pedagogy that demands a great deal of preparation and planning, but at the same time, requires spontaneity and flexibility. We had to give up some of our expectations about what should happen in a college classroom, and in the process, we were thrown into new ways of thinking about those questions that all of us in higher education ponder: Where does the learning take place, and what do we want our students to take with them?

We found that through practicing public work and deliberation we were able to answer these questions in different and more interesting ways than we could in a more traditional classroom. Students learned disciplinary knowledge (in this case, writing rhetorical arguments and thinking critically) through experience and practice. In addition, they began to experiment with ways of operating and affecting change in the public sphere. For our parts, we learned that our roles as professors are bigger than the tradition of our academic discipline. We could teach writing and English studies and also help our students experience the rewards of performing public work.

References

Barker, D., and Brown, D. (2009). *A different kind of politics.* Dayton, OH: Kettering Foundation Press.

Battistoni, R. (2002). *Civic engagement across the curriculum: A resource book for service-learning faculty in all disciplines.* Providence, R.I.: Campus Compact.

Bohman, J. (1996). *Public deliberation: Pluralism, complexity and democracy.* Cambridge: MIT Press.

Boyte, H. (2004). *Everyday politics: Reconnecting citizen and public life.* Philadelphia: University of Pennsylvania Press.

Boyte, H., & Farr, J. (1997). *The work of citizenship.* Retrieved from: http://www.augsburg.edu/cdc/publicachievement/pdf/probServiceLearning.pdf.

Butin, D. (2005). Service-learning as postmodern pedagogy. In *Service-learning in higher education: Critical issues and directions. New York: Palgrave.*

Campus Compact. (1999). *Presidents' Fourth of July declaration on the civic responsibility of higher education.* Retrieved from: http://www.internationalconsortium.org/about/presidents-fourth-of-july-declaration

Campus Compact. (2002) *The new students politics: The Wingspread statement on student civic engagement.* Providence, RI: Campus Compact.

Colby, A., Beaumont, E., Ehrlich, T., & Corngold, J. (2007). *Educating for democracy: Preparing undergraduates for responsible political engagement.* San Francisco: Jossey-Bass.

Cooper, D. (1998). Reading, writing and reflection. In R. Rhoads & J. Howard (Eds.), *Academic service learning: A pedagogy for action and reflection* (pp. 47–56). San Francisco: Jossey-Bass.

Cooper, D. (2004). Education for democracy: A conversation in two keys. In *Higher education exchange* (pp. 30–43). Dayton, OH: Kettering Foundation Press.

Cooper, D. (2008). "Turning student dissent into deliberation" *Inside higher education*, April 3. Retrieved 7 December 2009 from http://www.insidehighered.com/views/2008/04/03/cooper. Accessed 7 December 2009.

Dedrick, J., Grattan, L., & Dienstfrey, H. (2008). *Deliberation and the work of higher education: Innovations for the classroom, the campus and the community.* Dayton, OH: Kettering Foundation Press.

Dzur, A. (2008). *Democratic professionalism: Citizen participation and the reconstruction of professional ethics, identity, and practice.* University Park: Pennsylvania University Press.

Everyday Democracy. (2008). What is a study circle, and what is the process. Retrieved September 22, 2012, from http://www.everyday-democracy.org/en/Resource.126.aspx.

Eyler, J., & Giles, D. E. (1999). *Where's the learning in service-learning?* San Francisco: Jossey-Bass.

Fish, S. (2008). *Save the world on your own time.* Oxford: Oxford University Press.

Fishkin, J. (1995). *The voice of the people: Public opinion and democracy.* Binghamton, NY: Vail-Ballou Press.

Fraser, N. (1992). Rethinking the public sphere: A Contribution to the critique of actually existing democracy. In Calhoun, C. (Ed.) *Habermas and the public sphere.* Cambridge, MA: MIT Press.

Fretz, E., & Longo, N.V. (2010). Students co-creating an engaged academy. In H. E. Fitzgerald, C. Burack, & S. D. Seifer (Eds.), *Handbook of engaged scholarship: Contemporary landscapes, future directions,* vol. 1, *Institutional change* (pp. 313–329). East Lansing: Michigan State University Press.

Habermas, J. (1989). *The structural transformation of the public sphere: An inquiry into a category of bourgeois society.* Trans. T. Burger & F. Lawrence. Cambridge: MIT Press.

Harriger, K. J., and McMillan, J. J. (2007). *Preparing college students for democratic citizenship through deliberative dialogue.* Dayton, OH: Kettering Foundation Press.

Kiesa, A., Orlowski, A. P., Levine, P., Both, D., Kirby, E. H., Lopez, M. H., & Marcelo, K. B. (2007). Millennials talk politics: A study of college student political engagement. College Park, MD: Center for Information & Research on Civic Learning & Engagement.

Matthews, D. (2005). Listening to the public: A new agenda for higher education? In A. Kezar, T. C. Chambers, John C. Burkhardt, & Associates, *Higher education for public good: Emerging voices from a national movement* (pp. 71–86). San Francisco: Jossey-Bass.

Palmer, P. (1998). *The courage to teach: Exploring the inner landscape of a teacher's life.* San Francisco: Jossey-Bass.

Peters, S., Jordan, N.R., Adamek, M., & Alter, T.R. (2005). *Engaging campus and community: The practice of public scholarship in the state and land-grant university system.* Dayton, OH: Kettering Foundation Press.

Rice, E., & O'Meara, K.A. (2005). *Faculty priorities reconsidered: Rewarding multiple forms of scholarship.* San Francisco: Jossey-Bass.

Saltmarsh, J., Hartley, M., & Clayton, P. (2009). Democratic engagement white paper. Boston: New England Research Center for Higher Education.

Shor, I. (1996). *When students have power: Negotiating authority in a critical pedagogy.* Chicago: University of Chicago Press.

Ward, K. (2005). Rethinking faculty roles and rewards for the public good. In A. J. Kezar, A. C. Chambers, J. C. Burkhardt, & Associates, *Higher education for the public good: Emerging voices from a national movement* (pp. 217–234).San Francisco: Jossey-Bass.

Yankelovich, Daniel. (1999) *The magic of dialogue: Transforming conflict into cooperation.* New York: Simon and Schuster.

Zlotkowski, E., Longo, N., & Williams, J. (Eds.). (2006). *Students as colleagues: Expanding the circle of service-learning leadership.* Providence, RI: Campus Compact.

Service Learning and Civic Engagement as Preparation for a Life Committed to Working for the Common Good: The Michigan State University/Rust College Student Tutorial Education Project, 1965–1968

John S. Duley and Nicole C. Springer

During the summer months of 1965–68, 97 student volunteers and 10 faculty members from Michigan State University volunteered in a service-learning project at Rust College, a small African American liberal arts college in Holly Springs, Mississippi. The college was founded by the Freedman's Aid Society of the Methodist Episcopal Church in 1866 and celebrated its 145th commencement ceremony in May 2011. Like many colleges, Rust adheres to the three pillars of education: teaching, research, and community service. This project, called the Student Tutorial Education Project, was the result of the mutual involvement of Professor Robert L. Green of the College of Education and the author, the Presbyterian campus minister, in their local efforts to secure the passage of an Open Occupancy Ordinance to make it possible for people of color to rent and purchase homes in East Lansing. The project involved participation in a voter registration rally in Canton, Mississippi, at the invitation of one of Dr. Green's students who had participated in Freedom Summer and stayed on to work with the Council of Confederated Organizations in Canton. While participating in this event, feeling that Michigan State University should be making some educational contribution to the movement, we sought to ascertain what black colleges were in trouble with their boards of trustees or the state because of the involvement of their students and faculty in the civil rights movement. The name of Rust College kept being mentioned. On our return to Michigan State we recruited two students, Laura Lichlighter, a member of the All University Student government, and Frank Bianco, a graduate student in charge of the Student Education Corps, to accompany us on a visit to Rust College. As a result of that visit we were invited by President Smith and Academic Dean McMillan to develop and bring the STEP program to the college as a service-learning project.

Timothy K. Stanton and coauthors wrote about the history of service learning and attribute one of the first definitions of service learning to the work of the Southern Regional Education Board (SREB) in the year 1969: "The accomplishment of tasks that meet genuine human needs in combination with conscious educational growth" (Stanton, Giles, & Cruz, 1999, p. 2). The proximity of the people with these needs is not a limitation for a project. In fact, much can be said for the learning and growth that occurs when students step outside both their physical and, perhaps, their emotional comfort zones. At Rust College the services requested were threefold: (1) to better prepare African American high school graduates for the college level; (2) to help Rust College retain its accreditation; and (3) to provide a community recreation and cultural program for 11- to 14-year-olds. The learning phase of the project for the volunteers involved the applying of knowledge and skills acquired in the classroom in a very different culture. It also involved the development of new skills needed to plan, develop, and offer a curriculum to improve writing, reading, comprehension, and mathematical and study habit skills and prepare freshman to take full advantage of the education offered at Rust College. It also involved the volunteers in clarifying their values, leadership development, and personal growth through journal writing and continual reflection during and after the project and as they planned for the next year.

The purpose of studying the STEP project was to do some in-depth reflection on the subsequent professional and community activities of 12 participants. These reflections are part of a larger study of 77 participants in STEP conducted by Dr. Paul Herron, associate professor of anatomy and neurobiology, University of Tennessee, Memphis. Dr. Herron was a student in the 1966 STEP summer program and a student at Rust College for one year. He transferred to Michigan State University and became a tutor in STEP. His experiences from these two perspectives led to a study of the impact that the STEP program had on the MSU and Rust College participants. Dr. Herron's study was funded in part by President Lou Anna K. Simon of Michigan State University on the condition that upon the completion of the study she would host a reunion of the participants at MSU. On the weekend of Dr. Martin Luther King Jr.'s birthday, in January 2007, Dr. Herron gave a preliminary report on the results of his study to a reunion of 51 of the MSU participants. The interviews for this study were conducted during the reunion.

We wanted to explore the extent to which this service-learning experience was preparation for a life committed to working for the "common good." This commitment could be expressed in career choices and/or community involvement. We used the values and characteristics of persons interviewed by William Berkowitz in *Local Heroes: The Rebirth of Heroism in America* (1987) and by Parks Daloz and colleagues in *Common Fire* (1996) to determine the extent to which these same characteristics and values are held by the persons in this study.

What Do We Mean by "Common Good"?

One of the difficulties of ascertaining if STEP prepared people to live a life committed to the "common good" is the lack of clarity about the meaning of the phrase "the common good." The two sources used in this study take different approaches, but both imply a 24/7 commitment to living for the common good. The authors of *Common Fire* begin with recognizing the loss of a sense of place in our newly complex, globalized cultures; point to previous times in which there were "commons," places where people gathered to deal with the concerns of their communities: the village green, the wharf in coastal villages, the county courthouse grounds, Main Street and the restaurant with a round table in the back where the "regulars" gathered every weekday morning. This loss, for the authors, means that it is now necessary to find new "commons" that are global and diverse. The authors picked people who, lacking a local "commons," demonstrated a commitment that, in Frederich Buechner's phrase, is a vocation or calling in which "your deep gladness and the world's deep hunger meet," wherever that may be. These callings may take priority over traditional claims such as family, job, or career development. Having chosen people who meet these criteria, the authors explore the values and characteristics that have shaped and continue to shape their lives.

Berkowitz, in *Local Heroes*, selects folks who have made positive differences in their communities, mostly involving full-time commitments, like Candy Lightner of MADD, or Lois Gibbs of Love Canal, and identifies their values and characteristics.

The basic question raised by these two studies is whether or not "working for the Common Good" has to be a 24/7 commitment taking precedence over all other claims such as family and the personal and financial responsibilities that are related to these claims. This haunting question reminds me of a warning I have kept in the back of my mind since studying for the ministry. The warning is that most illustrations used in sermons are taken from the lives of people who have made a once-and-for-all-times dramatic decision to serve God in some dramatic way, usually in some foreign country for life, like Mother Teresa. The people who are listening to the sermon are everyday people who are pulled in many directions (e.g., family, professional responsibilities, and interests). They are making decisions on how to live day to day while choosing either the lesser of two evils or the better of two goods.

The STEP participants are like these parishioners; their commitment to living for the common good is seldom a once-and-for-all-time 24/7 commitment. In an effort to understand the manner in which STEP volunteers have lived lives committed to the "common good," I found three modes in which they expressed their commitments, not sharply distinguishable, but clear enough, although overlapping. These three modes of living for the common good are the following:

1. Working as change agents: those who strive to modify the societies or cultures in which they live and work
2. Making the quality of life of those they connected with better
3. Working for the common good through a deep commitment to their human service profession

This study helped me see that a commitment to living for the common good does not necessarily mean leaving behind the present claims of existing relationships and responsibilities. It may mean that your calling is to use the present context of where you live and work to make a commitment to live for the common good, that your deep gladness and the world's deep hunger may meet in the here and now.

We identified ten items that could be used to identify the common themes of those who have chosen to work for the common good. The chief characteristics and values identified in *Common Fire* and *Local Heroes* used in this study are the following:

1. Commitment
2. Naiveté
3. Risk taking, not in the entrepreneurial sense but in the personal sense (courage)
4. Persistence: perseverance and resilience
5. Belief in the power of one person to affect large events
6. Compassion (constructive, enlarging engagement with the other)
7. Spirituality
8. Living within the tribe and ability to break tribal barriers
9. Marginality as a factor in the development of compassion—both vulnerability based (thrust upon one) and value based (religious-inspired nonconformity)
10. Hard work and the belief that it pays off

We used two questions to determine the contribution of STEP as preparation for living a life committed to the common good:

1. How the experience impacted participants in their view of the world and themselves
2. How the experience contributed to the way they lived their lives

These interviews were shorter than those conducted by Berkowitz and by Parks Daloz and colleagues, 15 to 20 minutes each in comparison to three hours. The interviewers, in consultation with the director of the project, developed a common set of questions to be used:

How did you learn about/get involved in STEP?

Why did you get involved in STEP?

Were there objections from your parents?

What role did you play in STEP?

What was the most important thing you took away from STEP?

What impact did the experience have on your career?

What impact did it have on your inner journey, worldview, self-understanding?

What did you learn about leadership?

While the interviews did not focus on all of the characteristics and values identified in *Common Fire* and *Local Heroes*, the respondents spoke directly about ten of the characteristics. The brief autobiographical descriptions requested of the participants on the reunion registration form regarding their professional and community activities were used as evidence of their commitment to working for the common good. We present the autobiographical statements and portions of the interviews in support of our conclusion that this project did, and service learning does, prepare people to live for the common good.

The Interviews

Merrie Milton

Autobiographical Statement

I worked for three years teaching in South Carolina before returning to Michigan where I taught first and second grade in the inner city of Detroit for 20 years until I retired.

Commitment; Persistence

I taught for about 20 years in the Detroit inner schools. I loved teaching children in the first grade. I loved the kids and I miss it so much, so bad. Sorry I had to retire in 1988 for health reasons.

Risk Taking; Belief in Power of One Person to Make a Difference

After graduation I moved to South Carolina for three years to support integration. We protested in front of a store that was frequented mainly by African American people, but had no African American employees, and we succeeded in getting them to hire blacks. There was also a radio station that marketed to African Americans, but again had only a white disc jockey. We wrote letters to sponsors such as Coca-Cola, Johnson and Johnson, and Budweiser. When seven companies decided to cancel their advertisements, the station hired a black disc jockey. We also protested the murder of a young black man and tried to see what we could do to oust the offending police officer from the police department. We were not successful. During this time, I was harassed by the police many times. Once when I, a white woman, was in the car with Michigan license plates and a black man, a police officer stopped me and put a gun to my head and asked me what I was doing there.

Compassion; Commitment

Most of my students were Mexican and black.

When asked how she, as a white teacher, was able to reach out and connect with them, Milton replied:

I don't know; I took a lot of time with them, which was hard to do because I had as many as 35 children in the classroom, which is an awful lot of first-graders, but that's the Detroit school system. And a lot of times I would tutor some children after school because there was no way I could advance them up to the second grade without their being ready. The second-grade teachers loved to have my children because they were ready. There's no such thing as passing them along; passing means knowing what you need to know in order to progress. I loved my students; I miss them so much.

David Hollister

Autobiographical Statement

I'm presently the president and CEO of a nonprofit organization called the Prima Civitas Foundation that was launched by President Simon of Michigan State University to engage the university more fully in the economic and community development of this region. Prior to that, I worked as a member of Governor Granholm's cabinet as the director of the Department of Labor and Economic Growth, the biggest and most strategic department of state government. I had a budget of $1.4 billion and 4,200 employees. Prior to that, I was the mayor of the City of Lansing for just under 10 years and prior to that I served 19½ years in the Michigan legislature. And all of that, my 20 years in the legislature, my 10 years as mayor, my commitment to Governor Granholm and the Department of Labor and Economic Growth, was really guided by my experience in Mississippi.

How the Experience Contributed to the Participant's Life; Belief in Power of One Person to Make a Difference

The 30 seconds in which I met up with King, after his speech launching STEP, was probably the most significant event in my life. Before I met him I had an intellectual understanding of deeply personal commitment, but hearing that message and engaging his eye contact fundamentally changed my life. He was the essence of a great leader. I've always felt that you need four things to be a leader. You need a clearly defined goal . . . a clearly defined strategy . . . a sense of hope . . . and probably most important, you need courage. . . . King had the essence. He could capture people's imagination, he could give them hope and courage, he had a clear strategy and a clear goal. . . . I have always tried to take that experience with King and then the years in Mississippi and internalize them as I sought to be a leader on a local level.

Spirituality; Value-Based Marginality

Before I entered Michigan State University I was planning to study for the ministry, but I got married and started a family. I knew I needed to be able to support my family while in seminary, and I decided to become a teacher.

I never followed through on that original purpose of going into the ministry. So when King was killed in April 1968 that became a real transformational period for me. I decided to get involved in Bobby Kennedy's campaign. I took a group of Eastern High School students down to South Bend for the Indiana primary. And when Kennedy was killed right after the California primary in June, a group of us got together here at Michigan State University. There were probably 12 or 13 of us, and the question was, "Do we leave this country and go to Canada, get the hell out of here, or do we stay involved and try to change it, do we get involved politically?"

I didn't belong to a political party; I had never been involved, and everybody figured we'd run for something. We were sitting at a big table, and we went around: "Well, I'll run for State Senate, I'll run for the State House of Representatives, I'll run for this." It came around to me, and I was the last one at the table, and I said, "What's left?" "Well, a county commissioner will be elected for the first time in 1968." I said, "What does a county commissioner do? Ah, what the hell, nobody seems to know what a county commissioner does. Well, what does it take to become a county commissioner?" Someone said, "Well, it takes a minimum of 20 signatures to get on the ballot." I was leaving for Mississippi the next week, so I went to Cristo Rey Community Center. I got 50 signatures and submitted them, took off for Mississippi, and while I was in Mississippi I got a letter saying, "Congratulations, you are the Democratic nominee for County Commissioner." No one else had filed!

Coming back from Mississippi the second year and having made the decision to run for county commissioner changed my life, because I was close to going to Canada. Another Democrat running for county commissioner, Grady Porter, and I won that election. There were 19 Republicans and two Democrats; everyone in the courthouse was Republican—the sheriff, the registrar of deeds, all the judges. We were the only Democrats that had ever been elected to that board, and the first night we introduced two resolutions, one to stop the war in Vietnam and the other to support the grape boycott of Cesar Chavez. We were so disruptive, and they were so angry that we would bring social activism to the county commission, that it really was a very tense period. But within in four years we took control of the Board of Commissioners and did follow through on resolutions stopping the war and boycotting grapes. Eventually both ideas prevailed.

Risk Taking

But we didn't really think about the risk, it . . . was the right thing to do. We were going to go teach school, for God's sake! I was a schoolteacher, I had a teaching background, my wife was a schoolteacher; we were going to be teaching kids who were high school seniors who were from segregated schools that were so disadvantaged. It didn't seem like a big threat, but it turned out it was a life-transforming experience.

Phyllis Barten Harris

Autobiographical Statement

I am a church musician, director of music ministries at St. Pius V Church, dean of the American Guild of Organists—Houston Chapter, past president and president-elect of Bay Area Chorus, and I spent eight years in Mexico teaching English as a second language. I provide "Pipe Organ Encounters" for high school pianists (because education is vital), lead choir tours in Italy (you should never be afraid to go somewhere new and sing), organize community choirs (you should do things together and never stop learning), and engage in community theater (forget what people look like; what gifts do they have?).

Living within the Tribe; How the Experience Impacted the Participant's View of the World

Oh, I thought that I was going to teach them all how to read music and learn wonderful things about how to work together as an ensemble. I didn't quite expect to learn as much as I did about hand jiving and the correct way to do "Were You There When They Crucified My Lord?" . . . It was an eye-opening experience to find out that people who didn't read music were probably much more innately musical than I was. I was taught one evening how to do "Were You There"; the notes on the page, that which never changes, were the same, but while the first verse is done in a pretty regular tempo the second verse is done at a slightly slower tempo, and by the time you get to the nails it is so slow and so agonizing and every vowel and every consonant is there, and then when they roll the tombstone away the whole atmosphere changes; the brightness of the color in the voice is overwhelming.

Vulnerability-Based Marginality; Spirituality

At the time I went to Michigan State University I was majoring in music composition, and then in music education. I was a member of People's Church and got to know John Duley partly through some other campus work. I was very much interested in what he was doing in terms of working with blacks . . . in Mississippi, and when I was invited to go along and help with the music I jumped at the chance. My father was a minister, so I have probably always been aware of people

113

who had been underprivileged in one way or another, and as a preacher's kid you make a decision early on that you're either going to fight [being identified as a preacher's kid] . . . or you're going to accept it. And somewhere along the way I had enough grace to embrace it.

Risk Taking

The atmosphere of living on a small plot of land surrounded by people who would sometimes drive by in their pickup trucks with their rifles in the back window caused anxiety. Across the corner on one street was the Student Nonviolent Coordinating Committee (SNCC) house, and the people there had some run-ins with the law. I found it rather intimidating to walk with my students to a local store to try to buy some feminine supplies and realize that we weren't going to get waited on. One time we went to a restaurant and got seated, finally, in the back room, and discovered we'd been passed two different kinds of menus, one with higher prices and the other with lower prices, and we were told by the waitress that the lower prices were the old ones, and we were expected to pay the higher prices.

Kay Snyder

Autobiographical Statement

I am a college professor of sociology, and throughout my career much of my focus has been on issues of inequality based on race, class, gender, etc., an interest that . . . was deepened in significant ways by my involvement with STEP. I have taught classes on such topics as race and social stratification, which I again believe were shaped importantly by being in STEP. My involvement in community activities has reflected a commitment to greater equality for all, regardless of race, ethnicity, gender, sexual orientation, etc.—a commitment that I believe was deepened through STEP. This has included various involvements with women's issues and within our local Unitarian Universalist Church.

How the Experience Contributed to the Participant's Life; Belief in Power to Make a Difference

Dr. [Robert] Green was someone who was very involved in organizing this STEP project and he was the very first person who ever said to me, "You are to go to graduate school, you can do this." For my generation of women the idea was . . . get an insurance policy. In other words, we would get a degree so we could teach secondary school, so if something, God forbid, would happen to our husband along the way, we would be able to support ourselves and our children. And that was really the mind-set. That summer I realized that teaching was an interest to me, but I really . . . thought as my peers tended to think. Of course I'd never thought of going to graduate school. . . . But working with those entering freshmen—just the experience of thinking how do you communicate something to someone, how do you build those skills, was so engaging and I realized I could teach college students. You have to understand I had not had . . . a woman college professor in my freshman and sophomore years of college. So here I was . . . teaching students who were going to college and I realized I could do this. I was hooked on teaching . . . at that level. In working with these students I realized I could make a difference in their lives.

Spirituality; Compassion

I was a member of Edgewood United Church; there were deeply concerned people there. Truman Morrison, the minister, was very active locally in the civil rights movement and an outspoken advocate for the movement. Truman Morrison, Bob Green, and John Duley went to Selma and marched in the demonstrations. I knew Eleanor Morrison, the minister's wife, very well. This was a moral issue for me, very much so, and it was very much grounded in ethical concerns and so . . . I felt it as a calling and in fact I say now to students, "Whatever you do, find something that is a calling for you." . . . This became a calling for me. What was interesting was it was about social justice, it was about ethical, moral issues. . . . Through the experience in Mississippi I later worked for Southern Christian Leadership Conference (SCLC) for a summer in Chicago, connected with Bob Green, and it was an "Oh, my goodness" experience. I came to realize that there are issues out there that women face; there are inequalities there, including the women's civil rights movement, and that was very transformative.

So looking at my adult life . . . I teach sociology and my areas of interest are inequalities. . . . I never studied the sociology of gender in graduate school; gender certainly wasn't an issue at that time, but . . . if we're going to talk about justice and inequality, . . . it isn't just in one domain. We have to think of what's happening to women. So the seeds of all this were planted in the work of STEP.

How the Experience Impacted the Participant's View of the World

I want to say something about the moral issue. I look back, and I look at my journal, and I realize some of the things that I believed going to Mississippi were wrong. There was certainly a moral issue there that needed to be addressed, but what I realized repeatedly, from the students that we worked with . . . was that it was really very presumptuous and very ethnocentric for whites from the North to go down and think, "Oh Mississippi, they have such a problem, and we need to help with this problem." So . . . I came back . . . to my own situations to realize what kinds of inequalities existed in my community. . . . There were many things that . . . weren't being done in the North; there were many issues involving not just race but gender, and social class as well. . . . It was humbling.

Linda Garcia Shelton

Autobiographical Statement

My professional work is in the area of primary care psychology, largely within academic family medicine. My practice, teaching, and research have focused on medically underserved urban populations, which tend to be largely racial and ethnic minorities. My community involvement stemmed from my work. I worked with a community-based umbrella organization to develop plans for a multidisciplinary health care clinic that had services the community defined as important to them. The plans also included health professionals' education within the sites, as well as a health research program that was driven by the community's definition of what they needed to know, not the university's definition of what was important to study. I wrote grant proposals that were funded to support the health professionals' education and the health research programs for a span of three years.

Value-Based Marginality

When asked about her family background and the extent of family involvement in protest movements, Shelton said,

> I didn't learn about it until my husband secured immigration status in Canada to avoid the draft. My family was in all kinds of trouble in northern Spain because of one of my grandfathers, who had a little more education than most and was involved in writing things for the labor movement and organizing and was about to be drafted and sent to northern Africa, which is what they did to people that they wanted to disappear, and so he fled. Because we were going to flee the draft, we went and told my parents. We might just drop out of sight, and I wanted them to know where we were going, why we were going, and how they could get in touch with us. Contact with us would have to be through an organization related to a campus religious community. When I told my family this, I thought my parents would go through the roof, but that's when I heard the story of my grandfather. So, no, they weren't going to go through the roof. They said, "There are precedents for this in our family." In fact, I had a grandmother on the other side who was a real activist. She was an anarchist; we have pictures of her marching with a big banner across her chest down Woodward Avenue in Detroit in the thirties.

Living within the Tribe; How the Experience Impacted the Participant's View of the World

> There are two things that, to this day, majorly influenced me. One is very broad and not cognitive. In addition to the formal teaching we did with the entering freshmen, we had a community program . . . for kids from 11 to 14. . . . They came from the community around campus, and their families welcomed us. I can remember the warmth and the safety that they provided and the kindness and the time they gave us. They told us about themselves, and they asked us about ourselves, and they were truly interested, and this is in contrast to walking downtown.
>
> If . . . you needed to buy something you'd walk downtown, and it was like you could've been in Alaska in the winter, it was so cold. It just didn't feel good; you'd walk into a store and it was like . . . you were invisible. Usually after an incredibly uncomfortable time somebody would come up to you and ask you what you needed. . . . The closer you would get to the black area, I mean it was like we would speed up, but wouldn't run, then we'd get there, and we'd go up to some parent of the children we were working with because they said, "Come up to our house, come up to our porch, knock on the door and if nobody answers just come on in." Oh yes, and that went on that first year. We were there six weeks, and it was just so palpable, and then again the second year. Of course the second year is even bigger because they all remembered us, and it was great.
>
> I'd go back each time to Michigan State and I saw black people I never saw. Before I went I didn't think that there were any African Americans at Michigan State. But after I came back I saw them; there weren't many, but I saw them! So then it was clear to me that what I see isn't necessarily what is; and I saw differently. And naturally, when I did see them I did gravitate toward them, and I felt part of it because I was looking for that warmth again and that person-to-personhood, because Michigan State was big, and you could be anonymous. And I felt it.
>
> Okay, so race ahead ten years maybe, and that's gone, and I don't know at what point it dawned on me that it was gone. I no longer had that natural vision, that natural attraction, and I no longer had that sense of friendliness and welcoming and ease and connectedness, no I didn't. I had stranger, different, fearful feelings, and when that dawned on me, it was like, damn, this is powerful, this is social, this is learned but not consciously so. I think for me that this is a most

important insight: racism is just everywhere. It's powerful, and I didn't think I could ever change back! I didn't think I could change back! And I did. And it was so disgusting to me. And even now, it's like I have to watch it all the time.

Christina Lundberg

Autobiographical Statement

Rust College, two years as teacher, coach and counselor; Drew High School, one of two white teachers at black junior/senior high school; Mississippi Head Start Training Coordinating Council, five years as parent involvement coordinator; Small Business Development Center, multicultural business expositions. I also served on the Berkeley County Community Relations Advisory Committee in Martinsburg, West Virginia.

Persistence

The above description of Lundberg's work on behalf of social justice and civil rights shows the extent of her persistence, resilience, and perseverance.

Belief in Power to Make a Difference; Risk Taking

It's interesting just listening to Dr. King's talk again today about legislation. . . . Legislation can do much, but what else can we do to really change people? I think that one has to step up, if one knows in her heart that it's the right thing to do, and if you believe in nonviolence, because that was the other thing we learned very early, that you got to step up. And that doesn't mean that you necessarily have to be at the front of the march, but you have to be in the march; you have to be there to be counted. It doesn't mean that you have to take the leadership role on everything, but at some point you do have to be there.

Commitment; How the Experience Contributed to the Participant's Life

I didn't participate in STEP twice; I just stayed on at Rust College and helped with STEP during the summer of 1967. After the summer of 1966 I was looking for a job, and Dr. Frank Beeman of MSU called me and said, "Chris, President Smith is looking for a physical ed teacher, do you want to teach at Rust College?" I said, "Hey, why not?" So I went back that fall, and I worked at Rust College in 1966–67 and 1967–68.

I left Rust College and went down to Drew, Mississippi, and I taught for two years there. I was one of two white teachers in the black high school. I lost that job because I was out in a march picketing for equal employment opportunities for blacks, so my contract was not renewed that year.

I went down to Jackson, Mississippi, and worked with some people in the Mississippi Head Start Training Coordinating Council. Mississippi had the largest Head Start program in the country. So we had a staff of five or six of us; James Meredith's sister was the nutritionist in the program. I met a great number of people. Actually when I was up in Drew, Mississippi, I had a chance to meet Fannie Lou Hamer and was involved in many marches with her.

When I was down in Jackson, I got involved with the NAACP Legal Defense Fund. Many people do not know this, but Alice Walker was down there at that time because her husband was with the Legal Defense Fund. We got a little women's group going, so I had a chance to meet Alice Walker.

After that I moved to Washington, DC, and you name the marches, whether it was for the Equal Rights Amendment, abortion rights, women's health rights, gay rights, antiwar; I mean, I don't know how many miles I've put on this body marching.

Lewis C. Rudolph

Autobiographical Statement

I manage grants and community benefits for the Sisters of Providence Health System, Springfield, Massachusetts. Previously, I was vice president, community building, United Way of America, Alexandria, Virginia, served as president/CEO of local United Ways in Rochester, Minnesota, Northampton, Massachusetts, and Lewiston, Maine, senior VP at Berkshire United Way in Pittsfield, Massachusetts, and senior planner of United Way Community Services, Detroit, Michigan. Immediately following STEP, I served as a teacher intern in the Detroit Urban Corps, Detroit Public Schools. In the late 1970s, I served as educational coordinator training specialist at Focus HOPE of Metropolitan Detroit. Over the course of my career with United Ways I collaborated with national leaders and institutions, including the Kennedy School of Government at Harvard University and the Annie E. Casey Foundation. My work focused on changing the United Way business model, transforming it from being primarily a fund-raising campaign into a "community impact" or community-building organization.

Risk Taking

When I was a student at Michigan State University I studied psychology and philosophy and during my senior year I applied to the Peace Corps to go to Brazil and was accepted. I remember being in the Holly Springs movie theater, sitting in the balcony (this is all part of our low-key social activism; we had blacks downstairs, whites upstairs, interracial dates on Saturday night). A man by the name of Roundtree, who was rumored to be the head of the local Ku Klux Klan in Holly Springs, ran the theater. Here I was, sitting in the balcony, and I heard my name being called, paged by Roundtree, and I thought of the worst-case scenario because we were outside agitators, and we were reaching for this cultural tipping point in local social relations. Hearing my name called in a dark theater had all kinds of fear going through it. I followed him out to the lobby; strangely enough he knew exactly where I was sitting, and he said, "There's a phone call for you," and I thought, "Okay I'd better be ready for anything," and he said, "It's your mother," and it was.

Belief in Power to Make a Difference

Rudolph's long list of achievements in his work with local United Ways and United Way of America indicate his commitment to change bureaucratic structure to improve the quality of life for those dependent on agencies related to the United Way.

How the Experience Contributed to the Participant's Life; Commitment

During my senior year I applied to the Peace Corp to go to Brazil. . . . So while I was down in Mississippi I was awaiting my airline tickets . . . and Paul Herron, who had an instrumental trigger effect on my decision making, asked me "Why are you going to Brazil? You should think about going back to Detroit and doing work in your own community." This was one year after the

Detroit riots. That question had a searing effect on my decision making and I thought about it overnight.

I remember being in the Holly Springs movie theater (the next evening) and being paged by the manager. My mother had called Rust College and they transferred her to the movie theater. She said, "Your tickets for the Peace Corps have arrived." I said, "Send them back: I'm not going."

And I began applying for the Detroit Urban Corps and was later accepted and entered the Urban Corps in Detroit, Michigan, in September of 1968. I taught first grade and second grade. And that's the kind of the transition I made from being a civil rights activist, going to Mississippi from Detroit, going back to my hometown and beginning to do the work that I saw that needed to be done. In addition to my work in the Urban Corps I also worked for Focus Hope of Metropolitan Detroit. I found out that they were looking for someone with a civil rights background who was also familiar with Jewish culture because there was one particular school in metro Detroit, Southfield Lathrup High School, which had a fairly high influx of Iraqi Christians coming into a Jewish community. They needed a conflict resolution person.

I also worked as a trainer in the larger Training for Trust Program conducting race relations training in Detroit high schools that had recently undergone court-ordered busing.

How the Experience Impacted the Participant's View of the World

I think being able to put your body in a situation, rather than just being able to reflect, is very important. Being academic and cerebral was an important start for me. Being in the academic community prior to STEP, I was very good at lining up arguments, lining up data, analyzing policies, but until STEP I didn't understand the absolute necessity, for me, of putting my body in the situation where I was not only at risk but part of the connections that would create a solution, and that's very pragmatic. But it is also important to have a vision of an ideal future. That's what, of course, Martin Luther King Jr. presented us again and again and again, and especially for me to experience his speech in 1965, that vision of that future propels me as a leader.

When asked what it was like to hear Dr. King's speech again, Rudolph replied:

I was crying; I was crying kind of tears of beauty, realizing a profound set of truths that were being expounded. I understood then that he wasn't reading a word of it, and that it was a form of old school rhetoric and public address that was embedded in his brain. There's something about the directness of that encounter that will always stay with me. I am grateful for this university being enlightened and inspired enough to provide me with an educational experience that drew me out to meet the world. So I am eternally grateful to this institution.

Elizabeth King Snodgrass

Autobiographical Statement

Snodgrass is an art teacher of first- and third-grade students in a small rural community. She participated in STEP in 1967 and 1968 and feels that the experience made it possible for her to help her students have that time period become "real" for them because she can speak personally about it. In regard to community activities, she said:

I have been very active in my community, belonging to various organizations; how much stems from STEP or my upbringing I cannot say.

How the Experience Impacted the Participant's View of the World

It expanded my world a lot. I came from a small town. The town I came from only had actually 790 people at that time, so STEP expanded my horizons. I saw a larger world than what I had been seeing.

Spirituality

Something I hadn't thought of actually, until a long time ago, was probably some of my experiences as a child. My father was a church architect, and one of the churches that he did was in Flint called Quinn Chapel. . . . As a family we would go to the church dedication and groundbreaking and stuff, and so we got to know the Quinn Chapel people. They actually sent their choir to our little town church and helped us celebrate our 100th anniversary when I was a child, and that had to have an influence. The minister, who was Reverend Mitchum, when he'd come to talk to my dad about building the church, he would come to our home and eat dinner with us. I would say that he had an influence.

Thom Peterson

Autobiographical Statement

Master's degree in public administration, Grand Valley State University, 1989. Taught solar energy studies, Lansing Community College, in the Vocational-Technical Program. Energy efficiency workshop presentations and training, Grand Rapids Public Schools and Michigan School Business Administrators since 1984; [also] energy management, preventive maintenance, computer problem solving, interactive personal skill training. I am supervisor of energy management at Grand Rapids Public Schools, and I've been there over 20 years, but my role in that position as facilities manager is really translating the technical gizmos for human use so staff and students feel comfortable with the technology and equipment we have for people in the buildings. We want to make them comfortable, keep an environment that works for them, so our job is to maintain the facilities so that learning can occur in a comfortable environment.

I have also participated in the West Michigan Environmental Action Council, Transportation Working Group, since 1991; advocate and activist for bicycling, transit, and transit-oriented development. I have been a mediator and mediator trainer for the Dispute Resolution Center of West Michigan since 1991, and involved in the Creative Response to Conflict, International (Grand Rapids branch) 1996–2000; trainee and trainer for Children's Creative Response to Conflict, which are techniques for classroom management.

Spirituality

The word "calling" makes me think about something that we discussed in Sunday school class once a long time ago. It was the issue of vocation or a calling, and what we concluded in our discussion was that when we're thinking about it as young people we are wondering what we're to do with our lives. Some young people have that all figured out, and they're ready to go. And then there's folks like me who haven't a clue, you know, who're ready to go and curious and interested, but not in any specific direction, but the idea of the voice in the night giving you direction is kind of what I was looking for.

What we said in that Sunday school class was, well maybe your calling or vocation becomes clear once you have made a selection, made some choices, and there you are. So then you look back, and then you see it's a straight line. Your experiences helped shape you and direct you into that thing. So the idea was to follow your instincts, and follow what fulfills you, makes you happy, or satisfies your intellectual curiosity. Whatever floats your boat, you go for that, you take something that you're interested in and you go ahead and do that. Not knowing exactly what the outcome of something like that might be, but going on those instincts, then using your intelligence once you get into that situation to see where you go from here.

Commitment; Persistence

Peterson's commitment to the "common good" is through the environmental movement:

I have worked in the Grand Rapids Public Schools for a number of years as the person responsible for energy management and preventive maintenance. My community involvement is with the West Michigan Environmental Action Council, the Transportation Working Group. I am an advocate for and active in promoting bicycling, transit, and transit-oriented development.

Risk Taking

Peterson was a participant in the 1967 STEP. He dropped out of Michigan State University in the fall of 1967, and enrolled in the University of Mississippi (Ole Miss) in Oxford, Mississippi, with the intent of recruiting Ole Miss students to participate in STEP. He was unsuccessful in recruiting there, but the chaplain at Ole Miss helped him make contact with some Methodist colleges in the South, and he did recruit at least one student, Alex Valentine, who taught in STEP in the summer of 1968.

John Schuiteman

Autobiographical Statement

Becoming a STEP volunteer gave me the experience of being a teacher, which I enjoyed very much. Following service in the Air Force from 1966 to 1970, I returned to MSU and earned my PhD in political science. This permitted me to teach political science classes at MSU, Lansing Community College, Texas Tech University, and Virginia Commonwealth University. I was hired to testify as an expert on elections in a case initiated by the Virginia ACLU in 1983. The case sought to increase the probability of Afro-Americans being elected to the Town Council of Farmington, Virginia. Since 1985 I have served as a research and evaluation specialist with the Virginia Department of Criminal Justice Services. My STEP experience, and particularly the experience of marching in the Meredith March Against Fear, is a factor that encouraged my participation as an activist in support of Gay (GLBT) rights. My wife and I have marched in national gay rights parades and I have worked in my church to ensure a welcoming atmosphere for GLBT persons. It also gave me the courage to march as a Veteran Against the War with Iraq in the 2005 NYC Veterans' Day Parade.

How the Experience Contributed to the Participant's Life/Impacted the Participant's View of the World; Living within the Tribe

I came from a pretty conservative background. . . . My father was a state trooper. . . . Mom went to college, but my dad didn't. My brother's gay, and I actively marched in gay rights parades, which I don't know if I would've ever done had I not had the experience on the march in Jackson. Yeah, it instilled in me the idea that if you see a situation where everybody is not talking about what needs to be talked about, then I'm going to ask people to talk about it. I haven't been a great leader of anything in particular, but I believe in participating; I've been standing out in front of the courthouse once in a while down in Richmond against the Iraq war, against the misuse of . . . our troops . . . and the chaos that we've been putting them into and not having any clear indication as to the national interests. So the inner journey has definitely been affected by it; this whole reunion experience has put me . . . back in touch with that. I don't know what would've happened had I not participated in STEP, but . . . it makes me feel good when I think about that chance and opportunity. It is probably the first thing in my life that I did, on my own, that seemed to be approved by the world, you know, or at least my world.

Belief in Power to Make a Difference; Risk Taking

When Dr. Green came and asked us to participate in the last day of the March Against Fear I knew people make a difference. I learned in STEP that it has a ripple effect. I got a letter, for instance, from Fannie Mae Winston; I had her son as one of my students. She wrote me thanking me for paying attention to her son. STEP was a source of future courage, knowing that it was important to step over that line in terms of telling people this is not right; it gave me a little more fortitude in that way.

Caroline Wong

Autobiographical Statement

For 16 years I served as a high school and middle school teacher, and piloted the high school Ethnic Studies Program for the State of Hawaii. I have been serving as the principal of the Moanai Middle School for the last 16 years. I also piloted the Character Education Program for state schools. My school was recognized as the National Service Learning Leader School in 2001. I served as the president of the Hawaii Secondary Principals Association from 1998 to 2004. I also served as the ASFS state representative from 1980 to1990, and was actively involved in community outreach work through church education, building expansion programs as well as community service; actively involved in youth athletic programs, parent-teacher organizations, and served as president of the Hawaii Association of Secondary School Administrators.

Compassion; Commitment

I think that leaders have to make hard decisions, but they have to be based on real clear premises. In the leadership role that I hold, it has to be what's right for kids. And when you're in an organization, change is a process, it's not an event. My school is not going to change until people change. As a leader, and as I guide teachers through a change process, it's like, "You may not want to make this change, you may not feel comfortable with it, but this is a change we need to make based on data, on research, based on friendly help, and we're going to support you through this change process. But we have to do what's right for kids." We make decisions in this learning organization based on research, practice, and it's based on what's best for the kids.

Persistence

I was majoring in social studies for a graduate degree and I was taking a lot of ethnic studies courses and was very interested in black American history. I was taking a lot of these courses knowing that I would be going back to Hawaii to teach in a multicultural place. I was really interested in being a part of the teaching experience with the entering freshman at Rust College as preparation for my work in Hawaii.

Spirituality

I was raised in a Christian family, and there was always that sense that you're given gifts, and they're not for you; you should use the gifts that you've been given. There's not only this concept, but I saw my parents live it out; doing for others and involving themselves in other people's lives. And I suppose that was an expectation. . . . It's kind of like, you go from accepting your parents' values to making them your own.

How the Experience Contributed to the Participant's Life

I looked to a lot of leaders to see what type of leader I wanted to be, and I have defined myself as a servant leader. When I first became a principal the writers that influenced me significantly in this regard were Robert Greenleaf, Sergiovanni, and Roland Barth. All of them wrote about servant leadership and moral leadership. Barth even identifies principals as the lay clergy! More recently, many more have written about this—for instance, Michael Fullan in *The Moral Imperative of School Leadership.*

When asked, "Did you see leaders in STEP who demonstrated that particular leadership style?" Wong replied:

I did, I did. And I saw it in a quiet way. I saw John Duley especially—he definitely had this philosophy. He wasn't a loud or outspoken person; he just modeled it and lived it.

When Wong was asked, "Do you think your career as a leader and as an educator was shaped by this experience?" she replied:

Oh definitely. This project was a key for me in understanding and clarifying many things. I had planned to be a teacher, but it definitely clarified for me the steps that I would need to take as a classroom teacher and as a leader.

William Skocpol

Autobiographical Statement

I was a Danforth Foundation Graduate Fellow 1969–74, Department of Physics, Harvard University, assistant professor of physics, Harvard University, 1974–78, associate professor of physics, Harvard 1978–81, resident visitor, AT&T Bell Laboratories 1978–81, Distinguished Member of Technical Staff, AT&T Bell Laboratories 1980–87, professor of physics, Boston University, 1987–present, chairman, Boston University Faculty Council, 2001–3. I did not engage in any specific community activities outside of the University.

How the Experience Impacted the Participant's View of the World

> In regard to teaching, I think that right away you learn that what you plan to say is much more than you actually get across in class, so you interact adaptively, and that's been a good lesson for the rest of my career as a college teacher. And there at Rust College the best-prepared students learned the least, and the least-prepared students learned the most.

In response to the question, "Why was that?" Skocpol replied:

> There was one student who never really engaged in the class; he'd been fairly well off, had been to private school that had educated him pretty well, and he sort of just took the easy attitude towards it, and just enjoyed the social aspects, but didn't really engage with the material. Then there was at the other extreme a large, slow-speaking, very young man with huge hands who wrote very laboriously, and at the beginning it seemed that he didn't have a clue. To see him catch on and then actually do quite well in the space of four weeks was wonderful, and it wasn't just that he learned. He learned, and that was important. But the sense of accomplishment that you could see was great. He undoubtedly had been through a school system with very low expectations; he'd been led to expect very little of himself, and the glimpse that he could learn, that he had more abilities than he realized, was really a satisfying thing to see.

Belief in Hard Work

Skocpol's belief in hard work and that it pays off also was demonstrated by his efforts to track down on the Internet, for Paul Herron, the addresses of 36 of the 77 participants in STEP who received the research questionnaires. This trait was also demonstrated by his assuming, voluntarily, the responsibility of archivist, collecting photographs, journal entries, lesson plans, and papers written by the Rust students, and newspaper clippings about the project for the Special Collections of the Main Library at Michigan State University.

The individual interviews show that each person experienced or exhibited a variety of the characteristics and values that lead people to live a life for the common good. While it may not be evident as you read through the interviews, there are certain characteristics that tend to be discussed more than others. Figure 1 shows the classification and frequency of each of the ten characteristics and values previously identified.

Closing Reflections

In an effort to understand the manner in which the STEP participants have lived lives committed to the common good, I found three modes in which they expressed their commitments, not sharply distinguishable, but clear enough, although overlapping. These three modes of living for the common good are the following:

1. Working as change agents: those who strive to modify the societies or cultures in which they live and work. Of these there were five: Merrie Milton, Christina Lundberg, David Hollister, Linda Garcia Shelton, and Lewis Rudolph.
2. Making the quality of life of those they connected with better. Of these there were five: Kay Snyder, Thom Peterson, Caroline Wong, John Schuiteman, and Phyllis Barten Harris.

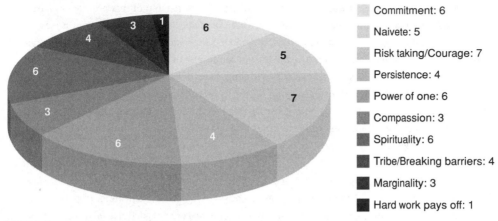

Commitment: 6
Naivete: 5
Risk taking/Courage: 7
Persistence: 4
Power of one: 6
Compassion: 3
Spirituality: 6
Tribe/Breaking barriers: 4
Marginality: 3
Hard work pays off: 1

FIGURE 1 Frequency of Characteristic/Value

3. Working for the common good through a deep commitment to their human service profession. This category included two teachers: William Skocpol and Elizabeth King Snodgrass.

My reflections on these interviews also raises, in my judgment, a fruitful field for further research in service/learning and civic engagement: Can service learning and civic engagement be the seedbed for developing engaged learners as leaders who live for the common good? Engaged learning is grounded in an ethos of mutuality, respectfulness, and stewardship; it proceeds through dialogue and fosters inclusive well-being. It is an approach, an expression of being, a leadership and management ethic, and a way for scholars to connect otherwise diverse activities thematically, coherently, and meaningfully (Fear, Bawden, Rosaen, & Foster-Fishman, 2002). The interviews plus the following quotes seem to support a positive answer.

Kay Snyder

I was a participant in the 1965 STEP. I was very involved in the organizing and the fund-raising that occurred before we went the first year. I was the social science coordinator that first year. There was a core group of students who knew director John Duley and the faculty members who were setting up the program. They involved us from the very early stages of the planning, so when I think how it was that this program had such an impact on my life, it was because we were working alongside of faculty who were committed to civil rights and for whom this was a very serious operation. You have to realize that the first year wasn't just fund-raising; it was figuring out what we were going to teach, how we were going to teach it, how we were going to organize these students. None of us had done this before; none of us had been teachers. So it was working with faculty and being listened to that made us realize that we could do all of those things.

William Skocpol

I was a participant in the 1966 STEP. I met my wife there. We were married on June 10, 1967, and on June 17 we were back at Rust. We participated as curriculum coordinators for that year and went for the beginning of the 1967 program to make sure that everything got off to a good start.

Another incident in which it was evident that students had ownership of this program occurred during the second or third week that we were there in 1966. Bob Green had taken a leave of absence from Michigan State University and joined Dr. King's staff as an educational consultant during 1965–66. When James Meredith was shot as he began the March Against Fear from Memphis, Tennessee, to Jackson, Mississippi, Dr. King asked Bob Green to assume the leadership role in the march for the Southern Christian Leadership Conference (SCLC). Dr. Green came to the Rust College campus the day before the last day of the march and invited students from the campus and STEP volunteers to participate. I have notes from a long student steering committee meeting where we discussed the principles of what restrictions we should observe because we were an educational project. The ground rules that were set up were: Since the last day of the march was a Sunday, which was not part of our academic program, people could participate. Also, if you were under 21 you needed your parents' permission. There were a number of parents who did not give permission, including my future wife's parents, so I did not go. But it was an experience for all of us, connecting us to the whole civil rights movement in a very, very direct way.

Lewis Rudolph

I remember meeting with Larry Klein, Roy Bryan, and Paul Herron, students who were engineering the interview process. The interview process was quite intimidating. It was one of the first interview processes that I had taken part in, and the whole premise was, "Why should we even be wasting our time talking with you about this kind of commitment; you certainly can't be ready to undergo this kind of an experience; you're not prepared." So, it really throttled me.

Linda Garcia Shelton

I was involved right from the beginning; I was in the first group in 1965 and again in 1966. During the 1967 year I was again involved in the planning retreat, in raising money, and in setting it up, but I did not go.

Linda and her husband, Harold, met in the project in 1965, were married in early summer of 1966, and spent their honeymoon in the project at Rust College during that summer.

Caroline Wong

Interviewer: Bob Green earlier today said, "Leadership is what it's all about." You are a principal; you've been recognized in the state of Hawaii for your leadership. Was there anything in the STEP program that affected your leadership style?

Caroline Wong: As a leader I look to a lot of leaders to see what type of leader I want to be, and I would define myself as a servant leader. I'm here to live but I'm also here to serve you and serve your needs, and that concept was integral to the Holly Springs experience. We were there, not because we had something more or something better, but we were there to walk beside people and live with them and share with them and be of service to them to meet their needs.

Interviewer: Did you see leaders there who demonstrated that, who were exemplars of that?

Caroline: I did, I did. I saw the project organizer as a person who definitely had the philosophy. He wasn't a loud and outspoken person; he just modeled and lived it.

It is not surprising that the people who participated in STEP have committed their lives to working for the common good. At the time when these students were most open to change and new ideas, they spent quality time being exposed to a group of people who came from very different backgrounds, yet still they were able to develop both physical and emotional bonds. They were able to reflect on the reasons why service learning is important and grasp the deeper reasons behind the Rust College community need.

Notes

Special thanks to Dr. Dwight Giles, professor of higher education administration and senior associate at the New England Resource Center for Higher Education in the Graduate College of Education, University of Massachusetts, Boston, longtime colleague in the National Society for Experiential Learning (NSEE), and friend, for his encouragement and support in the development of this document; to MSU's Associate Provost for University Outreach and Engagement, Hiram Fitzgerald, for his continuing support for my work; to Karen McKnight Casey, director of the Center for Service-Learning and Civic Engagement at MSU, for her support in this venture; to Tina Houghton for her insistence that autobiographical information be requested on the registration forms for the STEP reunion; to Suzanne Buglione, CmUnityBuild@aol.com, for her diligent and careful work in transcribing the interviews; to Dr. Dale Herder, professor of writing at Lansing Community College and personal friend and mentor, for his careful editorial revisions; and to Linda Chapel Jackson, MSU University Outreach and Engagement, for also adding her editorial prowess to the completion of this chapter.

References

Berkowitz, W. R. (1987). *Local heroes: The rebirth of heroism in America.* Lexington, MA: Lexington Books.

Buechner, F. (1993). *Wishful thinking: A seekers ABC.* San Francisco: Harper Collins.

Fear, F., Bawden, R. J., Rosaen, C., & Foster-Fishman, P. G. 2002. A model of engaged learning: Frames of reference and scholarly underpinnings. *Journal of Higher Education Outreach and Engagement, 7*(3), 55–68.

Honnet, E. P., & Poulsen, S. J. (1989). *Principals of good practice for combining service and learning.* Racine, WI: Johnson Foundation.

Parks Daloz, L. A., Keen, C. H., Keen, J. P., & Daloz Parks, S. (1996). *Common fire: Lives of commitment in a complex world.* Boston: Beacon Press.

Stanton, T. K., D. E. Giles Jr., & N. I. Cruz. (1999). *Service-learning: A movement's pioneers reflect on its origins, practice, and future.* San Francisco: Jossey-Bass.

PART 2

Community Engagement and the Scholarship of Practice

Introduction

Judy Primavera and Hiram E. Fitzgerald

The "new scholarship" set in motion by Boyer, Lynton, and the Kellogg Commission is a scholarship of *action*, a scholarship of *practice* that takes place both *in* and *with* the community. This scholarship of practice challenges higher education's age-old accepted epistemologies and requires a new set of norms regarding what counts as legitimate knowledge and what methodologies are acceptable means of acquiring such knowledge (Schön, 1995). It is a scholarship that frees the academy from the confinement of its myopic, reductionist, patriarchal, and self-serving scope of intellectual inquiry by offering a more expansive, more egalitarian, and more socially utilitarian model as to how knowledge is defined, communicated, and used. This new scholarship is founded on the premise that the academy is not the sole proprietor or distributor of knowledge (Barker, 2004). Knowledge also originates from and flourishes in the community. Within the framework of this new scholarship, the mission of the academy does not begin and end with intellectual discovery and fact-finding. Rather, the academy join forces with the community, and together they use their knowledge and their resources to address our society's most pressing social, civic, economic, and moral problems (Boyer, 1996).

There is no doubt that there have been great strides made in the last 25 years related to the acceptance, implementation, and institutionalization of the scholarship of engagement in higher education. However, universities were much faster to "talk the talk" than they were to "walk the walk." The stories told in the chapters in part 2 of *Going Public* are a testimony to the fact that we have moved far beyond the rhetoric of civic engagement to the reality of a very vibrant and change-producing scholarship of practice.

The chapters in part 2 are proof that the practice of *good* scholarship can happen anywhere; that the acceptable context for scholarship is not limited by geography or setting. The scholarship of practice presented here occurs in schools, prisons, museums, nonprofit environmental initiatives, and a Mayan Women's Weaving Cooperative. The university-community partnerships involved are local, statewide, and international.

Finally, as a collective, these stories might be considered models of the new epistemology of how knowledge is defined, acquired, communicated, and perhaps even judged. Each of the chapters tells a "story." Some contain reports of more traditional "data" and others do not, but again, as a collective, they suggest that the best measure of a "significant result" is not always a statistically derived low p-value. Each of these stories documents the process of positive change; they provide evidence that the "work" that was done by the university and community partners did, indeed, have a significant impact. Glassick, Huber, and Maeroff (1997) encourage us to move beyond the convenient practice of counting professional "products" when assessing the value of our work, and that is precisely what these stories illustrate. Working in the real world is messy. When our work takes place in real communities, with real people, living their real lives coping with real social-political-economic issues, a good deal of the "value" lies in the process of *how* we did what we did, and oftentimes the most valuable *product* is something that eludes precise measurement. Each of the chapters tells a unique story of community engagement and the scholarship of practice; they tell of our successes, our failures, the unintended consequences, and the questions yet to be answered. More importantly, they tell the stories of how trust was built, how attitudes and behaviors were changed, and how people and communities became empowered. *Going public* with these stories and others like them is something we should do more of—it "pushes the boundary" of the old epistemology and it brings us one step closer to Boyer's vision of a civically engaged and civically responsible academy.

The Scholarship of Practice

A crucial component of the scholarship of practice is the engagement process. The type of mutual trust required for *good* community engagement to happen is not something that happens overnight, nor is it something that proceeds in a smooth and linear fashion. There are often false starts and bumps to be smoothed over before the "real work" begins. Work *in* and *with* the community has a courtship period; in other words, the scholarship of practice typically begins "before the beginning" described in our professional writings (Kelly, 1986; Sarason, 1972). The first chapter in part 2 describes the early stages of a partnership between university researchers and the State of Michigan's American Indian/Alaskan Native Tribal Early Head Start/Head Start programs. Fitzgerald, Farrell, Barnes, Belleau, Gerde, Thompson, Lee, Calatera, and Parish discuss the process of relationship building and the steps taken to build trust before the real work toward the goal of improving Michigan's Tribal Head Start programs could begin. They describe how the potential obstacles of differences in culture and program implementation across significant geographic distance were overcome. This story, like several others in *Going Public*, illustrates the fact that events and projects that are planned for one purpose often lead to a variety of unintended consequences. In this case, the planned goals of creating an assessment tool and developing a program to improve services were achieved. The real "gold," however, lies in the deep and rich relationship that now exists between university researchers and community partners.

The university-community partnerships formed via the scholarship of practice unilaterally involve the mixing of disparate cultures as defined by an array of different characteristics: race, class, gender, sexual orientation, faith, values, culture, education, geography, etc. Faculty, students, and community members all face, to some degree, the experience of being "the other." Even the college student who grew up in an underprivileged urban setting and returns to a similar environment to engage in service learning is "the other" in that setting by the very fact that having the opportunity to attend college makes them "different." In her chapter, Dunlap uses Kübler-Ross's model of death and dying as a framework for how university and community partners experience the cross-cultural learning experiences inherent in the community engagement process. Using the reflections of her service-learning students, Dunlap illustrates the process of loss, grief, and growth set in motion when individuals with life experiences different from their own come together and take part in a meaningful community engagement experience.

O'Connor contends that by its very nature, scholarship that incorporates community service necessitates a long-term commitment to the community being served. O'Connor's three decades of work in prisons in the greater Washington, DC, area is a poignant reminder that significant impact and meaningful change require time, flexibility, and knowledge of and respect for the cultural system you are entering. Before attempting to work *in* and *with* a community, it is imperative that we appreciate social-ecological context (i.e., the history, the rules, the traditions, the values, the power structure, etc.) of that community setting (Kelly, 1970). Working within community settings, especially "total institutions" like prisons, takes a great deal of control out of the hands of the university researcher. Thus, the ability to adapt to changing situations and unexpected, sometimes irrational, obstacles is more valuable than any academic pedigree. Most importantly, O'Connor's work points to the fact that if we are going to call what we do "community-engaged scholarship," we'd best be prepared to commit ourselves wholeheartedly and for the long haul.

Earlier we shared a celebratory note acknowledging the progress made in embracing the best practices of community engagement scholarship by American universities in the past two decades. However, the results of Crawford, Rauhe, and Machemer's exploratory study of the contemporary "terrain" of community engagement in landscape architecture education remind us that different academic disciplines have different ways of engaging with the community and that different disciplines face different challenges when implementing community-engaged scholarship. The new scholarship heralded by Boyer, Lynton, and the Kellogg Commission lends itself most readily to the social sciences and applied professional programs such as public health and nursing. But for other disciplines the translation is not as easily accomplished, even when that discipline has a long history of using real-world community service projects to foster student professional development.

Beckman and Long raise an important question about how we measure the long-term impact of our community engagement efforts. They contend we need to shift our attention to the impact that our scholarship of practice is having in the communities we partner with. Beckman and Long argue that a coalition model of community engagement might best be suited to achieving the goal of long-term community improvement. They stress the importance of embedding our community engagement activities in a larger "trajectory of action" focused on community change. Beckman and Long use the "story" of the development, the ethos, and the work of South Bend, Indiana's Education Collaborative Group to illustrate how the resources of all coalition partners can be moved beyond the more typical forms of university-community engagement to increase the likelihood of long-term, meaningful community change.

The work presented in the chapter by O'Donnell offers an example of public sociology focused on grassroots community organizing. It illustrates the fact that sometimes in our work as "public" academic professionals, our role as "active citizen" participating in the life of a community takes us far beyond the stereotype of university teacher and researcher. The story of O'Donnell's democratic partnership with the Oneonta Community Alliance for Youth (OCAY) illustrates two noteworthy caveats inherent in the scholarship of practice. The first is that much can be accomplished when the partnership formed with the community and the resources drawn upon are more personal than institutional. The second is that the professional "product" of civically engaged work is often the *process* of the work itself. The "outcome" of this work is not the fact that OCAY is now a fully functioning 501(c)(3) non-profit corporation or that the Oneonta Teen Center thrives in its own dedicated physical space; nor is it a handful of peer-reviewed journal articles. In this case, the real professional product is the mobilization, the day-to-day management of the initiative, and the sharing of professional expertise with less experienced university students and community members so that they might become more civically engaged citizens themselves.

Rood's story of the Ocmulgee River Initiative (ORI) also points out the important question of what "counts" as valid and valuable faculty and student research. This question is especially germane for academic disciplines like the natural sciences, where work outside of a traditional laboratory setting is still somewhat of an anomaly. Rood reminds us that the enormity and complexity of local, regional, and national public health concerns underscore the need for natural science experts to *go public* and share their expertise and skills. Although the ORI has achieved and even superseded its original goals, Rood contends that the real measure of success is the ORI's ability to engage a diverse group of people—faculty and students from multiple universities and citizens from multiple communities—in a host of research, educational, and advocacy activities in the hopes of improving the region's environmental quality of life.

The next two chapters provide examples of community engagement of a transnational nature. Dewhurst and MacDowell review the scholarly-engaged work that began as a partnership between the Michigan State University Museum and the Institute of Ethiopian Studies and evolved into a multimember consortium of U.S. and South African organizations now known as the South African Cultural Heritage Project. The story of the bonds forged and the many successful outcomes of this partnership attests to the fact that the scholarship of practice has no geographic boundaries and that the mutual benefits to all involved can, and do, exceed initial expectations.

O'Donnell's story of her work with the Mayan women's weaving cooperative Jolam Mayaetik in Chiapas, Mexico, represents a blend of community-based pedagogy and feminist-inspired community-organizing work. She proposes a civic solidarity framework as a model for doing social justice-focused scholarship of practice. O'Donnell highlights two significant dilemmas faced by faculty doing solidarity-based work in an international arena: How do you remain true to your commitments to satisfy the social justice needs of your global partners? And how do you elicit committed and meaningful "buy-in" from students when the "real action" is occurring somewhere across the globe? O'Donnell also raises the nagging question of sustainability and suggests that if academic institutions cannot offer social justice and economic solidarity with groups such as Jolam Mayaetik, then faculty activists might do well to align themselves with nonprofits and other groups in the nonacademic sector.

This volume ends with a chapter by Primavera and Martinez that describes the potential for community-engaged scholarship to produce systems-level transformational change in the institutional culture and functioning in both university and community settings. It is the continuation of the story of the development and evolution of a 20-year university-community partnership designed to both enhance low-income preschoolers' school readiness skills and provide meaningful educational experiences for undergraduates that would increase their commitment to future community service (Primavera, 2004). When this partnership began, there was no plan for changing the underlying infrastructure of either institution. Primavera and Martinez contend that because the transformational changes occurred naturally, the factors found to be instrumental in influencing that change are particularly salient. That is, the future course of any attempt at civic engagement depends, first and foremost, on the quality of the relationships that are developed between the people involved (faculty–community member; faculty-student, student–community member, etc.). Likewise, personality is important. Careful reading of the stories in this volume attests to the fact that not just anyone has the demeanor, the value system, or the stamina for this type of work. It is crucial that the metaphor upon which the partnership is based reflects equality, mutual respect, and shared governance. Finally, Primavera and Martinez warn that the role of serendipity, simply being in the right place at the right time with the right set of people, cannot be ignored.

References

Barker, D. (2004). The scholarship of engagement: A taxonomy of five emerging practices. *Journal of Higher Education Outreach and Engagement, 9*, 123–137.

Boyer, E. L. (1996). The scholarship of engagement. *Journal of Public Service and Outreach, 1*, 11–20.

Glassick, C. E., Huber, M. T., & Maeroff, G. I. (1997). *Scholarship assessed: Evaluation of the professoriate.* San Francisco: Jossey-Bass.

Kelly, J. G. (1970). Towards an ecological conception of preventive interventions. In D. Adelson & B. Kalis (Eds.), *Community psychology and mental health* (pp. 126–145). Scranton, PA: Chandler.

Kelly, J. G. (1986). Context and process: An ecological view of the interdependence of practice and research. *American Journal of Community Psychology, 14*, 581–605.

Primavera, J. (2004). You can't get there from here: Identifying process routes to replication. *American Journal of Community Psychology, 33*, 181–191.

Sarason, S. B. (1972). *The creation of settings and the future of societies.* San Francisco: Jossey-Bass.

Schön, D. A. (1995). The new scholarship requires a new epistemology. *Change, 27*, 26–34.

Wiba Anung: Co-creating a Sustainable Partnership with Michigan's American Indian Head Start Programs

Hiram E. Fitzgerald, Patricia Farrell (Taos Pueblo), Jessica V. Barnes,
Ann Belleau (Ojibwe), Hope K. Gerde, Nicole L. Thompson (Menominee/
Mohican), Kyung Sook Lee, Mary Calcatera (Sault Saint Marie Ojibwe),
and Arnie Parish (Ojibwe)

It is often the case that an event planned for one purpose leads to unintended consequences. In this chapter, we describe an unintended consequence that has produced a multi-year partnership between researchers at Michigan State University and the Early Head Start and Head Start programs operated by the Inter-Tribal Council of Michigan, Inc. (ITC Michigan), the Grand Traverse Band of Ottawa and Chippewa Indians, and the Sault Saint Marie Tribe of Chippewa Indians. The original event was organized by the leaders of the American Indian / Alaska Native Head Start Research Center (AIANHSRC), located at the University of Colorado–Denver, and funded by the U.S. Department of Health of Human Services' Administration for Children and Families (ACF). Individuals invited to join the steering committee of the AIANHSRC were asked to help design a national study that could answer critical questions related to creating more vibrant and effective American Indian / Alaska Native (AI/AN) Tribal Head Start programs. Two of the members of the steering committee (Hiram Fitzgerald, MSU, and Ann Belleau, ITC Michigan) met for the first time in Colorado, beginning a story of partnership development and sustainability between Michigan State University and Michigan's AI early education programs.

Individuals attending the first meeting of the AIANHSRC in February 2006 included eight AI/AN Head Start program directors, 12 staff from the AIANHSRC, two staff from ACF, three university researchers, and a representative from the Academy for Educational Development. Early discussions among the steering committee members led to an understanding that several critical issues needed to be addressed before any national study could be designed. First, several nontribal members of the committee felt that they did not have sufficient knowledge of AI/AN cultures to engage in drafting concrete recommendations for assessment tools, evaluation strategies, and research methods appropriate for AI/AN Head

Start programs. Second, the small literature on early childhood development in tribal communities presented a barrier for conceptualizing a large-scale national study designed to enhance the quality of AI/AN Head Start programs. In effect, we did not know the set of questions that would easily guide a structured national study. Third, having met for the first time, we had no opportunity to develop the level of interpersonal relationships and trust necessary to guide our collective work. Because the AIANHSRC partnership consisted of AI/AN and non-AI/AN investigators, trust building was essential for assuring open discussion and transparency in order to move the planning agenda forward (Galligher, Tsethlikai, & Stolle, 2012). Ultimately, group consensus led us to emphasize three key aspects of systems change: Enhancing the qualifications and skills of Head Start teachers, building more effective cultural competence skills for nontribal teachers, and infusing culturally appropriate curricular components into existing evidence-based curricula being used in AI/AN Head Start programs.

After receiving recommendations from the steering committee, the Administration for Children and Families issued a request for proposals that highlighted nine core areas for potential funding. The Michigan State University team contacted Ann Belleau to determine whether the Intertribal Council of Michigan would be interested in a joint submission for a grant that would focus on professional development for teachers in order to enhance positive outcomes for children, particularly with respect to their academic and behavioral school readiness skills. The Inter-Tribal Council of Michigan coordinates the Early Head Start and Inter-Tribal Inc., Head Start programs offered by the Bay Mills Indian Community, Keweenaw Bay Indian Community, Nottawaseppi Huron Band of Potawatomi, Hannahville Indian Community, Lac Vieux Desert Band of Lake Superior Chippewa Indians, Little Traverse Bay Bands of Ottawa Indians, and Pokagan Band of Potawatomi. Ms. Belleau's invitation to two other Michigan Head Start programs, the Sault Ste. Marie Tribe of Chippewa Indians and the Grand Traverse Bay Band of Ottawa and Chippewa Indians, was successful, and all of the program directors agreed to the partnership. As indicated in figure 1, Michigan's AI Head Start programs are distributed over a wide geographic space. For example, Dowegiac and Watersmeet are approximately 610 miles apart, with estimated driving time of 10 hours in good weather, and considerably longer in winter weather conditions. In addition, the Intertribal Council of Michigan is located in Sault Ste Marie, approximately five hours from the university. These geographic realities posed new challenges to university researchers for managing an evaluation project that would include on-site data collection from teachers, parents, children, and community members. In this chapter we describe how our partnership developed and how the use of community-based participatory research enabled it to grow into a collaboration between university researchers and Michigan's AI Early Head Start / Head Start programs that is far deeper than any of us imagined was possible.

Initial Partnership Goals

The Wiba Anung partnership was formed in 2006 in order to improve the school readiness of children enrolled in AI Head Start programs in Michigan. Initially, we sought to effect these changes by focusing on five key aims: (1) to cocreate and deliver a staff development

Keweenaw Bay Start/Early Head Start
L'Anse, MI

Bay Mills Head Start/Early Head Start
Brimley, MI

Sault Ste, Marie Head Start
Stault Ste, Marie, MI

Inter Tribal Council of
MI Inc. Central Office

Lac Vieux-Desert
Head Start/Early Head Start
Watersmeet, MI

Little Traverse Bay
Band Head Start/
Early Head start
Pellston, MI

Hannahville Head Start/Early Head Start
Wilson, MI

Grand Traverse Band
Peshawbestown, MI

Huron Potawatomi Head Start
Grand Rapids, MI

Pokagon Head Start
Dowagiac, MI

FIGURE 1 Locations of Tribal Head Start Programs in Michigan

plan that would increase the competency skills of teachers in AI HS/EHS classrooms, (2) to cocreate a culturally appropriate teaching training curriculum based on established curriculum models for early childhood education developed at MSU and Bay Mills Community College (BMCC), (3) to conduct focus groups to assess community response to the proposed curriculum, (4) to randomly select six sites to evaluate the effectiveness of the curriculum model with response to teacher effectiveness and child cognitive, social-emotional, and cultural outcomes, and (5) to revise the curriculum based on the initial evaluation and implementation statewide using an outcome-based effectiveness evaluation model.

Theory of Change Related to Specific Aims

Our theory of change posited that bolstering teacher preparation in early childhood education and cultural competence would expose children to a more culturally relevant curriculum and improve their preacademic achievement skills (see figure 2). The model also posited that tribal elders (cultural traditions) and parents would play a key role in program effectiveness by mediating or moderating program impacts on child achievement outcomes.

Recent Head Start policy initiatives to increase the number of teachers with bachelor's degrees and specialized training in early childhood education is primarily driven by the

139

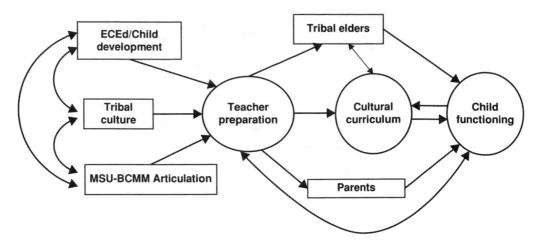

FIGURE 2 Heuristic Model of the Dynamics of Teacher Effectiveness and Influence on children over Time.
NOTE. ECEd = Early Childhood Education

substantial literature indicating that teacher's educational background is closely linked to the quality of early childhood education programs, and subsequently to the outcomes for children in pre-K programs (Burchinal, Cryer, Clifford, & Howes, 2002; de Kruif, McWilliam, Ridley, & Wakely, 2000; NICHHD, 2002). Although similar studies in Head Start have found mixed results (e.g., Early et al., 2007), largely due to the use of global measures of program quality that do not focus on teacher-child interactions or specific teaching practice, work measuring teaching behaviors has found the level of education (Gerde & Powell, 2009) and specialized training in early childhood education (Garet, Porter, Desimone, Birman, & Yoon, 2001) to be important predictors of classroom quality and children's developmental outcomes in Head Start. Currently, the percentage of teachers with degrees in both migrant and AI/AN EHS/HS programs remain far under the 50% legislative mandate (Marks, Moyer, Roche, & Graham, 2003). Whereas 52% of regular HS teachers nationwide had a minimum AA degree in early childhood education or in a related field at the end of 2002, only 27% of the teachers in AI/AN and 21% of teachers in migrant HS programs had associates degrees. Clearly, there are discrepancies between desired teacher credentials and tribal teacher credentials. The core question, however, is whether these credentialing differences are linked to differences in child development outcomes. Table 1 summarizes teacher credentials for Michigan's AI Head Start programs at the beginning of the grant (2006) and teacher educational degree status in 2010.

In 2006, 26% of teachers across the system had bachelor's degrees (BA/BS), 50% had associate's degrees (AA), and 24% had child development associate's (CDA) credentials. By 2010, the number of teachers increased from 54 to 65, but the distribution of degree status remained relatively the same (20% BA/BS; 51% AA; 29% CDA). As in all Head Start programs, increasing and maintaining teachers with bachelor's degrees is difficult. Head Start teachers are not well paid, and most must pursue academic degrees on a part-time basis. Because they also work and many have their own families, many AI/AN HS teachers can only take courses offered in summer sessions or online during evening and week-end hours. Once bachelor's degrees are earned, many teachers move to higher-paying positions

Table 1. Teacher Degree/Credentials for Michigan AI Head Start Programs in 2006 and 2010

HS region	Teachers with degrees (2006)		Teachers with degrees (2010)		
	AA or BA/BS	CDA	AA or BA/BS	CDA	No. of classrooms
Sault Ste Marie/ St. Ignace	9 (4AA, 5BA)	1	HS: 1 AA, 2 BA EHS: 3 AA, 1 BA	HS: 1 EHS: 3	4 HS 4 EHS
Bay Mills	7 (AA)	6	HS: 2 AA, 3 BA EHS: 7 AA	EHS: 4	3 HS 5 EHS
Keweenaw Bay	6 (4AA, 2BS, 1MA)	3	HS 4 AA EHS: 2 AA	EHS: 5; 2 in training	2 HS 4 EHS
Hannahville	5 (4 AA, 1 BA)	0	HS: 3 AA, 1 BA EHS: 4 AA, 1 BA		3 HS 3 EHS
Little Traverse Bay Band	1 AA	1 (pending)	HS: 1 AA, 1 BA EHS: 1 AA		1 HS 1 home-based EHS
Pokagon	2 AA	0	HS: 2 AA		2 HS
Huron Potawatomi	5 (3BA, 2AA)	0	HS: 2 AA, 2 BA		2 HS
Lac Vieux Desert	5 (1BA, 1BS, 3AA)	3 (1 pending)	HS: 1 BA EHS: 1 AA, 1 BS	EHS: 3, 3 pending	2 HS 4 EHS
Grand Traverse Band	Not Available				Not Available

in other educational settings. Nevertheless, during the course of the project, all teachers developed an educational plan to enhance their formal education, particularly in early childhood development. Moreover, as will be described later in the chapter, we were able to institute a professional development program designed to enhance teachers' classroom practices.

Community-Based Participatory Research

The decision to use community-based participatory research (CBPR) was based on clear indications from the literature that use of CBPR or tribal participatory research (TPR) was critical for success when working with AI/AN communities (Allen, Mohatt, Markstrom, Byers, & Novins, 2012; Galligher, Tsethlikai, & Stolle, 2012). Although this decision did not change our basic theory of change, it did lead to changes in our original specific aims. During the first two years of the grant we focused heavily on use of CBPR practices in order (1) to build a trust-based partnership with the ITC Michigan, BMCC, and each of the EHS/ HS program sites, (2) to develop articulation agreements between BMCC and Michigan State University to facilitate degree attainment for HS teachers, (3) to conduct focus groups designed to enhance the MSU research team's knowledge of tribal culture, (4) to conduct focus groups to generate baseline information about the extent to which cultural knowledge was used in HS classrooms and integrated into evidence-based curricula, and (5) to build a tribal-university CBPR team to develop and implement the research study.

We quickly learned that our original specific aims were too ambitious for the degree of systems change needed. For example, a nearly two-year effort to develop articulation agreements between Michigan State University and BMCC was set aside when we finally realized that the university's academic policies were barriers to creating a successful articulation process with the community college.

The CBPR process also led us to change the name of our partnership from "Building Teacher Capacity in American Indian Head Start and Early Head Start Programs in Michigan," to "Wiba Anung (Early Star): Promoting Academic and Social Success in Michigan Tribal Head Start Programs." The name change shifted project emphasis onto tribal assets as the basis for building systems change, created better balance among the various components of our theory of change model, and focused our efforts on changes in children as the key outcome.

Emphasis on inclusiveness in developing and executing the research plan fostered a shared vision for program outcomes and for selection of indicators of success. Inclusion involved creating a research team with individuals drawn from all components of our theory of change. The Tribal Partnership Team (TPT) of parents, HS directors, teachers, community members, and university researchers embraced the CBPR approach because it emphasized cocreative and participatory input to all facets of the proposed work. Within this context, the TPT developed three primary goals for the research partnership.

First, the TPT reiterated the importance of developing a strong research partnership among the tribes and Michigan State University. This partnership served to link the university with the communities to jointly assess, prioritize, and address community needs. They emphasized the importance of increasing the number of AI teachers in the EHS/HS tribal system.

Second, the TPT identified three aspects of early childhood development that required attention if we were to better understand AI/AN Head Start educational contexts: (1) understanding the quality of the environment in AI/AN Head Start and Early Head Start programs, (2) understanding the strengths and needs of the home environment of Head Start and Early Head Start families, and (3) understanding factors that promote child development.

We agreed to assess the socio-emotional development and school readiness of participating Head Start children, and to identify program approaches to the integration of culturally appropriate content and activities to the EHS/HS curricula consistent with the Office of Head Start Performance Standards. The TPT developed an assessment tool protocol. This began with the identification of potential instruments. MSU researchers distributed a large list of instruments to the TPT and discussed the types of constructs measured by each tool and the reasons why researchers believed such constructs were necessary to understand program outcomes. TPT members then voted on the specific content areas for assessment, thereby having a direct impact on the theory of change. The larger set of instruments was then pared down to a working set based on TPT objections to content domains or to length of a particular instrument. In the final step of instrument selection, TPT members received a copy of every instrument in the final list, and proceeded to review each individual item to determine whether the item was culturally appropriate. Then the TPT finalized the assessment package and constructed protocols for teachers, parents, and children (table 2).

Table 2. Core Components of the Assessment Package Adopted by the Tribal Partnership Team

Program Outcomes
  Teacher survey
  Parent involvement and support
  Staff interactions and support

Classroom Outcomes
  Classroom environment
  Classroom management

Family and community context
  Parenting behaviors
  Parenting beliefs
  Parenting discipline strategies
  Home environment
  Parent physical and mental health
  Family environment
  Parenting stress
  Parent depression
  Parent physical health

Community Health Indicators
  Child health
  Family health
  Education outcomes

Child Outcomes
  Cognitive and language development
  School readiness (literacy/numeracy)
  Language development
  Cognitive development
  Social-emotional development
  Behavior problems
  Externalizing
  Internalizing
  Inhibitory control
  Physical health
  Immunizations

Physical checkups
  Height and weight (BMI)

Finally, the TPT developed a research protocol to allow tracking of short- and long-term results of program enhancements, and to revise them within the context of both qualitative and quantitative indicators of success. The Wiba Anung TPT members focused on outcomes in relation to (1) more science-based university-community collaborations, (2) more highly qualified teachers in AI/AN EHS/HS programs, (3) stronger infusion of tribal culture within all AI/AN EHS/HS programs, (4) higher quality Head Start and Early Head Start programs, and (5) children who are tribal-culture embedded, and who are ready to be successful through the transition from HS to K-12 educational programs.

The TPT also generated a set of operational guidelines for the Wiba Anung project:

1. Site and tribal diversity requires sensitivity to the specific needs of each community. Therefore, efforts to promote staff professional development and early childhood education must be informed from within communities as well as across communities in order to achieve common and specific objectives.

2. The TPT must have representation from all tribal communities and all constituents within the communities. Full inclusion ensures that project activities can be implemented at every participant program site.

3. Identification of realistic timelines for the implementation of a professional development system is critical to achieving targeted outcomes across all sites.

4. Sampling perspectives of parents, community members, tribal elders, AI/AN HS and EHS teachers, and program directors is an essential step to achieve all guidelines. Sampling was achieved by use of focus groups and surveys across sites.

Cultural Context

The majority of mainstream educational practices directed toward AI/AN students have historically lacked a cultural component (Demmert, 2001). Research concerning the development and testing of educational alternatives for AI/AN children is limited, especially options that incorporate AI/AN linguistic and cultural patterns (Demmert & Towner, 2003). A number of historical accounts attribute this primarily to a history of assimilation practices of educators, the federal government, and religious denominations (Reyhner & Eder, 1989; Marr, 2010). Moreover, they note that the consequences of such efforts created a historical trauma that extended beyond removal of AI/AN children from their families and infiltrated the very fabric of AI/AN community life (Campbell & Evans-Campbell, 2011; Demmert, 2001). Because the traditional methods of education are no longer in practice, AI/AN students are less likely to experience academic success.

Voices of Parents and Community Members

Because the extant literature provided little direct guidance for developing culturally competent teacher training models or for developing children's culturally relevant curricular components, the TPT shifted attention away from aims 3–5 and instead focused efforts on gaining the background knowledge needed to contemplate the infusing of cultural content in to standard HS programs. We conducted seven focus groups and included education professionals and parents to explore relevant topics such as participants' perceptions about the role of formal education in their children's lives, participants' relationships to the current structure of education and educators in their community, and participants' perspectives on incorporating culture into formal education (Gerde et al., 2012). Participants were recruited for these focus groups through the Intertribal Council communities.

Focus group members were asked to identify a range of participation on several criteria, including current level of participation in the schools. Each focus group included, on average, eight members. A semistructured, open-ended uniform focus group protocol developed by the research team (based on work by Kruger & Casey, 2000) was used, and all focus group discussions were audio recorded by participant observers. Focus groups were moderated by tribal members not directly affiliated with the specific communities in which the focus groups were conducted. Findings suggested several important themes (Fitzgerald et al., 2008). First, definitions of success for children stressed the importance of self-esteem, confidence, health, happiness, sound decision making, and success in the workforce. One individual expressed this theme as being "educated to a level that they can make real choices in life. You know, not drop out of high school so they're limited to certain jobs."

The issue of workforce preparedness was expressed by many community members as they contrasted their aspirations for their children against the reality that American Indians are vastly underrepresented in many vocational areas, particularly among vocations that require education beyond high school.

Second, participants stressed the importance of enhancing cultural education in their communities while simultaneously acknowledging that there are resource gaps in this area. For example, there is a need for more Native language speakers, particularly in early childhood education settings where children can more easily master language skills. In addition, they specifically discussed issues related to learning styles, suggesting that AI children may approach learning differently than other children. As one participant stated, "It seems to me . . . [American Indian children] learn more global . . . they're not linear; they don't learn things in a linear fashion. It's not first do A, then B, then C. It's . . . it's different."

Third, many participants expressed deep concerns about the public education system. Ninety-three percent of respondents drew attention to the impact of racism and micro-aggression on the quality of education their children receive. As one participant related, "They actually told the Title VII lady, 'Tell the Native kids they can't walk more than three together because they could scare the white kids. Then they're like a gang.' . . . That was a very racist thing. We've had really huge problems in this area."

Voices of Elders

In 2009, a focus group consisting of eight experts in Ojibway and Potowatomi culture and language met and agreed to allow their session to be videotaped (Gerde et al., 2012). The focus group session lasted 10 hours across two days in which the team asked the experts to identify which components of culture and language young children should know, be aware of, and use regularly in their lives. Across the two days, essential information about Ojibway and Potowatomi cultural content and processes was gathered. We learned that for these individuals, culture and language are entities that young children should know, and that in their judgment, it is appropriate for schools serving young children to support the integration of culture into classrooms. Further, important information was gained about which cultural content knowledge is important and appropriate for young children and how it would be taught in culturally appropriate ways (i.e., what were the culturally appropriate processes for teaching such information; e.g., storytelling is a wintertime activity). The information gathered from the cultural summit was later coded using a constant comparative analysis to identify important themes as a way to begin the development of a culturally relevant preschool curriculum. Thus, we learned a great deal about the importance of understanding current cultural practices of the programs. Since that time we have systematically observed classroom practice across all classrooms and centers to identify approaches to promoting culture and Native language in the classroom. Second, a questionnaire was created and responses were gathered from program directors regarding center-level approaches to cultural and language integration in the programs (Gerde et al., 2012).

Voices of HS Staff

Part of the AIANHSRC project involved supported fellowships for early career American Indian faculty members who were already conducting research with young children, or wanted to transition to such work. One of the AIANHSRC Fellows was Nicole L. Thompson, who at the time was a faculty member at Mississippi State University. Thompson had planned to conduct her research with a local American Indian community, but when that community decided to disengage from the project, the Wiba Anung team invited her to consider conducting her research in Michigan. During a visit to Michigan, we introduced Thompson to PhotoVoice, a participatory action research method (Wang & Burris, 1994) designed to combine documentary

145

photography and empowerment education (Freire, 1970) into a methodology that allows participants to educate others about their lives, communities, and concerns (Wang, Burris, & Xiang, 1996). Based extensively on Freire (1990) and feminist theory, PhotoVoice engages participants by giving them cameras and asking them to take photos to answer research questions. Accompanying the photos is narrative text that explains the significance of visual images. PhotoVoice enables people who tend to be left out of decision-making processes to share meaningful images from their personal experience and to effect change. Participants are empowered through the research process and become catalysts for change within their communities (Foster-Fishman, Newell, Deacon, Nievar, & McCann, 2005). Essentially, participants reveal intimate images of their realities of the world and generate meaning associated with the images to facilitate an understanding of the world of the "other." Nicole received training in PhotoVoice methodology by Pennie Foster-Fishman, a community psychologist who uses this approach extensively in her work with underserved youth.

Using PhotoVoice, Thompson recruited AI staff from the nine partner sites and used their stories to create a visual representation explaining how life in Michigan's AI communities is different from life in other places and how HS has impacted their lives and communities (Thompson & Belleau, 2011). Moreover, they identified elements of the HS programs that policymakers should know about and collaboratively work to implement change.

Participants' stories revealed the following:

1. AI children from these communities are prepared for school.
2. These HS programs provide more than an education—they support entire families.
3. These HS/EHS programs provide safe and nurturing environments for AI children.
4. These HS teachers and staff demonstrate true commitment to their profession/children given the workload, minimal salary, and high expectations.
5. Economic conditions of these communities adds stress to an already economically stressed population, the effects of which trickle down to children in the HS programs.
6. Sustaining and teaching Native culture is paramount in these programs as that is what truly sets them apart. These themes and the 25 posters in Thompson's PhotoVoice exhibit were participant generated—they examined and documented their worlds so that these data could be used to inform, educate, change, and empower. The PhotoVoice project has led to improved facilities, acquisition of materials, and formation of relationships that support culturally and developmentally appropriate practice for these young AI children.

According to Thompson and Belleau (2011), the findings from the PhotoVoice project can be placed into three large themes:

1. The preservation of AI language and culture in the Head Start classroom and implications for AI children's development
2. Challenges faced by AI Head Start families, communities, and programs
3. Issues of consistency, security, attachment, and socio-emotional development of AI children's mental health in Head Start

The issue of young children's mental health stood out as particularly significant and matches the concern expressed by several of the Head Start directors who are members of the AIANHSRC. The next step in Thompson's research is to engage parents/caregivers of children enrolled in AI Head Start programs and non-AI staff members in the PhotoVoice process, with a focus on infant/young children's mental health. Images and explanations from the first PhotoVoice project revealed that young children in the AI Head Start programs in Michigan encountered issues with attachment, family separation and reconstitution, and security—all of which may negatively impact children's social-emotional development and mental health. This project would therefore seek to provide a better understanding of the mental health needs of young AI children in Michigan; how Head Start does or does not address these needs; what community supports are or are not available to children and families; the impact of children's mental health issues on the Head Start classroom; parental and community awareness of young children's mental health needs; and what should be done to address these issues.

Teacher Professional Development

AI/AN Head Start children are at risk of entering kindergarten without the academic skills they need to be successful in K-12 learning environments. Specifically, recent work with AI HS programs identified that at the end of Head Start only 55% and 49% of these children met expected national norms in literacy and mathematics skills respectively (Barnes, Gerde, Belleau, Farrell, & Fitzgerald, 2010). Risk factors include economic disparity of families (i.e., 31% of AI/AN children under age 18 live in poverty [U.S. Census, 2000]), low-quality educational environments, and low educational requirements for teachers (Marks et al., 2003).

Professional development can impact teachers' classroom practice and thus child academic outcomes (e.g., Powell, Diamond, Burchinal, & Koehler, 2010; Wasik, Bond, & Hindman, 2006). Because the AI/AN HS programs are geographically isolated and dispersed, the design of a distance learning delivery system had great potential for engaging the teachers of these remote programs in professional development. The addition of Hope Gerde to our research team made possible implementation of a research project designed to enhance teacher classroom practice through professional development. The professional development program includes the use of videotaping classroom practice and a coach, an expert in early childhood education, to provide concrete feedback to teachers regarding their classroom practices. The professional development is focused on enhancing the teacher's support of children's mathematics and literacy skills.

To understand child cognitive effects of the professional development program, children were tested individually at the beginning and end of the school year by trained AI and non-AI research assistants using standardized measures of cognitive school readiness, including mathematics and literacy skills (Chew & Lang, 1990). One hundred twenty six children (mean age 58 months, range 51–66 months) participated in the assessments. Although most children were AI (85%), other racio-ethnic groups included 9% Caucasian, 2% Hispanic, 1% Pacific Islander, >1% African American, and 2% multiracial, non-Native.

Teachers were randomly assigned to a wave 1 or wave 2 participation year, with teachers in the wave 2 initial assignment serving as control classrooms for wave 1. Several variables measuring the implementation of the professional development were gathered as a measure of fidelity (e.g., number of content suggestions from coach). Teachers practice was video-taped prior to, immediately following, and at a follow-up point in relation to the professional development implementation. Children's math and literacy skills were measured across the year to identify change as an outcome of the professional development. This initiative led the TPT to add the Peabody Picture Vocabulary Test (PPVT-4, Dunn & Dunn, 2007) to the assessment protocol in order to measure children's receptive language (table 3).

Preliminary results indicate that all treatment teachers successfully participated in the professional development, completing seven to eight video reviews across six months. Also, all teachers completed three to four self-reflective reviews of their own work. Results also suggest that children in classrooms of treatment teachers made significant increases over children in control classrooms in numeracy skills, but not in literacy skills.

Thus far it is clear that teachers of the AI/AN HS programs can successfully participate in a distance learning professional development program that includes video recording their classroom practice, uploading videos, and retrieving expert coaching feedback on a secure interactive webpage (Gerde et al., 2011). In addition, these teachers successfully wrote self-reflective feedback based on their video recordings and discussed this feedback with their coach on-line.

Preliminary Findings

What have we been learning during the past two and one-half years of data collection, teacher professional development, and continuous quality improvement feedback to AI HS program parents, teachers, and program directors? The answers to this question will emerge from the extensive data collection that we have obtained from three cohorts of children and families in AI/AN HS programs. In this chapter we will only refer to portions of data from the initial first cohort to illustrate directions that our more substantive analyses will take in the coming months.

The core question is whether children's skills are enhanced in relation to improvements in teacher practice, the quality of the home environment, and the quality of the learning environment. We developed a measurement model that would enable data collection to address each of these issues, with the exception of the evaluation of the physical space within which Head Start programs are located. The first indicator that we used to assess whether there were significant changes from wave 1 to wave 2 within cohorts was the standard p-value. However, because extant literature addressing early learning environments for very young American Indian children is so limited, we opted to utilize a more liberal p-value ($p < .10$).

The second indicator we used was Cohen's d estimate of effect size. For every dependent measure in the assessment package and for every subscale within measures, we compared parent ratings for boys and girls, teacher ratings for boys and girls, parents versus teachers, American Indian teachers versus non–American Indian teachers, and all possible combinations not listed here. Across the three cohorts, this produced well over 1,500 comparisons. Because of the sample size and the number of significant tests that were performed, Bonferroni corrections resulted in extremely conservative criteria for accepting statistical significance, usually requiring a $p < .001$. Because so little is known about early childhood development in AI samples and

Table 3. Number of Children, Parents, and Head Start Teaching Staff Involved in Data Collection across Three Cohorts

Participant category	Cohort 1				Cohort 2				Cohort 3	
	Wave 1		Wave 2		Wave 1		Wave 2		Wave 1	
	Individual inventory	Self-report inventory	Individual inventory	Self-report inventory	Individual inventory	Self-report inventory	Individual inventory	Self-report inventory	Individual inventory	Self-report inventory
Child	122		108		150		123		120	
Parent		100		67		170		186		167
HS staff		22		20		24		29		27

NOTE: Wave 1 = Fall; Wave 2 = Spring.

Table 4. Wiba Anung Statistical Statements: Distribution of Cohen's Effect Sizes for Significant Findings Reported for Preacademic Achievement Skills for Cohorts 1, 2, and 3, Respectively, for Children's Behavior, Parent and Teacher Surveys, and Parent Substance Use

Cohort	Number of significant findings (criterion: $p < .10$)	Small effects $d = .07-.3$		Medium effects $d = .4-.7$		Large effects $d = .8-above$	
		n	%	n	%	n	%
1	290	90	31.0	159	54.8	41	14.1
2	488	319	64.4	157	32.2	12	2.5
3	78	60	76.9	18	23.0	0	0

within the context of HS, we opted to focus more heavily on effect size as an indicator of meaningfulness rather than corrected p values. Therefore, in reporting these findings we have included all $p < .10$ values with small to large effect sizes. For the 874 significant findings across the first two cohorts, the mean effect size was $d = 0.478$ (range 0.076 to 2.301). Table 4 shows the distribution of small, medium, and large effects for all significant findings.

Parent and Teacher Survey Information

Parenting Behaviors

Expectations of Children and *Empathy for Children* were two aspects of parenting that were assessed. For *Expectations of Children,* parents who had appropriate expectations understood children's development and were supportive of their children's display of developmentally appropriate behaviors (Bavolek, 1984). Parents who had inappropriate expectations for children's development were overly demanding and had inappropriately high expectations for children. Seventy-two percent of parents in cohort 1 scored in the average expectations range, 10% scored in the overly demanding range, and 18% scored in the appropriate expectations range. The relationships between parent expectations for children and their ratings of their own children's adaptive behavior were different for their sons and daughters. Parents with appropriate expectations for children rated their daughters lower and sons higher on both externalizing and internalizing behaviors (Lee, Farrell, Barnes, Gerde, & Fitzgerald, 2011; Farrell et al., 2011). Parents with overly demanding expectations for children rated their daughters higher on externalizing and internalizing behaviors, and rated their sons lower than normative standards.

For *Empathy for Children,* parents who exhibit high levels of empathy and nurturing behaviors recognize and value children's needs and feelings (Bavolek, 1984). Eighty percent of parents scored in the average empathy category, 15% scored in the low empathy category, and 5% scored in the high empathy category. Parents who exhibit low levels of empathy and nurturing toward children's needs often have difficulties coping with the stresses associated with parenting. In this sample, parents higher in empathy rated their children higher in social skills (competence). In addition, boys with high empathy parents were less likely to be rated higher on externalizing behavior problems, whereas girls were more likely to be rated higher (Lee et al., 2011).

Family Environment

Family environment was assessed by asking parents to report on items indicative of family cohesion (the family is supportive of each other and gets along) and family conflict (the family experience of conflict in the home) (Moos & Moos, 1994). Items were rated by parents as strongly disagree, disagree, uncertain, agree, or strongly agree. For Family Cohesion, 82% of parents agreed with the statement, "We get along well with each other," 80% agreed with "There is plenty of time and attention for everyone," and 94% agreed that "We help support one another." For Family Conflict, 14% agreed that "We sometimes hit each other," 21% agreed that "People get so angry they throw things," and 8% agreed that "We fight a lot in our home." In the data reported above, family conflict was related to higher levels of externalizing behavior and lower social skills in children, and higher levels of internalizing behavior problems in boys and girls, but especially for girls (Lee et al., 2011).

Family Support System

The presence of various support systems was reported by parents on a scale of "Not Available," "Not Helpful," "Sometimes Helpful," "Generally Helpful," "Very Helpful," and "Extremely Helpful" (Dunst, Trivette, & Deal, 1988). Sources of support were considered to be available and helpful if the parent reported the source as "Generally," "Very," or "Extremely" helpful. The top five sources of support in order were Head Start / Early Head Start, My Parents, Spouse/Partner, Relatives/Elders/Kin, and other Parents (Lee et al., 2011).

Ethnic Identity

Ethnic identity for AI parents was assessed using a number of questions regarding beliefs about their identity and engagement in various cultural activities. Three scale scores were created from these items, with each reflecting a specific aspect of ethnic identity. The first scale, "Exploration of Ethnic Identity," contained two items regarding the individual's participation in activities to learn more about being American Indian (Phinney, 1992). The second scale, "Participation in Cultural Activities," contained 10 items about participation in various cultural activities, customs, and traditions (Phinney, 1992). The third scale, "Perception of Positive Views by Others," contained four items about the individual's belief that others have a positive perception of American Indians (Crocker, Luhtanen, Blaine, & Broadnax, 1994). For "Exploration of Ethnic Identity," the percentage of respondents reporting High Levels, Moderate Levels, and Low Levels were 78%, 18%, and 4%, respectively. For "Participation in Cultural Activities," the percentages were 66%, 30%, and 4%, respectively, and for "Perception of Positive Views by Others" the percentages were 64%, 32%, and 4%, respectively. Clearly the vast majority of American Indian parents reported being moderately or highly invested in activities supportive of American Indian culture and identity.

Parental Educational Supports for Children

Parents rated their participation in educational supports for their preschool-aged children on a scale of "Rarely," "Sometimes," "Often," and "Always" (Fantuzzo, Tighe, & Childs, 2000). In general, parents reported "Often" or "Always" with respect to keeping regular morning and bedtime schedules, maintaining clear rules at home, exposing their children to learning opportunities in the community, spending time working with their children on literacy and numeracy skills, and on creative activities.

Parental Risky Behaviors

Parents reported on their own endorsement of and engagement in risky behaviors. Parent report of substance use behaviors was rated by the number of days the substance was used in the past 30 days. Parents reported on cigarette use and binge drinking (consuming five or more alcoholic drinks in a row within a couple of hours). Although we assessed a variety of indicators of dosage for both smoking and drinking, in this report we only refer to findings related to smoking within the 30 days immediately prior to assessment. We focus here on smoking because prevalence rates in the United States are highest for AI/AN teenagers and adults. In general, exposure to secondary smoke is related to low birth weight, decreased lung growth, respiratory disorders, otitis media, risk for obesity, attention deficit/hyperactivity disorder, behavior problems, neurocognitive deficits, inattention and oppositional behavior (DiFranza, Algno, & Weitzman, 2004; Fergusson, Haywood, & Lynskey, 1993; Glass et al., 2006).

Smoking

Health statistics maintained by the Intertribal Council of Michigan indicate that slightly more than 35% of Michigan's American Indian mothers reported smoking during pregnancy. In the Wiba Anung evaluation, we did not have access to information about prenatal smoking, but we did ask questions about smoking during the postnatal period. Maternal smoking during the past 30 days was related to ratings of their children's adaptive behavior (Fitzgerald et al., 2011). Using odds ratios to estimate the probability that children exposed to secondary smoke were more or less likely to experience particular problem behaviors, we found that children were more likely to be rated as having more physical problems (somatization), and a wide range of self-regulatory problems than were children whose parents did not smoke during the past 30 days (table 5). The same outcome was found for children whose parents

Table 5. Likelihood of Head Start Children Receiving Higher Parent Ratings on Subscales of the Behavioral Assessment Scales for Children in Relation to Self-Reported Parental Daily Smoking within the Past 30 days ($N = 88$; 41 smokers)

Child behavior scale	Odds ratio	Problem behavior
Anger control	3.00	More anger control
Aggression	3.69	Higher aggression
Anxiety	1.56	Higher anxiety
Depression	1.75	Higher depression
Somatization	5.71	More somatization
Internalizing behavior	3.00	More internalizing
Atypicality	2.40	Less atypical
Withdrawal	1.71	More withdrawn
Behavioral symptoms	1.71	More symptoms

Table 6. Likelihood of Head Start Children Receiving Higher Parent Ratings on Subscales of the Behavioral Assessment Scales for Children in Relation to Self-Reported Parental Smoking at Least ½ packs per day (N = 99; 48 smokers)

Child behavior scale	Odds ratio	Problem rating
Anger control	3.00	More anger control
Aggression	1.85	Higher aggression
Anxiety	1.71	Higher anxiety
Somatization	1.91	More somatization
Internalizing behavior	2.33	More internalizing
Atypicality	2.33	Less atypical
Withdrawal	1.71	More withdrawn

who smoked more than 10 cigarettes per day (table 6). These findings are consistent with a broader literature on the effects of secondary smoking on very young children. Note that all of our indicators were linked to parent perceptions of behavioral outcomes. We do not know what effects parental smoking may have had on children's physical health (e.g., asthmas, illnesses), although this work is an important target of future research and of great interest to our community partners.

Teacher Behavior

Stress

In order to understand the level and source of stress in the lives of Head Start teachers, we asked teachers to report on the occurrence of a variety of different events (Frequency of Life Events). We asked teachers to then report on how stressful it was to experience the event.

During the fall, compared to AI teachers, non-AI teachers reported significantly fewer difficulties with Other Workers ($d = 0.96$), but more hassles with Relatives ($d = 1.05$) and Household ($d = 1.04$). By spring, compared to AI, non-AI teachers reported less difficulties with Money ($d = 0.36$) and more hassles with Friend ($d = 1.08$), Supervisor ($d = 1.00$), Other Worker ($d = 1.62$), Relatives ($d = 0.78$), and Health ($d = 0.91$).

In the spring, AI teachers reported decreases in hassles with Other Worker ($d = 2.06$), whereas non-AI teachers reported increases in hassles with Other Worker ($d = 0.40$), Relatives ($d = 1.13$), and decreases in hassles with Household tasks ($d = 1.27$). Clearly the life experiences of both AI and non-AI teachers fluctuated over the year. What impacts these fluctuations may have on children's classroom performance remain to be determined.

Perceptions of Children's Adaptive Behavior

One set of analyses focuses on children who are perceived to be sufficiently troubled that they fall in the clinical and at-risk distributions as assessed by the Behavior Assessment Scales for Children (BASC; Reynolds & Kamphaus, 2002). For example, the percentages of children in the fall who were rated in the combined clinical and at-risk ranges for Aggression, Hyperactivity, Attention Problems, and Atypicality were 16%, 18%, 19%, and 12% respectively, whereas by spring, these percentages were 20%, 18%, 16%, and 17% respectively.

The percentages of children who were rated in the combined clinical and at-risk ranges for Anxiety, Depression, Physical Concerns (Somatization), and Withdrawal were 18%, 16%, 9%, and 12% respectively; at the spring assessment these percentages were 23%, 22%, 30%, and 11% respectively. What accounts for these overall changes in perceived difficulties remains to be determined.

The percentages of children in the fall who were rated in the combined clinical and at-risk categories for Adaptability and Social Skills were 15% and 12% respectively, whereas in the spring, the percentages were 15% and 7% respectively, suggesting that something was positively influencing social skill development over the course of the year.

Parent Teacher Perceptions

The BASC assesses others' perceptions of children's behavior within three important behavioral domains, labeled clinical, adaptive, and content. The TPT was interested in evaluating the extent to which parents and teachers perceived children similarly (table 7). Overall, parents tended to perceive their children as having less difficulties than teachers did, with the clear exceptions of attention problems and developmental social disorders.

Equally interesting is that within cohort 1, AI and non-AI teachers also did not fully share perceptions about children (table 8). For example, American Indian teachers tended to perceive children as higher in internalizing behaviors and physical complaints (somatization), but they perceived girls as having less difficulty with externalizing behavior and hyperactivity

Table 7. Cohort 1, 2008–2009: Behaviors Assessed by the Behavioral Assessment Scale for Children on which Parents' Rated Children Higher (H) or Lower (L) Than Did Teachers

BASC scale	All children		Boys		Girls	
	Fall	Spring	Fall	Spring	Fall	Spring
Clinical scales						
Externalizing behavior problems	L	L				
Internalizing behavior problems	L	L	L	L	L	L
Aggression	L	L			L	L
Anxiety	L	L	L	L	L	L
Depression	L	L				
Attention problems	H	H	H	H	H	H
Adaptive scales						
Adaptability	L	L	L		L	L
Somatization	L	L	L	L	L	L
Withdrawal	H	H				
Social skills		L	L		L	L
Content scales						
Bullying	L	L			L	L
Developmental social disorders	H	H	H			H
Resiliency	L	L				

Table 8. Cohort 1, 2008–2009: Behaviors Assessed by the Behavioral Assessment Scale for Children on which American Indian Teachers Rated Children Higher (H) or Lower (L) Than Did Non–American Indian Teachers

BASC scale	All children		Boys		Girls	
	Fall	Spring	Fall	Spring	Fall	Spring
Clinical scales						
Externalizing behavior problems						L
Internalizing behavior problems	H		H		H	
Aggression					L	
Anxiety	H		H			
Depression						
Attention problems						
Hyperactivity						L
Adaptive scales						
Adaptability					H	
Somatization	H		H		H	
Withdrawal						
Social skills				L	H	
Content scales						
Bullying						
Developmental social disorders				H		
Resiliency						
Negative emotionality						

than did non-AI teachers. All of these contrasts between teachers and parents, and within teacher categories will be examined in more detail to determine whether their influences on children's behavior and/or academic skill attainment are direct, or whether they are important mediators or moderators of other influences on child outcomes.

Children's Academic Skills

Ultimately, efforts to change educational systems and the life space within which children develop must have positive outcomes on children's behavior and academic readiness skills. In our work we are primarily focused on determining the extent to which the enhancement of teacher skills, parenting practices, and culturally appropriate learning environments affects children's preacademic skills, the skills that prepare children to be ready for the transition to kindergarten and the early elementary years. First, however, we needed to have a solid understanding of children's current levels of academic skill attainment, particularly with respect to numeracy, literacy, and perceptual motor skills. Therefore, we assessed children's behavior relative to performance for age groups on a standardized test of very young children's skills related to numeracy, identification of shapes and colors, basic preliteracy skills (picture description and spatial recognition),

Table 9. Preacademic Skills: The Percentage of Children Who Met Expected Norms in the Fall on the Lollipop Test Subscales for Colors and Shapes, Picture Description and Spatial Recognition, Identification of Numbers and Counting, Identification of Letters and Writing

Scale	Cohort 1		Cohort 2		Cohort 3	
	Boys	Girls	Boys	Girls	Boys	Girls
Colors and shapes	77.6%	82.5%	68.9%	83.6%	70.7%	86.7%
Picture description and spatial recognition	70.7%	81.0%	55.4%	64.4%	70.0%	70.0%
Numbers and counting	43.1%	50.8%	41.9%	47.9%	31.7%	51.7%
Letters and writing	25.9%	39.7%	24.3%	41.1%	21.7%	51.7%

and letter identification and writing (Chew & Lang, 1990). In this instance, we present data from all three cohorts of children.

Table 9 depicts the percentage of children who met or exceeded the expected norms on all four scales of school readiness in the fall. Data, shown by gender and cohort, indicate that while the majority of children in this project are meeting the expected norms for color and shape identification as well as basic preliteracy skills, far fewer are meeting the expected norms for numeracy and letter knowledge. We also see a trend for girls to be slightly more likely to meet the expected norms as compared to boys in all four subscales.

However, over the course of the school year, a large percentage of children who did not score within the normative range of children improved their skills enough to move from not meeting the expected norms in the fall to meeting the expected norms in the spring. Upon examination of the data from all three cohorts, approximately 50% of the children who did not meet expected norms on Colors and Shapes increased their capacity in this subject to the extent that they were able to score high enough to meet the expected norms in the spring. For Picture Description and Spatial Recognition, approximately 66% of the children who did not meet expected norms increased their capacity in this subject to the extent that they were able to score high enough to meet the expected norms in the spring. For Numbers and Counting and for Letters and Writing, 37% and 41% of the children who did not meet expected norms increased their capacity in these subjects to the extent that they were able to score high enough to meet the expected norms in the spring. Thus, many children did make significant gains in their academic knowledge. However, fewer children made these gains in number and letter knowledge. Given the importance of these subjects, we have shared these findings with our partners, and they are actively implementing plans to address this need.

Summary

Wiba Anung is a research project guided by a heuristic model that posited that enhancing teacher skills would result in better child academic and behavioral outcomes. Because the project was anchored in community-based participatory research methods, all project activities were developed with strong input from members of Michigan's HS AI communities. Three cohorts of data collection have been completed and the descriptive information positions the research team to proceed with model testing. Thus, the "conclusions" in this chapter speak to critical areas of model testing more than they provide definitive answers to program effects on child outcomes.

Therefore, the most appropriate conclusions from this collaborative work with our community partners are as follows:

- Use of community-based participatory research methods assured that all facets of the project were cocreated. The emphasis on cocreation included training tribal members in data assessment techniques, and participation in annual research report and discussion sessions in which participants developed skills for identifying program strengths and needs from child outcome data. The strength of the TPT assures that we will continue to cocreate measurement models to test the various hypotheses generated by the heuristic model and the descriptive findings from three cohorts of data.

- Slow but steady progress is being achieved with respect to increasing the number of teachers with degrees in child development / early childhood education. Turnover in teachers with bachelor's degrees continues to be a problem due to salary differentials between tribal HS programs and public/private schools.

- Teachers of the AI/AN HES programs can effectively engage in professional development delivered through a distance learning online platform for improving teachers' practice and children's mathematics skills. Future work will study elements of the professional development curriculum and process, including dosage as contributing factors for the lack of significant growth in literacy skills for treatment versus control children.

- Qualitative studies of tribal culture and language have broad implications for teacher training (the majority of teachers are not AI) as well as program curricular modifications and classroom environmental quality. PhotoVoice qualitative methodology was an especially effective way to bring tribal voices to bear on our understanding of American Indian culture and community aspirations for their children.

- Parents, AI, and non-AI teachers often differ in their ratings of children's behavior. We will assess the extent to which these differences are related to variations in children's academic, cognitive, and social-emotional development.

- Sufficient evidence exists indicating that a minority of parents are heavy smokers. We will assess the extent to which these factors have direct or mediating influences on children's academic, cognitive, and social-emotional development.

- Teachers vary in the frequency of daily problem areas and the extent to which they perceive these events to be particularly stressful. We will assess the extent to which these factors influence teacher's perceptions of child behavior, as well as children's academic, cognitive, and social-emotional development.

Community-based participatory research provides magic moments to enhance the research and evaluation knowledge of diverse members of tribal communities. CBPR approaches provide space and time for university researchers and AI parents, teachers, program directors, and elders to build relationships based on trust and mutual work on behalf of AI children and programs. In addition, it provided the process to build sustainable assessment skills among AI staff so that monitoring of teacher classroom practice and assessment of children's performance can proceed independent of university involvement.

Notes

All data referred to in this chapter have appeared in various presentations as listed in the references and eventually will be published in full detail in peer review outlets.

We express thanks to everyone associated with the Wiba Anung evaluation project: parents, elders, directors, teachers, aides, support staff, children, and researchers. Without everyone's cooperation and involvement, the Wiba Anung partnership would not have been successful.

References

Allen, J., Mohatt, G. V., Markstrom, C. A., Byers, L., & Novins, D. K. (2012). "Oh no, we are just getting to know you": The relationship in research with children and youth in indigenous communities. *Child Development Perspectives, 6*(1), 55–60.

Barnes, J. V., Gerde, H., Belleau, A., Farrell, P. A., & Fitzgerald, H. E. (2010). Improving children's academic readiness through high quality tribal Head Start programs. Paper presented at the American Psychological Association Division 45: Society for the Study of Ethnic Minority children. Ann Arbor, MI.

Barnes, J. V., Gerde, H., Fitzgerald, H. E., Farrell, P. A., Calcatera, M., & Parish, A. (2011). Growth in children's language and cognitive skills across one year of American Indian Head Start. Poster presented at the 12th Annual Meeting of the National Outreach Scholarship Conference, East Lansing, MI.

Bavolek, S. (1984). *Handbook for the AAPI (Adult-Adolescent Parenting Inventory)*. Park City, Utah: Family Development Resources.

Burchinal, M. R., Cryer, D., Clifford, R. M., & Howes, C. (2002). Caregiver training and classroom quality in child care centers. *Applied Developmental Science, 6,* 2–11.

Campbell, C. D., & Evans-Campbell, T. (2011). Historical trauma and Native American child development and mental health: An overview. In M. C. Sarche, P. Spicer, P. Farrell, & H. E. Fitzgerald (Eds.), *American Indian children and mental health: Development, context, prevention and treatment* (pp. 1–26). Santa Barbara, CA: Praeger Press.

Chew, A. L., & Lang, W. S. (1990). Predicting academic achievement in kindergarten and first grade from prekindergarten scores on the Lollipop Test and Dial. *Educational and Psychological Measurement, 50,* 431–37.

Crocker, J., Luhtanen, R., Blaine, B., & Broadnax, S. (1994). Collective self-esteem and psychological well-being among white, black, and Asian college students. *Personality and Social Psychology Bulletin, 20*(5), 503–513.

de Kruif, R. E. L., McWilliam, R. A., Ridley, S. M., & Wakely, M. B. (2000). Classification of teachers' interaction behaviors in early childhood classrooms. *Early Childhood Research Quarterly, 15,* 247–268.

Demmert, W. G. Jr. (2001). Improving academic performance among Native American students: A review of the research literature. Charleston, WV: ERIC Clearinghouse on Rural Education and Small Schools.

Demmert, W. G. Jr., & Towner, J. (2003). A review of the research literature on the influences of culturally based education on the academic performance of Native American students. Portland, OR: Northwest Regional Education Laboratory.

DiFranza, J. R., Algno, C. A., & Weitzman, M. (2004). Prenatal and postnatal environmental tobacco smoke exposure and children's health. *Pediatrics, 119*(4), 1007–1015.

Duncan, G. J., Dowsett, C. J., Claessens, A., Magnuson, K., Huston, A. C., Klebanov, … Japel, C. (2007). School readiness and later achievement. *Developmental Psychology, 43*, 1428–1446.

Dunn, L. M., & Dunn, D. M. (2007). *Peabody Picture Vocabulary Test* (4th ed.). *(PPVT-4)*. Circle Pines, MN: American Guidance Services.

Dunst, C. J., Trivette, C. M., & Deal, A. G. (1988). *Enabling and empowering families: Principles and guidelines for practice*. Cambridge, MA: Brookline Books.

Early, D. M., Maxwell, K. L., Burchinal, M. R., Alva, S., Bender, R. H., Bryant, D., … Zill, N. (2007). Teachers' education, classroom quality, and young children's academic skills: Results from seven studies of preschool programs. *Child Development, 78*, 558–580.

Fantuzzo, J. W., Tighe, E., & Childs, S. (2000). Family involvement questionnaire: A multivariate assessment of family participation in early childhood education. *Journal of Educational Psychology, 92*(2), 367–376.

Farrell, P., Lee, K. S., Barnes, J. V., Gerde, H. K., Fitzgerald, H. E., & Belleau, A. (2011). The relations of quality of family environment and parenting belief to young children's socioemotional functioning. Poster presented at the biennial meeting of the Society for Research in Child Development, Montreal, Canada, April.

Fergusson, D. M., Haywood, J. H., & Lynskey, M. T. (1993). Prevalence and comorbidity of DSM-III-R diagnosis in a birth cohort of 15 year olds. *American Journal of Child and Adolescent Psychiatry, 32*, 1127–1134.

Fisher, P. A., & Ball, T. J. (2002). The Indian Family Wellness Project: An application of the tribal participatory research model. *Prevention Science, 3*, 235–240.

Fitzgerald, H. E., Barnes, J. V., Farrell, P. A., Belleau, A., Calcatera, M., & Paris, A. (2008). Bridging the gap: Understanding cultural factors relevant to American Indian Head Start programs. Poster presented at the biennial meeting of the Society for Research in Child Development.

Fitzgerald, H. E., Lee, K. S., Barnes, J. V., Farrell, P., Gerde, H. K., & Belleau, A. (2011). Maternal smoking is related to Head Start children's risk for behavior problems. Poster presented at the 12th Annual Meeting of the National Outreach Scholarship Conference, East Lansing, MI.

Fitzgerald, H. E., & Farrell, P. (2012). Fulfilling the promise: Creating a child development research agenda with Native communities. *Child Development Perspectives, 6*(1), 75–78.

Freire, P. (1990). *Pedagogy of the oppressed*. New York: Continuum.

Foster-Fishman, P., Newell, B., Deacon, X., Nievar, M.A., & McCann, P. (2005). Using methods that matter: The impact of reflection, dialogue, and voice. *American Journal of Community Psychology, 36*, 275–291.

Galligher, R. V., Tsethlikai, M. M., & Stolle, D. (2012). Perspectives of Native and non-Native scholars: Opportunities for collaboration. *Child Development Perspectives, 6*(1), 66–74.

Garet, M. S., Porter, A. C., Desimone, L., Birman, B. F., & Yoon, K. S. (2001). What makes professional development effective? Results from a national sample of teachers. *American Educational Research Journal, 38*, 915–945.

Gerde, H. K., Barnes, J. V., Belleau, A., Rau, L., Farrell, P. A., Parish, A., ... Fitzgerald, H. E. (2012). A Systematic Evaluation of the Cultural Content and Language Instruction in American Indian Head Start. *Journal of American Indian Education, 51*, 40–63.

Gerde, H. K., Barnes, J. V., Whitty, H. E., Belleau, A., & Fitzgerald, H. E. (2011). Effects of distance learning professional development for teachers of the American Indian Head Start on children's math and literacy outcomes. Poster presented at the biennial meeting of the Society for Research in Child Development, Montreal, Canada, April.

Gerde, H. K, & Powell, D. R. (2009). Teacher education, book-reading practices, and children's language growth across one year of Head Start. *Early Education and Development, 20*, 211–237.

Glass, J. M., Adams, K. M., Nigg, J. T., Wong, M. M., Puttler, L. I., Buu, A., ... Zucker, R. A. (2006). Smoking is associated with neurocognitive deficits in alcoholism. *Drug and Alcohol Dependence, 82*, 119–126.

Gottman, J., & Declaire, J. (1997*). Raising an Emotionally Intelligent Child: The Heart of Parenting.* New York: Fireside.

Jollie-Trottier, T., Holm, J. E., & MacDonald, J. D. (2008). Correlates of overweight and obesity in American Indian children. *Journal of Pediatric Psychology, 33*, 1–9.

Jones, D. S. (2006). The persistence of American Indian health disparities. *American Journal of Public Health, 96*, 2122–2134.

Krueger, R. A., & Casey, M. A. (2000). *Focus groups: A practical guide for applied research* (3rd ed.). Thousand Oaks, CA: Sage.

Lee, K. S., Farrell, P. A., Barnes, J. V., Gerde, H. K., & Fitzgerald, H. E. (2011). The relations of the quality of family environment and parenting beliefs to young children's socioemotional functioning. Poster presented at the 12th Annual Meeting of the National Outreach Scholarship Conference, East Lansing, MI.

Marks, E. L., Moyer, M. K., Roche, M., & Graham, E. T. (2003). Summary of research and publications on early childhood for American Indian and Alaska Native children. Washington, DC: U.S. Department of Health and Human Services.

Marr, C. J. (2010). *Assimilation through education: Indian boarding schools in the Pacific Northwest.* University Libraries Digital Collections, University of Washington.

Moos, R., & Moos, B. (1994). *Family Environment Scale Manual: Development, applications, research (3rd ed.).* Palo Alto, CA: Consulting Psychologist Press.

National Institute of Child Health and Human Development Early Child Care Research Network (NICHHD). (2002). Characteristics and quality of child care for toddlers and preschoolers. *Applied Developmental Science, 4*, 116–135.

Phinney, J. (1992). The Multigroup Ethnic Identity Measure: A new scale for use with adolescents and young adults from diverse groups. *Journal of Adolescent Research, 7*, 156–176.

Powell, D. R., Diamond, K. E., Burchinal, M. R., & Koehler, M. J. (2010). Effects of an early literacy professional development intervention of Head Start teachers and children. *Journal of Educational Psychology, 102*, 229–312.

Reyhner, J., & Eder, J. (1989). A history of Indian education. Billings, MT: Eastern Montana College.

Reynolds, C. R., & Kamphaus, R. W. (2002). *A clinician's guide to the BASC.* New York: Guilford Press.

Reynolds, C. R., & Kamphaus, R. W. (2004). *Behavior Assessment System of Children* (2nd ed.). San Antonio, TX: Pearson.

Sanchez, S. Y., & Thorp, E. K. (2010). Teaching to transform. *Zero to Three, 31*, 44–49.

Starnes, B. A. (2006). What we don't know can hurt them: White teachers, Indian children. *Phi Delta Kappan, 87*, 384–92.

Thompson, N. L. (2009). Understanding the importance of Head Start in Michigan's nine American Indian communities: A PhotoVoice project. Presented as part of P. G. Spicer and M. C. Sarche, Advancing Research on Early Childhood Education in Indian Country, Society for Research in Child Development, Denver, CO, April.

Thompson, N. L., & Belleau, A. (2009). Viewing and applying voices and visions from Michigan's American Indian Head Start programs: A PhotoVoice research project to document program needs. Presented at the National Indian Head Start Directors Association 19th Management Training Conference, Oklahoma City, OK, June.

Thompson, N. L., & Belleau, A. (2011). Methodological engagement: Using PhotoVoice to empower American Indian communities. Poster presented at the 12th annual meeting of the National Outreach Scholarship Conference, East Lansing, MI.

Thompson, N. L., & Miller, N. C. (2009). Voices and visions from Michigan's American Indian Head Start Programs: A PhotoVoice project. Paper presented at the American Educational Research Association, San Diego, CA, April.

United States Census Bureau. (2000). *Census 2000*. Washington, DC: Author.

Wang, C., & Burris, M. (1994). Empowerment through photo novella: Portraits of participation. *Health Education Quarterly, 21*, 171–86.

Wang, C., Burris, M., & Xiang, Y. P. (1996). Chinese village women as visual anthropologists: A participatory approach to reaching policymakers. *Social Science and Medicine, 42*, 1391–1400.

Wasik, B. A., Bond, M. A., & Hindman, A. (2006). The effects of a language and literacy intervention on Head Start children and teachers. *Journal of Educational Psychology, 98*, 63–74.

Cross-Cultural Community Engagement, Elizabeth Kübler-Ross's Model of Death and Dying, and Racial Identity Development

Michelle R. Dunlap

Scholars have proposed that Elizabeth Kübler-Ross's model of death and dying can be applied to any change that requires loss or, vice versa, to any loss that requires change (Goldsworthy, 2005). The community engagement process is one that involves significant change, negotiation, adaptation, and even loss. Within the community engagement process, constituents are challenged to try to understand one another, to work in partnership, and to evolve. Many times partners are traversing socioeconomic, racial, ethnic, cultural, gender, sexual orientation, and/or religious differences. For those who grew up in relatively homogenous environments, the community engagement process can provide major challenges and adjustments (Dunlap, 2000; Dunlap & Webster, 2009; Evans, Taylor, Dunlap, & Miller, 2009). One of the greatest challenges that those engaged in the multicultural community engagement process must navigate is that of coming to terms with the injustice that they find in communities that are different from their own (Dunlap, 1998; Dunlap, Scoggin, Green, & Davi, 2007). Engagers also may enter the community engagement process at different levels of awareness of, and preparedness for, talking about the role and impact of race, culture, discrimination, oppression, and so forth, on their and others' experiences. Students exposed to diversity, regardless of their own race, ethnicity, or other identifying factors might feel more comfortable in diverse settings. But because factors such as race, ethnicity, socioeconomics, and so forth influence our access to diverse experiences, they then also can play a role in how we respond to such experiences. But it depends on what kind of experiences, how in-depth, how frequent and consistent, how stereotypical or varied, those experiences are throughout our development (Dunlap, 2000). Thus, engagers—both because of, and regardless of, race and other differences and backgrounds—may come to the community

163

engagement process at different levels of preparedness for observing, discussing, and otherwise appropriately responding to the diversity that they may encounter (Dunlap et al., 2007; Tatum, 1992). All of this may prompt a loss of what feels normal to many involved in the cross-cultural engagement process.

The Kübler-Ross model of death and dying offers five stages through which a person negotiates when coming to terms with death or other major trauma: denial, anger, bargaining, depression, and acceptance. This chapter will present this five-stage model and will propose it as a useful model for helping community engagers understand the processes that they may experience when participating in cross-cultural community engagement. Parallels will be proposed between Kübler-Ross's model and experiences that those participating in cross-cultural community engagement may have. The usefulness of Kübler-Ross's model for thinking about community engagement and the diversity learning process also will be explored in light of racial identity development models.

Stage 1: Denial

Elizabeth Kübler-Ross described denial as "a healthy way of dealing with a painful situation" with which a person has to cope for a relatively significant period of time (1997, p. 52). She said that it serves as a "buffer" that allows us to "collect" ourselves, "mobilize others," and keep from overreacting (p. 52). As with any of her stages, a person can move in and out of, and backward and forward within, denial, which can blend with the other stages; a person can even skip denial altogether and later return to it (Goldsworthy, 2005; Kübler-Ross, 1997). Connecting the concept of denial to the experience of community engagement, and to service learning specifically, some student engagers have never had to think critically about racism and other forms of oppression, while others have had to grapple with such issues on a regular basis. Therefore, when high school or college students go into the community to engage in service either as volunteers or as part of service learning or other curriculum-based learning programs, they may be at different levels of preparedness for encountering the diversity and multicultural issues that they may face (Dunlap, 2000 & 1998). For example, a European American (or white) student from a very privileged environment—and especially if it's one lacking a diverse educational or experiential curriculum—may not anticipate the similarities and differences that they may observe among community partners and environments (Dunlap et al., 2007). They may expect very negative and inaccurately stereotypical behavior and simple explanations for the challenges that they observe. Further, they may not yet understand why in an economically challenged minority community, partners may not welcome engagers with opened arms. They could fret as to why people with whom they are attempting to engage may seem less open, or more cautious, toward them upon their initial meetings. They may not understand the sociohistorical factors, influences, and experiences that may contribute to some community partners' initial wariness of them. Therefore, some students or other community partners may be very unaware of, or unknowledgeable about, the community in which they are trying to engage, especially if they are from different racial, ethnic, and/or socioeconomic backgrounds. If inexperienced in a diversity of cultures and backgrounds, they even may be unwilling to recognize the similarities and/or broad or nuanced differences between their home community and their service-learning community (Dunlap et al., 2007). These students or other community partners may be committed to very well-intentioned, but somewhat color-blind, philosophies where they do not allow themselves to consciously observe or perceive intergroup differences in personal or community challenges, cultural behavior, or treatment by others. On the other hand, a student who has grown up in a very diverse community or who has had exposure to a very diverse educational curriculum regardless of their own race, ethnicity, or other backgrounds, may not be as put off by the cautious worldviews and other adaptive tendencies of some of their community partners, and therefore may not be as likely to let them impact their motivation and participation. They may have had a wide enough range of multicultural experiences that allow them to not be discouraged right away by initial cautiousness in partners.

To offer an example of possible denial, in an educational context that was known for its diversity challenges (e.g., the children consisted of 95% African American and Latina, and the teachers were 94% European American, and the teaching staff had little in-depth diversity training at the time), a European American service-learning student reported in her course journal that in her four months at the site, she saw no indications of socioeconomic, racial, gender, or other disparities or incidences. This may be true; however, it also could be an indication of lack of awareness and/or her denial about the uncomfortable and sometimes painful concept of racism and discrimination. A service-learning student shares from her journal:

> The classroom I volunteer at has contained a very diverse group of students. From what I have been able to observe, the children get along very well and do not discriminate. . . . the children often chose to work with other students who were very different from them, and everyone including the teachers get along.

Thus, the service learner conceptualized the environment as apparently free from discrimination and other issues because the children seemed to play well together. She seemed not to notice, or tended to deny, disparities in the diversity of the student-staff ratios, the tendency for the few European American children to escape disciplinary action, and the lack of diversity in curriculum materials.

Another student, who up to this point also had little to criticize about the same environment, begins to use the language of difference or diversity wherein she acknowledges that most of the children are African American whereas she is not. Further, she seems to grasp that because of the children's experiences as African Americans, she might need to anticipate some possible differences (e.g., Lynch & Hanson, 2006) as she continues her work in that environment in order to be culturally competent and effective:

> My experience today was educational. I realized that, as most of these children are African-American, they may be more sensitive and need to feel-out a person before trusting them. The aesthetic cues I gave them might have been misinterpreted, and I will try to talk to them more as a peer than a teacher. Although there is around an eight-year age difference, they talk about the same things I discuss with my friends. I need to make a stronger bond of trust before making demands upon them. Although it will be difficult to form this bond because I only volunteer once a week, I hope that by the end of the semester they will trust me, and friendships can be formed.

165

So this student is able to connect that she may need to spend more time than she first expected, building rapport with these children. She begins to move away from denial of any differences toward a greater place of awareness of the cross-cultural nuances that may exist within her site compared to the contexts of which she has been accustomed.

Stage 2: Anger

Anger in Kübler-Ross's model is characterized by the rage, blaming, envy, and jealousy over the unfairness of the unexpected death process (1997). It is proposed here that community engagers may also experience shock and anger as they begin to observe and witness the disparities that exists in communities outside of their own—the poverty, oppression, racism, sexism, exploitation, discrimination, and so on (e.g., National Urban League 2008). The disparate conditions that can exist and be observed by them over time can be not only overwhelming, but also disillusioning (Dunlap, 1997; Dunlap et al., 2007). Some engagers may then try to withdraw from and avoid the community engagement experience altogether (perhaps a form of denial), while others may become overly sensitive and may try to fight every instance of unfairness that they witness and then quickly burn out. While hopefully finding a healthy balance, they may become even more committed over a longer duration of time in their fight against the systems of oppression that they observe (Dunlap, 1997). Two European American students express their initial disappointment and anger in reaction to instances involving prejudice and racism:

> Today, while [engaged in service learning at a high school], one of the teachers made a reference to being in an airplane. One of the minority students said she had never been in an airplane, and [the white male teacher] responded with disbelief and teasing. I was totally outraged! There are a million and one reasons why she may have never been in an airplane, but especially if the reason was fear or simply lack of funds it was completely inappropriate for him to act like that. I was just really struck by his insensitivity. . . . The students say explicitly that they get the feeling that the majority of their teachers don't care about them, don't know them, and don't want to know them.

> This is the first time that a racist situation has affected me personally, and I just don't understand some people in this world. . . . Although I know that racism does exist, I have a hard time dealing with the extent to which it exists. . . . Just last year, my sister married a Cuban man. . . . He has very dark skin, and it is actually darker than the rest of his family. His skin color is what some people think make him different, or not as good as the dominant culture. When they were trying to find a church to get married at, they could not find a Catholic priest who would marry them because they were an interracial couple. Then, when they were trying to find an apartment to live in, they were told there were none available. This happened in a white, upper-class, suburban neighborhood. Although they eventually did find a place to live, they had a hard time doing so. I am 21 years old, and racism still confuses me. I cannot figure out how so many young children, especially children other than white children, deal with racism on a day-to-day basis. I think that is very sad, but we owe the young children in society a lot of credit for dealing with such hard issues.

Once becoming more aware of the prejudice, racism, discrimination, and everyday disparities that exist across communities, some engagers can, for a period of time, find themselves
feeling frustrated by almost everything that they encounter that has any hint of unfairness,
prejudice, racism, or discrimination. In the course of a couple of days, the following European American student found herself frustrated by numerous race-related observations.
Noted here are her upset with the lack of bilingual education, the lack of multicultural
materials, and the rude behavior of a male staff member at a training event, to illustrate a
few of her concerns:

> M. is the only child of color in the class, and from what I've seen in the halls, she's one of the very
> few children of color in the school. . . . The teacher was very excited about [a concept she had
> learned] until I mentioned that M. had said it in Spanish. Then [the teacher] just said, "Oh" and
> sounded disappointed (the teacher has told me to take note of the numbers, colors, and shapes
> M. knows in English. The ones she knows in Spanish don't count). . . . I find it very frustrating that
> the teacher does not care about M.'s Spanish. . . . The fact that she can recognize the number 8
> and say it in Spanish is not insignificant. At the very least, it shows that M. understands the
> concept. . . . The environment seems restrictive enough for the English-speaking children, but for
> K. and M., who have a hard time being understood even when they are allowed to, the environ-
> ment must be even more oppressive. . . . [Further,] from what I have seen, the teachers do not
> make any effort to teach any kind of a multicultural curriculum. . . . How can one expect these
> children to see other cultures as valid and not to be biased toward their own culture?. . . . [In
> addition, at a talk I attended] I was annoyed and offended by a man in the audience who kept
> asking questions and making comments. It was not what he had to say that bothered me. In fact,
> I do not even remember what he said. What bothered me was the fact that he felt so free to inter-
> rupt [an internationally renowned minority female scholar]. What immediately occurred to me is
> that no one interrupts when a man gives a presentation. Since this presentation, I have gone out
> of my way to try to recall a time, and I have yet to remember ever seeing a member of an audience
> do this to a man. With men, the audience members do not interrupt like this. They either wait
> until the question time or ask questions at other appropriate times. What this man was doing was
> just jumping in whenever he felt like saying something. He was making comments as if she
> needed help with her argument. It annoyed me, and I wondered if [the scholar herself] noticed.

So as you can see, this student is finding herself feeling critical of many things that are coming into her awareness as her knowledge of multicultural and diversity issues increase. The
community engager's parallel stage of anger, over a prolonged time, could possibly become
tiring, and engagers may find that they have to start choosing their battles carefully (perhaps
a function of the bargaining stage ahead). The following student shows signs that she is
beginning to move out of the anger stage and perhaps to a new stage when she admits that
she does not know what to do, or how to, by herself, tackle societal problems that are so
large:

> After reading so much literature on African-American children, and in particular low income
> African-American children, it seems as though the less money a family has the more difficult it
> is for the children to succeed. It truly angers me for this becomes a horrible, self-perpetuating
> cycle. . . . It seems so disheartening to think that the kindergarteners that were sitting in front of
> me today all come from unequal planes merely due to factors that they had no control over. . . .

167

The hurdles they must overcome seem greater than their competitors' and it seems unjust. So what do you do? I'm not sure how to correct the imbalance. But I'm still thinking about it.

So this student appears to be in the process of admitting to herself that she alone cannot fix this very complex problem, but that she will cognitively and emotionally grapple with it nonetheless. The following student, also European American, grapples with disheartening and anger-provoking experiences, and asks many questions. She struggles to not jump to conclusions and to not respond too hastily. She attempts to "choose her battles carefully" rather than fighting them all at once, and channels her energy into thinking about goals for herself for the future when she becomes an enlightened educator:

After this, we went downstairs for school pictures, and I noticed many interesting things that I previously overlooked before! The [white] staff wanted all the [predominantly minority] children to stand in the same way, and they took it upon themselves to "fix" these children's appearances so they looked decent for these pictures. The photographer gave all the children these small, black, fine-toothed combs for them to "fix" their hair. J. [an African American child]'s photo was first, and he was jokingly combing his hair with his comb, which was far too small for his curly hair. The photographer joked with him, "Hey boy, you look like you need a really big comb for all that hair." . . . I am hesitant to make any generalizations or judgments about this, but I do think that many of their comments and their philosophy to correct the children's appearances seemed inappropriate. Doesn't this assume that something is wrong with the children's looks in the first place? Shouldn't pictures reflect how the children want to look themselves?. . . . I did not bring the topic up with [the teacher] after class, because I thought about choosing my battles carefully and that this probably would not be the most crucial of issues. This classroom is hers, and I need to work with what she wants her children to do. I did think about this sort of [situation] for my own classroom and my own group of children. I think I want to nurture their ideas and their personal style. People are different and should we not nurture and accept that in the classroom?

Therefore, although this student was upset by the treatment of the minority children during the class photos, she elected to postpone reacting right away in favor of processing the situation further first. So the latter two students both suggest that they are struggling with their anger, but they also illustrate a move away from anger in the direction of bargaining.

Stage 3: Bargaining

Kübler-Ross's third stage, bargaining, is characterized by an attempt to negotiate to avoid death and gain an extension of life. During this stage, many what-ifs are considered, and the patient struggles to begin making sense of the situation and its expected permanency (Kübler-Ross, 1997). Conceptualized in terms of community engagement, a parallel may be the "grappling" that partners experience as they try to make sense of their diversity-related observations, experiences, and emotions involved in their work with community partners. Students illustrate this grappling in their journals:

The [multicultural] environment that these children are in is very different from the one that I grew up in. My pre-school and early schooling was in a predominately white area. Our education was nowhere near as politically correct as these children receive. Noticing this today made me realize that I have to work hard to remove my preconceived notions, or at least understand the restrictions these notions put on me. . . . I must confess that I am very wary of making observational judgments that are based on race. I think that it is definitely beneficial for me to be in this diverse setting, for this reason alone. It is easier to take a color-blind approach, but for the first time I am having the opportunity to observe the differences in learning styles. These differences can be brought about by race/ethnic differences, gender, or socioeconomic. This [preschool] takes great care to teach that these differences are not deficits. Different cultures are explored, not ignored. . . . Teachers there are also quick to acknowledge differences in racial and ethnic backgrounds when the children bring them up. The discussions help the children to understand why their differences make them unique, but that they are no better, or worse than anyone else.

The above student does not deny differences, and is in an emotionally healthy environment to explore them. She is able to work on sorting out her own past, and attempts to reconcile it with the new experiences she is having. The next student, also from a European American upper-middle-class background speaks of the "shifting" that occurs while in the stage that may parallel Kübler-Ross's bargaining stage. While reflecting on this, she also tries to understand some of her fellow classmates who do not yet appear to be making the shift:

In class today we discussed the possible cognitive, learning styles of African-Americans. I thought it was a very interesting class because it raised a lot of issues and clarified a lot of my own thinking. . . . I could not stop thinking about it, and I could feel everything shifting in my brain as I was trying to figure out what it all meant. . . . For me, what we were learning has implications for my whole life as a human being, and particularly as a teacher. Racism, discrimination and sexism are still big problems in our world, and really the best way to combat them is through education. Schools are institutions of learning and socialization, and as such are probably the best vehicles we can use to teach children (and adults) about these issues, so that we can end racism. Someone said knowledge is power, and I think some of the people in the class are reacting so strongly to what we are learning because it's so unfamiliar to them. This shouldn't be surprising in an educational system that has taught academics using a standard set mostly by white males. Luckily, this is beginning to change, which is why multi-culturalism is where it's at in education right now. Learning about different cognitive styles, where they come from and how to avoid misinterpreting different behaviors of children can only help us. I guess what made me the most angry was I didn't understand how everyone couldn't see this. Or maybe they could, but they just saw it differently because of their own particular experiences in their own culture in respect to their gender, economic class or race.

Such grappling is not limited to white students from privileged backgrounds. Minority students from economically privileged backgrounds may grapple with thoughts and feelings of guilt, loyalty, and heavy desires to fix observed disparities (see Dunlap 2000, pp. xvii–xxvii, "Passage"). A minority Hispanic student placed at an after-school program finds himself grappling with the pros and cons of the Hispanic children there not having Spanish-speaking teachers. "In one respect I feel that our Hispanic students are being underserved because none of our teachers can communicate with them in Spanish. But, on the other hand, I feel that being exposed to the English-speaking teachers in a not so structured setting will benefit the students in the long run." This student also appears to go back and forth in his reflections as he questions the pros and cons of the language exposure that the students have in the program. Again, such grappling is useful, but if prolonged, perhaps can be tiring. In response, service learners and other community partners may find themselves emotionally withdrawing or retreating for a period of time in order to regroup.

Stage 4: Depression

Kübler-Ross's conception of depression was that it is a time when the patient may cry, grieve, and disconnect from others in order to fully process the situation. The patient is no longer in denial, is consciously aware of the severity of the situation, and may feel overwhelmed enough to need to retreat (Kübler-Ross, 1997). Likewise, a similar process may occur concerning adapting to the realities that community engagement may bring to our awareness. Partners significantly engaged in community work may become sad, overwhelmed, and depressed and may need to retreat at times, especially during periods of stress or disillusionment. This stage may be indicated in the following student journal:

> [My service learning today] reminded me of when I was in [a social science class] last semester; one of my classmates gave a presentation about American schools around the turn of the century as they tried to assimilate Mexicans into English-only schools. My classmate reversed the situation for us, setting up a mock "Spanish-only" classroom in which a friend of hers, a Spanish major, played the part of the teacher. Those of us in the class who had very little knowledge of Spanish really felt sad and lost. The "[student] teacher," to drive home my classmate's point, [pretended to] consider us idiots because we couldn't speak Spanish, and we found these comments hurtful. For a long time it was a feeling that was difficult to shake. [The child I tutor in my service learning] is lucky to be in a preschool environment where people don't reject his ability to speak Spanish. I hope that when he gets to elementary school this ability is seen for the gift it is, rather than a hindrance.

Thus, this student speaks of the sadness and hurt that she feels as she encounters experiences that enlighten her to the realities of prejudice and racism. She connects these experiences to the community about which she cares deeply. She seems to have moved past denial, anger, and bargaining, and now experiences sadness and hurt. Another student describes her sadness as she reflects on a series of incidents from the previous semester involving her young community partners:

> [I worked with] a young boy named "C." C was a confident, energetic African American boy around the age of four. . . . I worried about him though because as he was developing such a positive attitude, it was being counteracted by a teacher that did not see these valuable qualities in C. He'd get in trouble often and for the most part any child would have been punished for the same acts, but C. became a focus. The teacher would always assume that he was the one causing trouble in every situation and never gave him a chance to prove that he could handle things differently. I remember one particular incident when we were coming in from the playground and a child at the back of the line with me was screaming and making inappropriately loud noise to enter the building. I was in the back, and from where I was I could see who was doing it. But the teacher did not even ask me anything before yelling at C. to be quiet. C. looked up with a confused look on his face, because he had been standing quietly waiting to head into the building. I quickly pointed out that it was not C., and the teacher sort of half-heartedly apologized but it was pretty

much too late. It had already affected C. and made him feel bad. This kind of thing happened all the time. On another occasion . . . she began to complain about [C.] and stated right to me, in front of the other children, "He is an awful child, a really terrible child." I cannot tell you how sad I felt over these incidences. I could not believe that someone could say something like that about a young child. This is the kind of thing she taught C. to believe about himself. I was so frustrated with this and still am to this day because as a volunteer I knew there was no way to counteract this negative situation by my two-hour placement once a week. Our class this semester has brought some of this into perspective. . . . I was not educated about all the possible styles in children from different racial/cultural backgrounds, I just knew that I did not believe that this was appropriate, fair treatment for any child.

Like some of the previous students, the above student takes her sadness and frustration and uses it to help motivate her to become a culturally competent teacher in the future. She both realizes that she cannot fix this situation in two hours per week and commits to making the most, however, of the two hours a week that she does have. Her method suggests she also may be approaching the acceptance stage.

Stage 5: Acceptance

In Kübler-Ross's conception of Acceptance, the patient stops fighting, accepts that death is impending, and begins preparing for it (1997). Patients at this stage may withdraw from others, but not necessarily in a state of denial, anger, or depression, but to conserve energies and prepare for their final days. Drawing parallels from Kübler-Ross's theory, within the multicultural community engagement process this final stage may be characterized by the partner accepting that the multicultural and diversity issues they observe are very complex, that they alone cannot correct all of the social ills that they encounter. They may find themselves committing to social activism to change what they can (Dunlap, 1997; Dunlap et al., 2007). They may chose their battles carefully and may try to conserve their energies for those battles. Those engaged in the cross-cultural diversity process that are in the acceptance stage may have learned to not only choose their battles and conserve energies, but to also rally support and resources. They also may move more toward working in collaboration rather than isolation, and may appreciate diversity and multicultural awareness and understanding as a process or journey rather than a destination. Further, they may not see or expect clear, definitive "black and white" answers to the diversity-related questions that they ask, having learned that, with the complex issues and dynamics involved both across and within cultures, simple and quick answers may not be possible. As examples, the following students illustrate their developing maturity with respect to various diversity issues that they encounter in their cross-cultural service-learning environments:

[A middle school teacher] had her students do a very interesting activity today. She had them draw an outline of themselves and then write their internal characteristics (personality traits) inside the figure and their physical characteristics around the figure. As the students drew, I wandered through the classroom and talked to the students about their drawings. I quickly noticed many trends. Every African American child in the class put black as one of their external characteristics. Not one of the white children in the class put white as an external characteristic.

171

This really struck me because about 75 percent of the class are children of color. It made me realize how being black is something children are always aware of, even at such a young age. It is such a major part of who a child is. For the white children, however, being white is not something they use to identify themselves even in a situation where they are the minority, because being a part of the dominant culture, the color of their skin will never be an issue. . . . Because the classroom was very diverse, with the majority being African-American children, I was able to make a lot of connections concerning the different cognitive, learning and social orientation styles we learned about. I was very aware of when the teacher was successful (and unsuccessful) in incorporating these different styles into her activities and teaching methods. I was pleased to see her use of collective and cooperative activities, which were always a big hit among the children. For the most part, she was tolerant of the energy many of these children had, but sometimes I felt the room get chaotic.

The above student appears to not be in denial, anger, bargaining, nor depression, but rather seems to be making powerful synergistic connections between her course in-class curriculum and her service-learning experiences. She also appears to be internalizing both theoretical and applied kinds of learning for her own future use. She does not idealize her service-learning site, nor does she condemn it. She is able to process and critique its faults, and praise and build on its strengths. If she were in a capacity of staff or management, she might rally resources and collaborate to further and favorably impact her sphere of influence.

The following student also seems to possibly have moved past denial, anger, bargaining, and depression in this journal posting:

[A] situation that interested me occurred while we were all coloring. Each of three little girls wanted me to draw them a picture of a woman with a big billowing hairdo. I found it so cool when [the only African American girl among them] picked up a brown marker matching her own skin, and colored in her woman's skin tone. It made me happy because I felt that she felt comfortable with, and proud of, her own color.

Of course had there not been multicultural crayons available, reflections on diversity might have gone unnoticed (denial), might have upset the service learner (anger), might have caused her to question why (bargaining), or may have saddened her over an extended period of time (depression)—we really can't say for sure. However, the following student encounters a similar situation, but the multicultural materials are indeed lacking. She processes this in light of her past and present experiences in a way that suggests she also may have moved beyond the stages of denial, anger, and so forth:

One problem struck me when playing with a young black girl with the Mr. Potato Head dolls. This may seem trivial, and did to me in some senses. But at the same time in light of what we have learned, it is important. The basket of parts for this activity include about four large bodies to decorate with clothes, and body features such as eyes. There are two with Caucasian skin tone and two with a dark reddish, brown complexion. I felt this was good because some children may relate better to one or the other but the problem is that many of the pieces for the activity are missing. More specifically pieces needed to decorate the dark complexioned bodies were missing. This made it impossible for children to complete these characters and deterred them from using these bodies. This could encourage children to view one of these as less significant, as less of a "person."

This same student reflects further on the importance of multicultural materials and appreciation of diversity for all children, and how that appreciation for diversity was subtly, but systematically, instilled in her by her parents:

> I have been in environments where there were no materials supporting multiculturalism and this was interesting as well. I grew up in a small town in New Hampshire. My parents had moved there from [the Midwest] after my brother was born. The town is essentially all white. There are a few Indian-American, Asian-American, and African-American families but there are no significant numbers that show up in this town. I have been hopeful when noticing more and more families moving into town, but it scares me at the same time because it shows you how few there actually are if I can recognize all of them. I worked in a daycare center there this summer. Besides one young girl of a mixed Caucasian/Asian-American background, all the children were white. Now to many, the logic is easy, if there are no children of different racial backgrounds then the materials are not needed. This could not be further from the truth. I do not recall my childhood to a great degree and do not remember my parents verbalizing specific values I should take on. My mother told me recently that the communication was not so blatant as just saying "You will like African-Americans," but they used more consistent, subtle ways to communicate that. They modeled acceptance of others, and they provided books and materials in support of multiculturalism. The problem is in my town families do not always provide this education, and the classrooms must take over. If the children do not have exposure to people of other backgrounds in their communities and then do not gain any understanding at school, how will they know how to cope with feelings or interact with others? This kind of system breeds ignorance and seems to show that these things are not important because they are not present. . . . It is interesting for me now to be able to recognize and identify problems in regards to multicultural environments. With each new [service-learning] placement, I get a new look at how someone else handles these issues. The information I get in classes like this one help me to also identify what needs to be done, and hopefully in some instances my experience will help me have a positive impact in other settings.

Thus, this student illustrates discontent with prejudice and racism, but also a determination and commitment to work toward change. Because of her upbringing, she likely already has had both time and opportunity to work through denial, anger, bargaining, and depression. Even so, for some, current events can trigger previous stages for a time (Goldsworthy, 2005; Kübler-Ross, 1997). Thus in trying to apply Kübler-Ross's model to community engagement, we cannot definitively predict a person's stage, but we can draw parallel's in order to anticipate where an engager might be developmentally in their adjustment to the cross-cultural community engagement partnership.

While it would be ideal to follow individual students through a complete cycle of adjustment from denial to acceptance, it is not feasible in the context of this chapter for several reasons. First, students come into the service-learning or other community engagement experience already at different stages of familiarity, comfort, preparedness, adjustment, and loss, so they do not all start out at the early or proposed denial stage of adjustment. Second, as with death and dying, the community engagement adjustment process also surely does not occur in a straight or linear trajectory. But rather, again, as with death and dying stages, people within the community engagement process likely sometimes skip stages, return to previous stages, and so on. Third, because of the relatively short periods associated with service learning and other community engagement experiences, even if individual students did neatly traverse through all five stages, there likely would not be enough time to observe the progression of all five stages within a typical 12- to 16-week semester period. However, such progression could possibly be observed as a future study among community engagement researchers who have access to students for longer periods of engagement, wherein all stages and their trajectories could be observed.

Death, Dying, and Racial Identity Development

Racial identity development is defined as the degree to which individuals perceive themselves as a member of a racial group that shares common heritage, challenges, and/or benefits (Helms, 1990; Tatum, 1992). Students and other stakeholders come into the community engagement environment with varying degrees of experiences with multiculturalism and diversity, and with different degrees of understanding with respect to the role of race, racism, systems of oppression, and so on, in our society, and this influences their stage of racial identity development (Tatum 1992). In this chapter Elizabeth Kübler-Ross's model of death and dying has been proposed as a model for helping to explain the process that community partners may experience as they deal with cross-cultural community engagement experiences—especially in situations where different partners may be at different stages of understanding with regard to multicultural and diversity issues. It is further proposed that the less experience one has with diverse communities and cultures, the earlier stage of "death or loss" will accompany their initial adjustment as they engage with community partners (e.g., denial) (Dunlap, 2011). But does the death-and-dying process really have anything to do with diversity and multiculturalism? Many of the racial identity development models do appear to follow a process similar to Kübler-Ross's model of death and dying. Parallels can be seen, for example, in three of the most popular racial identity models, Helms's white racial identity model (1990), Cross, Parham, and Helms's black racial identity model (1991), and Atkinson, Morten, and Sue's racial/cultural identity model (1989).

Outlined in further detail in Dunlap (2011) and summarized here, the Helms (1990) white racial identity model consists of six stages: Contact, disintegration, reintegration, pseudo-independence, immersion/emersion, and autonomy. The Cross, Parham, and Helms (1991) black racial identity model consists of five stages: pre-encounter, encounter, immersion/emersion, internalization, and internalization-commitment. The Atkinson, Morten, and Sue (1989) racial/cultural identity model consists of five stages: conformity, dissonance, resistance/emersion, introspection, and integrative awareness. Examining these models together, we see that each begins with a stage that connotes naiveté in one's thinking with regard to racial or cross-cultural issues—thus a conformity or lack of questioning that would suggest that there is no oppression or disparities about which to speak, complain, or engage in activism (i.e., contact, pre-encounter, and conformity, respectively). These stages may parallel Kübler-Ross's denial stage, because the new community engager may initially be in a state of unawareness or nonacceptance concerning the existence of racial disparities and other cross-cultural issues, oppressions, and/or challenges. Each of these three racial identity models also include a second or third stage wherein, like Kübler-Ross's "anger," upset begins to manifest itself as one becomes more aware that there are issues of unfairness, disparity, and/or oppression with which to contend (i.e., the disintegration/reintegration, encounter, and resistance/emersion stages, respectively). Each of these racial identity models also involves a stage of cognitive grappling, or possible "bargaining" to use Kübler-Ross's term, wherein individuals gather information and try to make cognitive sense out of all of the new truths to which they may now be exposed in their courses, readings, and/or personal experiences (i.e., the pseudo-independent, immersion/emersion, and dissonance stages, respectively). Each of these three models also include a fourth stage wherein to one extent or another individuals, rather than continuing to exhaust themselves, begin to introspectively retreat, withdraw, prioritize, and/or prepare to reemerge (i.e., the immersion/emersion, internalization, and introspection stages, respectively). And each of these models, similarly to the Kübler-Ross model, also ends with significant growth, maturity, and greater ability to critically reflect, negotiate, and/or engage in activism for positive change (i.e., autonomy, internalization-commitment, and integrative awareness, respectively). While none of these theories is identical to another, they do all involve a process of change, loss, and gain—change in how one sees oneself in relation to the cross-cultural world, a loss in some of one's beliefs and assumptions about oneself and the world, a possible gain in maturity and a better understanding of one's diverse world. Each model has usefulness for assisting community partners in better understanding one another, and therefore may assist them in working more successfully together. The Kübler-Ross model could be used in conjunction with models of racial identity development when trying to prepare engagers for cross-cultural work. The Kübler-Ross model may have a strong appeal in the cross-cultural engagement context because any community partner, regardless of racial, cultural, gender, socioeconomic, sexual orientation, religious, or educational background, may be able to relate to the experiences of loss, grief, and growth. Partners with a wide range of backgrounds and experiences may be able to easily apply concepts of denial, anger, bargaining, depression, and acceptance to their own development within a cross-cultural context.

Implications for Higher Education and Community Engagement

The commonalities that exist between Kübler-Ross's death-and-dying model and racial identity development models, such as the move from naiveté to dissonance and cognitive grappling to strategic adaptation and resolution, are noteworthy and potentially very useful as we try to find ways to help community partners prepare for self-reflection and engagement with others who may come from experiences completely different from their own. Considering the cognitive and emotional losses and changes involved in the cross-cultural community engagement process may be useful to all stakeholders involved in the community, including community partners, students, professors, administrators, and staff. The application of Kübler-Ross's model here is intended to inspire discussion, theory development, research, and application to help further prepare service learners and other community partners for cross-cultural engagement in the future.

References

Atkinson, D. R., Morten, G., & Sue, D. W. (1989). A minority identity development model. In D. R. Atkinson, G. Morten, & D. W. Sue (Eds.), *Counseling American minorities* (pp. 35–52). Dubuque, IA: William C. Brown.

Cross, W. E. Jr., Parham, T. A., & Helms, J. E. (1991). The stages of black racial identity development: Nigrescence models. In R. Jones (Ed.), *Black psychology* (3rd ed., pp. 319–338). San Francisco: Cobb and Henry.

Dunlap, M. (1997). The role of the personal fable in adolescent service learning and critical reflection. *Michigan Journal of Community Service Learning, 4,* 56–63.

Dunlap, M. (1998). Multicultural service learning: Challenges, research, and solutions for assisting students. In N. Kent, E. Frengel, & D. Carey (Eds.), *Removing the Vestiges: Research-Based Strategies to Promote Inclusion* (pp. 27–34). Washington, DC: American Association of Community Colleges.

Dunlap, M. (2000). *Reaching out to children and families: Students model effective community service.* Lanham, MD: Rowman and Littlefield.

Dunlap, M. (2011). Thriving in a multicultural classroom. In C. P. Harvey & M. J. Allard (Eds.), *Understanding and managing diversity* (5th ed., pp. 12–21). Upper Saddle River, NJ: Pearson/Prentice Hall.

Dunlap, M., Scoggin, J., Green, P., & Davi, A. (2007). White students' experiences of privilege and socio-economic disparities: Toward a theoretical model, *Michigan Journal of Community Service Learning, 13*(2), 19–30.

Dunlap, M., & Webster, N. (2009). Enhancing inter-cultural competence through civic engagement. In B. Jacoby (Ed.), *Civic engagement in higher education.* Hoboken, NJ: Jossey-Bass, 140–153.

Evans, S. Y., Taylor, C. M., Dunlap, M. R., & Miller, D. S. (Eds.). (2009). *African Americans and community engagement in higher education.* Albany: SUNY Press.

Goldsworthy, K. (2005). Grief and loss theory in social work practice: All changes involve loss, just as all losses require change. *Australian Social Work, 58*(2), 167–178.

Helms, J. E. (Ed.). (1990). *Black and white racial identity: Theory, research and practice.* Westport, CT: Greenwood Press.

Kübler-Ross, E. (1997). *On death and dying.* New York: Simon and Schuster/Scribner.

Lynch, E., & Hanson, M. (2006). *Developing cross-cultural competence: A guide for working with children and their families.* Baltimore, MD: Brookes.

National Urban League. (2008). *State of black America.* New York: National Urban League.

Tatum, B. (1992). Talking about race: The application of racial identity development theory in the classroom. *Harvard Educational Review, 62*(1), 1–24.

Hard Time: What We Can Learn from Long-Range Community Involvement in Prisons and Jails

Patricia E. O'Connor

Privilege

The day we volunteers brought free-reading novels
into cellblock 5
and committed the sin
of giving them to the inmates,
the officers locked *us* up,
sang to us the Control Center Blues:
"You got no right
You got no right
You got no right to leave those novels here!"

Entered then—one Rickey Bryant—
on his way to the hole,
beaten,
baton-bloodied,
constrained
arms and stumbling feet interlaced in silvery links.

Inmate, scholar, and poet, Bryant once wrote for me:
"I am not of color I am of being."
That night he mouthed through crimsoned lips,
cocking the less-bloodied eye, smiling an incongruous welcome:
"What brings you here, Ms. O?"
"Books," I replied softly.

177

"And you?" I asked,
as if every day I met swollen-eyed students in chains.
"Refusal to comply," he said with wry pride.

We had that in common that cold Lorton night,
our obstinancy
our True North determined
by will alone.
We would neither of us go by the book
But only Rickey was bound to pay the price.

I wrote that poem as I become sharply aware of the privilege I had as a college educator coming from Georgetown University and going inside a maximum security penal institution. Astonished that our goodwill as volunteers was being questioned, we grumbled as the zealous guards reported to the "white-shirt" officers that we had given away books to inmates in our college courses instead of carrying those books back out with us when we left. We were struck by their underlying image of education as something that occurred only in a discrete class session. How could books not be a part of the preparation for the next class? Was it the flammability of paperback pages that so outraged the guards? Or was it the acquisition of something valuable that the guards did not themselves have the opportunity to explore? Was prisoner educational attainment itself under review? How dangerous were those books? Or was it just that we had *failed to comply* in our benign ignorance that a teacher providing supplemental reading material to her students would be a violation unless accompanied by a specific, written, stamped, and suitably duplicated documentation? Rickey Bryant, on his part, was set in chains for failing to submit to drug testing, a much easier rationale to comprehend, though that did not explain the bloodied face.

Over time we who do community service work, we who volunteer, learn the intricacies of compliance as well as the changing modes of behavioral expectations and shifts in staffing in the communities we serve. We also learn through nuanced experience to adjust to changes in the bureaucracies that we ourselves represent. We who dwell in the work of community service are always at a crossroads, an intersection of autobiographies where our input and impact are shifted and changed by the involvements we share with others over time. Time, long time, even "hard time" is the hallmark of successful service. Such sustained work in communities frames successful research into causes of and solutions to entrenched social ills. By its nature, community service sets up longitudinal research and long-term commitment and works best accompanied by patience to overcome obstacles.

This chapter discusses the importance of both long-term service and flexibility in those affiliated with universities and colleges who set up programs that reach out into communities, especially those "total institutions" (Goffman, 1961) such as prisons, jails, and treatment centers. In these settings where the total round of life is contained, constrained, and seemingly *static*, we who enter in as guests, visitors, teachers, tutors, and/or researchers must ironically maintain a maximum tolerance for *change*. Based on over 30 years of my outreach service and research with inmates, ex-inmates, and institutions of incarceration, I examine how we can achieve long-term community involvement by preparing for shifts made in services, in learning, and in research agendas within communities. Flexibility and high standards yield long-term possibilities for long-term impact within shared communities. Thus, as Hiram Fitzgerald proposes with the title of this volume, we can "go public" with how educational institutions committed to service in communities can move progressively to interact with communities to foster social change and social justice. We promote this through shared exchange of stories of how we overcome obstacles, enrich educational expectations, and fine-tune research.

Background: Prisons, Jails, and Service in America

In 1984 when I first became involved with America's maximum security prisons, the Bureau of Justice Statistics (BJS) noted we were incarcerating in state and federal prisons and local jails 681,282 people at a rate of 188 persons per 100,000 (Bureau of Justice 2010a; 2010b). BJS reported that those incarcerated in state prisons, federal prisons, and local jails in 2008 numbered 2,396,002 persons (Bureau of Justice, 2009, p. 1), over three times as many. If we include all those under court supervision, "all persons incarcerated, either in prison, jail, or supervised in the community (probation or parole)," then the combined total of all these persons in the United States is 7.3 million people (Bureau of Justice, 2009, p. 1). In this time of greatly expanded imprisonment, the population of America grew from 226.5 million in 1980's census to 311.9 million in the most current total (U.S. Census Bureau, 2010), but incarceration rates greatly outstripped mere population growth.

Only in the last two years has the rate of incarceration begun a modest decline: "At year-end 2011, there were 1,537,415 prisoners serving sentences of more than one year, about 15,000 fewer than at yearend 2010" (Carson and Sabol, 2012, p. 6). In the figures for year-end 2009, we incarcerated 2.235 million with a rate of 502 persons per 100,000 (Bureau of Justice 2010a), though individual cities often have rates much higher, as did Washington, DC, when I did my teaching and research in their institutions. In 1999, the nation's capital had 1,594 per 100,000 persons incarcerated (Beck, 2000, p. 3).

Much of the work of those who are involved in community service addresses needs in the urban zones of poverty that fill prisons, areas that Jonathan Kozol (1995) in *Amazing Grace* refers to as "urban Lazarettos," pieces of a "perfectible ghetto" in which, he asserts, the poor are quarantined in public housing (p. 136). His interviews conducted with poor children and their families in the Bronx assert that children in such poverty zones have much dignity, but little chance. As in Washington, DC, children from these blighted zones are more likely to enter prisons than go to college. Students from affluent and privileged backgrounds have trouble even imagining the psychological and social costs of such overincarceration. College-based community service in such areas aims to thwart these seeming inevitabilities. One of the first elements of awareness comes in not overessentializing race in matters of incarceration. Yet in the settings in which service work takes place, we confront a dismal entropy, resulting from a loss of black and Hispanic youth to the worlds of crime and criminal justice.[1]

To clarify this dire setting, the Sentencing Project's Marc Mauer (2006, p. 130) opens his chapter "African Americans in the Criminal Justice System" in *Race to Incarcerate* with the hypothetical scenario of a childbirth class in which nine black women pregnant with nine male children listen to a discussion of childbirth. As well as details on delivery, he imagines them being told that "three of your nine boys will spend time in prison" (p. 130). The statistical interpolation comes from a Bureau of Justice publication by Thomas Bonczar (2003) on the likelihood of imprisonment in the United States from 1971 to 2001 that contrasts the probability for men—6 out of 100 white males, versus 32 of 100 black males and 17 of 100 Hispanic males—to be locked up (cited in Mauer, 2006, p. 139). Bureau of Justice researcher Bonczar (2003) notes, "About 1 in 3 black males, 1 in 6 Hispanic males, and 1 in 17 white males are expected to go to prison during their lifetime, if current incarceration rates remain unchanged" (p. 1). The publication's calculations are based on data from federal and state prisons and do not include jail time; thus even these shocking rates underreport incarceration probability. Into this arena of likely incarceration we who conduct service work in distressed communities enter, carrying with us or becoming quickly apprised of, a seeming inevitability of incarceration as an alternative kind of higher education, a tertiary education of a grim sort for the poor and minority populations.

Not only are those in prison overrepresentative of the population of blacks and Hispanics in America, but the population inside prisons is far less educated and far less able to perform well on literacy tasks. This assessment suggests a deep need for more community oversight and involvement in how time is spent once imprisonment is determined as the punishment. Measures used by the U.S. Department of Education in its National Adult Literacy Survey (NALS) in 1992 and the National Assessment of Adult Literacy (NAAL) of 2003 show that the incarcerated are very greatly educationally disadvantaged. In both surveys, prisoners scored much lower than householders on prose, document, and quantitative tasks (Haigler, Harlow, O'Connor, & Campbell, 1994, p. xviii; Greenberg, Dunleavy, & Kutner, 2007, pp. v–vii). Prisoner scores on prose and quantitative tasks in 2003 were somewhat higher than in 1992, with black inmates in particular showing an increase over the prior study, but still trailing the results of white inmates (Greenberg, Dunleavy, & Kutner 2007, p. v). The only area of comparison in which prisoners outscored householders was in those categories without high school diplomas. In the 2003 NAAL, inmates without diplomas "had higher average literacy on all three scales than adults living in households" (Greenberg, Dunleavy, & Kutner, 2007, p. vi). Such a finding may suggest a greater urgency on the part of inmates to address their literacy deficits. (See also the Bureau of Justice compilation on education in prisons by Caroline Harlow [2003].) For those who have left the fast life of the streets, the time and opportunity inside prison to do education can be taken seriously, if programs are available. Thus, a prison population with its overrepresentation of the poor, the minorities, and the less educated is a prime location for involvement by an institution of higher education such as Georgetown University, whose Jesuit mission of *cura personalis* seeks to educate the whole person and to educate women and men who are in service to others.

Into that setting of the less educated and the overly minority incarcerated come outside programs who work along with inside-the-prison practices that try to address the inequities and inadequacies of imprisonment to foster rehabilitation. This work takes place in a climate of reactionary increases in sentencing and movements to get tougher on crime while the prison counts, prison complexes, and expenses expand. According to the Bureau of Justice, total expenditures on incarceration were $68.7 billion in 2006, over six times the $10.5 billion in 1984, when our outreach into prisons began (Bureau of Justice, 2006).

Anyone working, whether volunteer or paid, inside prisons reckons immediately with the particulars of the individual setting in which they labor. Each state's prisons and penitentiaries and each local jurisdiction's jails operate in differing circumstances for funding, staffing, and modes of incarceration. We, newly welcomed into such an enclosed community to perform educational service, had to acclimate to the immediate setting. To do so, we had to contextualize this federal institution whose purview was a locus for criminals in a federal city, the District of Columbia. Part of the work we did in prison outreach meant growing more familiar with changing aspects of incarceration over that time span, by also understanding the past and current political climates of the place in which we volunteered, a climate that would change drastically over time and create obstacles for our university's continuing involvement in prison outreach.

Just as do the prisoners, the staff and volunteers must figure out the new round of life expectations peculiar to the setting and in contrast with the home environment. Volunteers in community service come to know this as a kind of culture shock akin to foreign travelers' surprise, enjoyment, frustration, and eventual adjustment to the culture of the Other and to also being the Other themselves. The particulars of my campus and its involvements both educationally and in research with maximum and medium security prisons of the District of Columbia and the jails of Arlington and Alexandria, Virginia, suggest ways of entering and growing within the changing situations of incarceration. Faced with obstacles, we adapted. These details reflect the workings and reworkings of necessarily flexible programs[2] over the three decades of this community outreach that began in 1983.

The Prison Complex at Lorton, Virginia

In 1910, the federal government had leased land for 99 years from Fairfax County, Virginia, to build for the District of Columbia its remote workhouse prison (famous for housing and force-feeding suffragettes in 1917) and later its prison farms and seven large facilities, some for youth detention, most for adults who were separated into minimum, medium, and maximum security. Inmate labor was used to build the workhouse complex that eventually became Maximum Security, buildings that bear an uncanny resemblance to the University of Virginia's famous Jeffersonian Quad. The prison's redbrick warehouse-style buildings are connected by covered and arched brick walkways inside a classic castle wall surrounding the whole with an imposing block of concrete at its base about 16 feet wide and about 30 feet tall. This exterior "Wall" with its additional perimeter fence topping of supplemental razor wire replicated the iconic idea of a prison kept at a great remove from community (see Oakey & Swanson, 1988). Such remote facilities, while funded with tax dollars, are designed for security reasons with little to no access to the general public. This presents a major obstacle in establishing volunteer work. Another obstacle is the problem of offering a service that might not be appropriate, a problem that many in service learning realize when merging a desire to be benevolent and in service to others without providing a community-member-recognized need. Our best aid in overcoming such barriers came from inside the prison walls themselves within the community of need, the prisoners.

Starting Our Outreach: Invited in by Inmates Seeking Help

In summer of 1983, inmate Elvin J. Johnson of the District of Columbia's prison at Lorton, Virginia, wrote a letter to all the presidents of the various universities in the District of Columbia, on behalf of inmates in Cellblock 5 of the maximum security facility that housed DC offenders. In his letter he noted that no educational services other than secondary level were available to inmates in maximum security. These inmates were serving long sentences and also had little access to programs for vocational work. The men in max were forgotten, but eager to learn. Georgetown University president Timothy Healy, S.J., responded by having one of his young assistants, Jack DeGioia,[3] respond to the letter. That young graduate student in philosophy asked a fellow graduate student Robert Braumiller to organize a reading group in Cellblock 5. The graduate students soon reported back that the men in the unit were adept readers of philosophy and literature and they recommended Georgetown start a college credit course there. President Timothy Healey and Dean Michael Collins of Georgetown's School for Summer and Continuing Education gave approval, and I was asked to teach. Thus, a letter, and groups of believers in potential on both sides of the walls, started building an educational network through the social networks they shared, working together in service to a larger community much affected both by crime and by wasted potential.

A graduate student and teaching assistant in literature and composition at that time and a veteran teacher in secondary education in Ohio, West Virginia, and DC, I accepted that challenging opportunity and began a three-credit Expository Writing course inside Maximum Security in January 1984, along with a group of Georgetown undergraduate and graduate volunteer tutors to assist the ten inmates selected. Facing negative assumptions about credibility for issuing college credits to prison students, we kept the syllabus as rigorous as those taught on campus. Students read widely and wrote copiously. To this day, the students from that first class have one key word they say when they speak of that class: "Revise!" Thus, we began what appeared to be a small experiment, testing to see if the men in maximum were up to the challenge of higher education, Georgetown University style. This meant a deep commitment to analytical writing and the value of a liberal arts education to shape the whole person, what the Jesuits who founded Georgetown call the *cura personalis*. That refrain to "revise" within the contexts of care and responsibility to those with whom we serve also became a mantra for maintaining our prison programs over the ensuing three decades. When obstacles came up, we adapted and revised our approaches.

How We Taught

Throughout the years teaching and tutoring in District of Columbia's Department of Corrections (DCDC), our groups had to be very flexible—both on a large scale and inside the small-scale life of teaching in rooms designed for detaining or interrogation. Some areas were about the size of three cells combined with either too little or too much heat for comfort and a few folding chairs. Others were actual classrooms. We went about delivery of courses within a climate of constant change. From the prisoners' side, maximum cleverness was also needed to guarantee materials were available and inmate students were prepared for the weekly sessions. We heard of inmates trading shower and laundry times with other men in their cellblocks so they could show their respect by being presentable for class. Inmates in our classes became tutors in the prison's Adult Basic Education and secondary GED programs so that they could ensure a steady pipeline of new and serious students for subsequent courses. These men shared textbooks when cell searches and sweeps emptied and "stored" contents of fellow classmates' cells. And most important of all, men in the classes kept us apprised of who had been locked down or who had been transferred to another cell block, to Administrative Segregation, to another prison, or just to the limbo called "in transit." During the years of our college course work in DC's maximum security facility, the complex was under federal mandate to reduce overcrowding. According to inmates and to staff,[4] this at its extremes involved some shuffling of prisoners onto buses on occasion to keep them "in transit" while numbers of inmates to beds were being carefully calculated.

More devastating to the work of the mind we offered in the classes, however, was the prison system's answer to overcrowding through renting bed space in other institutions nationwide. This forced the sudden shifting of prisoners to county jails in other states and eventually to federal institutions and built-for-profit prisons operated by the Corrections Corporation of America (traded on the NY Stock exchange along with several other such enterprises). Removed inmates could not finish the courses they left. The *Washington Post* covered the first of these diasporic journeys to Spokane County Jail in the state of Washington, a venture that whisked inmate William T. Lawson almost 3,000 miles away from one of our early literature courses in 1988. Our class had been stopped early that night for an unexplained reason, which later became all too clear when I read Lawson's remarks in the newspaper about his sudden relocation to the other coast of America: "I'm a lifer. I got to have something meaningful to do outside of just sitting here" (Hockstader, 1988, p. A1). Lawson communicated by mail with us and on occasion by telephone, but the work of that semester remained interrupted. Adult education has usually had a lower finish rate on coursework than traditional college, as life responsibilities often intervene in the routines of those who return to school while older adults. So too in the prison setting, where everyone on the outside imagines (and endlessly jokes) that you have a "captive audience," much outside one's control can still interfere with an inmate finishing a course.

In addition to adjusting to inmate relocations, we became adaptable to change in schedules and to students being absent due to a variety of issues: lockdowns for behavior infractions, fires, or weapons; drug searches that could prevent their or our entry into (or out of) the cellblocks; medical visits that sometimes required inmates to travel supervised (and in chains) for six- to eight-hour trips to have vision screened and glasses ordered. Inmates, too, adapted: they often borrowed glasses to try to do their reading, since getting prescriptions filled for corrective lenses could be a wait of several months. I mastered flexible teaching. I had several lesson plans for each evening to accommodate condensed or stretched schedules. I planned in the fashion of a news story: strong lead with the who, what, when, where of the night's work and a series of subsequent activities that I could rank in the realm of more to lesser urgency. We always left a script behind that detailed the plans and clarified the assignments. We always brought paper and pens and spare handouts of syllabi, as often the inmates' materials had been confiscated. Rather than waste time complaining, we overprepared and we adapted. The inmates, themselves, were the MacGyvers of invention. They

183

relocated a blackboard and chalk for me when I despaired of trying to teach with only a circle of folding chairs, notepads, and pens in the tiny 10- by 20-foot fishbowl room where we conducted our early courses in Cellblock 5. What became routine was the joint effort by inmates, teachers, and tutors to be inventive and to provide quality education. We were often assisted by officers at the prison who saw our work as helpful in promoting calm on the units.

Student Involvement

As a way of overcoming some of the gaps in inmate educational skills, we always included tutors in the teaching model to give one-on-one support, especially in polishing writing skills, but also in promoting enriching discussions. We were expanding the model of education beyond what Freire (2006) critiqued as the banking concept where the teacher only makes "deposits" into the minds. We engaged in problem solving. The student tutors we brought along were interested in teaching and in learning more about the criminal justice system. Some aspired to law, some to pedagogy, some to ethics, some to social work, and others to prison reform. All became aware of social justice through the seat-of-the-pants learning that comes with work inside total institutions. We often felt that we had "broken into" prison, so rare was the experience of long-term association over education inside the walls and barred spaces. We realized, though, that the real break was the shift into new paradigms of expectations. We were not there as voyeuristic tourists. In prison, we became complicit in a liberating educational venture. The student tutors came with obvious curiosity, but—surprising to the inmates and even to the tutors themselves—they came with growing respect for the intellectual successes the men were making.

Small-group discussions became a key to success of the program for inmates, teachers, and for tutors. Being held accountable for close readings became a shared responsibility. Tutors mentioned their surprise at the number of times inmates mentioned reading chapters twice or even three times, discussing the events, for instance, of a novel like Richard Wright's *Native Son* with others in their cell block who could not attend the class. Inmate comments on scenes in that novel showed keen attention. They probed scenes where black Bigger Thomas is on the run, scenes where he is shown smothering the white boss's daughter out of fear (yet candidly revealing desire as well), scenes of extremely well-articulated violence such as when Bigger takes a brick to the head of his black girlfriend Bessie. Such scenes evoked a viscerally close, careful, critiqued reading. We who entered into that prison work from Georgetown had little shared understanding of what Wright so accurately detailed and what the inmates so eerily understood. Our discussions in the van drive 26 miles back to campus showed an excitement about learning and teaching that made this volunteer program as exhilarating as it was humbling. It was not without obstacles for the volunteers.

Our students and faculty were mostly white; the inmate population was 99% black. We found ourselves in a minilab on cross-cultural communication, learning to listen closely to bridge dialects, idioms, attitudes, and assumptions. Many of the inmates challenged the students, assuming wealth, privilege and snobbery. Student assumptions of all inmates' past lives as downtrodden also were revised. Female tutors learned that locked-up men would flirt and that they needed to establish firm, appropriate, and public responses to prevent jeopardizing our work. After retraining workshops, and serious discussions by inmates with inmates and by tutors with tutors and mentor, if I felt an inmate (or a tutor) could not establish a professional educational relationship, we removed the person from the program.

On Georgetown's campus we encountered students who wanted to tutor strictly for resume building. That sort of student did not pass through our screening, which asked for a serious and long-term commitment to the project. Required trainings by our current tutors and faculty, inmate alumni, and prison volunteer coordinators explained the rigors and rewards. In addition all volunteers underwent background security checks and fingerprinting. All this and an essay application weeded out the voyeurish. Several tutors worked with us for all four years of their undergraduate career, marveling at the growth in the educational attainment that they saw develop over the time that men were serving their sentences and as students were matriculating—all of them grappling with texts, ideas, and perceptions in college.

Key Texts and Courses

Books we brought inside broadened our reach. We were charmed by inmate Elvin Johnson's description of first hiding the slim novel *The Little Prince*, carefully turning it over so as not to show the cartoonish cover drawing of a little prince in a blue gown. He worried that the depiction of the small, blue-robed prince standing on a globe might arouse queries about the grade level of this "college" work. He says he hid the cover until, that is, he had read the deep wisdom in Antoine de St.-Exupery's fine and philosophical book first published in 1943. The fox's advice to the prince, "You're always responsible for your rose" (p. 64), became a set phrase in the class for taking on the work of tending to family, friends, community—a poignantly difficult task when one is locked away from society, especially a society one has been guilty of damaging. Johnson proudly reported later conspicuously placing the book alongside his dinner tray, waiting for the inevitable: "What kind of college class is that?" He reports loaning the book to many inmates who were unable to be in our small classes. Such moments of shared understanding over the deeper insights found in literature readily united the class, the professor, and the tutors in ways far surpassing the main campus setting. Gone was the suspicion that the tutors would be rich snobs. Gone as well was any thought that prisoners would not be ready for college thinking. Jointly, the level of analysis of texts rose and rose.

We faced obstacles in scale of the program as we tried to include more inmates and more tutors. In one ambitious course, Prison Literature, we arranged dual enrollment. All tutors were enrolled in the same course with a main campus College of Arts and Sciences number. Inmates took the course with a Continuing Studies number. Main campus students attended class once a week at Georgetown's Washington, DC, campus and once a week in the DC Department of Corrections' Maximum Security Unit at Lorton, Virginia. (The inmates, of course, could not make reciprocal trips! They attended two weekly sessions in the cellblock.) The course involved reading, speaking, analyzing, performing, and researching various aspects of prison culture inspired through literature composed by inmate writers and researchers.

New Jersey prisoner Miguel Piñero's controversial play *Short Eyes* (1986) not only frankly discussed heinous crimes of child molestation, but also brought front and center the issues of inmate loyalties and guard complicities in violence inside prisons and jails. Prisoner journalists Ron Wikberg and Walter Rideau's *Life Sentences* (1992) modeled the strength of investigative reporting inside Louisiana's Angola prison, suggesting ways to create outlets for new talents in composition and research as well as a way to redress overcrowding, prison violence, lack of health care, even executions. Most challenging as a text for both sets of students was Michel Foucault's (1979) dense *Discipline and Punish* and its uses of the history of the movement from corporal punishment to imprisonment in European and Western society as a model for knowledge construction and power.

Inmate Andre Derrington-Bey brought out nuances to reading Foucault's opening chapter on the public execution of an attempted regicide. Without having read any biographies on Foucault, Derrington-Bey astutely reacted to the elongated passages of torture of the would-be slayer of the king that open that famous volume: "Is that guy Foucault into S & M?" Reading between the lines of texts as well as perceiving the ellipses in people's spoken words was a forte of the inmates who daily discerned the shifting and deadly nuances of prison regulations and inmate practices. Inmates challenged *Discipline and Punish* in its premise that modern-day prison no longer involves corporal punishment, noting the ease with which guards can turn a "blind eye" to instances of rape and other brutality inflicted by inmates or even other guards.[5]

Collaborative Endeavors in Learning

Most fulfilling in that conjoined course was the opportunity for paired term papers and collaborative writing: each inmate student and each main-campus student jointly explored various aspects of prison culture in these jointly researched and jointly composed papers. Inmates had access to interviewing guards, other inmates, and to their own considerable expertise of prison life. Students from the main campus could access library, newspaper, and database resources well out of the reach of the typical prisoner trying to study a college curriculum and with limited access even to a federally mandated law library. Students from the campus grew ever more accountable in order not to disappoint the waiting inmates who pored over the duplicated articles, chapters, and documents they retrieved for inmate partners. Drafting and revising became an artful negotiation of purpose, audience, and voice/s in a class that was sadly not replicable due to impending shifts in populations and closing of facilities. This model is also in use in a much-replicated program by Temple University professor Lori Pompa, who started the Inside Out program that takes Temple students into prison to take courses alongside enrolled inmates.

Built "from a single pilot class [in 1997] into a model program that's being replicated by colleges and universities across the country," Pompa's program has taken over 500 Temple college students into prison to be educated alongside inmates (Baals, 2005). Similar to that paired enrollment college course on Prison Literature that I taught once at Lorton, Pompa's Inside inmate students and the Outside Temple U students all take the criminal justice course for credit (Tiger, 2004). In the class they "explore issues of crime, justice, race, class and victimization" (Baals, 2005). Funded by the Soros Foundation Justice Senior Fellowship, Pompa now runs training programs to assist others in setting up similar programs across the United States.[6] Pompa (2004) writes of this teaching that it involves the "gift of disturbance" and engenders a "literacy of layers" that is unpacked as the two groups of students create dialogic understandings (pp. 24–26). Clearly an exciting form of education and deep commitment to understanding criminal justice underpin such a successful enterprise. Joining the disparate communities overrides the walls and bars that keep citizens out as much as they keep criminals in.

Learning of other programs and sharing information on their successes and failures has been a rich aspect of long-term community service work at our campus. Graduate student Martin Mitchell presented his volunteer drama work several times alongside other longtime educators such as Michigan Prison Arts educator Buzz Alexander[7] at Theatre of the Oppressed conferences recognizing both the pedagogy of Paulo Freire and activist theater of Augusto Boal. Our prison outreach involvement in national service-learning groups such as Campus Compact, the Invisible College (now Educators for Community Engagement), and the National Council for Experiential Education helped us negotiate the changing environments for volunteer work as budgets for incarceration increased amid climates for less rehabilitation.

More Obstacles: Location Shifts

As well as adapting teaching models in Washington, DC, Department of Corrections maximum security cellblocks, we soon had to adapt to major institutional shifts of inmates to other buildings in separately managed prisons on the large Lorton complex. Though we had taught in two different maximum locations Cellblock 5 and Cellblock 1, we eventually had to move our no-tuition, pro bono classes to Medium Security when Maximum was closing, as the entire institution was soon to be closed. At Lorton's Medium Security we used space from the University of the District of Columbia's facility there. UDC had used Pell Grants to fund the large tuition-charging program that helped many men improve the quality of their lives inside prison and also prepare them for life back in the community. Here we met up again with William Lawson. After his first relocation to a West Coast county jail, he was returned to the DC area and landed at Medium Security "on the Hill " and was able to take classes again through Georgetown's program. Lawson took a final GU class in a drama course I team taught with MA graduate student Martin Mitchell.[8] Thus, we experienced continuities and connectedness even amid disruptions.

Long Time Yields Variety of Services: Not "Bowling Alone"

In Robert Putnam's *Bowling Alone*, a critique on American communities' dangerous insularity, he suggests we engage, not as individuals, but in and with community. The work we at GU Prison Outreach took up could have become a cult of one personality, as sometimes happens in service projects. We worked against that by being, first of all, a community ourselves. As faculty and tutors we bonded during the "van time" we spent en route through rush-hour traffic in the DC suburbs, traveling the 26 miles each way to the prisons, preparing for, and then on the return trip debriefing on, the experience. As a program requested by inmates and cowritten by them in our founding documents as the "Friends of Lorton Prison," we set out to be collaborative and committed (if you will pardon the pun). We also connected as fellow students and faculty struggling to achieve our goals.

In long-term community work, one adjusts not only to changes in locations, but changes in requests for involvement. Our program spun off or assisted in the formation of other service work including the Georgetown University After School Kids program, set up by John Zoltner and Daniel Porterfield, which mentors adjudicated youth and is funded by the U.S. courts. Enthusiastic tutors developed further outreach to DC youth held in detention at Cedar Knoll (now called New Beginnings) in Maryland. Besides our programs, we also learned of others who worked with area prisoners, creating a climate of concerned practitioners who addressed the needs for variety of programming that could assist in rehabilitation of those under court scrutiny.

We also were not alone in our work as volunteers who crossed into that DC prison system. Our educational enrichment group composed of inmates and university students and faculty, called Friends of Lorton Prison, at that time, followed smoothly on the heels of a long-term involvement by Georgetown's Law School professor Richard Roe, who had set up courses at DC's prisons in Street Law, a class designed to apprise prisoners of their rights as citizens. That course was also taught pro bono in area high schools in the 1970s and 1980s, in years in which civil rights, especially of African Americans, were in stages of disarray on the streets as well as in the prisons of America[9]. In the subsequent years, I and a number of faculty and student volunteers conducted many courses inside the walls in English, philosophy, drama, business, and history. We never offered a degree-bearing program, just courses that we promised were the same standard as on Georgetown's campus in DC. Georgetown University, through its School of Continuing Studies and the benevolence of Dean Michael Collins, charged no tuition to the over 200 different inmates who enrolled over the years in these college courses.

We were not the lone representative of higher education in the DC prisons, though in 1984 we were the only institution serving maximum security prisoners. The University of the District of Columbia (UDC) ran many educational programs in the larger complex of medium security facilities at Lorton. They offered associate's and bachelor's degrees in a few disciplines such as urban studies.[10] Especially after a series of disturbances and riots in the 1980s, inmates we taught inside "The Wall," as maximum was called, had no access to those courses, which were only taught in the medium and minimum security areas "On the Hill," the compound that housed the most vocational instruction as well as the Education Facility for UDC's programs, along with the largest numbers of DC's incarcerated.

Working with Others Builds Capacity

Inmates readily entered into a variety of enriching programs beyond our college courses, including various offerings of religious study and services. Often the imprisoned students brought insights gleaned from the studies they made in these other programs. For instance, many discussed paintings they produced in art classes taught by long-term individual volunteer Mia Kemensky. The rich association of painting to literary analysis was brought to my classes via the alert inmates who appreciated the nuances of multiple interpretations rather than the reverse path of me informing them of such complexity. Though I never got to know Ms. Mia, the respect for her talent and her decades of dedication to the life of the mind through somatic expression enriched our work inside the walls.

Several religious groups also entered Maximum, bringing Christian as well as Muslim outreach to inmates. One man in that first class who was serving a life sentence said he attended all the religious services. He said he first attended as a way to fight the boredom of so much time incarcerated. Eventually he said he found this a way to expand his understanding of faiths and peoples. Programming into activities is a positive aspect of prison life in most jurisdictions. It can help reduce an indeterminate sentence with what is called "good time." Along with prison industry jobs, such activities provide a much-needed reacquaintance with a life of work and a life of the mind that can also bring about communication with those outside the walls. Such contacts can help the inmate transition into healthy aspects of community should the incarcerated person return to the community.

Though the primary motivation can be to ease ennui, the results of such involvements can be powerfully inspiring and lasting. Sadly, not much coordination is facilitated among the variety of programs that operate inside prisons, though facilities usually have an official who regulates entry and does security checks on those who volunteer or who work in programs with inmates. Sometimes an appreciation of volunteers event or an annual awards ceremony for inmates can bring together all such people who spend time connecting the incarcerated to the larger community outside the bars and walls. The inmates themselves who participate in educational, religious, and vocational programming, however, are the major and often untapped resource for coordination. As is often true in settings where "help" is given, the recipients are the central locus of information on the situation. We learned to tap that potential.

We who worked toward educating—whether it be adult basic literacy conducted by inmates and staff, college courses by faculty and tutors from outside, art lessons or religious education by volunteers, or legal workshops by Law School graduate students—we had built up a culture of learning and a culture of expectations of personal improvement inside the chaotic round of life inside the prisons. We were a motley crew, but we had in common a belief in rehabilitation and in the adage many prisoners quoted: "Education is the key to success." These examples of varieties of programs that reached into the prison suggest that continuity of programs rests on cooperation to strengthen the capacity and create deeper foundations of community involvement, especially important in places such as prisons that are shuttered from view and often lacking in frequent community oversight and investigation. Allies inside the prisons include inmates, educational, religious, and vocational staff as well as wardens and officers who seek more opportunities for normalcy to help inmates practice the routines that help them transition to the larger community or adjust to a life permanently behind bars.

Long-Term Service Yields Responsive Research

Interests in contextualizing the teaching resulted in research into the lives of those incarcerated. For me it started with the phrase "I caught a murder charge," spoken by a scholarly inmate of whom I, in my puzzlement at a locked-up man's adept skills in literary analysis, had asked: "How did you end up at Lorton?" As a sociolinguist I pondered that passivizing remark about "catching a charge," rather than "killing a man," and stepped away from my teaching agenda to do research while others took on the teaching role. I pursued a two-year collection of life stories of inmates inside maximum security that yielded the book *Speaking of Crime: Narratives of Prisoners* (O'Connor, 2000) and made my reentry to prison teaching more grounded in understandings of the whole round of life that entailed imprisonment. I suggest research "in the middle" is a credible model for service learning in higher education. Years spent in providing services yield (1) a developing trust, (2) research questions, and (3) a basis in fathoming the bureaucracies for community-based research. Returning to the teaching after extracting the interviews signals a commitment to the whole process, not a selfish agenda for the researcher alone. Information from the interviews helps our programs focus on surmounting difficulties for education within the violent worlds of crime-riddled communities and overcrowded, understaffed prisons. This research also brought to light how my discipline of sociolinguistics can help discern the social and moral positioning of criminals and their stories that suggest for some a sense of agency and for others a lack of agency in the crimes they committed.

Our community-based service also assisted others in forming their own queries. For me, I had the incredible experience of becoming involved in the prison work and then pursuing a doctorate degree that helped me to be able to understand the power of words inside the walls that locked in those with whom we worked. This became true also for Martin M. Mitchell, who worked as a teaching assistant with me on Georgetown's campus and also inside the prison setting. His MA thesis examined action theater in prison teaching. He later did a doctorate in theater arts at Cornell, writing his thesis on uses of drama with the incarcerated (see Mitchell, 1993 & 2007). What connected both these studies was the engagement of one inmate in particular, Elvin Johnson. Mr. Johnson, who with his 1983 letter had initiated the first courses we taught at the DC Department of Corrections, upon his release, became a speaker on imprisonment and on rehabilitation through education. In this personal outreach together we discussed the role of education in rehabilitation with a variety of audiences across America from Florida to Rhode Island, from Pennsylvania to Tennessee to New York and to California. City Year volunteers, service-learning conferences, the Modern Language Association, Educators for Community Engagement meetings, the Highlander Folk School, and also Mitchell's program at the Lou Gossett Junior Youth Residence near Cornell all heard Elvin Johnson discuss what it had meant to be asked to think deeply and to study hard in the company of the volunteers. In these settings we saw, over and over, that sharing our stories built capacity to strengthen our outreach.

Georgetown University undergraduate tutor Terra White (2004) conducted a study of learning disabilities and their impact on education in jails, using her tutoring in one of our programs at the Arlington County Detention Facility, a local jail, as springboard for her service and research questions. With guidance from Bill Muth, education director in the federal prison system, she discerned a strong correlation between incarceration and learning disabilities in self-reports from jail inmates in one jurisdiction. Thus, inquiry about what one learns in service leads to a spread of inquiry and knowledge, a fitting result for service learning from universities whose missions are teaching, research, and service.

Accessing such larger circles of knowing maximized our understandings of volunteering, community service learning, and community-based research. This ultimately resulted in a deeply engaged practice that brought greater strength to our efforts and enlarged what philosopher Richard Rorty and composition theorist Kenneth Bruffee have called our community of knowledgeable peers. Mitchell, White, and I thus used direct service, education, and research, in concert with the community of incarcerated, to open up to others ways to communicate with those whom many had written off as worthless. Such committed engagement leads to engaged scholarship that we can hope leads to positive change. Or as inmates say: "What goes around, comes around." What we who engage in activist research are about, then, is building new conversations not only in individual lives, but in multilogues of scholarship and discussion that examine and question the growing stressors on communities. Engaged commitment and engaged scholarship join to enhance communities in productive uptake to combat social ills. This long-term community service-learning model forefronts the service *as* teaching, and it has developed research *in* service to communities as it promotes new kinds of knowledge.

Continuity and Change in Community Service: Politics, Land Use, Control

For university volunteers entering into educational service, the immediate, hands-on work of educational tutoring is the draw. The difficulty for the volunteer is appreciating the depth of contexts that surround the simple acts of explication or help. The longer a program lasts, the more rings of context grow around the acts of reciprocal exchange. Universities and colleges are ideally equipped to help ground students and communities in wider historical, social, and political matters. We found we could only teach in the prisons and learn with the inmates if the political and even geographical concerns around us could be fathomed.

At the time of our 10-year anniversary in the prisons we faced our biggest obstacle—the nationwide zeal and polling appeal in the 1990s for those seeking election to get tougher on crime. The Omnibus Crime Bill of 1994 had ended many prison programs, though ours remained, as it had been internally funded by Georgetown. Simultaneously a boom in real estate values paralleled the expanding suburbs of Washington, DC, which had filled in all around the prison farm's 3,000 acres of land 25 miles south of the city, land leased from Virginia's Fairfax County by the federal government. Escapes and fears of escapes, and riots by inmates over religious freedom, work conditions, medical services and food services, merged with local Virginia citizens' increased interest in more housing and recreation areas for the suburban community that had grown up around the prison complex. By 2001, the federal land lease was ended; Lorton Correctional Complex was closed.[11] Inmates were dispersed to federal institutions across America.

Unable to relocate our program into the chaotic DC jail that was scrambling to cope with those changes in incarceration for DC criminals, we looked elsewhere. Georgetown undergraduate tutor Alex Belser arranged for the program to move into Arlington County at the local county jail, the Arlington County Detention Center (ACDC) in Virginia, ironically much closer than Lorton's complex to our campus at Georgetown. We launched a few college credit courses at that jail, including creative writing with the help of Dr. Carole Sargent. However, the need in that setting was for more basic education. Thus, we adapted. The programs center now on preparation for the test for general education (GED) and in various years, computer skills, Spanish GED, and adult basic education, always depending on the needs of the jailed population. We worked for the first time with female prisoners in the Arlington County Detention Center, necessarily expanding our contextualization to include that fastest-growing cohort in American imprisonment.

Our program soon faced another challenge in 2005: I embarked on a path teaching abroad for the university. This meant more letting go of the reins, a difficult task in community service, but one that universities are actually well equipped to undertake. I asked other faculty to advise the group, calling on the talents of a junior colleague Dr. Jennifer Fink, whose expertise in community creative writing helped the students retailor the volunteer work.

An obstacle to university community service can be the committed ownership we mentors command. Conversely, doing too much yields burnout. As noted by the mention of student Belser and the growing role for tutors as coordinators, our program had been putting more weight in the late 1990s and in the new century on the student roles for leadership: attracting volunteers, coordinating training, and interfacing with the bureaucracies. This was a welcome relief for me as an overcommitted professor who had managed to achieve a master's and a doctoral degree and tenure and promotion while mentoring the program. During that overbooked time, Georgetown tutor Dan D'Orazio, who later became a social worker, had spearheaded the first efforts to put recruitment and selection of tutors into the capable hands of the student tutors. Rather than burnout (though always scarily close) I soon enjoyed the peace of seeing a program churn out its own tutoring and administrative "progeny" by having tutors take on full leadership roles and using the university-wide mentoring and training from Georgetown's community service umbrella, the greatly expanded Center for Social Justice, Teaching and Research. Recent tutor coordinator for GU Prison Outreach Jessica Chafkin has helped expand our services to another Virginia jail in Alexandria.

The Residuals: Long-Term Connections and Giving Back

What resulted from these interactions with prisoners? Even with the diaspora of Washington, DC, prisoners, inmates have maintained a fruitful contact through letters and phone calls. When they are released we have the pleasure of educators the world over in seeing what has become of our students. As the example of Elvin Johnson showed, inmates of Maximum Security Cellblocks 1 and 5 have reentered our sphere. We see them showing up at the campus to relish the fact of being finished with their sentences and able to see the campus for the first time.

Poignantly, I recall a box of fresh peaches appearing around the corner of my office door one summer day in the hands of former inmate Brian Harris, who said: "I'm working now at an orchard in Maryland, and brought these Early Red Havens for you." Harris had been out before and worked for a while in auto maintenance on our campus, but had slid away from us and back into the world of addiction, robbery, and then to prison in another jurisdiction. That second sentence of eight years of his life had not diminished the desire to change, as he stated when he took on the simple orchard job. Desire and doing, however, are compounded by past mistakes, new bad choices, and addiction's enormous grip. A few years after I visited the peach orchard and Harris's new life, I received the saddest of calls from a woman who had hoped they would both recover from heroin addiction: Brian Harris had been murdered in a downtown DC zone known for its danger and drug trafficking.

Besides such a vignette being a warning for those of us who pin too much hope (or ego) on how our community service affects others, this also confirmed my decision to increase my research agenda. Addiction's tight association with original incarceration (as revealed in my first book) and recidivism (as revealed in several of the inmates' returns to prisons) has become now a new area of my research. Thus, adaptation is key, as well, in what we research in connection with changing situations in service. We learn to shift our agendas and bring our expertise to what is needed, not just what we have already done.

Other stories of past inmate scholars have given more hope. One of the few women prisoners whom I taught, J. D. from Arlington County Virginia's Detention Center, has kept me abreast of her educational achievements after being released. A discerning student in my last college-credit-bearing jail course, she attended Smith College after her release. She has also given back to our campus by assisting me in fostering more community involvement as a speaker at a night for foreign visitors from the Georgetown Qatar campus to the DC Georgetown campus. The students from eight different countries heard her tell of the inspiration she gained through education to believe in herself that she could surmount barriers she had to overcome both as a prisoner and as an ex-prisoner. J.D. has recently graduated from Smith and begun applications to graduate schools.

William Lawson has, as of summer 2009, been released from prison after serving 32 years. For 25 of those years I shared in his amazingly diasporic imprisonment. Lawson, as noted above, was not only a student in our first classes, but was one of the first inmates sent across the nation to occupy a cheaper prison bed in 1988. That was not, however, the end of Lawson's travels, nor of his involvement in educational enrichment. In correspondence he detailed his odyssey, which is representative of the diverse numbers of prisons in use now that house DC's felons in the wake of the closing of the Lorton complex: USP Leavenworth, Kansas; FCI El Reno, Oklahoma; USP Terre Haute, Indiana; FCI Oxford, Wisconsin; Stutsman County Correctional Center in Jamestown, North Dakota; Corrections Corporation of America, West Tennessee Detention Facility; Corrections Corporation of America, Northeast Ohio Correctional Center; Sussex II Super Maximum Penitentiary in Waverly, Virginia; USP Atlanta, Georgia; USP Coleman II in Coleman, Florida. That long list of shifts and changes included Lawson's participation in many programs of learning, though never again in college classes, as few were on offer, especially to inmates who were in relocation. Letters and phone calls had paramount importance for such inmates to keep in touch with families and also to keep in contact with those of us who had partnered with them on learning.

Remaining connected is an aspect of service that reminds us of the larger and changing contexts in which we work with local as well as increasingly diasporic communities. Time, long time, hard time, but most importantly, quality time surrounds the dynamic in which service affects the whole person, the conjoined communities, and our larger society deeply in the grips of economic, cultural, racial, and psychosocial factors that shape us.

I hear often from the inmates and former inmates about our collaborations on learning. They speak to the humanization of education. Not just books, not just papers to be written, but human exchange and debate about knowledge. These "new conversations" inside the cellblocks replace the ponderously mundane and sometimes shockingly deadly remarks inside the walls. They prepare, as well, a path back to society if we can increase the community uptake for released and soon-to-be released prisoners. Former Lorton inmate Rashim Grey, after his release, worked one semester as a special consultant attending and assisting in one of my GU Prison Literature sections. The former Lorton inmate and poet Rickey Bryant, mentioned in the opening poem for this chapter, was released in 2010 and is continuing the youth outreach he began while serving the last decade of his 32-year sentence in Lewisburg Federal Penitentiary in Pennsylvania. Former inmates Johnson, Lawson, and now Bryant regularly speak with student groups and classes on our campus, giving back to the community that had long ago sent its youth to volunteer in prisons. For example, they and their friend Juanita, all part of the very large community of former prisoners in DC, recently volunteered as consultants to Georgetown's Nomadic Theater as it produced Marsha Norman's play *Getting Out*. They advised student actors, directors, and stage crew on what they knew of the worlds of guards and prisoners on the inside as well as the difficult world of trying to restart a life outside. These experiences included looking for jobs, avoiding former associates, and realizing what to do when families may have given up on them.

Prisoners inside have made extraordinary efforts to retrain themselves and others to lessen the impact of their disappearance from the families they left behind. Lorton inmate and former student in our program Stuart Anderson helped start the Concerned Fathers Organization inside Medium Security at Lorton. This group continues to advocate for maintaining family ties in spite of the diasporic incarcerations for DC felons all across America. Families in that program now use new technologies for contact through teleconferencing in a few prisons. Such advocacy work has helped Anderson continue this project as a released inmate and has made his daughter—now grown and deeply attached to her father—a new advocate for families who try to stay in communication with their incarcerated members. Such inmate expertise and family resources can be tapped and channeled for the good of communities. We who foster community service learning realize that we all have the potential to become reciprocal educators on the social and emotional frameworks that affect our communities.

I hear, too, from the former tutors how compelling was that experience of devoting one night a week to prisoners for one, two, three, or—in a few cases—four years of their college time. Several "long timer" tutors' examples suggest ways that this formative volunteer experience has impacted the trajectories of the lives shared in service. Undergraduate Ellen Kelly gave four years to the program as an undergraduate and has kept up a 20-year correspondence and belief in one inmate whose potential she recognized. Now a lawyer, Kelly has celebrated through his letters the slow changes in status from prisoner to truck driver to proud husband and father that former inmate Milton Greene became. Martin Mitchell now directs fine arts and teaches drama at Flint Hill in Virginia. Tutor Jannie Bui, who fostered the writing of poetry by inmates in the very first years of our work, teaches in Cleveland. Alex Belser, who helped reorganize our group to enter jails when the Lorton Complex closed, did his master's degree at the Institute of Criminology at Cambridge, where he developed a research tool to assist in evaluating prisoner capacity for reentry to society. Belser is now in a doctoral program in criminal psychology. Enthusiasm of former tutors has led to small educational intervention programs in other states and nations started by alumni/ae volunteers and those affected by the work we did at DC's Lorton Prison complex and the work we continue doing in DC area jails. Some became educators in Teach for America, others worked for public defenders, some became social workers. All of us have shared a strange and perplexing intersection in our autobiographies—a crossroads inside the walled and barred universe of punishment.

More Than a Novelty

While one's first visit to a prison or jail might have a residue of novelty, sustained work inside the systems of incarceration removes both voyeurism and rose-colored glasses. We suffered disappointments when some of those we championed recidivated. We reexamined complexities in institutional, social, and economic systems that attracted and ensnared so much lost potential. Those new to the volunteering always bring enthusiasm to the task of change in a society that seems bent on destruction with the drug trade appearing, ironically, as the most equal opportunity employer around. Tutor groups have expanded outward, drawing in former inmates to help recruit new tutors and hosting forums to help the larger campus community confront psychological and social issues that contribute to the massive incarceration rates and the rate of criminal activity.[12]

In a way, we who have been immersed in and affected by this work are rather like Bigger Thomas and the Little Prince, the two central characters in two of the novels from that very first course I taught inside Cellblock 5 in 1984. Bigger Thomas in Wright's *Native Son* reacted via murders to the immediate fear and survival instinct amid stifling social disillusion for black Americans in the 1930s. St.-Exupery's *Little Prince*, written shortly after Bigger's time while St.-Exupery was in exile from occupied France during World War II, recounted the Prince's search for knowledge to care for the life of a treasured and endangered entity, a rose. The prince was met with deception, delusion, bureaucracy, inanity, and finally the wisdom that nurturing is what matters to keep his beloved rose from dying. We in service need such concern for those whose lives are, like Bigger, a wandering prince, and a neglected rose, withering before they take root. A constancy of concern, expansion of understanding of complex contributors to crime, and belief in the potential of all of us can nurture and sustain outreach programs. We need to affect positively the incarcerated and those en route to the nation's youth "camps," jails, and prisons. Each criminal, each tutor, each of us who taught or coordinated or incarcerated others was born with potential, a potential we need not only to value, but to rediscover and redeploy.

Going public with the stories of our successes, our failures, our research findings can bring about a reconnected commitment to education that helps people reach full potential.

In the current climate of change in America, I can relish the words of mountain musician Bill Staines in his lyrics "I can feel the sweet winds blowing through the valleys and the hills" as I witness new interest in working with the incarcerated (qtd. in Carawan & Carawan 1996, p. 5). Two research groups, one from Harvard's Houston Institute and another from the University of Illinois, are now compiling nationwide information on educational enrichment via college programs in America's prisons. New programs are starting, such as that begun by a consortium of educators from Goucher College and Loyola University in Maryland now serving the Maryland Women's Detention Center. (I have just taught a course there in 2011.) Lori Pompa's Inside Out program at Temple University expanded and is now replicated in many states, bringing inspiring experiences for those moving from the outside to educational exchanges inside the walls. "I can hear the people stirring as I go, as I go" say those lyrics that inspire me and have me welcoming queries about doing more of this work in other communities.

Thus, unbelievably, over 30 years have now passed and Georgetown University can still count educational outreach to prisoners as part of its continuing commitment to the community. Much developed, much changed in that time. Adaptability has been the keystone of this community service, integral to maintaining commitment to community renewal. On a macro level we learned to maintain a program in spite of national political climates of mistrust in rehabilitation. Locally, we focused on shifting programs to meet needs and circumstances. We developed research agendas that sprang from the experiences and needs of the inmates, the institutions, and the larger society. In a way, we who have become involved in longtime service have "failed to comply" with hopelessness. Our continuing contact and work becomes a dynamic intervention in which we all have the privilege to become part of creating new and reflective selves. We become intellectually informed communities who continue to serve each other and who learn the value of long time, even hard time, together.

Notes

1. The picture of incarceration becomes even more of a concern when we factor race into the frame. In 1991, the Bureau of Justice Statistics (Maguire & Pastore 1995, p. 548) noted the ratio of 740 whites per 100,000 in lockups. They state that adult black males were incarcerated at a rate six times that of whites, with 5,717 blacks incarcerated per 100,000 (p. 548). As time passed, such rates of incarceration for men of color continued to increase. In 1997, "The rate among black males in their late twenties reached 8,630 prisoners per 100,000 residents compared to 2,703 among Hispanic males and 868 among white males" (Beck & Mumola 1999, p. 1).

2. See the special issue "Prison Literacies, Narratives and Community Connections" in *Reflections: A Journal of Writing, Service Learning and Community Literacy* edited by Tobi Jacobi and Patricia E. O'Connor for more community service programs inside U.S. prisons and jails.

3. Currently John J. DeGioia is president of Georgetown University.

4. An amateur video about the closed Maximum Facility available on YouTube has a maintenance employee verifying reports I heard from inmates about this bus shuttling. This material was assembled for a George Mason University class IT314. *The History of Lorton Prison*, IT413.http://www.youtube.com/watch?v=dBUtDfDZ7_Q.

5. I eventually took up these topics in my research on life stories of prisoners in *Speaking of Crime: Narratives of Prisoners* (2000) in which inmates recounted instances of being targets of, or perpetrators of, hit squads and other violence.

6. By 2005, teams from "Penn, Indiana University, Mount Holyoke, Amherst and the College of Wooster. . . . Vanderbilt Divinity School, Gettysburg, Bucknell, Chestnut Hill College, the University of Delaware and North Carolina State" had all attended and instituted the program (Baals 2005).

7. Alexander's 20-year look back at his prison arts project is chronicled in *Is William Martinez Not Our Brother: Twenty Years of the Prison Creative Arts Project* (2010).

8. Mitchell later wrote his thesis on teaching drama inside prison enlisting action theater techniques as well as the work of Augusto Boal on people's theater.

9. Professor Rick Roe's long-term work, his textbooks on street law, and his initiation of legal clinics and services for inmates stand as testimony to community service.

10. Eventually, in the large, sad wake of the get-tougher-on-crime climate and the 1994 Omnibus Crime Bill that ended the use of Pell Grants for prisoners to pay tuition, UDC's college programs closed, affecting not only the inmates but the solvency of the institution itself, which counted on the Pell moneys for operating expenses.

11. Currently the old workhouse, locus of some of our courses, is home to a fine arts studio for local artists and a museum focused on the prison. See Lorton Arts Foundation at http://www.lortonarts.org/.

12. Tutor coordinator Jessica Chafkin in 2011 and 2012 organized current GU tutors to visit SingSing (Osining) Penitentiary and Bedford Women's Prison in New York to widen our students' understanding of the complexities of imprisonment nationwide.

References

Alexander, B. *Is William Martinez not our brother: Twenty years of the prison creative arts project.* Ann Arbor: University of Michigan Press, 2010.

Baals, B. (2005). Program breaking down prison walls. *Temple Times Online*, November 3. Retrieved February 26, 2010 from http://www.temple.edu/temple_times/11-3-05/insideout.html.

Beck, A. (2000). *Prisoner and jail inmates at midyear 1999.* Washington, DC: U.S. Department of Justice, Bureau of Justice Statistics.

Beck, A., and Mumola, C. (1999). *Prisoners in 1998.* Washington, DC: U.S. Department of Justice, Bureau of Justice Statistics.

Boal, A. (1993). *Theatre of the oppressed.* New York: Theatre Communications Group.

Bonczar, T. (2003). *Prevalence of imprisonment in the United States population, 1974–2001.* Washington, DC: U.S. Department of Justice, Bureau of Justice Statistics.

Bruffee, K. (1984). Collaborative learning and the "conversation of mankind." *College English, 46*(7), 635–52.

Bureau of Justice. (2006). *Total expenditures: Direct expenditures by criminal justice function, 1982–2006.* Washington, DC: U.S. Department of Justice, Bureau of Justice Statistics. Retrieved March 15, 2010, from http://bjs.ojp.usdoj.gov/content/glance/tables/exptyptab.cfm.

Bureau of Justice. (2009). *Total correctional populations mid-year 2008.* Washington, DC: U.S. Department of Justice, Bureau of Justice Statistics. Retrieved February 28, 2010, from http://bjs.ojp.usdoj.gov/index.cfm?ty=tp&tid=11.

Bureau of Justice. (2010a). *Key facts: Incarceration rate, 1980–2009.* Retrieved March 31, 2011, from http://bjs.ojp.usdoj.gov/content/glance/tables/incrttab.cfm.

Bureau of Justice. (2010b). *Key facts at a glance: Correctional populations, 1980–2008.* Washington, DC: Bureau of Justice Statistics. Retrieved February 28, 2010, from http://bjs.ojp.usdoj.gov/content/glance/tables/corr2tab.cfm.

Carawan, G., & Carawan, C. 1996. *Voices from the mountains.* Athens: University of Georgia Press.

Carson, E. A., & Sabol, W. J. (2012). *Prisoners in 2011.* Washington, DC: U.S. Department of Justice, Bureau of Justice Statistics.

Foucault, M. (1979). *Discipline and punish: The birth of the prison.* Trans. A. Sheridan. New York: Vintage Books.

Freire, P. (2006). *Pedagogy of the oppressed.* New York: Continuum.

Goffman, E. (1961). *Asylums: Essays on the social situation of mental patients and other inmates.* Chicago: Aldine.

Greenberg E., Dunleavy, E., & Kutner, M. (2007). *Literacy behind bars: Results from the National Assessment of Adult Literacy prison survey.* Washington, DC: U.S. Department of Education National Center for Education Statistics.

Haigler, K., Harlow, C., O'Connor, P. E., & Campbell, A. (1994). *Literacy behind prison walls.* Washington, DC: U.S. Department of Education.

Hamilton Institute for Race and Justice. (2010). Harvard Law School. Retrieved March 30, 2010, from http://www.charleshamiltonhouston.org/Projects/Project.aspx?id=100000.

Harlow, C. (2003) *Education and correctional populations.* Washington, DC: U.S. Department of Justice, Bureau of Justice Statistics.

The history of Lorton prison. (2008). George Mason University IT314. (Video). Retrieved February 10, 2010, from http://www.youtube.com/watch?v=dBUtDfDZ7_Q.

Jacobi, T., & O'Connor, P. E. (Eds.). (2004). Prison literacies, narratives, and community connections. Special issue of *Reflections: A Journal of Writing, Service Learning and Community Literacy,* 4(1).

Kozol, J. (1995). *Amazing grace: The lives of children and the conscience of America.* New York: Crown.

Hockstader, L. (1988). Sudden move severs inmates' ties to D.C. *Washington Post,* December 17, A1. Retrieved from LexisNexis Academic.

Lorton Arts Foundation. (2010). *Workhouse arts.* http://www.lortonarts.org/.

Maguire, K., & Pastore, A. (1995). *Sourcebook of criminal justice statistics, 1994.* Washington, DC: U.S. Department of Justice, Bureau of Justice Statistics.

Mauer, M. (2006). *The race to incarcerate.* 2nd ed. New York: New Press.

Mitchell, M. M., III. (1993). Stars behind bars: Prison pedagogy, performance theory, and the social construction of identity. MA thesis, Georgetown University.

Mitchell, M. M., III. (2007). Theatre of the oppressed in United States prisons: Eight years of working with adult and youth prisoners examined. PhD dissertation, Cornell University.

Oakey, M., & Swanson, B. (1988). *Journey from the gallows: Historical evolution of the penal philosophies and practices in the nation's capital.* New York: University Press of America.

O'Connor, P. E. (2000). *Speaking of crime: Narratives of prisoners.* Lincoln: University of Nebraska Press.

Piñero, M. (1986). *Short eyes.* New York: Broadway Play Publications.

Pompa, L. (2004). Disturbing where we are comfortable. *Reflections: A Journal of Writing, Service Learning and Community Literacy,* 4(1), 24–34.

St.-Exupery, A. (2005). *The little prince.* Trans. R. Howard. London: Harcourt/Egmont.

Staines, W. (1996). I can hear the sweet winds blowing. (Lyrics). In G. Carawan and C. Carawan (Eds.), *Voices from the mountains* (p. 5). Athens: University of Georgia Press.

Tiger, C. (2004). Turning lives inside out. *Philadelphia City Paper,* September 30. Cover. Retrieved February 26, 2010, from http://citypaper.net/articles/2004–09–30/cover.shtml.

U.S. Census Bureau. (2010). U.S. and World Population Clocks. Retrieved April 2, 2010, from http://www.census.gov/main/www/popclock.html.

White, T. (2004). Learning disabilities among the incarcerated. *Reflections: A Journal of Writing, Service Learning and Community Literacy, 4*(1), 51–60.

Wikberg, R., & Rideau W. 1992. *Life sentences: Rage and survival behind bars.* New York: Times Books.

Wright, R. *Native son.* 1940. New York: Harper.

Illuminating the Terrain of Community Engagement in Landscape Architecture Education

Pat Crawford, Warren Rauhe, and Patricia Machemer

"Illuminating the Terrain" is an exploratory study of how professional academic programs integrate community engagement around the issues of community design and land use. Real-life design projects are a mainstay of landscape architecture (LA) studio courses across North America and a lively topic with many CELA (Council of Educators in Landscape Architecture) members. However, a systematic look at how we do it, why we do it, and what we know does not exist. The perception of engagement activities as less scholarly or rigorous than traditional research remains a challenge in many universities. The weaknesses are attributed to lack of consensus or clarity in how engaged scholarship is defined, assessed, and documented (Finkelstein, 2001).

This study begins to answer these questions with a profile created from interviews with 20 accredited LA programs in the United States and Canada with formal community engagement initiatives or programs. It started out as a simple idea and quickly grew into a rich qualitative database generated from the interviews. Questions range from the details of staffing, number of projects, and funding to broader questions of student benefits, stakeholder roles, and assessment. The questions are grouped into related topics or layers, much like the contours on a topographic map, which in combination create the terrain.

The types of engagement described are as diverse as the landscape architectural profession itself. What binds them all together is an intense enthusiasm and ethic for quality student learning and the use of real-world projects to foster professional development through community service. A study goal is to articulate what we do and how we do it so that we may foster dialogue for sharing, learning, and growth. Landscape architecture programs have an opportunity to blend together student learning, community service, and scholarship in a manner that addresses the needs of students, faculty, and communities. Feedback from the 20 interviews documents the potential while also pointing out apparent disconnects.

Landscape Architecture Education and Community Engagement

Landscape architecture is a design profession that applies artistic, cultural, ecological, scientific, and technical knowledge to the planning, design, and management of the landscape. It requires an understanding of natural and social processes, a creative imagination, technical expertise, and a commitment to protect and improve the quality of the physical environment for optimum human use and enjoyment. The core of the profession is visual, experiential, and three-dimensional.

The twenty-first-century movement in higher education from teacher-centered to learner-centered (Huba & Freed, 2000) is a natural fit for landscape architecture programs. The educational foundation in landscape architecture is built on an experiential, learning-by-doing process (Wagner & Gansemer-Topf, 2005) including problem-based learning, community-based learning, service learning, integrative learning, undergraduate research, and capstone courses.

Over 100 years ago, in 1898, the first U.S. landscape architecture program was established in Michigan with influences from the Beaux Arts traditions and design studio pedagogy. In a design charrette, students are given a design problem and a specified amount of time (often short) in which to create a solution. They are then judged on the merits of the solution and the artistry of the presentation. During the Great Depression and World War II, U.S. schools began to broaden from a purely aesthetic base to include environmental, cultural, psychological, and engineering aspects. Today, communities are often engaged to bring social and participatory components into the design process and learning experiences with site-specific issues, opportunities, history, and resources. These types of experiential immersion are advocated as critical for students to learn the complex disciplinary components of the profession and how to integrate their skills in practice (Council of Educators in Landscape Architecture, 1998).

Higher education across the country is challenged to increase accountability to its stakeholders (including student learning), increase revenue streams (especially for those with government funding), reinvigorate civic responsibility, and reevaluate what constitutes scholarship (Boyer, 1990; Dubb & Howard, 2007). Community-based design is one way of meeting these challenges while creating real-life learning experiences, expanding applied research venues, and increasing community service compatible with the institution's mission (Scholarship of Engagement, 2006). This understanding of community engagement is aligned with the definition articulated by the University Outreach and Engagement office at Michigan State University. Community outreach and engagement "occurs when scholarship is applied directly for the public good and when the relationship between partners is reciprocal and mutually beneficial" (Michigan State University, University Outreach and Engagement, 2010). Engagement also brings with it many challenges. Learning from the Milwaukee Idea (2006), Wergin found that faculty tend to be unaccustomed to the messiness of engagement in real-world projects, and they often lack experiential knowledge of the situation and issues. Engaged work can challenge traditional notions of what is scholarship and research, and engagement is time-intensive because of the need to develop trust and social networks. Peters has gone so far as to say that "the skills, capabilities, and dispositions that are required to do excellent scholarship that is recognized as such by the academy are not necessarily the same—and may even be in conflict with—what it takes to do excellent public work that contributes to civic learning and development in ways that are recognized as being valuable by citizens beyond the academy" (Peters, Jordan, Adamek, & Alter, 2005, p. 438).

Comparative Case Study and Survey Respondents

The study targets accredited LA programs with formal community engagement initiatives. An initial inquiry was sent to 53 LA programs and 23 (43%) self-identified as having a formal engagement process. The profile is derived from the 20 programs that agreed to participate in a telephone interview survey, giving an 87% response rate. The interviews range from 60 to 90 minutes in length, and the respondent programs are geographically distributed across the United States and Canada. Three programs are located in Canada, and 17 are located in the United States. Of the U.S. programs, four are in northeastern states, six are in midwestern states, five are in southern states, and two are in western states (figure 1).

It should be noted that this work focuses on formal processes and many of the programs use community service learning in their studio classes without a formal engagement structure in place. It also does not include external Community Design Centers, which may include community design projects or participation of landscape architecture students.

Survey Development

Developing the survey began with a brainstorming session of the principal investigators around formal community engagement in LA to identify who does it, what do we do, how we do it, why we do it, and how do we measure it. Given the 40-plus years of practice and teaching experience represented, questions came quickly and were often very specific. Examples include the following: how many projects per year, is there a director, who provides funding and how much, how are LA professional practitioners involved, how are projects identified, what is the impact on the community, and what products do the students create? The questions were grouped using a pile-sort technique that allowed us to see the bigger picture of the types of information we were looking for, where we had duplicate questions and what information was missing. Because of the need for specific information, we selected a semistructured interview format to develop the protocol.

The question groupings are much like the contours on a topographic map, which in combination create the terrain. While the contours hold the related details, the terrain forms the bigger picture and connects the contours together. The terrain is community engagement in landscape architecture education and the six contours are the following:

Contour 1: overview of engagement and history

Contour 2: administration and funding

Contour 3: project identification and engagement process

- ## 60-90 minute phone interviews

- ## respondents

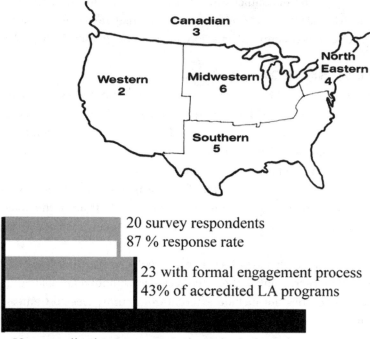

20 survey respondents
87 % response rate

23 with formal engagement process
43% of accredited LA programs

53 accredited LA programs in U.S. & Canada

FIGURE 1 Survey Respondents

Contour 4: products

Contour 5: impact

Contour 6: effectiveness and assessment

Each contour includes seven to 12 questions, beginning with broader questions and probing down into specific topic areas. The protocol was pilot tested to check for question phrasing, flow, and thoroughness. Figure 2 is an example of the interview protocol for contour 3, which focuses on the engagement process.

The telephone interviews were audio recorded for accuracy, and the transcribed responses resulted in over 350 pages of qualitative data. Each interview had a unique numerical identifier and the question responses were cut and pasted into the interview protocol for data input. The responses were collated by contour and question in an Access database for analysis. The Access database allowed for storing and viewing numerical data alongside text data. Each question was analyzed independently and common themes were identified for the qualitative data by the investigators for coding. Data tables and a summary statement were generated for the findings of each question. Figure 3 is an example of findings of contour 1,

3) **Contour 3: Process**

3-1) How are community projects initially identified? How did find out about them?

3-2) How do you select which community projects to accept for the _____? Is this an application process or an informal set of guidelines?

3-3) Once a community is accepted, who defines the project scope and anticipated products?

3-4) Would you describe the community engagement process as:
__ more informal than formal, or __ more formal than informal

3-5) Do you have a process or set of techniques that you typically use with community projects?
Yes ___ No ___ Please elaborate.

3-6) A variety of people can work together on community engagement projects. Of the following list of potential participants, do they participate in the _____ and how would you describe their role?

Community role:
Faculty role - LA:
Faculty role - other disciplines: which disciplines?
Student role:
Practitioner role:
Other:

3-7) How is the _____ integrated into LA curriculum classes?

3-8) How does LA faculty engage in or utilize the _____ meeting service/outreach expectations?

3-9) How does LA faculty engage in or utilize the _____ for research activities?

3-10) Does the _____ provide financial resources to the faculty? No __
If yes ___, please elaborate.

3-11) Do they provide financial resources to support the student work No___
If yes please elaborate.

FIGURE 2 Sample Interview Protocol

question 6: What is the most important thing the program does? The data were organized by contours to structure the findings and are available in a "Final Survey Report on Illuminating the Terrain of Community Engagement in Landscape Architecture Education" (Crawford & Rauhe, 2007). These data were used by the investigators to interpret the terrain and identify exploratory themes of commonalities, differences, balance and compromise, and future recommendations.

1-6) Most important thing the program provides.

Five themes emerge as important program provisions. A focus on student learning, with real-world projects, fostering professional development and exposure to the realities of working with people, is the most common theme (40%). A community service focus is expressed by six (30%) of the respondents. Descriptions of service include products, such as planning and design documents, and community development, such as education, empowerment and consensus building. Three (15%) of the programs highlight the blend of teaching and community service through engagement. Fostering university/community relations and building department credibility at the state and university level is identified by two (10%) of the respondents. The nexus of research, community service and teaching is a theme articulated by one respondent.

Provision Themes	
Student learning	40% (8)
Community service	30% (6)
Blend of teaching and service	15% (3)
Relations / Credibility	10% (2)
Nexus of research, service, teaching	5% (1)
	100% (20)

FIGURE 3 Sample Findings Summary and Table

Illuminating the Terrain

The terrain of community engagement is explored through each of the contours. The contours illuminate details within each of the subject areas that can remain hidden or masked in the overall picture.

Contour 1: Overview of Engagement and History (Figure 4)

Community-based teaching is a traditional component of LA education, and the survey bears this out, with over three-quarters of the formal processes in existence for 10 or more years. The oldest program began in 1960, and the turn of the century (2000–2001) marks a high point in community initiatives with LA engagement programs initiated at six universities. The number of projects taken on each year varies significantly, from one project over multiple years to 11 projects yearly. Collectively, up to 125 engagement projects are taken on each year by the 20 programs participating in the survey. This number could be significantly

• program age

Oldest program: began in 1960
Average Age: 14 years

                        6 programs initiated in 2000-2001

• number of projects / year

123 projects combined each year

5 run one project over multiple years
        6 run one to five projects each year
            4 run six to ten projects each year
                    5 run eleven plus projects yearly

• description emphasis

Student learning opportunities	45%	(9)
Community benefits and outreach	45%	(9)
Applied research	10%	(2)

• most important provision

Students	Real world projects Professional development Service engagement	55%	(11)
Community	Products for communities Community development	30%	(6)
University	University / community relations Department credibility	10%	(2)
Nexus	Teaching/research/service	5%	(1)

FIGURE 4 Contour 1: Overview of Engagement and History

raised if informal engagement projects taken on by studio, practicum, or capstone courses were added.

The primary impetus for starting a community engagement program falls under three main reasons. The first is a need to formalize the work already being done by the faculty and students with communities. The formalization increases project coordination, maximizes benefit potential, and creates a centralized place for communities to bring their requests to the departments. Another equally represented reason is to create a mechanism to meet the outreach and service requirements of the departments within the university setting. A quarter of the programs were initiated to meet specific teaching goals such as working with real sites and community members. This was the third most common reason articulated by respondents. Two of the community engagement programs are an outgrowth of applied research efforts.

Descriptions of the types of engagement reflect the breadth of the landscape architectural profession. Design projects range from countywide master plans, to community visioning, to small-scale design projects culminating in actual construction. Some programs target specific groups such as small towns or low-income communities, while others work with a broad range of communities. Planning and regional projects include community sustainability, watershed stewardship, and shoreline management. Nine (45%) of the descriptions emphasize student learning opportunities through community-based learning, problem-based learning, and service learning. The community benefits are emphasized by an equal number of the respondents and include the university outreach and service aspects of their work. Two respondents emphasized the applied research component of the engagement, reflecting the reason for program initiation.

Across the programs, objectives have an equal emphasis on student learning and community service. The objectives also bring out secondary benefits to the university departments, communities, and LA profession. Department-level objectives include coordinating projects that support course curricula, raising operating funds, and increasing awareness of the department within the university. Promotion of the landscape architecture profession at the community, state, and university levels is achieved in concert with the engagement activities. Community education about the importance of planning and design enhances the ability to participate in the current project and enhances the community's knowledge as future consumers of professional services. Finally, the engagement projects create a venue for research activities, which can be a mechanism for generating external research funding.

Six of the programs are similar today to when they were initiated, including one that has been in place for over 25 years. Seventy percent of the respondents indicate notable changes have taken place. The major change is one of focus. This is expressed as either broadening and diversifying types of projects or narrowing to target community groups or subject areas. Programs have also increased in formality of procedures and rigorousness of student products over time. Other comments include changing with technology and adding a research element. Attitudinal changes toward the value of community-based learning is expressed by one respondent: "[In the beginning] we thought it compromised our students' education. Today it has become a key educational tool."

Contour 2: Administration and Funding (Figure 5)

Respondents indicated that program administration on a day-to-day basis is conducted by Landscape Architecture faculty. A specific person responsible for program administration (often with a "director" title) is the predominant situation. Directors, faculty, staff, and student interns represent the breadth of support scenarios across all the programs. Six of the programs have both support staff and student interns, while seven of the programs have

- ## support

Staff and/or student interns	65% (13) + + + + + + + + + + + + +
No support	35% (7) + + + + + + +

- ## faculty "sweat equity"

High	70% (14) + + + + + + + + + + + + + +
Medium	20% (4) + + + +
Low	10% (2) + +

- ## 15 multiple funding sources (average %)
+ + + + + + + + + + + + + + +

community	university	external
44%	33%	23%

- ## 5 single funding source (100% by)
+ + + + +

community	university	external
2	1	2

FIGURE 5 Contour 2: Administration and Funding

neither. Over half of the programs operate with only student interns. Executing the engagement projects is substantially provided through faculty "sweat equity." This is ranked as high by 70% of the respondents. Four respondents rank sweat equity as medium and two rank it as low.

Support for LA faculty to work with the engagement program is provided by just over half (55%) of the programs. Three programs include summer funding and/or salaries for faculty members. Direct costs, such as travel, supplies, and some equipment are supported by six of the programs on a project basis. Other support includes conference expenses and teaching assistants. In the remaining 45%, faculty members work on projects with limited or no program financial support or seek funds independently from other sources.

Student financial support is provided by 80% of the engagement programs. Six include stipends, hourly wages, or tuition assistance for students working with the program. Minimal direct expenses, such as transportation, lodging, food, and production materials, are supported by 10 of the programs on a project basis. Twenty percent of the programs do not provide financial support for student costs associated with class projects.

A mix of funding sources is the most common approach to supporting the community engagement program. While the percentages vary, 14 programs receive funding from the community, 11 receive funding from the university, and 11 use external funding sources to support their engagement activities. On average, funding is 44% from the communities, 33% from the University and 23% from external sources. Five of the programs report a single source for full funding: two are community supported, one is university supported, and two are supported by external sources.

Contour 3: Project Identification and Engagement Process (Figure 6)

Almost all of the programs rely on communities contacting them to identify potential projects. This includes communities calling the program looking for assistance and "word of mouth" referrals. Five programs use a formal process including press announcements and RFPs (requests for proposal) or applications. Only one program self-initiates formal project proposals and targets connections that can garner financial support.

Project selection is predominantly (70%) an informal screening process. General screening issues include whether the project fits with the program's focus (such as community size or project topic), community need, community readiness, and ability to work with the program and/or students. Five of the programs require the community to have resources available to dedicate to the project. A direct fit with a specific class and curriculum needs is a primary selection criterion for a third of the programs.

Engagement techniques include client interviews, site tours, public meetings, design charrettes, stakeholder workshops, open houses, and presentations. The use of predefined engagement techniques, or a variable process depending on the project, is mixed. Using a predefined engagement process is slightly higher (55%) whether the project is defined by program requirements or a class professor. Projects are predominantly integrated into the LA curriculum. Twelve are in core required classes and five are in elective independent study classes. Three of the programs function independently, and projects are incorporated in LA courses on an ad hoc basis.

• project proposal by community

informal   75%   (15)
+ + + + + + + + + + + + + + +

formal   20%   (4)
+ + + +

**1 program self-initiates and targets   connections that
can garner financial support**   +

• engagement technique(s)

**Pre-defined
(5 by the program, 6 by the class professor)**   + + + + + 55% + (11) + +

Varies   + + + + + 45% (9) +

• primary roles

Community	**client -** **provide information, recipient of** **products/services**
Faculty	**teacher -** instruction, managing student involvement
Student	doing the work of the profession— reports, designs
LA Practitioner	juror / reviews (no role 30% - 6 of 20)

• teaching faculty financial support

salary/ summer   15% (3)
+ + +

direct expenses   30% (6)
+ + + + + +

other   10% (2)
+ +

no financial support   45% (9)
+ + + + + + + + +

FIGURE 6 Contour 3: Project Identification and Engagement Process

Respondents described the roles of communities, faculty members, practitioners, and students in their engagement program. Community roles are divided into three types: clients (60%), partners (25%), and drivers (15%). As clients, communities provide information, are a sounding board and reality check for ideas, and are recipients of the program's products. Communities as partners emphasize interaction, participation in product generation, and providing resources for the project. Community empowerment is the goal of the driver role, with organizing, facilitating, and self-actualization responsibilities.

Faculty roles include teaching, managing student involvement, and providing professional leadership in all of the LA engagement programs. In five of the programs teaching is the main role. Half of the programs include facilitation with the community as a faculty role, and five include project administration duties. Student roles include "doing the work of the profession," such as analysis and planning reports, design generation and presentation, and learning public participation techniques. Two of the respondents focused on the academic component, "meeting class requirements," as the primary student role.

Roles for landscape architecture practitioners in the engagement projects vary from none, to information provider, teacher, and/or juror. Three programs engage professionals at the beginning of the process to provide materials and background information. Twenty percent engage practitioners during the process as teachers and professional role models. The most common role is at the end of the process as a reviewer or juror. One-third of the programs do not involve practitioners or only sometimes involve them.

Contour 4: Products (Figure 7)

Products for the communities encompass the traditional range of academic landscape architectural materials. These include analysis and summary reports, design boards with master plans and site plans, design books, model and PowerPoint presentations. Nontraditional products communities receive include on-site construction by students (one program), written grant proposals (one program), and project websites (two programs).

Twenty-five percent of the respondents feel that products created for the communities are not valued in the current faculty promotion and tenure process. When the products are recognized, they fit easily into the "research, teaching, service/outreach" paradigm, with traditional corresponding values. Faculty product types are categorized as articles/publications, design competitions, grants, reports and "other." The most cited faculty product is published articles (10), followed by grants (7). Reports are faculty products for six of the programs, and design competition entries have been produced by faculty with two of the programs. Other types of products mentioned include a conference presentation, book, video, and websites. None of the respondents cite built works as faculty products, while this is considered a student product for two of the programs.

Contour 5: Impacts (Figure 8)

Program respondents perceive a wide range of impacts (changes or benefits from the engagement activity) for communities, faculty, students, practitioners, and institutions. The most frequently cited community impacts are educating the public and helping to change the way the community thinks about growth and development. This includes focusing efforts,

- ## community products

Analysis reports (8)
Design generation (12)
    Masterplans
    Site plans
    Design books
    Models
    Powerpoint presentations

On-site construction (1)
Grant proposals (1)
Web sites (2)

- ## faculty products

Publications/articles (10)
Grants (7)
Reports (6)
Competitions (2)
Other
    book
    conference
    video
    web site

FIGURE 7 Contour 4: Products

changes in local leadership, and guiding local decision-making. Use of community engagement products to support funding of potential projects is also perceived to have impact, as are good public relations within the community.

Predominant faculty impacts relate to personal rewards and professional growth as a landscape architect. These include a rewarding, creative outlet, personal satisfaction, community involvement, staying current, and quasi-practice. The flip side of community engagement is voiced as "a lot of work," exhausting, frustrating, and the cause of many restless nights. Strong impacts for teaching enhancement are also mentioned. Comments such as a teaching outlet, educational enhancement, supporting the education mission, real-life studio projects, and student development all reinforce this impact. Use as a research outlet is mentioned by a small portion of the respondents.

community impacts

95% feel that engagement program results in community impacts
citing:

	comments
Educating / guiding communities	(9)
Support funding proposals	
Public relations	
Design ideas	(5)

faculty impacts

citing:

	comments
Personal reward & connection to communities	(14)
Professional growth as an LA	(5)
Teaching enhancement	(7)
Research opportunities	(3)
Tenure requirements	(2)

- Also the flip side: lots of work, frustration, exhaustion and restless nights

student impacts

citing:

	comments
Professional growth / maturity	(9)
Improve skills / range of experiences	(7)
Realize value of working with people	(6)
Portfolio building / employability / opening doors	(5)
Rewarding / motivational	(4)

university impacts

citing:

	comments
Public relations	(10)
Recognition / visibility	(6)

FIGURE 8 Contour 5: Impacts

The primary student impacts revolve around three themes: professional growth and maturity, improving skills and range of experiences, and realizing the value of input and interaction with people. Comments such as a broadening vision of landscape architecture, gaining confidence, career deciding, and life changing all relate to the students' professional growth. Improving skills such as communication and looking at design decisions from a "reasonable" perspective were also mentioned. Negative impacts on students such as high stress, disappointment, and hard work were equally recognized and balanced by comments such as rewarding, motivating, fun, and significant. Community engagement projects impact students by increasing their employability, building portfolios, opening doors, and creating connections.

Practitioner impacts are few and vary considerably. Feelings that the practitioners participate in the community engagement program as a way to give back to the university and local communities split evenly with participation as a venue for exposure for future pay projects. Community engagement program impacts on practitioners are also seen as a two-way exposure between students and practitioners and an opportunity for skill sharing. Practitioners getting to know the students' skills and potential employability is cited as an impact from the faculty perspective.

By far the most significant university impact is positive public relations, as cited by half of the respondents. Positive visibility and recognition of the university/community interaction is the second most frequent comment. Additional comments include creating "goodwill," returning money/resources to the community, making lives better, and enhancing the prominence of the community engagement program on campus.

Contour 6: Effectiveness and Assessment (Figure 9)

Community engagement is considered most effective (to achieve something well, having an intended effect, producing a response) for teaching students (72%), with generating community benefits the second most effective. Commitment to the community-based pedagogy by faculty and students is a primary attribute of program effectiveness. Expertise, such as with technology or research, is the trait also cited as contributing most to effectiveness, along with a successful program reputation, demonstrated by past projects and a demand for new projects. Three (15%) respondents cite the community as the feature most contributing to the program's effectiveness. The community contribution is described as feedback, interaction, and collaboration.

Five types of constraints to effectiveness are identified from the responses: funding, logistics, human resources, community attitudes, and department support. Funding and the logistics of timing, travel distances to communities, and scheduling are the major constraints to effectiveness. A lack of human resources includes the burden on faculty, a lack of instructor continuity, and technical expertise needs. The community emerges as a constraint due to attitudes that limit student creativity and exploration of alternative solutions that may not be supported by a vocal majority.

The majority of the programs (85%) do not have assessment tools in place. Informal assessment techniques include student reflection papers, annual reports, and feedback from the students. The three programs with assessment tools each focus on a different group of people.

215

- ## most effective at

	Top	Runner-up
Teaching students	60% (12)	30% (6)
Generating community benefits	40% (8)	60% (12)
Generating research products	0	10% (2)

- ## What contributes most to effectiveness

Commitment to the community-based pedagogy	65% (13)
Faculty/program expertise	10% (2)
Reputation of the program	10% (2)
Community contribution to the project	15% (3)

- ## Constraints to effectiveness

Funding	35% (7)
Logistics	30% (6)
Human resources	20% (4)
Community	10% (2)
Department	5% (1)

- ## Assessment

15% have assessment tool
(participant survey, self-assessment reports, student product evaluations)

FIGURE 9 Contour 6: Effectiveness and Assessment

One focuses on the community with questionnaires, another completes self-assessment reports, and one assesses student products. Documenting outcomes is mixed, with just under half documenting outcomes. Examples of academic outcomes are papers, competitions, and professional presentations. Community feedback and news press are the most mentioned types of outcome documents. One respondent cites student employment as an outcome.

Interpreting the Terrain and Exploratory Themes

Contours are often the focus of hallway discussions, such as the need for funding or student benefits. Conference presentations extol the student design products and appreciation of communities. In this work, investigators illuminate the contours to identify the terrain and explore themes of commonalities and differences, and future recommendations.

Terrain of Community Engagement (Figure 10)

The most resounding characterization is that community engagement is a *passion*. Interview respondents bubbled over with excitement and welcomed the depth and detail of questions in the protocol. This is evidenced in that the original estimate for interviews was 40 minutes, yet the shortest was 60 minutes and several respondents spoke for 90 minutes. The most important aspect of the work is a balance of teaching and outreach. Community engagement programs are often initiated, and continue today, as a real-life venues to meet the needs of professional training and experiences in landscape architecture education. The passion for their work overshadows and outweighs the lengthy list of complications, frustrations, and often limited benefit for personal promotion in the university environment.

Commonalities and Differences

Community engagement is a strong component of landscape architecture curriculums in the United States and Canada. In fact, is can be said that community engagement is a passion. The most common theme across programs is a focus on student learning with real-world projects, fostering professional development, and exposure to the realities of working with people. The approach to community engagement is fairly consistent with studio-based design classes, with typical products of design boards or reports. Programs also recognize consistent limitations of the amount of funding and the ability to create sustainable funding streams.

Very few of the community engagement programs studied are able to achieve the trifecta of research, community service, and teaching embedded in their activities. The few programs that do include a research component are a reflection of the changing roles and expectations of professional programs in universities, especially research institutions. The inclusion of formal assessment techniques, whether on student learning or community impacts, is another of the strongest differences among the community engagement programs. Project or community contracts are not significant enough in size to support research or evaluation in addition to the project costs. Adding together the real costs of doing a project, a small amount for overhead, research funds, and some wage compensation (for faculty or students) quickly makes a university project more expensive than hiring a consult or

217

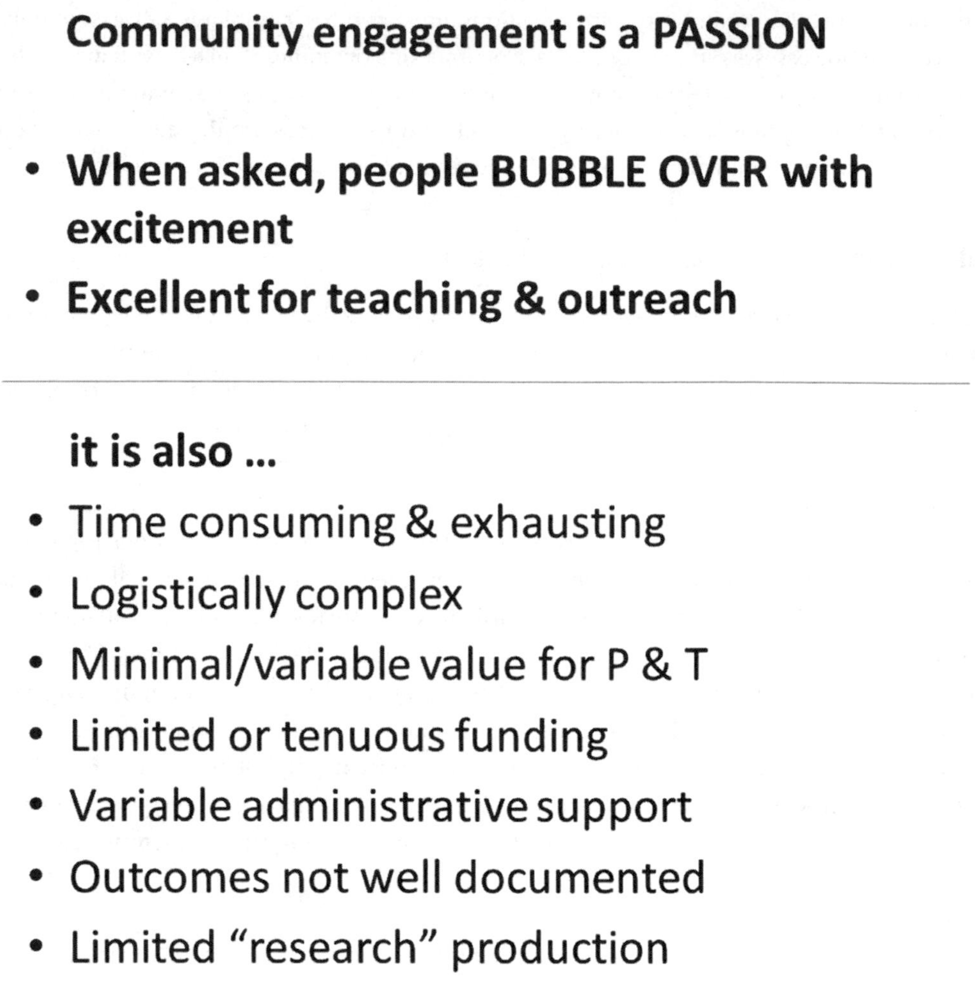

Community engagement is a PASSION

- **When asked, people BUBBLE OVER with excitement**
- **Excellent for teaching & outreach**

---

it is also ...

- Time consuming & exhausting
- Logistically complex
- Minimal/variable value for P & T
- Limited or tenuous funding
- Variable administrative support
- Outcomes not well documented
- Limited "research" production

FIGURE 10 Terrain of Community Engagement

design firm. Communities are not inclined to devote the few dollars they have to "research" activities that do not have a direct benefit to their community. They are also leery of being used as, or even perceived as, "lab rats" for work that benefits the university but does not directly help their community.

Future Recommendations

Future changes are recommended by all of the respondents and encompass funding, administration, and enhancement of knowledge. Funding is mentioned as the top change, as they express a need for sustainable sources and/or diversification of funding sources (to enhance sustainability). This is a basic need to be addressed head-on in the future. If the engagement programs no longer exist, the question of how to improve the practice or measure outcomes is moot. Administrative changes range from a desire for a community engagement center to a dedicated administrative position to oversee program growth. The suggested changes however, are short-sighted in that they focus on ways to continue what they do now, instead of revisioning a delivery system and product line, or reframing engagement as scholarship.

A critical piece will be the balancing of research and practice, engagement and teaching. Currently programs are weak at balancing research and practice and strong at balancing engagement and teaching. A significant aspect of the weakness is the time intensiveness of executing community engagement projects in the classroom and meeting current-day university research expectations for promotion and tenure. Successful role models in engaged scholarship are just beginning to move into the upper ranks of academia. Historically, LA faculty predominantly had master's degrees and were promoted through the academic ranks on teaching and outreach with minimal expectations for grant writing or peer review publications (Gobster, Nassauer, & Nadenicek, 2010). Programs today are seeking a mix of master's degrees with professional practice and teaching and PhDs with research experience to remain competitive in the university environment. Supporting engaged scholarship will require administrative changes to internal funding allocations and how faculty are evaluated in order to create collaborative teams that bring all of the skill sets together (Wade & Demb, 2009). To garner university support will require alignment of the program's goals with the university's overarching goals, just as they have historically aligned with the outreach and teaching goals.

Advantages of more formalized approaches (but not necessarily "centers") make an engagement program more efficient to operate and create venues for long-term studies to look at outcomes and impacts. Enhancing knowledge involves better assessment techniques as well as introducing more theoretical and cutting-edge design into projects. Potential research areas include community design principles, participatory techniques, community development, economic development and analysis, issues of sustainable development, measurable impacts of university-community engagement, active learning, impacts of community-based learning, service learning, incidental learning, and design pedagogy.

References

Boyer, E. (1990). *Scholarship reconsidered: Priorities of the professoriate.* New York: Carnegie Foundation for the Advancement of Teaching.

Crawford, P., & Rauhe, W. (2007). *Final survey report on illuminating the terrain of community engagement in landscape architecture education.* East Lansing: School of Planning, Design and Construction, Michigan State University.

Dubb, S., & Howard, T. (2007). *Linking colleges to communities: Engaging the university for community development.* College Park, MD: Democracy Collaborative.

Council of Educators in Landscape Architecture. (1998). Educating LAs. *Landscape Architecture, 88*(10), 100–145.

Finkelstein, M. (2001). Toward a unified view of scholarship: Eliminating tensions between traditional and engaged work. *Journal of Higher Education Outreach and Engagement, 6*(2), 35–44.

Gobster, P., Nassauer, J., & Nadenicek, D. (2010). Landscape Journal and scholarship in landscape architecture: The next 25 years. *Landscape Journal, 29*(1), 52–70.

Huba, M., & Freed, J. E. (2000). *Learner centered assessment on college campuses: Shifting the focus from teaching to learning.* Boston: Allyn & Bacon.

Michigan State University, University Outreach and Engagement. (2010). University outreach and engagement defined. Retrieved March 9, 2010, from http://outreach.msu.edu/approach/Defined. aspx.

Peters, S., Jordan, N., Adamek, M., & Alter, T. (2005). *Engaging campus and community: The practice of public scholarship in the state and land-grant university system.* Dayton, OH: Kettering Foundation.

Scholarship of Engagement. (2006). Evaluation criteria for the scholarship of engagement. Retrieved November 17, 2009, from http://schoe.coe.uga.edu/evaluation/evaluation_criteria.html.

Wade, A., & Demb, A. (2009). A conceptual model to explore faculty community engagement. *Michigan Journal of Community Service Learning, 15*(2), 5–16.

Wagner, M., & Gansemer-Topf, A. (2005). Learning by teaching others: A qualitative study exploring the benefits of peer teaching. *Landscape Journal, 24*(2), 198–208.

Wergin, J. F. (2006). Elements of effective community engagement. In S. Percy, N. Zimpher, & M. J. Brukardt (Eds.), *Creating a new kind of university: institutionalizing community-engagement* (pp. 23–42). Boston: Anker.

Beyond Tomorrow: Charting a Long-Term Course toward Community Impact in Local Public Education

Mary Beckman and Joyce F. Long

An important reason for "going public" is to improve the "public" with whom universities and their constituents are engaged. Although service learning and community-based research (CBR) have at least an implicit aim to do just that (Ehrlich, 2000; Parks Daloz, Keen, Keen, & Daloz Parks, 1996; Peters, 2005), many who are involved in all manner of higher education community engagement voice the concern that effects on communities simply do not get enough attention. Critics of common modes of higher education community engagement argue that initiatives are disjointed and driven by university or college and faculty interests rather than by the social challenges in need of remedies (Stoecker & Beckman, 2009).

The coalition, one word used to describe a form of community-campus collaboration that is growing in popularity (Gillies, 1998; Roussel, Fan, & Fulmer, 2002), seems promising for addressing some of the limitations of service learning, CBR, and other modes of higher education community involvement (Bayne-Smith, Mizrahi, & Garcia, 2008; Minkler, 2002). One aim of this chapter is to present an example of such a model, the Education Collaborative Group (ECG) in South Bend, Indiana. This group's story highlights how civic engagement that involves undergraduates, faculty, and community partners in CBR emerged and gained momentum over time toward addressing pressing social and academic concerns in the local public education community.

The second aim of the chapter is to push a step beyond what the ECG has already done, by interrogating its activities with an emerging framework explicitly intended to enhance the community impact of university civic engagement (Stoecker, Beckman, & Min, 2010). While the education collaborative has been admirably successful on some levels, it will be argued that its efforts can become more effectual by applying this alternative approach. We begin our discussion by examining the limitations of dominant modes of university-community engagement.

Limitations of Current Community-Campus Forms of Engagement

Typically, service-learning courses emerge from a faculty member's agenda. A professor wants to teach a course in his or her discipline, such as economics of poverty. He or she then seeks ways to engage students in the local area as an element of the class. Frequently, this requires the professor, or some mediator such as might be found in a campus service-learning center, to form a connection with a nonprofit organization, so students can make a contribution while also gaining real-world knowledge to take back to the classroom and integrate with their readings, writing assignments, and class discussion. In the example of an economics of poverty class, students may volunteer at a center for people who are homeless. While the students are presumably fulfilling a request of a local organization, the engagement of the students would not happen if the faculty member did not initiate the effort.

Community-based research, as a form of service for undergraduates in service-learning classes, requires students to address questions that come from a community partner, just as organizations where students serve through service-learning classes identify the work that students will do in their organizations. In a CBR class, the community partner is, ideally, involved in various ways in the actual research process. And the typical CBR class, like the traditional service-learning course, is developed out of the faculty member's teaching or research interests. Not surprisingly, other forms of university civic engagement tend to be similarly oriented toward aims of the higher education institutions (Stoecker, Beckman, & Min, 2010).

Another indicator of the primacy of the academic community's agenda in its civic involvement is the fact that very little evaluative work within the world of service learning has examined the effects of student contributions in communities. Instead, most of the evaluation literature in this content area has focused on the outreach's effects upon students rather than linking student efforts with long-term documented changes in the community sphere. One literature review that examined published articles during the five-year period from 2005 to 2009 (Beckman, Penney, & Cockburn, 2010) discovered that service learning's reported influence was primarily associated with general learning gains in students (e.g., Frazer, 2007; Paoletti, 2007; Scales, 2006), student attitudes (e.g., Brown, 2007; Dukhan, 2008; Keen, 2009), student development (e.g., Borden, 2007; Johnson, 2007; Joseph, 2007), or effects on teachers (Bollin, 2007; Hart, 2007; Kirtman, 2008).

In comparison, there have been modest efforts within CBR to document how communities benefit from such investigations. For example, Marullo and colleagues (2003) offer a grid to help practitioners consider the effects of CBR on individuals, organizations, and communities. This resource highlights the usefulness of considering multiple arenas or levels of effect. Another factor that has been described in the literature as important in assessing the effects of CBR is time (PAR Outcomes Project, 2007). Here it has been suggested that single CBR projects are unlikely to result in much impact in the short run, but need to be combined with action over a longer period.

These preliminary efforts to identify indicators for understanding CBR's effectiveness in communities suggest that practitioners desire to attain impact. We will argue here that collaborative efforts such as those that emerge within coalitions might be better equipped to bring about desired effects than the current emphasis on service learning and individual classroom experiences in CBR.

Campus-Community Coalitions

In contrast to the service and research efforts initiated through courses of individual faculty members, community efforts that emerge out of the activities of coalitions may be more likely to result in community impact. Next, we will explain what we mean by coalitions and why they have been growing as forums for university and community efforts.

Various literatures are liberally sprinkled with interchangeable terms for this form of collective participatory relationship—collaboratives, coalitions (Rowe, 1997), alliances (Bibeau, Howell, Rife, & Taylor, 1996), partnerships, interdisciplinary community collaborations, collaborative research partnerships, and consortia (Caplan, Lefkowitz, & Spector, 1992). These currently appear in a variety of settings and cross multiple disciplines (Bayne-Smith, Mitzrahi, & Garcia 2008; Currie et al., 2005; Himmelman, 1992).

According to Roussos and Fawcett (2000):

> The structure of partnerships can vary and may include formal organizations with a financial stake or interest (e.g. a consortium of health care providers) as well as individuals and grassroots organizations that have formed around a recent event (e.g. child homicide) or a local concerns (e.g. environmental pollution). In a similar manner, the vision and mission of the partnership may focus on a continuum of outcomes, including (*a*) categorical issues (e.g. immunization or violence), (*b*) broader interrelated concerns (e.g. education and jobs), and/or (*c*) more fundamental social determinants of health and development (e.g. income disparities and trusting relationships). (p. 370)

The same authors additionally found that the following assumptions generally undergird collaborative partnership approaches:

> (*a*) the goal cannot be reached by any one individual or group working alone, (*b*) participants should include a diversity of individuals and groups who represent the concern and/or geographic area or population, and (*c*) shared interests make consensus among the prospective partners possible. (pp. 370–371)

Such enterprises are proliferating in public health work (Gillies, 1998; Roussel, Fan, & Fulmer, 2002), and evidence suggests that they generally are well suited for addressing "complex social issues" (Currie et al., 2005, p. 401).

A number of factors account for the growth in these partnership activities. First, a general shift in the political and economic environment (Amey & Brown, 2004; Fogel & Cook, 2006; Soska & Johnson Butterfield, 2005), going back to the decentralization of welfare and other government programs in the Reagan years (Schorr, 1997), has placed greater responsibility for addressing social challenges on the local level. As this trend has unfolded, government funding agencies have put more pressure on universities to engage in collaborations with community partners; indeed, some federal funders require such collaborations (Eakin & Maclean, 1992). Second, philanthropic organizations have likewise been increasing their contributions to such efforts (e.g., Fawcett, 1999; Parker et al., 1998; Tarvlov et al., 1987; Yin & Kaftarian, 1997). Third, a record of services and successful advocacy over time has enabled many such partnerships to gain the trust of their constituents (Bayne-Smith, Mitzrahi, & Garcia, 2008; Minkler, 2002), another factor leading to their growth. In sum, these working groups represent an important mode of university civic engagement, that is, activities that "go public."

The Education Collaborative Group

The Education Collaborative in South Bend, Indiana, shows some of the ways in which partnerships of the nature discussed previously can move university-community engagement in the direction of community impact.

Phase 1: Building a Community-Campus Network of Academic Professionals

In March 2006, Notre Dame's Center for Social Concerns brought Dr. Emma Fuentes to campus. As a collaborator in a community-based research study related to race and achievement at Berkeley High School in California (Noguera & Wing, 2006), Fuentes was invited to conduct a CBR workshop for cross-campus faculty. During her time in South Bend, she also spoke about the study at a gathering of South Bend public school educators and faculty interested in local school issues. The intent of this gathering was to stimulate campus-community thinking on ways CBR could be used to address school challenges.

Shortly after Fuentes's visit, a number of faculty members, university personnel, local nonprofit organization staff, and public school educators and administrators met to discuss how they might move forward with ideas generated by the speaker. This preliminary gathering led to the formation of the Education Collaborative Group (ECG), comprised of approximately seven local public school principals, six faculty members from a wide variety of disciplines, several university staff, a physician, and a few other interested community residents. All the participants expressed their desire to be part of an ongoing group in which they could share local schooling concerns and problem-solve together.

To that end, the ECG has provided a supportive atmosphere for local principals and university people to reflectively share their concerns and resources. As the group has evolved, several categories of issues have consistently appeared on its agenda. First, university personnel regularly invite principals to ongoing campus resources and upcoming special events that teachers and students alike can utilize. For example, several physicists in the group have annually asked principals to send their teachers to professional development training sponsored by QuarkNet, a campus program funded by the National Science Foundation and the U.S. Department of Energy. As a result of these personal invitations, more teachers from schools with ECG principals have attended the sessions, and several principals reported that those who attended the program utilized the training to initiate a science fair with school-wide participation.

Principals also regularly update campus individuals on potential research topics, existing programmatic ventures with other university partners, and issues within their individual schools or the entire K-12 system. Similarly, university faculty members describe their ongoing instructional and empirical projects in schools (e.g., Visual Thinking workshops, Web 2.0 collaboration training, a teacher motivation study). Finally, as participants share a meal and simply enjoy being together, they forge mutually respectful and committed camaraderie within the group. The genuine care and trust that develops from these casual exchanges transcends the more formal relationships typical of many career-related activities.

Phase 2: Naturally Emerging Collaborative Educational Initiatives

The following two research projects provide examples of the kind of campus-community collaborations that can emerge from such cooperative groups.

Mobility Study

The first example involves economist Jennifer Warlick. At the original gathering with Fuentes, Warlick connected with Britt Magneson, who directed the district's Title I federal program. During their ensuing conversation, Magneson mentioned the district's large data sets that could be further analyzed; Warlick responded by sharing her curiosity in the district's high mobility rate. When Magneson agreed the issue needed to be investigated, the project was officially conceived. In this case, the choice of which project to research was neither solely driven by Warlick nor exclusively pursued by the community partner; instead, it emerged from the community need and the expertise and interest of the faculty member. The effort was identified and forged through the developing relationship between the two partners.

By the fall of 2007, Warlick offered her undergraduate students in Economics of Education three research options relative to what school administrators believed were effects of student migration: (*a*) Why do children withdraw and reenroll within the district, and why do newcomers and returnees choose South Bend schools? (*b*) Why or how does mobility affect student achievement? (*c*) How would reducing mobility affect student achievement at the individual, school, and corporate levels?

When the study began, the annual public school mobility rate in South Bend was reported to be 42% across the entire school district, meaning 42% of the children changed schools during the year. As national research (e.g., Rumberger, 2003) has shown that moving frequently tends to create psychological, social, and academic hardships for students, school officials were justifiably concerned about the high rate. The problem was also particularly noteworthy for two principals in the ECG, who had agreed to pro-actively try to reduce mobility between their specific schools. Consequently, ECG members had a vested interest in the issue—both in individual schools and at the systemic level.

From the onset, Warlick envisioned the project as a significant vehicle for creating community impact, and expressed that goal in her course syllabus: "In my career, I have found that the rewards of community involvement dwarf the frustrations, and that the best learning occurs when students have a chance to apply their knowledge to the investigation of current issues and the formulation of policies that affect the well being of their fellow citizens. I hope you recognize this project as such an opportunity and share my excitement and enthusiasm for it."

During the initial semester, Warlick's students met with Magneson and curriculum leaders from across the system, and invested effort in examining two different data sets, one using data collected at the state level, and one using local data. This preliminary effort demonstrated that the problem was worth investigating and laid the groundwork for a follow-up study in spring of 2008, which further addressed the negative outcomes of mobility. In April 2009, Warlick, her community partner, and a group of her students received a $7,000 Ganey community-based research minigrant from Notre Dame's Center for Social Concerns to continue working on this project, which is still under way. Cumulative findings indicate that mobility is a widespread phenomenon in SBCSC schools. Nearly 70% of the cohort that started kindergarten in the fall of 2003 changed schools at least once during their five years in elementary school, and 25% moved three or more times. Title I primary centers account for a disproportionate share of this churning within the system, and 50% of the moves occurring within the system involve five Title I primary centers located in the central city that enroll only one-third of all primary students. Ultimately, school switching was found to have negative effects on student achievement as measured by performance on Indiana's statewide test of educational progress.

Already Warlick has received local attention for the unfolding results, and one student group's paper was published (Smither & Clark, 2007–8). In addition, this topic presented Warlick with a new area for her own scholarship.

Parent Involvement Study

Professors Greene and Long and public school principal Darice Austin-Phillips provide a second example of the kind of work that can emerge from entities like the ECG. Stuart Greene is an associate professor of English. He is also the current director of the University's Education, Schooling and Society (ESS) minor program, which he founded. Since its inception almost nine years ago, ESS is an increasingly popular program for Notre Dame undergraduates. This is the avenue many students interested in teaching or educational policy take to learn about the field, as the University does not have an undergraduate education program. Joyce Long was a postdoctoral fellow with the ESS program at the time the ECG began; she was subsequently paid, alternately by the Center for Social Concerns, Notre Dame's Arts and Letters Dean's Office, and the Robinson Community Learning Center (an off-campus educational initiative of the University), for her time as a facilitator of the ECG.

At the ECG's initial meeting in August 2006, Darice Austin-Phillips noted that her primary school, Perley Primary Center, was struggling with low parent involvement. As she spoke, the remaining principals concurred that their schools faced the same problem, regardless of grade level. Greene and Long immediately offered to help investigate the issue. Greene also suggested that the first step should be to offer the problem to students in his ESS senior seminar, which requires each student to design and complete a research project on an educational issue of his or her choice. Within a month, the ECG hosted a roundtable discussion for senior ESS students to meet local principals from the group at the Robinson Community Learning Center. The evening provided students with the opportunity to learn about issues facing local schools, so they could potentially select one of those topics for their empirical investigation.

One of Greene's students, Joanna Mangeney, responded to Austin-Phillips's suggestion that they examine urban minority parents' perspectives on involvement at her school. Mangeney's study then stimulated Greene, Long, and Austin-Phillips to design a more extensive investigation that was initially funded by a $13,000 grant from the South Bend Community School Corporation. Their intervention study during the spring semester of 2007 utilized both teacher and parent participants and included a series of 12 workshops.

Initial results indicated that parents implicitly trusted teachers' effectiveness (although the majority of students had failed to pass the state's proficiency exam for several consecutive years), but teachers were frustrated and lacked confidence in parents' ability to help their children succeed in school. These results showed that parents and teachers were not collaboratively working together to help students learn, although parents began forming relationships with other parents and became more knowledgeable and engaged in helping their children with academic activities after attending the initial series of workshops. After these preliminary findings, Austin-Phillips, Greene, and Long realized the program needed to be expanded to multiple semesters and sites. The trio subsequently was awarded a three-year Community Health Enhancement Grant for $48,000 from Memorial Hospital of South Bend. This funding enabled the program—now named No Parent Left Behind—to extend the curriculum for additional semesters (e.g., workshops on nutrition, goal setting, resume building, brain-based learning) and expand to two more locations: another primary school whose principal is likewise part of ECG and South Bend's Center for the Homeless.

Their success at the two ECG members' schools recently led to the school corporation replicating the program in additional struggling schools under a two-year federal stimulus initiative. After attending workshops, initial qualitative coding revealed consistent parent gains ($n = 11$ schools) in the following categories: understanding (of the school and its programs; academic learning; the need for practice every day), knowledge (learning can be fun; learned a lot about myself, my city, and other parents), skill development (parenting; reading to children every day; how to teach; play math games with children; improved help with homework), communication (with teachers, children, principal), relationships (closer to children, made new positive friends, appreciate children), community connections (regularly visiting the library), and personal development (more patient, attentive). Parents also reported their children were more motivated (excited about learning, working harder in class) and had improved their academic performance (reading grades increased).

Mangeney's student work was later presented in a symposium with Long and Austin-Philips at the National Council of Teachers of English fall conference in 2007. Her research project is also cited in a chapter written by Greene and Long (2011) for an edited volume on parent involvement and literacy.

Benefits of University Community Engagement through Coalitions

The collaborative approach to campus-community civic involvement, as exemplified by the ECG, appears to offer some enhancements to more common approaches to university-community engagement. Since activities and agendas emerge organically within a framework of mutuality, they are of value to both sides of the partnership at the outset, but more importantly, they can continue to evolve with regular guidance from all parties. Projects can be changed and adapted due to input from campus or community side as they unfold, thus ensuring that they remain on track to attain desired aims.

Because each individual is honored as a source of valuable insight and wisdom, everyone freely contributes to each discussion, offering suggestions and resources, and collaboratively solving problems. It is not unusual for principals to generously offer their sites as research settings; similarly, faculty members readily incorporate principals' ideas and experiences into their teaching and research. Empirical projects or, in some cases, areas for service are thus determined by an explicit blending of expressed need on the part of the community members and the faculty members' expertise and existing or developing interests.

Warlick, Greene, and Long collaborated and participated in dialogue with school staff throughout their projects' duration. These were not simply situations where faculty discussed research topics with community partners, but scenarios in which campus members were part of ongoing conversations with their community partners during regular group gatherings. While any faculty member could forge such relationships with community partners on a one-to-one basis, the regular gatherings of the ECG kept Warlick, Greene, and Long in touch with their community colleagues and provided ongoing accountability. When campus or community partners shared regular updates in the group, everyone freely offered feedback, which provided a continual stream of strategic information that nurtured each project's development. Each gathering offered members motivation, inspiration, and critical support for integrating community relevance and academic theory.

The levels of strength, commitment, and affinity in the ECG's relationships contrast with many other community engagement experiences. For example, when community partner organizations where students are placed as part of service-learning classes are asked to assess their relationships with campus affiliates, they often report that they do not have enough contact with faculty members. Community partners contend that professors send their students out into the community by themselves and have very little connection with the organizations where students work. Some community partners participating in a study conducted by Sandy and Holland (2006) "voiced concern that higher education campuses and service-learning offices focus too much on individual courses and programs and not enough on the obligation of the higher education institution to participate as a partner in community matters" (p. 38). They found, moreover, that "experienced partners often desire more coordinated involvement in larger scale community development initiatives. . . . All of the community partners at the participating campuses stressed that they would welcome more opportunities to network with their campus partner and partnering agencies, and some recommended that the campus take on a leadership role in bringing community members together" (p. 37). We believe that a coalition approach to campus-community engagement facilitates this kind of leadership direction.

But what is the actual impact of such work in the communities in which it is undertaken? What improvements is the ECG facilitating? Can such collaborative groups bring about community improvement in significant ways?

In addition to the effects of the research described above—for example, more parent engagement in their children's schooling—the enduring success of the ECG so far has been in developing relationships. In some cases, those relationships have enhanced individual members' capacity for taking on greater roles in the local school community. One campus member is running for a position on the local school board, and another has shifted from a full-time position at the University to working as a consultant with the school corporation and teaching CBR courses as an adjunct. One of the ECG's principals now leads an arts-based magnet primary school in a building where ECG members introduced arts-based learning within several of its classrooms, and a former ECG principal has become the district's superintendent. In addition to this individual momentum, more educational connections are also blossoming across the community. For example, parents from Greene, Long, and Austin-Philips's project No Parent Left Behind (NPLB) led a workshop with parents from two other community groups (Women's Care Center, Life Lessons) at a local Upward Bound leadership summit. This opportunity not only provided a chance for NPLB parent graduates to share their experiences with other parents, but also offered attendees and panel members the chance to increase their capacity for building parent support networks throughout the region. Moreover, several parents from NPLB are currently helping to facilitate workshops for other parents.

But what about the research? Is it leading to long-term impact? While it is obvious that this research on mobility and parent involvement can make a difference in local communities, there is no guarantee findings will produce long-term results. There is nothing implicit in a community-based research project, or any service-learning activity, for that matter, that ensures the effects go beyond an initial output (e.g., a CBR report).

Indeed there is little evidence to date that alliances, coalitions, and the like, though used increasingly to address pressing social issues, are effective. There is an expectation that they will produce research that will have real-world implications and relevance (Baker, Homan, Schonoff, & Kreuter, 1999; Lynn, 2000), and the value of community involvement in studies that were previously the terrain of academic researchers is widely asserted through anecdotal accounts. Very little data, however, actually looks at the outcomes and impacts from such work to reach evaluative conclusions (Ansari & Weiss, 2006). According to Currie et al. (2005):

> The real-world impacts of research partnerships largely have been unexplored, making it difficult to determine if research is applicable and relevant from the perspective of community members. A search of the literature (including the fields of health promotion, education, community development, science and technology, and research utilization) uncovered no generic, comprehensive models of types of impacts that reveal the real-world relevance of research partnerships. (p. 401)

Thus, while intuitively and anecdotally the work of ventures such as the ECG seems to move in the right direction toward community impact, it is still important to question how substantive impact on communities can be encouraged and ensured through research or other forms of service.

A Framework for Enhancing Community Impact of University Civic Engagement

Participants in the ECG, some of whom have also been on the community or campus side of service-learning and CBR efforts over the years, view their ongoing work in the ECG as a better way, in a number of areas, for moving toward community improvement than other partnerships they have experienced. But they would like to do more to ensure that their work will lead to long-term improvements in public education. We believe that the following framework, based in part on the work of Stoecker, Beckman, and Min (2010) and continued by Beckman, Penney, and Cockburn (2010) and Beckman and Greene (2011), provides a conceptual understanding that can assist us in this venture. The framework will be described here, and then applied to the work of the ECG to show how the ECG might move further and more explicitly toward community impact.

The framework rests on a certain understanding of community impact. Impact is viewed as an accumulation of outputs and outcomes over time. Outputs are the short-run results of community engagement. In the case of CBR, this would most likely be the research results. Let's assume students in a CBR course on poverty are interviewing people who are homeless, to find out how they are reacting to a particular initiative through the center where they are staying. The "output" would be the results of this investigation. "Outcomes" are defined as the results of the use of the outputs. This might be, following the simple example just given, the alteration of the center's programming in light of what the research has shown, or the creation of an alternative program. It might be the creation of a new center-wide policy, instigated by the students' research. The impact framework we are talking about here, however, aims to shift action over time toward attaining community improvement in a larger sense that ultimately improves well-being across a community. In this example, an impact might be the reduction of homelessness. Ideally, the accumulation of enough appropriately designed outcomes could lead to such impact.

The community impact framework, then, has as an overarching goal that is a long-term community improvement result, such as the reduction in homelessness, a decrease in the crime rate, or some other big change that will enhance the quality of life in a community. Strategies are developed that will move efforts toward this aim. The first feature of the framework is this long-term goal and accompanying strategies. The second key feature of the framework is broad participation in all related initiatives. The third element is ongoing evaluation and revision of efforts under way toward the goal.

Long-Term Impact Goal and Strategies

Attainment of impact is guided by the long term, rather than by immediate results of campus-community efforts. Once the longer-term goals are devised and established, individual CBR projects, service-learning contributions, and other civic engagement activities can become part of the set or sets of strategies that, when followed through appropriately, become outcomes that are collectively aimed at reaching the longer-term goal. Another way to say this is that over time, outputs (i.e., the most immediate result, such as research reports) and outcomes (i.e., focused medium-term effects of action) geared toward the attainment of a larger and more *long-term* goal could result in impact. Within this framework, civic engagement activities must become part of a larger trajectory of action in order for impact to result.

Participation

At its foundation, this impact framework demands a base of support that involves diverse and broad participation. This component is valuable and, we suggest, essential for a number of reasons. First, including potential study participants in the determination of goals and strategies enables researchers to focus on the best questions to get the information they are seeking. For example, if breast cancer survivors give input into the research design of a study intended to learn why African American woman are less inclined to participate in breast screening, which is the case in our area, it can be intuitively concluded that there is a better chance that appropriate questions will be asked in the study. Inclusion of such voices in planning toward community impact is referred to by those in some fields as participation of the "target population" or "study subjects." Second, including clinicians and others who have access to study subjects often underrepresented in the literature will expand literal applications for the research among those most likely to benefit from the findings (e.g., African American breast cancer survivors). This is especially crucial for clinical researchers, who could be disconnected from their local communities. Third, involving community members who are able to take research results to the public—members of the media or politicians, for example—enhances the possibility that information about results will be widespread and actually influence public policy. Fourth, a broad base of participation can lead to more thorough results and extend the knowledge base within a discipline. In general, achieving change in marginalized communities requires input from multiple stakeholders (both nonprofessional and professional) with a broad range of expertise (Bayne-Smith, Graham, & Guttmacher, 2005).

Ongoing Evaluation and Revision

In addition to creating a broad base of participation for engaging in processes that are designed to reach an impact goal, the framework depends upon ongoing evaluation and revision of strategies. If a particular approach is not getting to the goal, or if information learned along the way indicates that an earlier-conceived strategy will not work, strategies should be flexibly revised. The importance of this step is demonstrated in the work of a local coalition aimed at reducing obesity. After reviewing literature on the importance of access to fresh produce in reducing obesity (Andrews, Kantor, Lino, & Ripplinger, 2001; Neault, Cook, Morris, & Frank, 2005), the group engaged researchers to study people's willingness to purchase fresh produce if it were accessible. Local results showed that, contrary to expectations, participants would still not purchase the produce even if such foods were available. Originally, the group had hoped to use the evidence to press policymakers and city officials to ensure greater access to fresh produce as one step toward reducing obesity, but there was no plan for revising direction if local evidence disconfirmed the existing theory. Consequently, progress toward attaining an obesity-related goal began shutting down; but if ongoing assessment and the ability to revisit subsequent plans had been in place, the research could have informed further action to attain the desired community impact.

This unfortunate example seems to provide some support for our contention that achieving impact requires long-term goals and strategies, considerable diverse participation, and continual evaluation and revision of strategies based on what is learned via evaluation. To examine how this interplay might influence community impact, we will now examine how this theoretical framework can be applied to the ongoing development of the ECG. As the local dropout rate in the community where the coalition operates is reported to be 26%, there is a definite need for the type of impactive changes that a coalition could potentially generate.

The ECG Revisited: Gaining Momentum for Long-Term Community Impact

Thus far, ECG-inspired research on mobility and parent involvement has resulted in both outputs and outcomes, as defined above. For the mobility work, one output is a report that provided a much more refined understanding of what characterizes mobility—which groups and schools are highly affected, for example. Another output is the identification of effects of mobility on children. Results suggest that introducing programs (e.g., adopting open enrollment policies that allow students to remain at their first school of record when their residential addresses change; providing free transportation to enable students to take advantage of this policy) to reduce the amount of school switching could decrease the amount of classroom chaos that occurs and contribute to students' sense of belonging to a stable community, thus raising the level of individual and aggregate achievement. In comparison, the parental involvement study has resulted in both outputs and outcomes, because the research findings—the output—have actually led to new programs within SBCSC—the outcomes. The Educational Collaborative Group sees all of these as successes.

Nonetheless, will such outputs and outcomes continue to build toward long-term impact? Will they contribute toward larger and enduring improvements in the local public schools and even the community as a whole? ECG leadership is currently reassessing how to attain the greatest possible impact from its work and examining the viability of applying the framework described herein to its operation.

What would this implementation look like? First, the group would need to determine if it is ready to collectively work on one overarching goal. Then participants should evaluate whether their group is sufficiently diverse to accommodate these new actions. It might be that the group decides to invite new members who represent groups currently missing from their discussions (e.g., directors of community foundations, business leaders, parents, and students).

After setting a clear goal, the group would need to discuss possible strategies for attaining that goal. This could include an assessment of the ECG's own assets—the expertise and interests of the people around the table—in order to guide some of its developing strategies. Finally, the group should devise a plan for evaluating accomplishments on a regular basis, and regrouping if new strategies are needed.

At the same time that the ECG is considering its own future, the University, under the guidance of a new vice president for public affairs and communications, has been developing a plan for focusing university resources in the local area. The plan began with an inventory of activities that university employees and students already engaged in. Subsequent focus groups of local area representatives also met to give their input about the University's contributions in the local community thus far as well as to express their opinions about where the University ought to be directing its resources. Results of these studies led to the identification of public education as an area warranting the University's resources in a more focused way than has been previously attempted. Leaders of the ECG have been involved in the undertaking of various parts of this university endeavor, and it is possible that the ECG can play a more strategic role in assisting with this part of the University's newly focused direction for resource allocation. At the same time, it also makes sense for university players from the larger university community engagement strategic plan to likewise inform the work of the ECG. The hope is that the ECG will work in conjunction with whatever larger goal might emerge from university-wide deliberations and planning.

In light of this campus-wide initiative, and the rethinking taking place within the ECG itself, members of the ECG will likely be considering how they might reorient their teaching and research to better contribute to attaining a new collective goal. In addition, they will undoubtedly seek out other university colleagues who teach service-learning classes, conduct research locally, or are simply involved in service, to determine if they will refocus their efforts on creating outcomes that could move toward fulfilling the larger community aim.

Conclusion

Universities "go public" in many ways. They do so through undergraduate engagement in service-learning course activities and faculty scholarship in geographical locations where the campus is situated. Similarly they can employ local individuals, and partner with community-wide projects, such as neighborhood redevelopment. These examples are just some of the many possible modes of university civic participation that can be ongoing at any moment.

The beauty of alliances, coalitions, and the like lies in their potential for involving participation simultaneously from various levels of universities and communities to address pressing social issues. They effectively offer the possibility of moving human and academic resources beyond more typical forms of university-community engagement that may be individually oriented and unconnected from other community efforts, because they directly engage faculty members and university staff with community partners in an ongoing manner. Within this enlarged proactively focused context, community engagement, as the examples herein show, can build upon existing respectful and trusting personal relationships to move the group toward broad problem solving.

When coalition activity is undertaken in a highly participatory manner, involving long-term goal and strategy determination with regular evaluation and built-in revision, the possibility of community impact is likely to be enhanced. Moreover, when this framework is operative, the more commonly disparate service-learning, community-based research, and other civic engagement activities can be focused more coherently toward the attainment of a broad goal, such as reducing homelessness or decreasing obesity or improving K through 12 public school outcomes. University civic engagement can be directed to community development—the furthering of healthier, safer communities—rather than to the achievement of unrelated outcomes such as the creation of reports or new programs. While the latter are generally goods in themselves, they do not necessarily lead to broader community improvement when done in isolation from other longer-term focused efforts.

In the past, many school personnel in South Bend have expressed frustrations with the University, feeling a sense of being used in various ways by campus staff and faculty. Fortunately, the ECG has been a counterforce, paving the way for broader participation, more extensive goals, continual evaluation, and ultimate impact. As the ECG explores how to use the framework described herein to promote educational impact in our local community, it will continue to partner with other endeavors at Notre Dame and in off-campus communities. It is hoped that through these collaborative ventures, others will likewise benefit from their commitment to "going public."

References

Amey, M. J., & Brown, D. F. (2004). *Breaking out of the box: Interdisciplinary collaboration and faculty work*. Greenwich, CT: Information Age Publishing.

Andrews, M., Kantor, L. S., Lino, M., & Ripplinger, D. (2001). Using USDA's thrifty food plan to assess food availability and affordability. *Food Review, 24*(2), 45–53. Retrieved September 23, 2012, from http://webarchives.cdlib.org/sw1bc3ts3z/http://ers.usda.gov/publications/FoodReview/May2001/FRV24I2h.pdf.

Ansari, W. E., & Weiss, E. S. (2006). Quality of research on community partnerships: Developing the evidence base. *Health Education Research, 21*(2), 175–180.

Baker, E. A., Homan, S., Schonoff, R., & Kreuter, M. (1999). Principles of practice for academic/practice/community research partnerships. *American Journal of Preventive Medicine, 16*, 86–93.

Bayne-Smith, M., Graham, Y., & Guttmacher, S. (2005). *Community-based health organizations: Advocating for improved health*. San Francisco: Jossey-Bass.

Bayne-Smith, M., Mizrahi, T., & Garcia, M. (2008). Interdisciplinary community collaboration: Perspectives of community practitioners on successful strategies. *Journal of Community Practice, 16*(3), 249–269.

Beckman, M., & Greene, S. (2011). The education collaborative, parental involvement in public schools, and undergraduate community-based research. Manuscript submitted for publication.

Beckman, M., Penney, N., & Cockburn, B. (2010). Maximizing the impact of community-based research. Manuscript submitted for publication.

Bibeau, D. L., Howell, K. A., Rife, J. C., & Taylor, M. L. (1996). The role of a community coalition in the development of health services for the poor and uninsured. *International Journal of Health Services, 26*, 93–110.

Bollin, G. G. (2007). Preparing teachers for Hispanic immigrant children: A service learning approach. *Journal of Latinos and Education, 6*(2), 177–189.

Borden, A. M. (2007). The impact of service-learning on ethnocentrism in an intercultural communication course. *Journal of Experiential Education, 30*(2), 171–183.

Brown, B. (2007). Service-learning elective to promote enhanced understanding of civic, cultural, and social issues and health disparities in pharmacy. *American Journal of Pharmacy Education, 71*(1), article 9.

Caplan, P. A., Lefkowitz, B., & Spector, L. (1992). Health care consortia: A mechanism for increasing access for the medically indigent. *Henry Ford Hospital Medical Journal, 40*, 50–55.

Currie, M., King, G., Rosenbaum, P., Law, M., Kertoy, M., & Specht, J. (2005). A model of impacts of research partnerships in health and social services. *Evaluation and Program Planning, 28*(4), 400–412.

Dukhan, N. (2008). Implementation of service-learning in engineering and its impact on students' attitudes and identity. *European Journal of Engineering, 33*(1), 21–31.

Eakin, J., & Maclean, H. (1992). A critical perspective on research and knowledge development in health promotion. *Canadian Journal of Public Health, 83*, 572–576.

Ehrlich, T. (2000). *Civic engagement.* Washington, DC: National Center for Public Policy and Higher Education.

Fawcett, S. B. (1999). Building healthy communities. In A. Tarlov & R. F. St. Peter (Eds.), *Society and population health reader: State and community applications* (pp. 75–95). New York: New Press.

Fogel, S. J., & Cook, J. R. (2006). Considerations on the scholarship of engagement as an area of specialization for faculty. *Journal of Social Work Education, 42*(3), 595–606.

Frazer, L. (2007). The impact of community clients on student learning: The case of a university service-learning course. *Journal of Experiential Education, 29*(3), 407–412.

Gillies, P. (1998). Effectiveness of alliances and partnerships for health promotion. *Health Promotion International, 13,* 99–120.

Greene, S., & Long, J. F. (2011). Flipping the script: Honoring and supporting parent involvement. In C. Compton-Lilly and S. Greene (Eds.), *Bedtime stories and book reports: Connecting parent involvement and family literacy* (pp. 15–26). New York: Teachers College Press.

Hart, S. M. (2007). Service learning and literacy tutoring: Academic impact on pre-service teachers. *Teaching and Teacher Education, 23*(4), 323–338.

Himmelman, A. T. (1992). *Communities working collaboratively for a change.* Minneapolis: Humphrey Institute of Public Affairs, University of Minnesota.

Johnson, L. R. (2007). Youth civic engagement in China: Results from a program promoting environmental activism. *Journal of Adolescent Research, 22*(4), 355–386.

Joseph, M. (2007). An exploratory study on the value of service learning projects and their impact on community service involvement and critical thinking. *Quality Assurance in Education: An International Perspective, 15*(3), 318–333.

Keen, C. (2009). Engaging with difference matters. *Journal of Higher Education, 80*(1), 59–79.

Kirtman, L. (2008). Pre-service teachers and mathematics: The impact of service-learning on teacher preparation. *School Science and Mathematics, 108*(4), 94–102.

Lynn, F. (2000). Community-scientist collaboration in environmental research. *American Behavioral Scientist, 44,* 649–663.

Marullo, S., Cooke, D., Willis, J., Rollins, A., Burke, J., Bonilla, P., & Waldref, V. (2003). Community-based research assessments: Some principles and practices. *Michigan Journal of Community Service-Learning, 9,* 57–68.

Minkler, M. (Ed.). (2002). *Community organizing and community building for health.* New Brunswick, NJ: Rutgers University Press.

Neault, N., Cook, J. T., Morris, V., & Frank, D. A. (2005). The real cost of a healthy diet: Healthful foods are out of reach for low-income families in Boston, Massachusetts. Retrieved September 23, 2012, from http://www.childrenshealthwatch.org/upload/resource/healthy_diet_8_05.pdf.

Noguera, P. A., & Wing, J. Y. (Eds.). (2006). *Unfinished business: Closing the racial achievement gap in our schools.* San Francisco: John Wiley.

Paoletti, J. B. (2007). Acts of diversity: Assessing the impact of service-learning. *New Directions for Teaching and Learning* (111), 47–54.

PAR Outcomes Project. (2007). The 31 August 2007 Paris planning meeting. Retrieved September 23, 2012, from http://comm-org.wisc.edu/wcbr/paris.html.

Parker, E. A., Eng, E., Laraia, B., Ammerman, A., Dodds, J., & Margolis, L. (1998). Coalition building for prevention: Lessons learned from the North Carolina community-based public health initiative. *Journal of Public Health Management Practice, 4*(2), 25–36.

235

Parks Daloz, L. A., Keen, C. H., Keen, J. P., & Daloz Parks, S. (1996). *Common fire: Lives of commitment in a complex world.* Boston: Beacon Press.

Peters, S. (2005). Introduction and overview. In S. J. Peters, N. R. Jordan, M. Adamek, and T. R. Alter (Eds.), *Engaging campus and community: The practice of public scholarship in the state and land-grant university system* (pp. 1–36). Dayton, OH: Kettering Foundation.

Rodriguez-Brown, F. V. (2009). *The home-school connection: Lessons learned in a culturally and linguistically diverse community.* New York: Routledge.

Roussel, A., Fan, N., & Fulmer, E. (2002). Identifying characteristics of successful researcher/community-based organization in the development of behavioral interventions to prevent HIV infection. Research Triangle Park, RTI.

Roussos, S. T., & Fawcett, S. B. (2000). A review of collaborative partnerships as a strategy for improving community health. *Annual Review of Public Health, 21,* 369–402.

Rowe, W. (1997). Changing ATOD norms and behaviors: A Native American community commitment to wellness. *Evaluation Program Plan, 20,* 323–333.

Rumberger, R. W. (2003). The causes and consequences of student mobility. *Journal of Negro Education, 72,* 6–21.

Sandy, M., & Holland, B. (2006). Different worlds and common ground: Community partner perspectives on campus-community partnerships. *Michigan Journal of Community Service-Learning, 13,* 30–43.

Scales, P. C. (2006). Reducing academic achievement gaps: The role of community service and service-learning. *Journal of Experiential Education, 29*(1), 38–60.

Schorr, L. B. (1997). *Common purpose: Strengthening families and neighborhoods to rebuild America.* New York: Doubleday.

Smither, C., & Clarke, B. (2007–8). The chaos factor: A study of student mobility in Indiana. *Journal of Undergraduate Research,* 1–25.

Soska, T., & Johnson Butterfield, A. K. (Eds.). (2005). *University-community partnerships: Universities in civic engagement.* Binghamton, NY: Haworth Social Work Practice Press.

Stoecker, R., & Beckman, M. (2009). Making higher education civic engagement matter in the community. Retrieved September 23, 2012, from http://www.compact.org/wp-content/uploads/2010/02/engagementproof-1.pdf.

Stoecker, R., Beckman, M., & Min, B. H. (2010). Evaluating the community impact of higher education community engagement. In H. E. Fitzgerald, C. Burack & S. D. Seifer (Eds.), *Handbook of engaged scholarship: Contemporary landscapes, future directions,* vol. 2, *Community-campus partnerships* (pp. 177–198). East Lansing: Michigan State University Press.

Tarvlov, A. R., Behrer, B. H., Hall, D. P., Samuels, S. E., Brown, G. S., Felix, M. R., & Ross, J. A. (1987). Foundation work: The health promotion program of the Henry J. Kaiser Family Foundation. *American Journal of Health Promotion, 2*(2), 74–80.

Yin, R. K., & Kaftarian, S. J. (1997). Introduction: Challenges of community-based program outcome evaluations. *Evaluation Program Plan, 20,* 293–297.

Steppin' Up: The Oneonta Community Alliance for Youth, Grassroots Democracy, and the Battle for Public Space

Katherine O'Donnell

Understanding the social forces that bring us together or keep us apart and the role of communities in that dynamic are central foci of the discipline of sociology. Connecting young people to their communities through institutions and traditions is a key task for societies, one with which we struggle as some of the formerly integrative dimensions of communities, like neighborhoods, crumble and new ones emerge, including youth culture itself. As families work longer hours and experience more stress in dealing with the demands of work, school, and home, communities, youth advocates, families, and researchers have realized that structured activities for after school, evenings, weekends, and summers at supervised sites are essential parts of today's families' realities.

At the same time that youth advocates are creating a proactive and youth empowerment approach, a rethinking of civic purpose is occurring in higher education (Knefelkamp & Schneider, 1997) with fundamental emphasis being placed on the complexity and richness of community life and education's purpose to prepare students to contribute to a world lived in common with others. Linking community challenges and educational mission allows us to create relationships based on mutual respect; to challenge the race, class, and gender privilege matrix that feeds town-gown conflicts, stereotypes, and insularity; and to use our collective wisdom to tackle the key issues of our time. This is the work of public sociology informed by a social justice-centered form of engagement (Ward & Moore, 2010).

A new framework for research stresses that primary attention be given to understanding adolescent identity development or "life at the border of school" (Weis & Fine 2000) and in other public spaces including clubs, neighborhoods, and community organizations. Weis and Fine (2000, p. 2) describe such places as "construction sites where youth create, invent,

237

reconstruct, critique, and reassemble identities" and where they "seek meaning, recognition, and comfort."

This research analyzes the emergence of a grassroots, youth advocacy social movement spearheaded by OCAY, the Oneonta Community Alliance for Youth, and the role of community-based service learning, research, and activism in moving the youth rights agenda. A local skate park, music performance space, teen center, and after-school program—"construction sites"—have emerged from that organizing as well as research in the public interest and teaching and learning experiences linked to organizational needs and student interests and skills.

While the Oneonta Teen Center was developed to meet teens' desire for a social, live music space, families' interest in a safe, supervised, and creative place for teens, and the local government's concern for youth, the community-based work that evolved in conjunction with my community organizing was also designed to increase the participation of college students as allies, mentors, and researchers working together with the teens on youth initiatives, thereby developing the leadership of community members, local teens, and college members in the process. Placing this organizing within the context of best practices for democratic and authentic partnerships is critical for future work and raises questions regarding the extent to which partnering institutions share visions, support systems, and values.

Partnering for Youth Rights

Feminist-Freire-activist underpinnings shape my training of students, writing, personal commitments, research design decisions, and community work. My community- based service learning (CBSL) courses have their roots in social movements and community organizing, a developmental trajectory that Stoecker and Beckman (2010) advocate. Generally, the overall nature of the relationships in these courses is one of mutual engagement (Petras & Porpora, 1993). College students and local teens have also engaged in community-based research with me. That research has emerged from the organizing and serves the purpose of identifying key problems and solving them. While I have conducted formal surveys to identify teen interests and community concerns, that scholarship as well as other reports, letters to the editor, public presentations, lectures, and grants informed by my research and academic training have been largely for the public arena. Conference presentations and publishing have taken a backseat to the demands of mobilization, management, and teaching.

Students who excelled at CBSL and possessed great capacity for forming and sustaining community partnerships later became interns and researchers who worked as staff at various organizations. Students have commented on a growing sense of community, recognition of community needs, increased sense of efficacy, clarification of career goals, and recognition of town-gown relationships and the politics of power.

As mentioned in the opening paragraphs, my emphasis is on creating community partnerships for social justice (Ward & Moore, 2010), and CBSL functions as the opportunity for students to align with community and social movement activists and community nonprofit organizations (O'Donnell, 2010). I embrace Holland's (quoted in Glass & Fitzgerald, 2010,

p. 15) definition of engaged scholarship as "a specific conception of faculty work that connects the intellectual assets of the institution (i.e., faculty expertise) to public issues such as community, social, cultural, human, and economic development. Through engaged forms of teaching and research, faculty apply their academic expertise to public purposes, as a way of contributing to the fulfillment of the core mission of the institution." I also accept Stoecker and Beckman's (2010, p. 11) community-organizing-based view of civic engagement as one that "sees university participation as one element in a broad-based effort for the benefit of the entire community. The involvement of faculty and students follows a community-led direction, of which the university community is only one participant. Student and faculty involvement occur[s] in response to the large agenda identified by a diverse coalition, rather than by a faculty member's class or scholarship interests."

In addition, the work may be characterized as youth-led organizing (Delgado & Staples, 2008) in that it involves youth in decision making, leadership development, goal setting, skills building, arts and culture, coalition building, democratic practice, and community service. From this perspective, adults are allies. In the earlier phases of this mobilization, youth were more engaged in the political processes of lobbying, letter writing, and petitioning. With the development of the nonprofit organization and the teen center, youth leadership has moved more to programming and center activities.

Since 1996, I have had the ability to work with the community to address emergent concerns and develop multiple forms of engagement as an individual faculty and community member but not within the context of an institutional partners program. Historically, outside of programs that require certification, faculty members develop, oversee, and maintain community relationships without having institutional infrastructure, transportation, or staff assistance.

In order to ensure that community organizations had the volunteer resources and projects they could use, I have worked with the same community partners for decades and have developed courses within my discipline to provide student volunteers and other resources across time. In the case of our local youth organizing movement, I spearheaded work with others to create OCAY, a nonprofit organization with a board of directors, a paid manager, and a Youth Leadership Council, and personally co-partnered with OCAY via sociology courses, internships, and research. The new campus center for engagement provides the college with the opportunity to institutionalize a formal partners program informed by civic engagement principles.

Contemporary History of Local Youth Development Agendas

In 2002, the Leatherstocking's Promise Research report and the 2001–2009 Otsego County Comprehensive Youth Development Plan outlined a series of programs and services devoted to fulfilling key America's Promises in relation to five youth risk areas: academic failure, community norms favorable toward drug use and crime, economic deprivation, peer influence on early initiation of high-risk behaviors, and family history of problem behavior. The report noted that barriers to the development of community-based prevention initiatives included staffing and lack of funding for area extended-day programs.

An examination of the summary of age groups served by existing programs at the time revealed that the services were greatest for elementary-aged children and fewest for junior high and high school teens. Local businesses and organizations (coffeehouses, youth centers) were noted as having the strength to produce programs designed by youth and attract youth not served by other programs. Gaps noted included funding, volunteers, and consistency of programming.

In following up on the mission to provide safe places with structured activities during nonschool hours for Otsego County youth, the Leatherstocking's plan made the following recommendations for community-based businesses and organizations:

- Establish a youth board in 2002, made up primarily with a minority of nonvoting adult members, to study and make recommendations for specific programs for middle school and high school students
- Increase elementary and middle school after-school programs to include later hours during school days, and full days when school is not in session
- Create incentives for community-based businesses and organizations to provide and participate in youth-centered programming via the Safe Places Team's work in 2002
- Encourage and find funding for informal neighborhood-based youth centers—a Safe Places Team 2002 initiative
- Wage a public campaign to educate public about need for Safe Places and the need for children to be in safe places

From the 2002 Communities That Care Risk Assessment Report perspective, risk was assessed at community, family, school, and individual/peer levels. Adolescent problem behaviors were operationalized as substance abuse, delinquency, teen pregnancy, dropping out of school, and violence. Key findings reported for Otsego county in 2002 included a dropout rate of 5.9% in Oneonta, higher than area towns, which reported rates ranging from 0 to 2.7%. The report also noted substantial rates of drug and alcohol usage, with 16% of teens reporting first drink at 11–12 years old and peaking at 30% for ages 13–14 years in 2000. Alcohol use, although basically unchanged between 1997 and 2000, was high, with 81% of high school students reporting ever having a drink and 35% reporting having more than five drinks a day in the past month. Drug usage and availability at school were also problematic, as 43% of students in 2000 reported having smoked marijuana and 28% of students reported being offered, sold, or given illegal drugs on school property.

College towns like Oneonta can create ample access to drugs and alcohol with few alternative social sites and scarce resources. Accessibility of drugs and alcohol and a community context where 75 local establishments served alcohol were noted as key risk factors.

The Otsego County Youth Risk Behavior Survey (2000) also reported teens having sexual activity without adequate access to frank and respectful discussions about sexuality, STDs, healthy relationships, and pregnancy prevention; 40% of high school students and 18% of middle school students reported having had sexual intercourse. Only 27% of respondents participated in service in their community one hour a week or more.

I mined the research in order to advocate for programming and funding for community youth projects, a teen center, and an after-school program. I also utilized these reports in courses with CBSL components and had students conduct additional research on youth programs in order to develop a proposal for the city council.

History of Area Youth Programs

From 1945 to 1965, Oneonta had a thriving teen center run by the city at the old YMCA. Later, several teen centers existed in town, and municipal ones were located in the county building, city hall, and the Oneonta High School.

In 1999, the city closed the existing public teen center, and the area was without one until 2006. Multiple organizations outside of the school were working on creating a supportive environment for teens including the grassroots group OCAY (Oneonta Community Alliance for Youth), the Boys and Girls Club, and the YMCA. Teen programs with religious affiliations included the First United Methodist Church, Ichthus Youth Center at the Episcopalian Church, and Main Street Baptist Church. All of the groups emphasized positive youth development by building on resources and connecting youth with their communities.

Teens and adults who helped organize OCAY wanted a non-religiously affiliated place. Church-based programs were perceived as a plus for some teens and a minus for others.

While most small communities around Oneonta had after-school programs for elementary schoolchildren to eighth-graders through CROP—a federally funded after-school program for low-income rural youth—Oneonta, with the largest teen population in four counties, did not. The one elementary school that met income requirements had an after-school program for children through sixth grade; the Oneonta school district did not pursue a program for middle school-aged children. After seven years of lobbying, OCAY opened the Oneonta Teen Center and after-school program in the former Armory (now the Asa C. Allison Municipal Building) in the fall of 2006 as an independent contractor.

Oneonta Community Alliance for Youth

In 1996, I organized a Stand for Children event and bus ride in conjunction with the Children's Defense Fund national rally at the Lincoln Memorial. On our bus ride back from DC, area activists and I talked about local problems with skateboarders and the lack of programs for teens. Following that bus trip conversation, I assembled key community leaders and area parents at my house for a planning meeting and coined the name OCAY for the organization. OCAY emerged as a grassroots response to community conflict over skateboarding, youth rights, safety, youth empowerment, and creative and safe after-school, weekend, and summer activities for teens. Like the Elvises or hippies of yesteryear, skateboarders represented social "others" who pushed limits, and 12-year-old kids were being punished with large monetary fines, notoriety in the local paper's police blotter, skateboard impounding, and arrest. Community residents, parents, and teens responded, and OCAY's mission became working across generations to bring community groups together in coalitions to address youth, family, and community concerns and needs and to develop youth leadership and give them a voice in their community. Ours was an assets-based approach. In 1996—the beginning of our organizing—we began mobilizing for a skate park and rights for young skateboarders. Youth and their advocates needed a place at the decision-making table.

OCAY was never only about skateboarding but also about cultivating grassroots citizen action, youth voice, creativity, and community. We were about the art of democracy and democracy of the arts. Our work included meetings, forums, fund-raisers, tons of music events, lobbying, community-based research, advocating, letter writing, networking, collaboration, and petition campaigns with lots of signatures.

From its inception, OCAY mobilized creative arts energy to fuel its imagination and campaign and fund its programs. From 1999 to 2006, after the closing of the existing city teen center, OCAY was a gypsy organization in search of a permanent space for youth performance and activities. Our local teen rock stars played benefit concerts across town in coffeehouses, restaurants, churches, and art galleries, and we inaugurated our Battle of the Bands at the Armory in 2004.

Our Summerfest skate and rock event created the opportunity for organizing, visibility, and petition signature collection. I delivered the hundreds of signatures that we collected calling for the development of an Oneonta Teen Center to New York State Senator Seward, and with his help, OCAY applied for a grant to cover operating costs including salary and equipment. I completed the grant application in 2005 in preparation for the hoped-for opening in 2006.

Over the years, our coffeehouses, battles of the bands, Rock & Bowl, and Summerfest attracted thousands of teens and their families and galvanized teen leadership, youth voice, youth talent, and parental, educational, business, civic, and government collaboration. Initial official city reluctance turned into civic pride, and OCAY youth leaders rose to prominent leadership positions in school and the region and garnered college scholarships in the process. Our house bands and local rock stars also translated their talents into related college careers, tours, and recording opportunities.

As noted by the Panel on High-Risk Youth (Commission on Behavioral and Social Sciences and Education, National Research Council, 1993), more and more young people are exposed to social institutions that are under strain. Increasingly, these settings and institutions fail to provide adolescents with the support and resources needed for healthy development. Nationally, millions of children have no place to go when school ends. Drug and alcohol use and early sexual activity are also more likely to occur without supervised programs and caring adults.

From 1999 to 2006, the time of our mobilization for a teen center, the mayor and several council members were initially opposed to the creation of a teen center in the Armory. After years of lobbying, when the ranking Republican on the finance committee altered his opposition, more supportive Republicans and Democrats on the council could move toward creation of the center in the Armory, which the city acquired from the state for $1 in 2003. Under the subsequent administration of Mayor John Nader, an Oneonta local who grew up in the neighborhood near the Armory, the city entered into a new level of support for the OTC. Key people involved in moving the youth center agenda were city council members, some with personal connections to youth musicians; others were motivated by interest in youth issues and public safety.

Support also came from area foundations and grants. I applied to the Parisian Foundation, the First United Methodist Church Patrick Fund, the Oneonta Arts Council (UCCCA) for New York State Council for the Arts (NYSCA) decentralization funds, the Hayes Foundation, and the New York State Senate through Senator Jim Seward. Local businesses helped us with fund-raising for the skate park and with our Summerfest event prizes and food and with new initiatives like providing DJ and film equipment for our classes. Building community support was central to the campaign for the skate park and the OTC. The local paper, the *Daily Star*, and local radio were extremely helpful in shaping our campaign.

In 2004–5, OCAY partnered with the City of Oneonta and our local arts council for a NYSCA arts program and inaugurated coffeehouses with teen musicians on the first floor of the Armory. Later, OCAY was relegated to the third floor due to the city's interest in renting out the first two floors to a dance studio.

The OTC's initial operating costs were covered by OCAY through previous fund-raisers. Our first grant was for sound equipment that could be used by any musicians working with us. A NYSCA grant and food sales funded the Summerfest skateboard competition and rock concert.

In the summer of 2006, we occupied and rehabbed a 30- by 60-foot space in the basement—the spot favored by the teen musicians—and officially launched the Oneonta Teen Center—"The Armory," as the teens call it. The rehabbing was done by the newly appointed site manager, a crew of 14- to 16-year-old teens, and myself and paid for by me. OCAY paid for a pool table and jukebox; private individuals donated other new recreational items. OCAY also solicited and received used furniture from area colleges and individuals.

Based on OCAY's experience with developing the skate park and promoting young musicians through live music shows, in fall 2006 the Oneonta Teen Center opened as a supervised, creative space for all teens of junior and senior high age in the City and Town of Oneonta area. OCAY created an after-school program (CASA) with a focus on arts and recreation. Our after-school program has included classes in DJ-ing and O TEEN TV, launched by a local, nationally recognized filmmaker Joe Stillman. We have a computer lab with free Internet. Classes complement teen interests and our Friday and Saturday night live music shows.

Ian Austin, our teen center manager, came full circle—being one of the first teens in OCAY in 1996 and designer of our first T-shirt. After completing his BA in art from the School for Visual Arts, he is utilizing his art training to design logos, posters, murals, and CD covers for the teens. He is also a key bridge person between his high school art teachers and our nascent teen center.

Between 2004 and 2006, OCAY hosted 4,500 attendees at events—mostly teens—and 2,621 at the new teen center and related events during 2009. The center's biggest draw is live music, with great local youth alternative/rock talent like Oneonta's Moby Strip, Cleveland Patrol, Wine Cellar, and current emerging phenoms Shasta Flock, as well as acoustic musicians.

Our current location is exquisitely amusing and appropriate. After its 1885 inception as a military outpost policing the Brotherhood of Railroad Trainmen in Oneonta, a second building was erected in 1904, and the Armory began life as a National Guard center and transitioned to an informal community center for a town without one.

243

Like swords to plowshares, guns morphed into guitars, and we are dancing to different drummers in a former military, as well as legendary sock hop, site, the Armory. An intergenerational coalition of young teen musicians, college students, and community members has led the millennial rebirth of the Oneonta Armory as the Oneonta Teen Center.

The OTC is made possible through the city's donation of space and utilities, OCAY's contract to provide youth services, previous county NYS Department of Youth grant funds, foundation support for equipment, fund-raising, and volunteer services for grant writing, accounting, education, development, outreach, supervision, and oversight. Private donations and fund-raisers performed by our youth bands also continue to support our operation. Future expansion of programs and staff will demand a new level of grant development and supervision—challenges that must be met by paid staff rather than continuing volunteer efforts.

Hartwick College Community-Based Research Connection

Hartwick College students have related and rallied as students, researchers, and citizens. Hundreds of college students have been actively involved in the development of the teen center through their organizing, mentoring, fund-raising, research, and chaperoning as members of CATs—community action teams—that are part of my courses including Children's Lives, Teens and Families, and Qualitative Methods. I created Teens and Families to train students in youth development issues and the theory and practice of youth activism. While my focus has been organizing within Hartwick College, where I work, local SUNY service fraternity Phi Kappa Psi has helped out, and the SUNY Oneonta music industry program students have worked with us over the years.

The most immediate goal of the CBR research project was to acquire survey, interview, and focus group data regarding youth perceptions of community youth resources and suggestions for youth programming. Research was used to develop grant proposals, link Hartwick students with area teens through mentoring relationships, and develop the Oneonta Teen Center and its programming. The ultimate goal was to create a collaborative partnership between youth, families, community organizations, and the campus to combine our resources and assets to cultivate young people's development in creative, safe, and civic-minded spaces for youth. OCAY youth leaders were also involved in the survey development and distribution process.

Hartwick College sociology students, being trained in both survey and research techniques like interviewing, participant observation, fieldwork, and focused group interviews, as well as in theory and research on issues affecting youth, have been central to the mobilization process. CBSL students work as mentors directly with youth in the Oneonta community, and upper-level students with advanced training and field experience complete research internships at the OTC with me.

Since 2002, within my courses, college students and I have conducted qualitative (Whynot-Vickers, 2002; 2005; Clutz, 2003; Janssen, 2003) and quantitative research to identify youth interests and programming needs for the area and establish a campus-community collaborative program that matches area priorities and needs with youth, college, and community strengths and capacities.

Preliminary Youth Interests Survey Research Findings

The risks reported in the Youth Risk Survey were identified in the initial focus group research that we conducted in 2002 at a teen after-school program. We asked if there were places for Oneonta youth. What places could be created? Responses included that youth thought a center would be "cool just to be." They wanted a big center with expanded hours and weekend programs, as there was "nothing to do on the weekends." They talked about a dance club. They also raised concerns about the availability of drugs, including at the high school.

Our fall 2003 youth test survey with 93 respondents revealed that 70% favored the development of a teen café; the three most frequent areas youth suggested for community development included live music, teen dances, and writing; 15 teens ages 12–17 volunteered to be part of the organizing work. We called all of the teens and eight became core teen leaders of OCAY. Teen suggestions became the backbone of programming as well as future research and planning. Survey, interview, and focus group data assisted us in charting that work.

In 2005, 662 students (of 1,007 total enrolled) ages 10–19 at Oneonta Middle School and Senior High School responded to a Teen Interest Survey that I developed and distributed through Social Studies courses with the help of the OCAY youth president and VP in conjunction with their high school Sociology course. Leia Mortenson, intern and senior sociology major, collaborated with me in the research analysis during 2006 and supervised 19 Hartwick students who worked at the Oneonta Teen Center that year. She also assisted with programming. Earlier classes of Hartwick students completed community-based research fieldwork, interviews, archival research, and participant observation studies for the research as well as volunteer mentoring, programming, fund-raising, construction, and chaperoning OCAY events as part of sociology courses.

Survey results indicated that the vast majority of teens said they needed "a place to hang out" and favored creating a downtown teen center. They said that they would participate in an after-school program and wanted information on jobs. Teens expressed the greatest interest in music, computers, games, films, and instruments—particularly drums—with poetry, dance, art, and photography/video next. As far as music tastes went, rock was the most popular, with alternative and country close behind; hip-hop was the favorite for about half.

When students were asked, "What activities would you like to see in the community for teens?" the majority responded that in addition to sports, they wanted live music concerts, a place to hang out, dances, and a juice bar.

When teens enrolled in Oneonta High School and Oneonta middle school were asked, "What are some teen issues that you think are not being addressed in this community?" they replied that drugs in the community were a major concern with no place to go second in unaddressed needs. Input from local teens informed the core programming initiatives for the OTC.

Teen leadership, both civic and artistic, has been a mobilizing force for OCAY. Parental involvement, business community recruitment and support, and cross-generation work as well as very active and well-advertised programs were helpful in pushing for the teen center initiative despite initial municipal reservations.

Youth-Organizing Challenges

Diverse Youth Cultures and Inclusivity

In reflecting on the first year of the new center, and particularly after the fall 2007 paid work program, I observed two different groups of youth emerging. One was composed of teens who were paid through the Youth Employment program. They were supervised by a paid employee through a contract with a different nonprofit. Their work consisted of maintenance at the OTC and staffing the door or snack bar during shows. They also worked at different sites across the city. The other group was teens who were musicians and volunteering. Sometimes musicians were paid for occasional work and received proceeds from a small door charge at music shows. The teens held different allegiances—some were committed to the idea of a center, social space, performance space, and others, primarily the paid workers, saw the center as merely a paycheck. This was painfully brought home to me one afternoon when I had asked to meet with teen workers about leadership at the OTC. The supervisor was going to pay the teens to be there and for this meeting I said that it needed to be voluntary. When asking the teens about what the OTC meant to them, one stated that it was only a job. Another added that he had never gotten paid before just to hang out. The only young women in the group summed up her group's feelings saying, "Kate, it is only your dream. To us, the teen center is nothing but a job." The responses made me feel bad but I responded, "Well, you are entitled to your opinions, but we are all sitting in my dream—it is a reality."

Eventually, most of the teens working through the city Youth Employment Program only showed up for labor and not programs. For weekend music events, they attended when paid to work, not otherwise. One home-schooled student attended the after-school program routinely at her mother's insistence. Eventually, she stopped coming as well. When the Youth Employment program abruptly ran out of money due to overspending, the city cut off the program, and none of the teens showed up again although most recently, several of these teens worked with the OTC manager to sponsor a Haiti fund-raiser. Although the OTC name was used to solicit donations to cover space rental costs, the organizers did not acknowledge the OTC's help in developing the program.

Another pattern that was evident in the first year was the lack of kids from the immediate neighborhood. I perceived this as a class, race, and social capital issue, as parents did not know of the OTC, and bands that performed were more affluent and white. The neighborhood youth did not hang out with the band members and their fans in school. These informal practices excluded youth from the immediate neighborhood, one with the largest concentration of poor youth and youth of color in the city. To open up the center to area families, I enlisted Hartwick College students in community outreach and began planning our first fall community open house. We only had one visitor on that rainy fall day, but it initiated our process of community outreach. In 2008, we hosted our first spring block party with music, African dance, food, dance competition, and kids' games and installed a small children's garden in the housing complex across the street from the teen center. In 2009 and 2010, we did so again.

During 2009, there was a noticeable change in the composition of youth at the OTC, as our after-school program had more kids from the neighborhood for the first time. They were also younger and more racially diverse. Developing outreach and programming for diverse youth audiences including the neighborhood will be important as the OTC matures.

Youth Leadership

The most creative energy for building the OTC has emerged from young musicians who wanted to play their music for friends who wanted a fun place to hang out. In 2004, young male and female leaders stepped forward to help with program development and teen center mobilization. They were a group of friends and included male musicians. This group remained in leadership positions from sophomore to senior year, with the guys doing more performing and programming and the young women taking on the formal roles of president and vice president. During their senior year, the girls' focus waned. The next year, 2006, we had to jump-start the leadership process and called together a small group of interested kids. A young male emerged as president. After his graduation in 2007, we once again faced a lack of leadership. Dylan Youngs, a musician member since 2004, was reluctant to take on the role of president. He was the informal leader. In his senior year, he finally became the OTC president. In 2008–9, we once again attempted to forge a youth leadership team and ended up opting for a team approach with loose and infrequent meetings. One young female became somewhat distant. The next year, one senior high school male musician took over the role of president and worked with the OTC manager and board on programming and initiatives. The dearth of female participation in leadership roles was worrisome and was quite a change from our earlier organizing experience. In 2009, the young women were there but usually as fans of the nearly all-male bands.

In order to increase youth participation and leadership and to cultivate diverse teen interests to form the backbone of a youth leadership council, I developed a new initiative for project development and youth leadership stipends. The board approved the program and we ran it in the local paper, but to date, we have not had any takers. In fall, 2009, I sent it through allied groups like the Boys and Girls Club, Oneonta High School, and the Girls' Group via my college student mentors. Expanding community service opportunities beyond musician fund-raisers is another way to cultivate leadership, and that has been initiated.

In 2010, we started a Youth Leadership Council and a Girls' Group. Both groups have been meeting, doing events, and developing programming ideas but need cultivation.

Communication

It has been challenging to learn to communicate with diverse audiences in multiple channels simultaneously. When we opened the OTC in 2006, we relied on the newspaper and posters for announcements. Soon, we created a website and a Myspace page, as most of the musicians were sharing their music through that site. Subsequently, we used Facebook to announce programs, share photos, and build networks. Using social networking media works best with teens, but adults at school and on the board are still used to more conventional communication. Improving communication with the local high school is a priority, one that has been attempted through the recruitment of school staff to the OCAY board. Despite our best efforts at publicity, there are still many in the Oneonta community who do not know about the OTC. The lack of transportation from the high school to the OTC is a continuing source of difficulty.

Conflicts

Early on in our organizing experience, OCAY had serious conflicts with city council members over skateboarding policy, band lyrics, the existence of a youth center, and the Armory as a location. Intense mobilization, long-term organizing, and networking resolved these issues.

There was also a debate with the city over OCAY resistance to being a partner with a local antidrug organization in an army-sponsored, antidrug event at the skate park. OCAY applauded the antidrug effort but was unwilling to be part of what was seen by us as military recruitment.

Sustainability and Best Practices

A 1999 decision made by the former mayor to separate the teen center from city recreation has meant that a grassroots group is providing what was previously a municipal service. After substantial lobbying for the city to reinstate a municipal youth program, OCAY's strategy became one of collaborating with the city to provide youth services on a contractual basis and obtain municipal buy-in via provision of a physical space and utilities.

In 2007, OCAY formalized its role and became a nonprofit 501(c)(3) corporation with a board. Later, the city did a RFP (request for proposals) competitive call for services, to which several organizations applied; OCAY got the contract in 2007. The capacity of OCAY to continue providing services with two part-time employees and college volunteers is of concern. While the focus of the OTC is local teens, the center also brings college and community youth together with adult mentors and grassroots groups in Oneonta, thus channeling college student energy and diminishing town-gown tensions.

As is developed in the Wingspread Principles of Democratic and Authentic Campus Community Partnerships (Wingspread Institute, 1998) and by practitioners of community-based research (Strand, Marullo, Cutforth, Stoecker, & Donohue, 2003), democratic partnerships are beneficial to all institutional partners in the relationship; they share vision and values. Building strong collaborations involves interpersonal relationships based on trust and respect. Sustaining these relationships over time entails incorporating partnerships into the mission and various support systems of partnering institutions and sharing communication, decision making, and evaluation capacities. At an institutional level, this requires adopting the best practices or standards for regulating campus-community partnerships, which Weideman (2010, citing Fitzgerald, outlines as shared mission, shared commitment to cross-site linkages, and shared outcome-oriented work plan, resource investment, development, learning, and scholarship. My personal community-organizing history and the lack of civic engagement institutionalization have pushed me to form alliances, work in coalitions, and develop departmental infrastructure and independent, community-based organizations when necessary to accomplish community goals.

Although OTC programming promotes healthy relationships among teens, mentors, college volunteers, and the community and provides community-based experiential learning and research opportunities, OCAY has no permanent link to the college to continue providing volunteers or training. If the college wishes to invest in this aspect of the community and support community youth programs in the future, it needs to develop a campus partner collaboration with the requisite communication, shared planning, training, and project development. Historically, community-based involvement has been largely dependent on individual faculty initiative, departmental courses, and time availability in the academic calendar. As the city benefits from the provision of services and the campus benefits from college student education, recreation, and leadership development, signing a memorandum of mutual understanding with OCAY regarding shared visions for the future would solidify this partnership. The new campus center for professional, service, and global civic engagement at Hartwick can become the institutional site providing faculty, students, and the community with a comprehensive and genuine partnership program that addresses community concerns, meets the standards of engagement, and provides a framework for scholarship.

From Swords to Axes: Youth, Creativity, and the Future of Oneonta

With the creation of the teen center and after-school program, OCAY has ventured into a whole new level of fiscal and social responsibility. Via personal relationships and board membership, new bridges have been built with the school, the colleges, the city, and the neighborhood as the Armory moves from militias to music, and bands are no longer roaming minstrels. The Oneonta Teen Center's programs and events, with mentoring by college students, staff, and adult volunteers, function as an alternative space for youth identity work—a place for youth to have fun, learn, and practice participatory democracy and community building. Challenges abound, but the crowded shows, community organizational support, college student rallying, and growing neighborhood interest give me hope that grassroots organizing around people's concerns and interests works.

References

Clutz, B. (2003). Developing teen identity: The Oneonta YMCA. Sociology 211 final community action research report. Unpublished paper.

Commission on Behavioral and Social Sciences and Education, National Research Council. (1993). *Losing generations: Adolescents in high-risk settings*. Washington, DC: National Academy Press.

Delgado, M., & Staples, L. (2008). *Youth-led community organizing: Theory and action*. New York: Oxford University Press.

Glass, C., & Fitzgerald, H. E. (2010). Engaged scholarship: Historical roots, contemporary challenges. In H. E. Fitzgerald, C. Burack, & S. D. Seifer, (Eds.), *Handbook of engaged scholarship: Contemporary landscapes, future directions*, vol. 2, *Campus-community partnerships* (pp. 9–24). East Lansing: Michigan State University Press.

Janssen, K. (2003). Challenging teen health risks through community advocacy with OCAY—Oneonta Community Alliance for Youth. Sociology 211 final community action research report. Unpublished paper.

Knefelkamp, L., & Schneider, C. (1997). Education for a world lived in common. In R. Orrill (Ed.), *Education and democracy: Re-imagining liberal learning in America* (pp. 327–344). New York: College Board.

Leatherstocking's Promise—The Alliance for Youth. (2002a). Otsego County comprehensive youth development plan, 2001–2009.

Leatherstocking's Promise—The Alliance for Youth (2002b). Community risk assessment report Otsego County.

Mortenson, L. (2007). Oneonta Community Alliance for Youth survey data analysis. Unpublished paper.

O'Donnell, K. (2003). Rural teens and communities confront the roots of adolescent pregnancy: The promise of Project REACH. *Practicing Anthropology, 25*(4), 23–27.

O'Donnell, K. (2010). *Weaving transnational solidarity: From the Catskills to Chiapas and beyond.* Boston: Brill.

Otsego County Youth Risk Behavior Survey. (2000). Cooperstown, NY: Otsego Public Health Partnership.

Petras, E. M., & Porpora, D. V. (1993). Participatory research: Three models and an analysis. *American Sociologist, 24*(1), 107–125.

Strand, K., Marullo, S., Cutforth, N., Stoecker, R., & Donohue P. (2003). *Community-based research and higher education: Principles and practices.* San Francisco: Jossey-Bass.

Stoecker, R., & Beckman, M. (2010). Making higher education civic engagement matter in the community. Campus Compact. Retrieved September 24, 2012, from http://www.compact.org/wp-content/uploads/2010/02/engagementproof-1.pdf.

Ward, K., & Moore, T. (2010). Defining the "engagement" in the scholarship of engagement. In H. E. Fitzgerald, C. Burack, & S. D. Seifer (Eds.), *Handbook of engaged scholarship: Contemporary landscapes, future directions*, vol. 1, *Institutional change* (pp. 39–70). East Lansing: Michigan State University Press.

Weideman, C. (2010). Types of engaged scholarship. In H. E. Fitzgerald, C. Burack, & S. D. Seifer (Eds.), *Handbook of engaged scholarship: Contemporary landscapes, future directions*, vol. 2, *Campus-community partnerships* (pp. 3–28). East Lansing: Michigan State University Press.

Weis, L., and Fine, M. (Eds.). (2000). *Construction sites: Excavating race, class, and gender among urban youth.* New York: Teachers College Press.

Whynot-Vickers, R. (2002). Community programming for youth at Ichthus Youth Center. Sociology 211 final community action research report. Unpublished paper.

Whynot-Vickers, R. (2005). *Adolescent Identity Construction in an Alternative Site.* Undergraduate thesis, Hartwick College, Oneonta, NY.

Wingspread Institute. (1998). Benchmarks for campus/community partnerships: Findings of the Campus Compact Wingspread conference on campus/community partnerships. Retrieved September 24, 2012, from http://www.e2e-store.com/compact/compact-product.cgi?category_id=10&product_id=132.

The Ocmulgee River Initiative: Engaging the Community in Aquatic Research

Brian E. Rood

The greatest joys of a researcher-educator are to "solve problems" and to see our students transform from pupils to professionals. For so many research scientists, the professional focus follows a reductionist perspective, asking questions about specific problems, developing testing strategies that address the problem statement, and conveying the outcomes of the experimentation to professionals who are involved in common reductionist endeavors. Consequently, a student researcher's success is measured by the student's capacity to delve effectively and productively in this reductionist mind-set, so many young scientists develop in specific realms of the sciences and their professional success is measured by their unique expertise in technique and theory. This aspect of scientific research generally isolates the technical experts from the community and from broader "problem statements" in the community and its environs (Pearce, Pearson, & Cameron, 2007).

Many universities struggle with the term "research" because its definitions vary so widely from the traditional sciences to the social sciences, humanities, and even engineering. For example, is a senior-level engineering design project to be considered "research"? If it were to be recognized as research by a cohort of engineers, would it be accepted by a chemist or physicist as such? If a historian is active in professional scholarship, how is this perceived or assessed by a scientist as they each strive to perform "research" as a component of their faculty professional development? In academic institutions, we clearly struggle with the value system that is placed on research "broadly defined." An inclusive definition of under-graduate research was proposed as "an inquiry or investigation conducted by an under-graduate that makes an original intellectual or creative contribution to [a] discipline" (Wenzel, 1997). To be sure, faculty who engage in interdisciplinary studies or interdisciplinary sciences programs will most readily greet the broadest definitions of "undergraduate research," while faculty from specific disciplinary backgrounds may be more defined in their definitions of research and scholarship. In the Department of Chemistry at Mercer University, a faculty member's article published in the *Journal for Chemical Education* is "weighted" for tenure and promotion at a level subordinate to an article published in *Analytica Chimica Acta*. So how does this bear on faculty (or students) when an environmental chemist (or his/her student) publishes an article in a multidisciplinary journal such as *Wetlands, Biogeochemistry,* or *Limnology and Oceanography?*

Increasingly, faculty-centered research programs are expected to define their contribution to society. Many federal and state funding sources use "real and demonstrated utility" as a significant criterion for grant approval. Further, academic institutions are now more inclined to attempt to break barriers between the perceived "ivory tower" of academe and the community at large (Pearce, Pearson, & Cameron, 2007). This effort has been achieved to a large extent through service-learning projects for undergraduate students. While communities have enjoyed outreach activities implemented for student learning in the social sciences and humanities (Flicker & Savan, 2006), such endeavors have been less noted for students of the natural sciences and of engineering.

Interdisciplinary sciences cast a broad net within the scientific and academic communities that, by its very nature, embraces collegial interaction that transcends disciplinary reductionism. Public health and environmental studies are two exemplary genres of interdisciplinary endeavor that, even within the confines of academe, spur on a multilayered sharing of ideas, strategies, perspectives, research, and scholarship. The holistic perspective permits faculty to capitalize on the expertise of colleagues across many disciplines (Dabrowski, 1995). So what do we do with these communications and collaborations? We work together, we engage students in broad-reaching conversations that identify problem statements that may even be beyond our own reach, and we engage the community.

Engaging the community in research creates learning opportunities for our students; it empowers the community and community change-agents and frequently teaches us that we still have much to learn. We are humbled by the scope and complexity of local and regional public health concerns, socioeconomic crises, and environmental quality, and we come to value the contribution of expertise, experience, time, and "elbow grease" that stems from the community. And so, "going public" with our contemporary understanding and application of our "science, engineering, and policy" fosters a multitude of benefits for everyone involved in such endeavor.

What is the Ocmulgee River Initiative?

The Ocmulgee River Initiative, Inc. (ORI) is a 501(c)(3) nonprofit organization that arose from such regional concerns as "You shouldn't eat the fish that you catch south of Macon" and "Somebody should find out what's in that water" (anecdotal). As a young Mercer University professor excited to share his technical expertise to address regional issues of concern, I along with colleagues had an opportunity to work with concerned citizens to establish an organization that was not a subset of the academic institution, but could draw from the expertise and energy of members of the academic community. The organization was spearheaded to establish a comprehensive water quality monitoring program for the entire 222 river miles of the Ocmulgee River. This activity developed into a collaborative quarterly sampling and testing event, where volunteers from the community learned the proper techniques for sample collection and handling and then assisted with water testing in the laboratory with university researchers and student interns. Because the effort was, from its onset, a fully collaborative endeavor, the founding of the organization, ORI, was facilitated but never governed by the university researchers. Four mission objectives arose from planning discussions among the participating members: (1) maintain a quarterly water quality monitoring program of the Ocmulgee River and its tributaries, (2) provide educational workshops and seminars for schools and social or civic community groups, (3) organize events such as river cleanups, and (4) produce a video documentary on the natural and cultural history of the Ocmulgee River watershed. As an independent nonprofit organization, ORI is not only invigorated by the university faculty at a single institution, but can effectively draw from the interest, drive, and motivation of faculty researchers from other nearby academic institutions. The objective of this chapter is to convey the strategies and accomplishments of our approach that engages the community in aquatic research and to characterize the transformations within this organization that have stemmed from a simple acknowledgment that great ideas and positive energy come in many forms from a wealth of sources.

Community-based research (CBR) is "conducted by, for, or with the participation of community members. . . . Community based research aims not merely to advance understanding, but also to ensure that knowledge contributes to making a concrete and constructive difference in the world" (LOKA Institute, 2002). In central Georgia, concerns about water quality in the Ocmulgee River watershed and its potential negative impact on public health led university scientists and community representatives to design a program to assess the quality of the regional environment and the potential health effects on the citizens of central Georgia. Unlike many CBRs where "Academics dominate most areas of the research process, . . . while community members *are* the 'least involved' partners" (Flicker & Savan, 1996), the Ocmulgee River Initiative was born of the expressed concerns of local anglers, hunters, concerned parents, and environmentalists in response to a perceived absence of concern or action by regional political and regulatory entities. And so, given the foundational necessity of technical expertise from the university scientists, the sense of ORI has always been that it is owned by the community and emboldened by the technical guidance of the researchers.

Who We Are and What We Do

The Ocmulgee River Initiative comprises academics, scientists/engineers, teachers, and interested community member volunteers in central Georgia who wish to participate in water quality research, monitoring, and education that focuses on issues of regional concern. The organization was definitively established as a nonpolitical, nonlitigious entity to encourage free and open communication with representatives of industry, government, community, and activist groups alike. The focus of this organization is on environmental research, education, and advocacy. ORI provides information and support to individuals and

253

communities to empower the community with a body of knowledge (an expansive water quality database) and the tools to make guiding decisions regarding the health of the environment (educational outreach).

The stated objectives of ORI in its articles of incorporation codify four primary activities: (1) to establish a volunteer-based water quality monitoring program, (2) to offer educational outreach programs for schools, and social and civic groups, (3) to organize river or watershed cleanup activities, and (4) to produce a video documentary on the natural and cultural history of the Ocmulgee River watershed. As a starting point, the objectives appear to have been well conceived. Three of the four stated objectives have endured the 15 years since the inception of the organization and have undergone positive transformational growth, while the fourth objective permits there to be a series of target accomplishments that will culminate in a long-term goal for new iterations of volunteers to shepherd.

The impetus to monitor water quality in the Ocmulgee River stemmed from both legitimate and fantastical claims made about the quality of this watershed system and the associated human health risks. Local media outlets would produce stories based on anecdotal, and frequently flawed, information about water quality in the Ocmulgee River watershed. At other times, significant stories would be well covered by the media, such as a 2009 break in the main sewer line in the city of Macon that spewed over 200 million gallons of raw sewage directly into the Ocmulgee River at the public boat landing of the Ocmulgee Heritage Greenway riverwalk (Bennett, 2009). The water quality monitoring program, called ORI-Riverwatch, strives to establish common ground and clarity to our understanding of the health of this river system. Another chronic dilemma is that environmental activists, local industries, and urban expansionists readily lock horns in public vitriol, leaving the "average citizen" without a voice, and, as an example, impoverished subsistence fisherman fish for bream and catfish along the banks of the river at the rather productive fishing spot found at the discharge pipe of the Lower Poplar Municipal Wastewater Treatment Plant.

ORI-Riverwatch is a quarterly volunteer-based activity where ORI volunteers collect water samples four times per year at 20 locations along the 222 river miles of the Ocmulgee from its origin at the Lloyd Shoals Dam of Lake Jackson, Georgia, to its confluence with the Oconee River in Lumber City, Georgia, where the Altamaha River is formed and meanders to the Atlantic coast. Samples are collected and delivered to the ORI testing laboratory, where the samples are tested for microbial activity (fecal coliform bacteria), physical parameters (pH, conductivity, turbidity, organic color), nutrients (phosphate, nitrate, nitrite, ammonium, and sulfate), metals (sodium, potassium, calcium, magnesium), toxic trace metals (arsenic, selenium, cadmium, cobalt, copper, chromium, iron, nickel, lead, and zinc), and organic priority pollutants (OPPS) (pesticides, herbicides, fungicides, xenobiotics, pharmaceuticals, and petroleum-based fuels). The data outcomes have been documented in annual reports of water quality such as the "First Annual Report on the 'State of the Ocmulgee River'" (Ocmulgee River Initiative, 1997). Currently, the ever-increasing database is being incorporated into an interactive GIS (geographic information system) (a geospatial database anchored in the central Georgia Ocmulgee River watershed) (Chang, 2010).

Educational Outreach

Environmental education modules are offered at local school and community groups by request. Volunteer representatives of the Ocmulgee River Initiative speak on various age-appropriate topics to schoolchildren of any age and to community groups ranging from area Chambers of Commerce to the Audubon Society or the Georgia Wilderness Society. By offering these educational outreach opportunities, interested individuals frequently maintain contacts with the organization and may become volunteer water samplers or participate in other activities of the group. Other educational outreach activities will be described later in this chapter.

Community Service Activities

One other primary activity of the Ocmulgee River Initiative is to organize river or watershed clean-ups. The group typically schedules two large clean-up events per year. The first event is marked as a local Earth Day activity (April) and the second event occurs in October in conjunction with a wonderful statewide effort called RiversAlive. By coordinating a local river cleanup event with a statewide collective of cleanup activities, citizens of central Georgia can feel that they are participating in an event that is broad-reaching and powerful at the grassroots level. The RiversAlive Program is administered through the State of Georgia Department of Natural Resources, Environmental Protection Division. This statewide effort began about the time of the inception of the Ocmulgee River Initiative and it permits participants to earn a T-shirt and an acknowledgment that the collective participation of individuals and groups statewide can truly make a significant difference with respect to environmental health, quality, and sustainability that spans well beyond the scope of that individual or group.

Video Documentary: "Natural and Cultural History of the Ocmulgee River"

Finally, there is an ongoing effort to produce a video documentary on the natural and cultural history of the Ocmulgee River watershed. Central Georgia has a rich cultural history that has been documented to reveal 17,000 years of continuous human habitation from Ice Age hunters and Paleo-Indians who roamed the land as hunter-gathers, transitioning to the Mississippian culture, an expansive agrarian society, capitalizing on the geographic relief of the transitional geologic feature called the "Fall Line."

With access to uplands and lowlands and the fertile soils of the riparian wetlands, this area became the "Cradle of the Muscogee Nation," the Muscogees being the society that was ultimately driven west to Oklahoma in the famed "Trail of Tears" (Foreman, 1989). Modern urban centers occur at the junction of Coastal Plain rivers and the geologic Fall Line because these locations were the furthest inland that riverboats of the 1800s could navigate to inland sites from the coast. Today, the "New South" is faced with the pressures and consequences of modern agriculture and silviculture as well as urban and suburban sprawl across the landscape.

The natural history of the region is rather interesting as well. The state of Georgia enjoys dramatic transitions from the mountainous regions to the northwest that give way to the Piedmont (foothills) region in the north, followed by a marked transition to the relict Coastal

Plain across a dramatic demarcation zone referred to as the Fall Line . The geologic features are not only distinguished by topographic relief but by distinct variations in mineral and soil substrata. The Ocmulgee River system changes dramatically from the direct-channel flow expressed in the "hard rock" geology in the Piedmont to the meandering riverbed in the sedimentary geology of the Coastal Plain complete with vast flanking riparian floodplains and vestigial oxbow lakes. Correspondingly, the plant communities of these geographic zones vary commensurate with the changes in topographic relief and geology.

The production of this video involves a process of gathering information that will be incorporated in the final script, designing the cinematography that will be the basis for the visual presentation of the information, and producing the final video documentary product. Much of the progress that has been made to date on this project is the gathering of information. This has been used as a comprehensive educational/research tool for students and will be discussed in the next section. An exceptional comparative guide for this work has been the pictorial "River Song: A Journey Down the Chattahoochee and Apalachicola Rivers," by Joe and Monica Cook (2000). ORI volunteers intend to publish such a pictorial adventure about the Ocmulgee River watershed as an intermediate stage in the production of the video documentary.

Engaging Students and Community

The success of the Ocmulgee River Initiative is measured, to a large extent, by its ability to engage students and members of the community in various activities of the organization. The other primary measure of success is through the gathering of water quality data that are incorporated into a comprehensive geospatial database and the resulting dissemination of that information. The foundational resource of ORI must, by its nature, stem from the expertise of the scientists and engineers of the universities that engage in the efforts of the organization. This becomes the spirit of "going public" with a program of this type.

Central Georgia has a number of colleges and universities, and to our great fortune these institutions are many and varied. As an example, in our state university system, Fort Valley State University (FVSU), Georgia College and State University (GCSU), and Macon State College (MSC) are within 60 miles of one another. FVSU is a "Historically Black College or University" (HBCU) that has a well-established history in agricultural sciences as a classified 1890 land-grant college. GCSU is a comprehensive university system and MSC is a rapidly growing local college that was originally established as a local community college (i.e., two-year degrees have more recently been developed into four-year degree programs that offer BA and BS degrees). Among our local private colleges and universities, Wesleyan College is the oldest women's college in the United States, chartered in 1836 as Georgia Female College. Mercer University is a comprehensive university with a heritage in the Baptist tradition that was founded in 1833 as Mercer College, a College of Liberal Arts, and has grown to include Schools of Education, Business, Engineering, Law, Medicine, and Nursing as well as the College of Liberal Arts. Although the Ocmulgee River Initiative was conceived by a Mercer University professor attempting to "go public" with environmental research and educational outreach in the community, because ORI was created as an independent organization, it is easier to engage university researchers from the other universities in the region.

A significant, and nearly exclusive, point of interaction among these institutions relies on the communication and active collaboration of colleagues from these institutions. Academic programs that embrace interdisciplinarity tend to spur on the most enduring collegial rapport. Collaboration of this type may ebb and flow in the hectic schedules of college faculty, but an independent organization like the Ocmulgee River Initiative can create a focal point that is steady, measured, and enduring. Currently, the Ocmulgee River Initiative is working with college faculty from four of these five listed institutions. Further, through the Bibb County Extension Office of the University of Georgia Cooperative Extension Agency (College of Agricultural and Environmental Sciences), the Ocmulgee River Initiative collaborates with on-site representatives of the Extension Office in Bibb County, and with University of Georgia faculty and staff in Athens. Faculty at these academic institutions have recognized the opportunity that is afforded by an independent entity such as ORI to facilitate enhanced interactions with folks in the community at large.

ORI as a Place for College Students to "Go Public"

College students are also drawn into the activities of the Ocmulgee River Initiative as citizens of their campus community through their social and service organizations (i.e., honor societies, fraternities, and sororities). Social and service organizations commit to activities of the Ocmulgee River Initiative. River and community cleanups are the most common activities that students become involved with because they are readily compartmentalized to a date and location. Because of the inherent visibility of river cleanup events, the media routinely covers cleanups as "public interest" stories in the newspaper or on local network television news. This attention spurs on additional excitement for the college students and reinforces in them the inherent value of community service.

Involving college students in ORI activities is handled separately from engaging kindergarten through twelfth-grade students because precollege students participate in the Initiative activities as a subset of the community at large. Increasingly, college students are encouraged to incorporate some form of "service-learning" activities into their course study plan. This option is expressed in various forms, both curricular and extracurricular. Curricular opportunities to participate in service-learning programs may be specifically characterized in the college curriculum as a plan of study (i.e., course offerings at Mercer University referred to as Programs in Leadership / Community Service Learning [PLS]) or in specific courses with an expectation of community service (i.e. Mercer University First Year Seminar—Experiential [FYS-X]). Some universities may be combining study abroad with service learning through credit-bearing activities like "Mercer-on-Mission." Each of these avenues that draw students out of the classroom and into the "field" create a wonderful opportunity to engage students in community-based scientific research or a form of community-based environmental protection (CBEP) program (Meyer & Konisky, 2005). The Ocmulgee River Initiative is a vehicle for science majors, in particular, to enjoy such opportunities.

For a course that includes a community service component, ORI representatives can coordinate with the course instructor, who might incorporate an ORI event or activity in the course syllabus. This arrangement works best with a single-day event like a river cleanup, a specially arranged water-sampling event, or an educational outreach activity at a local school or community group. Participation in an outreach activity requires that the college students first become informed about the specific topics that will be included in the outreach activity so their contribution to the objective is most effective. The students and course instructors also gain significantly by participating when an ORI volunteer returns for a classroom visit to facilitate a follow-up discussion and debriefing.

For colleges that offer a course plan of study (or a major) in community leadership and community service, an organization like the Ocmulgee River Initiative may seize the opportunity to develop a more concrete and enduring relationship with the department that offers this curriculum. In that collaboration, ORI is able to develop a longer-term rapport with the college students. These students are already interested in service learning, but may not have considered the option of service that relates to environmental quality and sustainability. Since many such programs would primarily focus on the critical areas of human health, public health, and socioeconomic crisis, the partnership with a CBEP program like the Ocmulgee River Initiative opens a variety of avenues for service learning not only specifically related to environmental research, monitoring, and educational outreach but also the intrinsically connected issues of public health, socioeconomic disparity, and regional "smart" planning. The Ocmulgee River Initiative, as an independent entity, may then serve the university and its student body in a unique way, but the organization is also made better by the nature of the collaboration with young energetic minds.

One unique contribution made by college students was accomplished as the focus of a Senior Seminar in Environmental Science course at Mercer University. College students produced and presented an extensive report on the Ocmulgee River watershed with particular attention focused on the natural and cultural history of the area, contemporary issues, and environmental assessments (Kennedy, 1999). This 242-page technical report serves as an extensive foundation for the ongoing development of a script for future video production. The students organized a formal evening seminar presentation and invited political leaders including the mayor of the City of Macon, executive board members of the Macon Water Authority, the superintendant of the U.S. Department of Interior's Ocmulgee National Monument, and representatives of the Georgia Departments of Transportation and Natural Resources (Environmental Protection Division). The presentation was covered by the local newspaper (*Macon Telegraph*) and a local television station (13-WMAZ), and the comprehensive document serves as the foundation for the script for the developing video documentary on the natural and cultural history of the Ocmulgee River watershed.

Engaging the Community

Community volunteers of the Ocmulgee River Initiative may become involved or connected as individuals or families. Community groups (Rotary Club, Kiwanis Club, etc.) and environmental groups (Georgia Wilderness Society, Audubon Society, etc.) coordinate with the Ocmulgee River Initiative with various objectives. Area businesses and industries (Sams Club, Imedia Corporation, etc.) support the Initiative and may encourage employees to become actively involved. Because ORI is focused on water quality monitoring and educational outreach and is neither political nor litigious, the organization enjoys the involvement of individuals and families with various perspectives and motivations, and it is uniquely able to develop strong ties with industries, municipalities, utilities (Macon Water Authority, Georgia Power—Plant Arkwright and Plant Scherer, etc.), and even environmental action groups that, indeed, are both political and litigious in nature (Altamaha Riverkeeper).

Individuals and families enjoy participating in activities of ORI because they "want to make a difference" either through water sampling, testing, and cleanup activities or by speaking to children in classrooms. They may wish to engage their own children in activities that support positive change in the community. In this regard, the fact that ORI is not political or litigious permits people to simply "make a difference with no strings attached."

ORI provides a clear opportunity for Boy Scout and Girl Scout groups to participate in activities that lead to earning badges related to environment, water resources, geology, and/or community service. One example of such participation is the current involvement of a local Boy Scout group that is learning the U.S. Army Corps of Engineers guidelines for wetland delineation (1987) to assist a group of environmental scientists and college students from Macon State College, Wesleyan College, and Mercer University to perform a wetland site assessment of critically sensitive riparian wetlands along the Ocmulgee River in a tenth-year reassessment of a previous study, "The Impacts of Highway Construction in the Ocmulgee Old Fields Reserve (Rood et al., 2001) and "The History of the Ocmulgee Old Fields Reserve in Carbon-Dated Peat Soils" (Rood & Lackey, 2001).

Community and civic groups typically have annual commitments that their members participate in community service. Some groups are inclined to coordinate with ORI in water sampling and testing, or cleanup events, because it empowers these groups and individuals to venture into scientific discoveries that are meaningful to them and to the community. The Macon Exchange Club, as a unique example, is a group of elderly Maconites who support the efforts of the group doing what they enjoy the best. They serve a classic barbeque meal for river cleanup volunteers! This kind of participation enhances the spirit of community for a group of very different people who come together for the common purpose to serve the community through these river-based events.

Environmental groups regularly invite ORI volunteers to give presentations at monthly meetings of their own members. Some groups wish to learn about the current status of water quality in the river and the watershed while others become more actively involved in ORI events. In this capacity, ORI may serve these groups by providing and interpreting our extensive water quality database or maybe provide input about some specific water resource issue that may bear on decisions or directives originating from that organization's mission.

ORI has developed a robust relationship with a "watchdog" organization, the Altamaha Riverkeeper . The Altamaha Riverkeeper was organized in 2000 and works to protect and preserve the quality of water and environment in the greater Altamaha River watershed that encompasses the Ocmulgee and Oconee Rivers, the two subwatersheds that combine to form the Altamaha River, which meanders to the Atlantic Ocean. The Altamaha Riverkeeper does not have laboratory testing capabilities nor an extensive budget allocated to environmental testing. Because of the political nature of this organization, in-house laboratory test results would risk being "held suspect," and opponents to the findings of the group's efforts would use this as a basis to disregard critical water quality data. However, in collaboration with the Altamaha Riverkeeper, the Ocmulgee River Initiative has coordinated independent studies of water quality in areas that the Altamaha Riverkeeper has identified as "areas of concern."

In 2009, point discharges into the Oconee River in Dublin, Georgia, were tested for fecal coliform bacteria, nutrients, and toxic trace metals. Astonishingly high fecal coliform bacteria counts were discovered not only at point source discharges but in areas of the river that were presumed to offer "baseline" data. The resulting media reports of hazardous water conditions in this area were summarily attacked by opponents of the Altamaha Riverkeeper because of the "presumed bias." However, these claims were definitively refuted because ORI carried out its water-sampling regime independent of the Altamaha Riverkeeper group. Recently, the Altamaha Riverkeeper documented its concerns with the U.S. EPA regarding dredge spoils at Andrews Island, Georgia, and the deleterious impact these contaminated sludges have had on the ecosystem near Brunswick, Georgia. The EPA committed to evaluating the claims that have been made by the Riverkeeper. ORI has been asked to coordinate another sampling program in this estuarine system of the greater watershed. The primary focus of the sample testing will be on the concentrations of toxic trace metals and organic priority pollutants. Local college students will be offered summer internship opportunities to assist with the planning, sampling, and testing of samples from this Andrews Island site.

A Representative Training and Development Opportunity

Since the late 1980s, there has been a contentious debate about a proposed segment of the southeast region's Fall Line Freeway that will connect major southern cities including Columbus, Macon, and Augusta to remedy a poor east-west transportation network in the state (Georgia Department of Transportation, 2012). The two primary concerns about this construction in the Ocmulgee River watershed are the perceived "cultural assault" on the Traditional Cultural Property (TCP) of the Muscogee Nation in an area referred to as the Ocmulgee Old Fields Reserve and of the potentially negative impacts on the riparian (floodplain) wetlands of the river. In 2000, a wetland site assessment was performed on these riparian wetlands with a fundamental assumption that the 1970s construction of Interstate 16 serves as a worst-case scenario for highway construction in this floodplain because it was constructed on a raised roadbed (essentially, a levee) with minimal bridging (Rood et al., 2001). A wetland site assessment was performed according to the U.S. Army Corps of Engineers Wetlands Delineation Protocol (U.S. Army Corps of Engineers, 1987). Two college faculty and five college students worked on this project throughout the summer.

It is believed that this area boasts the second deepest peat soil deposit (18 feet) in the state (Sylvia Flowers—Ocmulgee National Monument, personal communication), the famed Okefenokee Swamp deposits being the deepest. During the site assessment, an unusual peat soil core was collected. The core was collected and dated radiochemically by carbon-14 assay, revealing the deepest portion of collected material (six feet below ground surface) to be more than 9,000 years old (i.e., 9,000 yrs BP) (Rood & Lackey, 2001). This material was laid down at the end of the late Pleistocene, a time when this area was dominated by saber-toothed cats, camelids, giant ground sloth, three-toed horses, shovel-tusked gomphotheres (Lambert, 1992), and other animals of the distant past. Pollen stratigraphy was examined to identify the advent of the agrarian Mississippian culture by the occurrence of corn pollen. Paleoecological investigations further identified a history of fire and flood in the stratigraphy of charcoal horizons and sand/silt/clay strata.

The two resulting research projects, while ancillary to the primary mission objectives of ORI, provide unique multidisciplinary opportunities for college students to participate in aquatic and environmental research that is meaningful to the community. Students participated in the organization and implementation of the field-sampling regime for these projects with the supervision of university faculty who have expertise in these fields of study. They learned the federally mandated protocols for wetland site assessment, and they learned the elements of quality assurance and quality control protocols necessary to the collection and testing of environmental samples (U.S. Environmental Protection Agency, 1986).

The initial researchers on these two projects have coordinated with faculty from two other local colleges, college students, and community members (including a local Boy Scout troop) to return to the study location and this project. As a tenth-year return to this site, not only will the results of the current study enhance the interpretive value of the wetland assessment as an ongoing site survey, but this project embraces a strong collaborative spirit among faculty from various local universities/colleges and ORI. The educational value for college students and for members of the community is exceptional, and the positive contribution to the environment and to the empowerment of the middle Georgia community is clear.

Change Is Good: Enhancing Engagement

After a number of years, an outreach and assessment organization such as ORI may find that its efforts have become too routine to optimally engage the broadest cross-section of the community. In the case of ORI, it becomes so easy to rely on the most active participants in the enterprise that we concluded that there may be new or better ways to re-cast the net of inclusion. In July 2009, a concept plan was developed by ORI members to launch a Center for Environmental Testing and Learning (CETAL).

The CETAL facility serves as a fully QA/QC-compliant analytical testing laboratory that offers affordable certified laboratory testing services and hands-on laboratory and field sampling experiences for children and adults. CETAL also offers educational and training workshops permitting participants to earn CEUs (continuing education units), PLUs (professional learning units), and certifications (i.e., Certified Wetlands Professional, etc.).

The center offers a full array of analytical tests at prices that are affordable for individuals, families, special interest groups, and so on. Typical analyses include tests of air, water, soil/sediment, and biota for physical parameters (pH, conductivity, turbidity, color), nutrients (nitrate, nitrite, ammonium, sulfate, phosphate), metals (sodium, potassium, calcium, magnesium, iron, manganese, arsenic, selenium, cadmium, cobalt, copper, chromium, nickel, lead, zinc, and mercury), and organic priority pollutants (petroleum products, pesticides, herbicides, insecticides, fungicides, industrial chemicals, etc.).

CETAL is a resource for green job development and supports local industry with testing and compliance technical assistance. This includes, but is not limited to, the testing of industrial and economically significant materials, such as the research production and testing of alternative fuels (biofuels, biodiesels) with due focus on feedstocks, including algae and waste products that will be critical to sustain an alternative fuels market in middle Georgia and beyond.

Students are encouraged to participate in a work-study program to introduce them to the variety of exciting opportunities in the fields of chemistry, biology, environmental science, and policy/regulation. Adults may participate in training experiences that introduce them to an array of technical experiences to prepare them for opportunities in the workplace. Alternatively, children and adults may experience the daily operations of an analytical testing laboratory with guided tours and informational presentations. Informational displays and "hands-on" activities in a family-friendly "museum and literature resource atrium" provide an area for self-guided learning and create opportunities for a docent program for work-study students to develop skills in public speaking (i.e., by offering guided and impromptu tours of the displays and scholarly resources).

The center is funded by offering low-cost analytical services and consulting to families, groups, municipalities, and industries, and from nominal tuition from enrollees in scheduled training and certification programs. ORI also seeks external funding by submitting grant proposals to private and public funding sources. As a part of the Ocmulgee River Initiative, Inc. (a 501(c)(3) nonprofit organization) ORI-CETAL also invites private donations to support the activities of the center.

ORI-CETAL opened its doors in August 2010 at a location near the Ocmulgee Heritage Greenway in Macon, Georgia, to make the center readily accessible to the community and to enhance the preexisting success of the Ocmulgee Heritage Greenway. The anticipated outcomes of CETAL are to provide opportunities for children and adults to participate in studies of the environment, to introduce students to the concept that "science is fun" and accessible, and to empower individuals, groups, and industries with access to affordable analytical testing services for educational, research, and/or monitoring purposes. By centralizing and transforming the activities of ORI in a location that is readily accessible, college researchers and their students, going public with the central Georgia community, will markedly broaden the initial scope of ORI's previously established accomplishments.

Conclusions

Communities thirst for knowledge about their surrounding environment and seek opportunities to contribute to its betterment. By establishing a community-based environmental protection (CBEP) program, various cohorts of the community (individuals, families, industries, municipalities, special interest groups, etc.) may engage in any or all of the activities of the CBEP without imposed or self-imposed restriction. By initiating this CBEP from the expertise of the university community but outside of the construct of an academic institution, there is an even playing field for faculty of any regional academic institution to participate in the program. ORI attempts to engage the general community and college-aged students in activities of the group, recognizing that the positive outcomes will be as unique and varied as the sum total of all of the individuals involved. In an enduring CBEP, while growth occurs for each individual engaged in the program, whether the association is transient or ongoing, it is clear that growth occurs for the organization as well. The Ocmulgee River Initiative, founded in 1996, has striven to meet the needs of the regional environment and of its citizens. Current transformational growth and expansion of the Initiative, in its inception of a Center for Environmental Testing and Learning, is an indication that there will always be better ways to support the needs of the environment and to engage the community in aquatic or environmental research.

References

American Public Health Association (1986). *Standard methods for the determination of water and wastewater* (17th ed.). Washington, DC: American Public Health Association.

Bennett, J. (2009). Sewage stops pouring into Ocmulgee River. *GPB News*. Retrieved September 24, 2012, from http://www.gpb.org/news/2009/09/30/sewage-stops-pouring-into-ocmulgee-river.

Chang, K. T. (2010). *Introduction to geographic information systems*. (5th ed.). New York: McGraw-Hill.

Dabrowski, I. J. (1995). David Bohm's theory of the implicate order: Implications for holistic thought processes. *Issues in Integrative Studies, 13*, 1–12.

Flicker, S., & Savan, B. (2006). A snapshot of CBR (community-based research) in Canada. Wellesley Institute: Advancing Urban Health.

Foreman, G. ([1932] 1989). *Indian Removal: The Emigration of the Five Civilized Tribes of Indians* (11th ed.). Norman, OK: University of Oklahoma Press.

Georgia Department of Transportation. (2012). GDOT Fall Line Freeway fact sheet. Retrieved September 24, 2012, from http://www.dot.ga.gov/informationcenter/programs/roadimprovement/grip/documents/facts/falllinefreewayfactsheet.pdf.

Kennedy, J. (1999). *Natural and cultural history of the Ocmulgee River watershed: Contemporary issues and environmental assessments*. Technical Report. Macon, Georgia, Mercer University.

Lambert, D. (1992). The feeding habits of the shovel-tusked gomphotheres: Evidence from tusk wear patterns. *Paleobiology, 18*(2), 132–147.

LOKA Institute. (2002). About the CRN: What is community based research? Retrieved February 26, 2010, from: http://www.loka.org/crn/About%20CRN.htm.

Meyer, S. M., & Konisky, D. M. (2005). Community-based environmental protection: A status report and some new evidence. Paper presented at the Annual Meeting of the Midwest Political Science Association, Chicago, April 7. Retrieved May 25, 2009, from http://www.allacademic.com/meta/p86342_index.html.

Ocmulgee River Initiative. (1997). First annual report on the "State of the Ocmulgee River." Technical report. Macon, GA.

Pearce, J., Pearson, M., & S. Cameron. (2007). The ivory tower and beyond: Bradford University at the heart of its communities. University of Bradford.

Rood, B. E., & Lackey, L. (2001). The history of the Ocmulgee Old Fields Reserve in carbon-dated peat soils. Mercer University Office of the President, Macon, GA.

Rood, B. E., Lackey, L., Eden, J., Johnson, L., Swallow, C., Ratliff, H., & Hurt, M. (2001). The impacts of highway construction in the Ocmulgee Old Fields Reserve. Mercer University Office of the President, Macon, GA.

U.S. Army Corps of Engineers, Environmental Laboratory. (1987). Corps of Engineers wetlands delineation manual. Technical Report Y-87-1, U.S. Army Engineer Waterways Experiment Station, Vicksburg, MS. NTIS No. A.D. A176 912. Retrieved September 24, 2012, from www.wetlands.com/regs/tlpge02e.htm.

U.S. Environmental Protection Agency. (1986). Test methods for evaluating solid waste: Physical/chemical methods: SW-846 Methods. 3rd ed.

Wenzel, T. J. (1997). What is undergraduate research? *Council on Undergraduate Research Quarterly*, *17*, 163.

Going Public through International Museum Partnerships

C. Kurt Dewhurst and Marsha MacDowell

Museums face unprecedented opportunities to exert even greater influence in society. We are becoming places of dialogue, advocates for inclusion, places of values, and incubators of community. Without straying from our foundations, we can become places where consensus evolves around fundamental questions faced by people in every age. What is beautiful and what is ugly? What have we done well, what have we done poorly, and how can we do better? What is good, what is evil, and how do we know the difference? How can we work differently in order to reach our potential?

—*Robert R. Archibald*, introduction to Mastering Civic Engagement: A Challenge to Museums

University museums have a long and distinguished history in serving their campus communities of faculty, staff, and students as well as the residents of the towns and cities in which they are located. While today university museums continue to serve these traditionally expected constituents, many university museums are now also expected to be more broadly and deeply engaged within and beyond those previous spheres. They are using their unique campus-based resources (collections, facilities, programs, and staff expertise) to work with others outside the museum and campus to address local, regional, national, and even international needs. In "going public," many university museums are reflecting the now international museum community's expectations of good museum practice of being responsible to the multiple communities they serve.[1] At the same time, university museums are increasingly providing unique and innovative opportunities for universities to advance their agendas of scholarly engaged community-based work.

This chapter will examine the ways in which university museums are advancing engaged scholarship by focusing on the work of one American university museum that has been strategically using its assets to address needs within its academic home community as well

265

as in local, regional, and international communities. Specifically, this historical and reflective narrative will describe the development and implementation of a set of research, exhibition, collection development, and educational program activities of the Michigan State University Museum that reflect good museum practice in a global society and, at the same time, foster opportunities for university students, faculty, and staff to work with individuals outside academe on collaborative and meaningful projects that have relevancy for both the academy and the communities they serve. Within this context, the chapter will highlight three collaborations between the Michigan State University Museum (MSU Museum), located on the campus of Michigan State University in East Lansing, Michigan, and other partners both on and off campus, and both local and international, to advance engaged scholarship. The chapter will examine the challenges and opportunities that arise when university museums seek to plan and implement scholarly engaged activities with nonacademic public partners, communities, and organizations. It will also describe the ways in which this work has realized outcomes that are mutually beneficial to the university and respective community constituencies. Further, this essay will trace the development of these collaborations, summarize the primary project activities, provide a critical analysis of the collaboration, and offer some lessons for the future. Finally, this chapter will set this project within the context of the now accepted international professional practices for museums and within the context of the scholarly engaged, community-based work of universities.

The Michigan State University Museum: A Mission for Scholarly Engaged Work

University museums are uniquely situated to be leaders in demonstrating the positive impact of purpose-driven practice. Ultimately, this impact should demonstrate to the university administration, faculty, and students the value of visual literacy in a liberal arts education while attracting and retaining the support of the local community because they value a museum that demonstrates its commitment to learning. . . . Purpose has become not a lofty statement that covers all the bases, but a carefully crafted set of intentions that are easily understood, flexible, and meant to deliver particular experiences . . . with the knowledge that effective and inclusive planning, implementation, and evaluation continues to lead the university museum towards greater achievement of purpose, a course where everyone benefits.

—*Juliette Bianco*, A Purpose-Driven University Museum

Michigan State University Museum, initiated in 1857, is one of the oldest museums in the Midwest and is the state's only land-grant university museum. It is a public steward for nearly a million objects and specimens of cultural history and natural science from around the world, and is accredited by the American Association of Museums.[2] As stated in its mission, "The Michigan State University Museum will support and enhance the MSU mission of providing outstanding education to students, conducting research of the highest caliber and advancing outreach through engaged scholarship to Michigan and the world" (Michigan State University Museum 2009).

When the museum was first established, it was designed to serve faculty at the land-grant university that focused "on the teaching of agriculture, science and engineering as a response to the industrial revolution and changing social class rather than higher education's historic core of classical studies."[3] It was not until the late 1970s that the museum began to substantially reach and engage constituents beyond the campus when Clifton R. Wharton, then president of Michigan State University, provided the MSU Museum with new staffing and a charge to expand its cultural research, exhibition, education, and engagement activities. Since then, the MSU Museum has initiated programs and projects that greatly expanded its scholarly engagement within and outside the university and reached communities near and far. By the late 1980s, the MSU Museum was designated an anchor organization by the Michigan Council for Arts and Cultural Affairs, joining a select number of institutions whose work was highly regarded by its peers. By 2001, the MSU Museum became the first museum in the state to receive Smithsonian Affiliate status from the Smithsonian Institution in Washington, DC, the world's largest museum and research complex, thereby giving the MSU Museum broader access to Smithsonian's cultural and scientific resources to use in scholarly engaged work.

In 2006 the MSU Museum was administratively realigned from the MSU Office of the Vice-President for Research and Graduate Studies to the MSU University Outreach and Engagement, a unit of the Office of the Provost at Michigan State University. This change reflected the recognition of the MSU Museum's role not only in furthering the teaching and research activities of campus-based faculty and students but also in using its resources to foster unique scholarly based collaborations with communities outside the university. Consistent with the core principles of University Outreach and Engagement at Michigan State University, the MSU Museum staff "seeks to become more embedded in the communities with which we work, to stress asset-based solutions, to strive to build long-term community capacity, and to create and strengthen collaborative networks" (University Outreach and Engagement 2010). Today the museum reaches broad and diverse audiences through strong, varied, and accessible collections, field- and collections-based research, public service and education programs, traveling exhibits, and innovative partnerships that respond to needs and issues not only of campus faculty, staff, and students but also of communities around the world.

The Michigan State University Museum and Global Engagement in Cultural Heritage

Higher educational institutions and cultural heritage organizations share interests in fostering international interaction to exchange expertise, to create networks for communication, and to assemble resources to identify and address needs, whether local or global. Within the international community of museums, there has been an increased focus on aligning their missions to address issues related to tangible and intangible cultural resources policies and practices, such as those affiliated with intellectual property rights, cultural identity, and cultural patrimony. At the same time museums are engaging with communities to address contemporary societal issues such as sustainable resources, education, poverty alleviation, human rights, and health. It is within this context that museums, including some affiliated with universities, are now working hand in hand with other museums and cultural heritage organizations, including those with global perspectives such as the United Nations Educational, Scientific, and Cultural Organization (UNESCO), the World International

Property Organization (WIPO), and the International Council of Museums (ICOM), to address those issues.[4]

In 1990–91, the Michigan State University Museum began one of its first notable forays into global engagement in higher education and cultural heritage when the MSU Museum and the Institute of Ethiopian Studies at the University of Addis Ababa were awarded an International Partnerships Among Museums (IPAM) grant to collaborate on a project of shared interest.[5] The aim of the partnership was to build research capacity for graduate students at both institutions, enable staff members to become more deeply aware of the general culture and history of the respective countries as well as the particular museological practices of each institution, and to work together on a mutual project. The partnership resulted in the first major exhibition of contemporary Ethiopian craft traditions that opened at the MSU Museum in conjunction with the Third International Congress on Ethiopian Studies held at Michigan State University in 1993. A related scholarly publication, video materials, educational booklets, and events organized with students, faculty, and members of the mid-Michigan Ethiopian community and held during the exhibition run further extended campus and community engagement in learning. A smaller version of the exhibition then traveled to Dillard College, a historically black campus located in New Orleans, thus furthering the reach of the partnership. As part of the project, the MSU Museum acquired what is regarded as the most significant collection of turn-of-the-twenty-first-century assemblages of Ethiopian art and, as such, is an invaluable resource for future research and teaching—for both classroom and general audiences.

South African Cultural Heritage Project: An MSU Response to International Cultural Heritage Needs

In the late 1990s the MSU Museum became involved in its second major engagement in international cultural heritage work, this time with multiple partners in the United States and in South Africa. This engagement had its roots in the longtime work of many other members of the MSU community who had been engaged in responding particularly to the needs of historically disadvantaged tertiary institutions and, in general, the need to address the issues of transgressions of human rights under the apartheid government prior to the new democratic government established in 1994.

During the years of apartheid in South Africa, MSU faculty, staff, students, alumni, and community members were particularly active in antiapartheid efforts that led to MSU being the first American university to vote to divest of all stock holdings of corporations with economic interests in South Africa. Their continued activism led to the divestiture of the State of Michigan's investment holdings in South Africa—the first state government to do so, setting in motion the wave of divestitures across the United States that ultimately played a key role in the economic pressure levied on the apartheid government. The contacts initiated during this critical and tumultuous period of South African history between individuals at MSU and at various South African agencies (especially those now called "previously disadvantaged tertiary educational institutions") continued to be sustained after South Africa's negotiated transition from an apartheid government to a democratic government in 1994.

Once the democratic government was established, the national government quickly mobilized efforts to transform all sectors of activities in South Africa to reflect practices and policies that erased those of the previously white-dominated, apartheid nation. Since arts and culture had been valued and used as weapons in the antiapartheid effort, within the new democracy, arts and culture were seen as important tools for empowerment, healing, economic development, and nation-building. From the nation's highest level of governance came commissions, incentives programs, and mandates to transform the cultural heritage practices of the country. On November 4, 1994, the minister of arts, culture, science, and technology, Ben Ngubane, appointed an Arts and Culture Task Group that completed a first major report in June 1995, followed by one in 1996 in which it was clearly stated that a key value of the new government was that "participation in, and enjoyment of the arts, cultural expression, and preservation of one's heritage are basic human rights; they are not luxuries, nor are they privileges as we have generally been led to believe" (Ngubane 2005, p. 1; see also South African Department of Arts, Culture, Science, and Technology 1996). The report noted that the bill of rights of the Constitution of South Africa states,

> Everyone has the right to freedom of expression, which includes artistic creativity. . . . Everyone has the right to use the language and to participate in the cultural life of their choice. . . . It is the role of government to facilitate the optimum conditions in which these rights may be enjoyed and practiced. . . . Arts and culture may play a healing role through promoting reconciliation. Our approach to culture is premised on international standards in which culture is understood as an important component of national life, which enhances all our freedoms. . . . [We] have the responsibility to pursue and implement internationally agreed and accepted norms and standards in various sectors of our society, including arts and culture. (Ngubane 2005, p. 1)

The new Department of Arts, Culture, Science, and Technology quickly became an active force for cultural policy development, training, and cultural transformation. As expressed in a departmental report,

> The vision of DACST is to realize the full potential of arts, culture, science and technology in social and economic development, in nurturing creativity and innovation, and in promoting the diverse heritage of our nation. The mission of the Department is to support: the arts, culture, and heritage, by valuing diversity and promoting economic activity; the linguistic diversity of our country, as a resource in empowering all South Africans to participate in their country's social, political, and economic life; and the equitable development and preservation, conservation, promotion and cherishing of our collective history, national symbols, and heritage. (Ngubane 2002, p. 3)

The transformation activities within the cultural heritage sector were, however, difficult. The lingering presence of many historical, long-standing societal, economic, and cultural apartheid-era practices created a context in which change in the cultural heritage sector came slowly. Heritage institutions and heritage workers found themselves floundering in the aftermath of the cultural ravages caused by over 300 years of colonial and apartheid repression. Under the former apartheid government, professional training in museum, library, and archival work had been largely denied to persons of color within South Africa and the nation faced a shortage of skilled practitioners who were appropriately equipped with the skills and knowledge to enter the field of heritage work. Few people of color were members, let alone

269

leaders of the major cultural heritage associations—the South African Museums Association, South African Archival Association, and South African Library Association. Few networking opportunities existed for those trying to transform the cultural heritage sector. Entry-level professionals needed basic skill development, and those few persons of color already in the field, whose opportunities for advancement had opened under the new government, needed enhanced skill development.

While the new government and some institutions of higher education began to immediately address these cultural heritage sector needs, it was clear that the needs for skill development far outstripped the capacity of the government, higher education, or professional associations to quickly and effectively deliver services. There were many reasons why the sector was not ready to provide training, including lack of funding to initiate new programs. One of the most significant reasons, however, was that the culture of suspicion that characterized apartheid society continued to pervade both the nation and the cultural heritage sector. Attempts by individuals within South Africa to encourage greater communication and collaboration between institutions to address the cultural heritage sector deficiencies were met with resistance and lack of trust.

One strategy to facilitate collaboration across the heritage sector was put forward by Narissa Ramdhani, then the director of the Documentation Center at University of Durban–Westville (now joined with the former University of Natal as the University of KwaZulu Natal) and archivist, African National Congress. As a South African exile she had done graduate studies in archival management and worked in archives in the Unites States and believed that external agencies could help seek funding, provide training, and facilitate dialogue among cultural heritage workers. She knew, though, that given the landscape of distrust and the quickly changing political dynamics, the choice of an international partner to work with South African organizations would be a politically sensitive issue. When Ramdhani was brought together in a meeting in Durban in the summer of 1997 with Marsha MacDowell and Kurt Dewhurst, both museum professionals from Michigan State University working in South Africa, the seed for Michigan State University to become the primary partner was planted.[6] MSU was a potential partner that had a number of significant assets: the institutional commitment to engage in extending its resources to address worldwide problems; one of the world's major centers for African studies outside of Africa; an award-winning humanities technology center developing tools for research and education and delivering cutting-edge training, including in South Africa; and a university museum that was well known in the United States for its innovative and engaged research and educational programs. Importantly, Michigan State University had its long, deep engagement in antiapartheid activities and international aid through research and education.

In 1998, supported again by MSU, MacDowell and Dewhurst began consultations with individuals across the cultural heritage landscape to gather more input on needs and to begin exploring what strategies might be used to address the needs. During this same period, colleagues at MSU's matrix: Center for Humane Arts, Letters, and Social Sciences On-Line (a digital humanities center) and MSU's African Studies Center were working in South Africa to strengthen and expand linkages between MSU and South African higher education institutions, particularly those interested in developing technology capacity. When, back in

Michigan, the key individuals from MATRIX, MSU Museum, and African Studies met to share findings of their separate but related projects in South Africa, they began to see convergences of interests and needs and, consequently, began to work to bring together other U.S and South African colleagues to focus energies together. Thus a transnational, collaborative, multipartner project was hatched.

In 1999, a consortium of U.S. and South African organizations launched the South African National Cultural Heritage Project (SANCH), a multiyear, transnational, cultural heritage training and technology program to develop appropriate professional skills for the collection, documentation, preservation, and presentation of the rich cultural expressions of the peoples in the newly democratic South Africa. Three lead organizations in the United States based at Michigan State University (MSU Museum, African Studies Center, and MATRIX), and one lead organization in South Africa—the Documentation Centre at the University of Durban–Westville, were joined by two other U.S. partners—the Smithsonian Institution Center for Folklife and Cultural Heritage and the Chicago Historical Society—and a cadre of South African cultural heritage workers and organizations.[7] Over the course of six years, this program, funded by the Andrew J. Mellon Foundation and the Ford Foundation, provided cultural heritage training for over 300 participating individuals from museums, archives, and cultural institutions across South Africa. Over the duration of the SANCH project, the work included some projects/tasks that were short term and easy to implement as well as some that were multiyear and more complex. These varied projects helped foster trust and experience in collaborative work.

One of the most critical lessons learned in the planning and implementation of the SANCH project came at its first major planning meeting of over 60 stakeholders in South African cultural heritage work along with the U.S. team. In order to establish a framework to accommodate mutual desires to foster equity, communication, impact, and sustainable infrastructures, a set of "Principles of Partnership" was negotiated and became essential to the successful realization of the project outcomes. The principles are as follows:

1. At the heart of successful collaborations there needs to be *reciprocity or direct benefit to both parties*. Ideally, these reciprocal rewards, while not often the same, will enrich each partner in expected or unexpected ways.
2. The most successful collaborations *bring all relevant stakeholders to the table* to launch and implement the collaboration. This requires thinking broadly to identify potential participants representing a diversity of cultural background, race, gender, and sexual orientation—as well as geography and discipline within the cultural heritage sector.
3. The best collaborations usually have an *impact beyond the individual project*—they should build new collaborative opportunities, reach large audiences, and serve the communities involved in the project.
4. Whatever the product of the collaborative project, it should *result in the empowerment of those involved*, the development of skills, the transformation of participants' organization, and the building of new capacity within the individual and organization.
5. There should be *agreement on the framework for the partnership*: the structure of leadership, frequency of meetings, sharing of minutes/communications/results of planning, procedures for mediation in the case of conflict, and a clearly defined leadership team.

6. Those involved must have a commitment to collaboration and a *belief that more can be achieved by working together than working alone.*

7. There must be recognition that *individual participants in collaborative projects also represent institutions* and the development of knowledge and skills for individuals is a means to capacitate their respective organizations.

8. There is a real need for *transparency: open and honest expression of aspirations, expectations, and a process to ensure ongoing review and evaluation.* Real transparency takes time, energy, and a desire to build a sense of trust and respect.

9. *Regular communication, establishment of timelines, respect for deadlines, and willingness to share concerns and credit* are a fundamental part of successful collaborations.

10. *Continual consultation* must take place not only within organizations but also across participating organizations. New relationships demand investments of time, energy and goodwill.[8]

While some of these principles were tested during the project when points of potential conflict were encountered, these principles provided a valuable road map to resolve the tensions and have become incorporated into subsequent museum collaborative planning for community-engaged work. The positive relationships forged between the MSU Museum and other museums and cultural heritage organizations during the SANCH project laid the groundwork for a variety of subsequent collaborations, including ones with the Ahmed Kathrada Foundation, Durban University of Technology, Artists for Humanity, the Ifa Lethu Foundation, the University of Witwatersrand's Ethnology Museum, and, through the internationalization of the Quilt Index, with museums across South Africa. One particularly deep and lasting collaboration was established between the Nelson Mandela Museum and the MSU Museum.

Building a Community-Engaged Project: The Michigan State University Museum and Nelson Mandela Museum Experience

The challenge to museums to engage in civic processes and play an important role in community building is no small request. . . . This can be difficult, frustrating, and time and resource intensive. But the prospect of a more engaged and relevant museum holds much promise. In the long run, museums will benefit in many ways, as well the communities they seek to serve and inspire.

—*Maria Rosario Jackson,* "Coming to the Center of Community Life"

During the SANCH program, staff members of the Michigan State University Museum and the Nelson Mandela Museum began to identify a set of potential projects that would be of mutual interest and benefit. The Nelson Mandela Museum, an associated institution of the South African Department of Arts and Culture and one of South Africa's National Legacy Projects, was opened in February 2000 in Mthatha, a town in South Africa's rural Eastern Cape Province, near Mandela's birth and boyhood homes.[9] The museum consists of three campuses: a large exhibition facility in Mthatha that houses an exhibition on Mandela's life as well as displays of gifts presented to President Mandela from leaders and citizens around the world in recognition and appreciation of the role he played in the struggle for peace, freedom, and democracy; a heritage site and interpretation facility at Mandela's birthplace at Mvezo (also fondly called by South Africans Madiba, the name of his Xhosa clan); and a National Youth and Heritage Centre in Qunu, the site of Mandela's first school days.

The museum's mission is "to be a living museum that embraces development and is a fitting tribute to the legacy of Nelson R. Mandela, a product of *ubuntu* and to inspire and enrich humanity through exercising effective stewardship, learning and sharing the heritage resources linked to Nelson R. Mandela" (Nelson Mandela Museum 2010). The work of the museum is "guided by the principles of *ubuntu*, including respect for human dignity and a person is a person through people . . . [inspiring] people to be the best they can be" and is committed to "service, stewardship and conservation . . . [and being] a learning, reflective organization that is a development role player and helps people learn" (Nelson Mandela Museum 2010). Furthermore, according to the 2009 Nelson Mandela Museum's annual report,

> The aim of this program is to deliver quality memorable experiences for and with our audiences and communities, to ensure learning from the Mandela legacy, to achieve growth and diversity in visitor numbers, and to build sustainable relationships between the museum and communities and key stakeholders. The program draws direct inspiration from the requirement of legacy projects to contribute to national unity, and the imperatives of contributing to African renaissance and moral regeneration. These programs seek to inspire people to be the best they can be. Nelson Mandela himself "has insisted that the Museum should not simply form a tribute dedicated to him. Instead it should serve as both catalyst and springboard for the upliftment and development of the local community." (Nelson Mandela Museum 2009, p. 5)

After the SANCH project ended, the leadership of the two museums continued discussions on ways they could work together. The first concrete action was to include a visit to Mthatha as part of the new MSU Study Abroad Program developed by MacDowell and Dewhurst and launched in 2007. Students in this Expressive Arts, Cultural Heritage and Museum Studies program were able to experience the Mandela Museum firsthand and, more importantly, to hear about museology from the perspective of South African museum professionals. Discussions eventually led to the decision to pursue some joint international exhibitions that would respond to the mutual interests of the two museums. Key staff at both institutions thought that a major exhibition and community education project would increase awareness of youth in both countries of the contributions of Mandela and would help the Mandela Museum in development of sustainable economic growth, particularly if based on local cultural skills and knowledge, for the citizens who live in the communities near the Mandela Museum. Khwezi Mpumlwana, director of the Mandela Museum, was also interested in stimulating international and African continental use of the Mandela Museum's new youth educational conference center/gallery as a locale for conferences, especially those focusing on peace and reconciliation.

The Michigan State University Museum was simultaneously seeking (in the spirit of the mission of its land-grant university parent organization and in compliance with museum professional practices) to use its resources to assist in solving global problems and to create meaningful, experiential opportunities for university students, especially those enrolled in museum studies, African studies, art history, history, and other programs at MSU. The MSU Museum was also seeking opportunities to engage larger communities both in Michigan and

273

in South Africa in activities that would generate awareness and understanding of issues facing their respective locales and nations.

Staff of the Mandela Museum and the MSU Museum considered several ideas for possible collaborative projects, but none seemed to have a strong potential both for immediate sponsorship and for meeting the identified priority needs. Then, in early 2007, Gregory Reed, the personal lawyer of the late Mrs. Rosa Parks, announced a planned gift to the MSU Museum of a collection of letters written by children to Parks that had formed the basis of a book coauthored by Reed and Parks. Reed had also underwritten the development of an exhibition outline, based on her letters, that he and the MSU Museum had already been discussing. When MacDowell and Dewhurst discovered that the Mandela Museum housed a collection of letters written by children to Mandela that remarkably mirrored the collection of letters to Parks, an idea was launched to use these two collections *together* in a collaborative exhibition. It seemed that an exhibition based on these letters could make a powerful statement about the shared values and the lasting impacts of these two human rights leaders and, respectively, icons of the South African liberation struggle and the American civil rights movement and could provide unique opportunities for engaging both academic and public audiences in informal learning experiences. After agreement to pursue this exhibition idea, the staff of the MSU Museum and the Mandela Museum began to actively explore external funding opportunities to support the work on the exhibition and related community educational programs.

In 2007, the American Association of Museums (AAM) announced a new funding initiative program, Museums and Community Collaborations Abroad, and, by then, the MSU Museum and the Mandela Museum were ready with their compelling idea for an exhibition based on the two sets of letters. As the museums articulated in their grant proposal to AAM, the goals were to use the exhibition as a springboard to engage young children in activities that would, in both countries: (*a*) raise awareness of the contributions of these two champions of human rights; (*b*) stimulate communication of exhibition viewers' understanding and tolerance of diverse cultures as well as their own cultures (especially traditional practices and beliefs) through written form; and (*c*) expand viewers' awareness of United States and South African history and culture. In addition to the goals articulated above, the museums expected that the following specific learning outcomes would be achieved:

1. Visitors to the exhibition in the communities where the traveling exhibition is showcased will be able to identify the reasons why Parks and Mandela are internationally honored.
2. Students in Mthatha and surrounding communities will know more about the United States and be able to articulate similarities and differences with South Africa and be able to locate the United States and Michigan on a world map.
3. Students in communities in Michigan will know more about South Africa including being able to articulate similarities and differences with the United States and be able to locate South Africa and Mthatha on a world map.
4. Students in both countries who see the exhibition will be able to identify someone they know who exemplifies some of the key attributes for which Mandela and Parks have been honored and then to articulate why they admire this person.[10]

Evaluation for these outcomes was to include self-reporting on pre- and postvisit questionnaires, the documented participation of youth in writing new letters, and the use of the exhibition by educators and learners through in-school activities and visits to the museums. The application was approved by AAM, and the two museums were awarded one of the first four of the grants awarded in the inaugural year of this grant program. The Nelson Mandela Foundation provided an additional grant to underwrite an expanded version of the original conception of the exhibition so that the exhibition could serve as the Mandela Museum's core contribution to the 2008 celebration of Nelson Mandela's ninetieth birthday. Oryx Media, based in Cape Town, was engaged to collaborate on the design and fabrication of the exhibition and marketing components and also contributed invaluable images out of its extensive archive of media documentation on Mandela's life and on South Africa's political and cultural heritage. Planning for the exhibition included consultations of the projects leaders with community members in both the United States and South Africa (figure 1). The Nelson Mandela Museum organized a media launch about the project, and national radio and print media reported on the forthcoming exhibition (figure 2).

In June 2008, shortly before the exhibition was to open, Dewhurst approached MSU president Lou Anna Simon with a proposal to honor Mandela with a gift in honor of his ninetieth birthday and in honor of the honorary doctorate conferred on him by MSU in 2008. Simon immediately embraced the idea of establishing an MSU Museum / Nelson Mandela

FIGURE 1 C. Kurt Dewhurst (MSU Museum) facilitating consultation meeting of project leaders and community members in Cape Town. February 2008. Photo courtesy of Marsha MacDowell.

FIGURE 2 C. Kurt Dewhurst (MSU Museum) was interviewed by a reporter from the South African Broadcasting Corporation at the public launch of the project that was organized in Cape Town by the Nelson Mandela Museum. February 2008. Photo courtesy of Marsha MacDowell.

Museum Graduate Curatorial Fellowship and committed the first five years of funding for it. The fellowship was set up so that the selected graduate student would spend two months working in Mthatha and two months working at the MSU Museum, ideally on collaborative projects of the two institutions.

In July 2008, the exhibition "Dear Mr. Mandela, Dear Mrs. Parks: Children's Letters, Global Lessons" opened at the Mandela Museum's National Youth Education Center in Qunu as part of a weekend of celebratory activities in honor of Mr. Mandela's ninetieth birthday. The weekend began on July 17 with a Nelson Mandela Ninetieth Birthday Football Tournament hosted by the Mandela Museum in partnership with the Eastern Cape Department of Sports and Recreation. Hundreds of youth from communities near and far arrived for the day-long tournament and were then housed overnight at the museum's educational complex. At the evening sports banquet local dignitaries made speeches that connected the sports event to the exhibition and commented on Mandela's love (even while he was in prison) of sport, and the ways in South Africa that, under apartheid, sport was racially segregated.

Then, on Saturday, the exhibition formally opened. In addition to the scores of youth who had participated in the sports tournament, hundreds of members of the local community came by car, horse, and foot. Members of the cultural heritage sector from across South Africa, local traditional and political leaders, school groups, Mandela Museum board members, representatives of the MSU Museum, MSU African Studies Program, Keeper of the Word

Foundation, and the U.S. Embassy came to participate in the opening festivities.[11] The formal opening started with the showing of messages especially videotaped by then-senator Barack Obama, President Nelson Mandela, Archbishop Desmond Tutu, and MSU president Lou Anna K. Simon. These inspiring messages, also shown on video screens within the exhibition, reflected on the importance of learning about the lives of Parks and Mandela, as these excerpts attest:

> How wonderful there is this exhibition of two extraordinary human beings . . . how wonderful that our children and grandchildren will know the man who made that long walk to freedom . . . so that we all can reach for the stars. Thank you to both of you. We know that Rosa Parks is looking down on us and smiling. . . . to think that she is conjoined with you Madiba to give inspiration forever to successive to generations.[12]

—Archbishop Desmond Tutu

> When I visited South Africa a few years ago I had a chance to go to Robben Island and to stand in your cell. I reflected on your courage, conviction, and your fundamental belief that we do not have to accept the world as it is—but we can make the world as it should be. You, like Rosa Parks and Martin Luther King in the U.S., we all can work to tear down the barriers of prejudice and misunderstanding and to act every day to help build a world that is more free, equal, and just.[13]

—[Then] U.S. Senator Barack Obama

> It is an honor for us to be sharing this exhibition and platform with a person of the character of Mrs. Rosa Parks—an acknowledged mother of the civil rights movement. . . . Mrs. Parks and I had other things in common, one among the most precious was the gift of receiving letters from children around the world. We often say that children are our future, but they are also our present and our past. Children are so honest, uncomplicated and full of love. . . . If we can bring knowledge to children, we can help them realize their true potential. I hope many children will visit this exhibition. Thanks to all of you for bringing history to life in Qunu.[14]

—President Nelson Mandela

The videotaped messages were then followed by short speeches from local and visiting dignitaries, including Dewhurst, who announced MSU's gift of the Nelson Mandela Museum / MSU Museum Graduate Curatorial Fellowship. After Professor Kader Asmal (former South African minister of education and chairperson of the Mandela Museum board) cut the opening entrance ribbon, the hundreds gathered at Qunu began filing into see the exhibition, and afterwards enjoyed a dinner feast provided by the Mandela Museum. Throughout the day, local traditional musicians and dancers performed on the museum grounds and curators conducted live interviews with U.S. and South African radio reporters. On Sunday, July 19 (Mandela's actual birthday), and with only members of the museum staff and guest curators present, Mandela, along with his wife Graca Machel Mandela, toured the exhibition for about an hour. He then spoke about how much Rosa Parks was an inspiration to him and signed the guest book (figure 3).

The weekend was a joyous community celebration in which the exhibition, developed by the Mandela Museum and the MSU Museum, played a key role in bringing together many

FIGURE 3 President Nelson Mandela and Graca Machel Mandela visit the exhibition. Photograph courtesy of Oryx Multimedia.

sectors of society. What was perhaps the most memorable and lasting image of the weekend was the sight of the lines of hundreds of individuals walking along rural roads and pasture pathways from great distances from their villages, all headed to the site of the Mandela Museum. Old, young, individuals, families, groups of schoolchildren in uniforms, youth sports teams, and members of chiefly families garbed in their traditional clothing came to dance, sing, witness the opening speeches, see the exhibition, to enjoy a feast, and to learn.

The exhibition was showcased at the Mandela Museum through June 2010, and by the time it closed it had been seen by thousands of local citizens and visitors from near and far. Subsequently Mandela Museum staff completed a curriculum guide for youth education to accompany all of its long-term exhibitions, and museum educators led youth on tours of the exhibition and visited local schools. When MSU doctoral student Rachel Laws was in residence at Mthatha as the recipient of the first Mandela Museum / MSU Museum Graduate

Curatorial Fellowship, she helped develop exhibition education and visitor evaluation materials and visited schools to talk about the exhibition.

In Michigan planning commenced in early 2008 for the partnership activities that would occur in the United States. In the spring of 2008, project collaborator Gregory Reed and his staff at the Keeper of the Word Foundation (KWF), initiated a "Global Lessons" Essay/Letter Writing Contest and encouraged all youth in schools in the metropolitan Detroit area to submit an essay that "reflects on a person in your life that has the qualities or Mrs. Rosa Parks and/or Mr. Nelson Mandela that inspires you" or a letter to Mrs. Parks or to Mr. Mandela "about a 'Global Lessons' value that would inspire today's youth to make the world a better place."[15] The Keeper of the Word Foundation offered cash prizes for the top three entries of, according to Reed, the hundreds submitted, and the KWF staff worked closely with area educators to promote the contest. Comments from some of the awardees demonstrate some of the ways this project helped youth to think about the information and issues raised in the exhibition and how their own views and lives were changed.

[Ending] racism is one Global Lesson that became important to me during the project.[16]

—*Kechara Torrence*, eleventh grade, Crockett Career Technical Center, Detroit, Michigan

We are never too old to listen or record or even imagine what a lot a people went through just to help everyone in the future.[17]

—*Ron Collins*, ninth grade, Farmington High School, Farmington, Michigan

I learned that all people should be treated equally, no matter what their skin color or religion is.[18]

—*Miles Sutphen*, ninth grade, Farmington High School, Farmington, Michigan

Pictures of the award winners and other youth participants in the contest appeared in a special educational section of the *Michigan Chronicle*, the major print news source serving the state's African-American citizens.

Once the exhibition opened in Mthatha, MSU Museum staff met with MSU faculty, staff, students, and community members to solicit their collaboration in connecting the planned installation at MSU of a U.S. version of the exhibition to their students, organizations, and audiences. During the year input was also solicited from South African academic and museum professionals who came to campus; if they had a specific scholarly or personal link to Mandela, they were asked to give presentations to museum studies classes, local high school students, and groups of local educators. As planning ensued, the MSU All-University Martin Luther King, Jr. Commemoration Day Committee, of which MacDowell was a member, decided to open the exhibition in conjunction with the university's day of commemorative activities.

Thus, the duplicate version of the exhibition opened at the MSU Museum on January 17, 2010 (figures 4–6). The annual Martin Luther King, Jr. Day commemorative march across campus concluded at the MSU Museum, and scores of faculty, students, staff, and members of the general public poured into the exhibition. As part of the opening ceremony, students

FIGURE 4 Installation of the "Dear Mr. Mandela, Dear Mrs. Parks" exhibition at Michigan State University Museum, 2009. Photo courtesy of University Relations, Michigan State University.

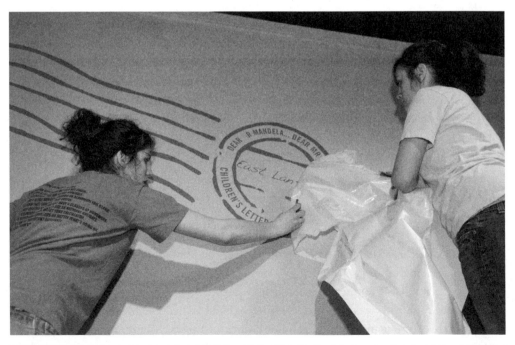

FIGURE 5 MSU Museum student workers help to install the exhibition "Dear Mr. Mandela, Dear Mrs. Parks" exhibition at Michigan State University Museum, 2009. Photo courtesy of University Relations, Michigan State University.

FIGURE 6 Visitors at the exhibition "Dear Mr. Mandela, Dear Mrs. Parks" exhibition at Michigan State University Museum, 2009. Photo courtesy of University Relations, Michigan State University.

from the MSU Residential College of Arts and Humanities' speech choir Act for Justice performed a new work based on a selection of the materials in the exhibition. Later that evening, at a dinner attended by over 400 individuals from the university and larger community, Act for Justice performed another version of their work, this time with two faculty members playing the roles of Parks and Mandela and with two child actors from the community reading "their" letters and asking questions of Parks and Mandela. As Dewhurst was quoted in one of the many news coverage's of the day's events, "This powerful collection of letters encourages visitors—especially youth—to understand and be accepting of diverse cultures and traditions and become aware of the ongoing struggle for human rights around the world. It also helps them recognize ways to honor individuals in their own families and communities who—like Mandela and Parks—have contributed to making a better world" (Dewhurst 2008).

Throughout the run of the exhibition at Michigan State University, many other programs were planned and implemented. MSU curators and educators collaborated with members of LATTICE (Linking All Types of Teachers to International Cross-Cultural Education), a "learning community and international network that cultivates and supports a global perspective in K-12 classrooms through personal and professional development opportunities" (LATTICE 2012), on planning and implementing the group's annual in-service professional development workshop. University faculty from many different departments brought their classes for tours of the exhibition led by MSU Museum staff and afterwards assigned students in-class letter-writing projects. Staff and students affiliated with the MSU Office for Cultural and Academic Transitions and MSU Museum curators organized in-service training workshops for student leaders of multicultural and diversity education.[19] The Nelson Mandela Museum/MSU Museum Graduate

Curatorial Fellow and the faculty leader of My Brother's Keeper, a program for encouraging minority male Detroit high school students to graduate from high school and advance to college, arranged for two bus trips for those Detroit youth to come to East Lansing to get a guided tour of the exhibition, after which they participated in discussion and letter-writing sessions.

Within the university community, the project was presented in the MSU African Studies seminar series featuring collaborations between MSU-based faculty and staff and individuals and organizations in South Africa. Information on the project has been disseminated in webcasts produced by the MSU Office of University Relations and the Michigan State University Museum communications manager—and reports on the project have been included in the *MSU Alumni Association Magazine* (Helou 2008), the annual reports of the MSU Museum and the Mandela Museum, and in the MSU president's 2009 State of the University report.

The original exhibition in Mthatha closed in June 2010, and the exhibition at MSU Museum closed in January 2011, but both museums prepared traveling versions of the exhibitions. On February 24, 2011, the South African traveling version opened at the Albany Museum on the campus of Rhodes University in Grahamstown. Simultaneously, the MSU Museum is seeking potential venues—particularly university museums, presidential libraries and museums, children's museums, and African-American museums—in the United States that will host the exhibition.

Other outputs of the exhibition project collaboration are under way. The MSU Museum, Oryx Media, and the Mandela Museum are working with matrix on a virtual version of the exhibition. MSU Museum faculty and graduate students are working with educators in both countries on developing curriculum materials aligned with U.S. and South African benchmarks and standards for K-12 students in both countries. The Mandela Museum and the MSU Museum are working on a publication that will showcase a selection of letters that have been written by visitors to the exhibition and by youth in special workshops and in K-12 classrooms. All of these activities will extend the impact of the original collaboration.

The MSU Museum and the Nelson Mandela Museum Collaborations: A Critical Review/Analysis of Engaged Scholarship

Research-intensive colleges and universities that are committed to public civic engagement also strive to ensure that there are scholarly products that present new knowledge and professional reflections on impact and effectiveness of practice. For this project, there was the immediate scholarly output of the exhibition itself and the various ways in which students and community members were involved in the development of the exhibition and participated in associated educational programs. Beyond those immediate scholarly engaged activities, there were presentations and papers given at meetings and conferences of diverse professional and academic groups and the preparation of manuscripts submitted for publication.[20] One significant instance of the relationship of the exhibition to a scholarly outcome is that the Nelson Mandela Museum planned and implemented a major symposium, "Critical Reflections on the Legacy of Nelson Mandela: Tracing the Making and Meaning of the Liberation Struggles in African Museums and Heritage," at the University of Fort Hare, East London, South Africa, in 2008. MacDowell and Dewhurst were two of the only four invited international guests to give papers, posters of the "Dear Mr. Mandela, Dear Mrs. Parks" exhibition decorated the symposium hall, and the video greetings by Mandela, Tutu, and Obama that were produced for the exhibition were played at the opening of the symposium. On the last day of the symposium, attendees traveled three hours by bus to Mthatha to partake in a tour of the exhibition led by MacDowell, Dewhurst, and a docent guide from the Mandela Museum.

The Nelson Mandela Museum / MSU Museum Graduate Curatorial Fellowship program provides an ongoing mechanism to connect university research and teaching with a defined community. The first two fellows, Rachel Laws (an MSU doctoral student in African and African-American Studies) and Adrianne Daggett (an MSU doctoral student in anthropology), both participated in the "Dear Mr. Mandela, Dear Mrs. Parks" project in substantial ways and both have testified to the impact that the project has had on their own scholarly careers; already both aim to combine museum practice and academic teaching in their professional futures.

There is no doubt that this exhibition fostered extensive community engagement that profoundly connected the Mandela Museum and the MSU Museum to community members and incorporated activities that were uniquely appropriate for both South Africans and American academic and general public communities. This project clearly facilitated the reach of the university museum both more deeply into the academic community and far beyond its physical walls in East Lansing.

The collaboration between the MSU Museum and the Nelson Mandela Museum benefited from the lessons learned in both the Ethiopian exhibition project and the SANCH project. Four years after the initial discussions of the possibility of focusing on the "Dear Mrs. Parks, Dear Mr. Mandela" exhibition as a first tangible collaboration, much, as noted previously, has been achieved. Now, though, a critical analysis of the development and implementation of this first major project reveals factors that were important to the success of the project as well as elements that served as challenges for the planning and production of this project. These factors and elements must be recognized and understood, as they are critical for replicating the process for other projects not only between the two institutions but between other university museums and potential partners; they are, in fact, cautionary notes for using this a project as a model for collaboration between other institutions.

One of the most important factors in the success of the Mandela Museum and MSU Museum collaboration was that the two institutions shared missions that contained similar core values and goals. The development of effective partnerships often rests on getting to know one another's values and aspirations as well as respective approaches toward community engagement. The Mandela Museum and the MSU Museum are both dedicated to an inclusive sense of cultural diversity, socially relevant scholarly based research, building community investment and ownership in projects, and community-engaged work in response to societal need. While there are still fundamental differences in terms of mission and reward systems for nonuniversity museums and university museums, in the case of the Mandela Museum and the MSU Museum each was able to produce outcomes that were appropriate for their institutions and multiple audiences/communities.

Second, the two institutions already had a shared history of several years of working together as part of larger team framework through the SANCH project. As such, key members of both staffs had worked directly together on developing and implementing symposia, workshops, and other educational programs. In some cases Mandela Museum staff had visited the MSU Museum in East Lansing and, vice versa, MSU Museum staff had visited Mthatha. This shared history of working together had engendered a familiarity and certain level of trust for working on additional projects.

Last, and perhaps most important, the two organizations openly discussed the importance of adhering to the Principles of Partnership that had been forged as part of the SANCH project. These principles were often referred to by both partners at various stages of planning and proved invaluable at moments of concern on the parts of either organization.

The Engaged Museum Experience in an International Context: A Critical Review/Analysis

Across the world, university museums are playing an increasing role in civic and regional cultural and social strategies; [including] examples in Bogota, Tartu and Sydney. . . . In the UK, a number of universities have recently been designated as "Beacons of Public Engagement" by the Higher Education Funding Council, giving them specific responsibilities for engaging with local and regional audiences. At the heart of this initiative lies the conviction that all universities have a duty to engage the public with what they do, and that such engagement should take the form of dialogue.

—*Sally MacDonald*, "University Museums and the Community"

As cultural heritage workers in a university museum committed to engaged scholarship, we have realized the importance of ongoing critical review as these collaborative projects have unfolded. In the museum and community collaborations described above, we encountered numerous issues, including contested power relationships between individuals and institutions; misunderstanding and distrust of motivations for engaging in collaborations; lack of clarity of mutual rewards in collaborative activities; and varying skill levels and capacities in project management. Despite the difficulties inherent in these international projects, the development of and adherence to the Principles of Partnership, a commitment to potential positive benefits of partnering, and the cultivation of patience, flexibility, careful listening, relationship building and—ultimately—a trust between partners aided the projects to move forward and succeed.

Corinne A. Kratz and Ivan Karp, scholars of museum practice, have written with keen insights about the challenges of connecting museums in meaningful ways to community:

Museum work is not without strife and conflict. Many in our field seek to avoid engaging in the issues that occupy their community and choose to be sites of only reflection and reverence. While museums do play a valuable role in these ways, today, museums are finding themselves more marginalized due to global forces and we are just beginning to understand the intensity of the challenge that lies ahead if indeed we want to be players in our civic landscapes and to be a central force in the cultural commons of our communities. (Kratz and Karp 2006, p. 2)

As Kratz and Karp express, museum work, especially that done with a commitment to collaborative actions that meaningfully address specific societal needs, can be challenging. When multiple stakeholders are brought to the table to plan and implement co-owned activities, the process of doing the work is often more labor intensive and takes longer, as the project plan ensures both that the multiple voices are included *and* that the work is, in fact, measuring up to the desired outcomes. Even when partners aim to adhere to principles of partnership, differences in cultural practices, technical and skill capacities, and economic resources brought to the table can impact the ease or difficulty in constructing harmonious partnerships. When the partnership is between museums and communities greatly divided by geography, it can be even more challenging. As an example, in the case of the Mandela Museum and MSU Museum it became apparent early on in the project that while electronic and phone conversations/meetings were valuable and necessary, it was also critical that lead staff needed to hold periodic face-to-face meetings and that the MSU Museum staff needed to keep in regular communication with the chairperson of the Mandela Museum Board of Trustees.

Final Thoughts / Lasting Impressions

There can be no doubt in my own mind that the arts play a crucial role in the life of the people. And it is important that people know that, in being creative, they become more than consumers. They can transcend their often horrendous circumstances and bring something new into being.

—*Desmond Tutu*, introduction to Resistance Art in South Africa

University museum-based, community-engaged scholarship endeavors, as exemplified by those of the MSU Museum described in this chapter, have revealed lessons and values that can be applied by other museums working in partnership with communities. They provide an opportunity to learn from the successes and the weaknesses of cocreated collaborative partnerships between museums.

The university museum international partnership of the Mandela Museum and the MSU Museum was clearly built on the conviction that both museums wanted to be significant players in their respective civic landscapes to help transform the cultural commons of their communities. Both museums have been deeply committed to participating more broadly in the educational, civic, and cultural structures in their communities to forge new sustained relationships that respond to pressing societal problems, particularly of their immediate audiences. The exhibition and related programs matched the relevant collection resources and appropriate design and educational strategies of each institution to ensure meaningful and effective responses to identified needs. In both the inclusive and collaborative way in which the exhibition and related activities were developed, the two museums increased their credibility and value in their respective cultural commons.

In the final analysis the partnership yielded significant dividends beyond their initial expectation of creating an exhibition that addressed community needs. It has set the stage for the planning of new additional collaborative initiatives that will continue to realize the goals of both museums as well as Michigan State University for sustained, scholarly engaged, international work.

Last, the two museums hoped that the "Dear Mr. Mandela, Dear Mrs. Parks" exhibition project would lead not only to the deliverables outlined in grant proposals but also to the establishment of a mode of collaboration that would set the foundation for an ongoing relationship and perhaps even serve as a model for other museums seeking to engage in effective partnerships with other museums and with their communities. What has been evident is that the *process* of planning and implementing the project was perhaps as important as the outcomes. The challenge of "going public" for university museums—regardless of whether on a local or a global level—can sometimes be daunting, but when the work respects and adheres to sets of shared principles of operation, of shared missions, and when it addresses community needs, it can enable museums to be essential forces in their respective civic and cultural community landscapes.

Notes

1. For more information on expectations of good museum practice, see Code of Ethics, Professional Standards, and Key Concepts of Museology documents at International Council of Museums (retrieved February 2, 2010, from http://icom.museum/what-we-do/professional-standards/key-concepts-of-museology.html), and Characteristics of Excellence for U.S. Museums and Standards for U.S. Museums (Washington, DC: American Association of Museums), retrieved February 2, 2010, from http://www.aam-us.org/museumresources/ic/index.cfm.

2. See Accreditation standards, American Association of Museums. Washington, D.C. Retrieved from http://www.aam-us.org/museumresources/accred/standards.cfm.

3. Land grant university, retrieved March 17, 2010, from http://en.wikipedia.org/wiki/Land-grant_university.

4. See United Nations Educational, Scientific, and Cultural organization (UNESCO), retrieved March 17, 2010 from http://whc.unesco.org/en/35/; World International Property Organization (WIPO), retrieved March 17, 2010, from http://www.wipo.int/portal/index.html.en; and International Council of Museums (ICOM), retrieved March 17, 2010, from http://icom.museum/.

5. International Partnerships Among Museums (IPAM) provides museums the opportunity to undertake a project with an international partner and establish lasting ties in another part of the world. IPAM is an institution-to-institution exchange program administered by the American Association of Museums with primary support from the Bureau of Educational and Cultural Affairs of the U.S. Department of State. Retrieved April 23, 2007, from http://www.aam-us.org/getinvolved/ipam/.

6. In 1997, a team of South African cultural workers at the Documentation Centre and Museum at University of Fort Hare in Alice, South Africa approached MSU, seeking assistance in addressing a number of needs related to their art and ethnographic collections, liberation archival material, oral history/fieldwork collections, and related public programming. Based at one of the historically disadvantaged tertiary universities (and the alma mater of many key Southern African leaders), the Documentation Centre was seeking to find an international partner—preferably university based—with a commitment to Africa, experience in conducting fieldwork on living cultural traditions, experience in cultural policy and planning work for museums and archives,

experience with documentation and presentation of intangible cultural heritage and with training students to gain the skills needed to work in new South Africa's changing cultural heritage sector. With support from MSU, Kurt Dewhurst (then as director of the MSU Museum) and Marsha MacDowell (as coordinator of the Michigan Traditional Arts Program and a faculty member in museum studies) traveled to Alice, a small town located in South Africa's Eastern Cape Province, an area once a designated homeland for people of color under apartheid. After MacDowell and Dewhurst provided assistance to the staff of the University of Fort Hare's Documentation Centre, they were asked by UFH staff member Janet Pillai to meet with Narissa Ramdhani in Durban. Ramdhani, in turn, introduced MacDowell, Dewhurst, and other members of the MSU team to key South African cultural professionals in government, museums, archives, and universities.

7. For more details on the history and development of this project as well as access to the Final Report of the South African National Heritage Project (2004), see http://www.sanch.org/. The SANCH project received financial support from these units at Michigan State University: College of Arts and Letters, African Studies Center, Michigan State University Museum, Office of the Vice President for Research and Graduate Studies, Office of the Provost, International Studies Center (South African Initiative Project), and MATRIX: Center for Humane Arts, Letters, and Social Science Online. The core leadership team at Michigan State University consisted of Mark Kornbluh, John Eadie, Christine Root-Wiley, David Wiley, Robert Vassen, Marsha MacDowell, and C. Kurt Dewhurst with invaluable input from Melanie Shell-Weiss, Jackie Shoppell, Joan Eadie, and other colleagues at MATRIX and the MSU Museum. After the first year they were joined by Peter Knupfer, who served as manager of the project for the last two years.

   The project benefited greatly from input from many individuals in South Africa and in the United States, but the authors want to single out Lou Anna K. Simon and Charlie Greenleaf for their roles in enabling the MSU participation, the contributions of Diana N'Diaye, Richard Kurin, and James Early at the Smithsonian Institution Center for Folklife and Cultural Heritage, and Russell Lewis and Doug Greenburg at the Chicago Historical Society. We also want to single out the following individuals who served on the Bi-National SANCH Project Advisory Council: Mandy Gilder, National Archives; Anthea Josias, Robben Island Museum/Mayibuye Archives; Khwezi ka Mpumlwana, Mandela Museum; Rooksana Omar, Durban Local History Museums; Michele Pickover, University of Witswatersrand Historical Papers; Narissa Ramdhani, Documentation Centre, University of Natal and ANC Archives; Professor Yonah Seleti, Campbell Collections, University of Natal; and Mwelela Cele, SANCH program administrative assistant. (Some of these individuals are currently affiliated with other institutions.)

   The staff of the Documentation Centre and the Library at the University of Fort Hare provided a rich introduction to the cultural heritage of South Africa through their important collections. We also benefited from the chance to work with Margaret Hedstrom, of the School of Information at the University of Michigan, while at the University of Fort Hare. We especially want to thank Narissa Ramdhani, Janet Pillai, and Mandy Gilder, who were among the first South African cultural heritage professionals who shared their knowledge and network of colleagues with us.

8. At the Durban conference, SANCH member David Wiley shared a set of "principles for partnerships" that he had used in previous collaborative activities. The SANCH team used his "principles" as a basis to form a set of principles for the SANCH project and added new elements based on contributed recommendations from the conferees in Durban. The resulting set of "Principles for

Partnerships" that came out of the Durban conference were critical to the SANCH project and could easily serve as useful principles in the development and implementation of any collaborative project.

9. Under the new democratic government, there was a movement effort by the National Department of Arts and Culture to establish commemorative symbols of South Africa's history and to celebrate its heritage, especially those aspects of cultural heritage that were excluded from commemoration and celebration during the years of the apartheid government. This included "monuments, museums, plaques, outdoor art, heritage trails, and other symbolic representations to creative visible reminders of and to commemorate, the many aspects of South Africa's past." See Legacy Projects 2010, 82–83.

10. Grant proposal project goals, Museums and Community Collaborations Abroad Program (Washington, DC: American Association of Museums), 4.

11. Representatives of the National and Provincial Departments of Art, Culture, Recreation, and Sport, as well as David Grier, deputy press attaché, U.S. Embassy, Pretoria, South Africa, were in attendance.

12. Video messages recorded by Archbishop Desmond Tutu for inclusion in the Dear Mr. Mandela, Dear Mrs. Parks: Children's Letters, Global Lessons exhibition. The message was recorded and provided by Oryx Media of Cape Town, South Africa, and premiered on July 17, 2008.

13. Video message recorded by Barack Obama for inclusion in the Dear Mr. Mandela, Dear Mrs. Parks: Children's Letters, Global Lessons. The message was provided by the senator's office for the Michigan State University Museum and the Nelson Mandela Museum, and it premiered on July 17, 2008.

14. Video message recorded by Nelson Mandela for inclusion in the Dear Mr. Mandela, Dear Mrs. Parks: Children's Letters, Global Lessons exhibition. The message provided by the Nelson Mandela Foundation of Johannesburg, South Africa, and it premiered on July 17, 2008.

15. The Global Lessons Essay/Letter Writing Contest was coordinated by the Keeper of the Word Foundation in cooperation with the Michigan State University Museum and the Nelson Mandela Museum. The Keeper of the Word Foundation is a Detroit-based foundation dedicated to the life and work of Rosa Parks. The competition was focused on schools in greater Detroit in March–April, 2008.

16. Kechara Torrence, letter submitted to Global Lessons Essay/Letter Writing Contest, Detroit, Michigan.

17. Ron Collins, letter submitted to Global Lessons Essay/Letter Writing Contest, Detroit, Michigan.

18. Miles Sutphen, letter submitted to the Global Lessons Essay/Letter Writing Contest, Detroit, Michigan.

19. MSU's Office of Cultural and Academic Transitions (OCAT) "supports individual students in their navigation of cross-cultural encounters, and in their own understanding, exploration, and development of cultural identity. Student-to-student interaction is the key to benefiting from diversity, and OCAT strives to bring together individuals as well as groups of students from diverse racial, ethnic, international, and domestic backgrounds for meaningful interactions." (Office of Cultural and Academic Transitions, 2010).

20. The presentations include those at the American Folklore Society Annual Meeting; the Michigan Department of Education's School Improvement Conference; National Outreach Scholarship Conference; the American Association for Museums Annual Meeting; the South African Museums Association Annual Meeting; and, forthcoming, the triannual meeting of AFRICOM (the International

Council of Museums' consortium of museums from the African continent). Scholarly publications have also been prepared for academic journals such as *Museum Anthropology Review* and the *South African Museums Association Journal*.

References

Dewhurst, C. K. (2008). News release. Michigan State University Relations, July 18.

Helou, L. (2008). Dear Mr. Mandela, Dear Mrs. Parks—a global education project. *MSU Alumni Magazine*, Spring, 25, 38–39.

Kratz, C. A., & Karp, I. (2006). Introduction. In *Museum frictions: Public cultures/global transformations* (pp. 1–32). Durham: Duke University Press.

Linking All Types of Teachers to International Cross-Cultural Education (LATTICE). (2012). What is LATTICE?. Retrieved September 24, 2012, from http://www.latticeworld.org/index.php/about-us/what-is-lattice.

Legacy Projects. (2010). *Experience the vibrancy of South Africa's cultural diversity: Arts and culture guide 2010*. Pretoria: National Department of Arts and Culture.

Michigan State University Museum. (2009). Mission statement. Strategic plan. Retrieved from http://museum.msu.edu/.

Nelson Mandela Museum. (2009a), *Nelson Mandela Museum activity book*. Mthatha, South Africa: Nelson Mandela Museum.

Nelson Mandela Museum. (2009b). 2008–2009 annual report of the Nelson Mandela Museum. Mthatha, South Africa: Nelson Mandela Museum.

Nelson Mandela Museum. 2010. Vision and mission. Retrieved September 24, 2012, from http://www.nelsonmandelamuseum.org.za/about-us/vision-and-mission.

Ngubane, B. S. (2002). *Strategic plan*. Pretoria: Department of Arts, Culture, Science, and Technology.

Ngubane, B. S. (2005). *A report of the arts and culture task force*. Pretoria: South African Department of Arts, Culture, Science, and Technology.

Office of Cultural and Academic Transitions, Michigan State University. (2010). Welcome to OCAT. Retrieved September 24, 2012, from http://ocat.msu.edu/.

South African Department of Arts, Culture, Science, and Technology. (1996). All our legacies, all our futures: White paper on arts, culture and heritage. Pretoria: South African Department of Arts, Culture, Science, and Technology.

University Outreach and Engagement, Michigan State University. (2010). Building collaborative partnerships. PowerPoint presentation. Retrieved February 12, 2010, from http://outreach.msu.edu/.

Poco a Poco: Weaving Transnational Solidarity with Jolom Mayaetik, Mayan Women's Weaving Cooperative, Chiapas, Mexico

Katherine O'Donnell

If you want to have a "global partnership" with an artisan co-op you should in the first place have respect for their lives and their work.

—*International advisor*

The above quote, from a *compañera* with whom I worked during the last fourteen years in Chiapas, Mexico, captured the bottom-line realities involved in an emerging, dynamic, and complex transnational and intercultural partnership. Organizing with Jolom Mayaetik, an autonomous, Mayan women's weaving cooperative composed of 200 members from the highlands of Chiapas, within the context of the academy, I moved from tourist to academic observer and finally to a solidarity relationship through what is referred to in Latin America as the "accompaniment" of *compañeras*–fellow political allies in Chiapas. Accompaniment is a horizontal relationship of mutual learning, building collective commitment and trust along the way. As our relationship has deepened and we have grown to trust each other and know each other, my role has emerged as a bridge person between academic, business, fair trade, health, and human rights individuals, organizations, and networks in the global North and South. Consequently, in brokering relationships for grants, speaking tours, or the marketing of textiles, I have been in the middle of many conversations and have had to translate actions and decisions back and forth.

A principal job that the members of Jolom Mayaetik have asked me to take on is finding new U.S. markets for their textiles, and each time that I visit the women co-op members in their villages or at the center for training and development, I am reminded of that duty and thanked for my work with them. This work involves large-scale, direct retail marketing and, more often, networking and correspondence with solidarity members around the world,

291

grant writing for health initiatives, and formal and popular education on indigenous rights, economic justice, and globalization.

Within the first year of working with the cooperative in the United States, I realized that using the conventional course that I had developed for students would meet neither the hopes nor the needs of the cooperative. I learned that my academic course succeeded at raising consciousness, but the short duration of the course and lack of follow-up affiliation and organizational structure intensified the "chameleon complex" (Kiely, 2004), the struggle to reconcile shifts in worldview, and precluded alignment with the solidarity relationship and commitment to the long haul by all but the most highly motivated students who had completed intensive intercultural and social justice work in high school long before their Chiapas college experience.

I also realized that without an institutional level approach to social-justice-centered engagement, which Ward and Moore (2010) describe as working as equal partners within communities to collectively build community, solve problems, and increase social capital, it would be difficult to create genuine solidarity relations within the context of the college and recruit people to become part of an international network. If I went only the conventional course route to satisfy the college and students, I would violate the expectations and bottom line needs of my global partners and fail to accomplish our shared social justice goals. On the other hand, if I worked to satisfy the commitments and demands of economic solidarity, I could bring students in occasionally through courses and small-scale events, but the economic and social justice bottom lines would have to be met largely outside of the academic context and there would be looser buy-in on the part of students. The persistent economic and political inequalities in Chiapas, my deepening commitments, the relationships and insights (accompaniment) of my *compañeras* in Chiapas, and the academic context's constraints led me to choose the pursuit of solidarity in the more public realm.

In the following sections, I develop my conceptualization of the solidarity process and consider long-standing transnational models that utilize a solidarity-based praxis and structural approach. Next, I turn to the work with Jolom Mayaetik and discuss how our alignment with our partners' struggle for economic and political justice shapes the solidarity relationship.

Introduction to Solidarity-Based Practice

Long-term activist, Freire- and feminist-inspired grassroots community-organizing work is my foundation for community-based pedagogy and partnerships informed by a human rights framework. Such a position makes explicit the intersection of gender, race, culture, and class oppression and sees student activism and community-based service learning (CBSL) as alignment—the first step in a solidarity process (refer to figure 1). Students and solidarity network members are accompanied in their growing awareness by community mentor-partners from both the United States and Chiapas, Mexico. Economic solidarity evolves through the increasing commitment of individuals to the shared value of social and economic justice. Developing mechanisms to market both the fair-trade textiles made by members of the Chiapas weaving cooperative and the educational message of social justice is work undertaken in the solidarity relationship.

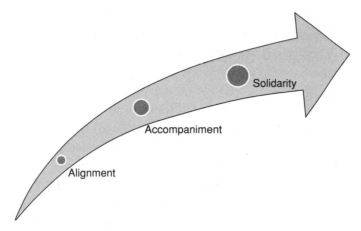

FIGURE 1 Solidarity Continuum
SOURCE: O'Donnell, 2010

Acting on feminism as a transformational ethic seeking social justice leads potentially to the development of challenges to structural violence and a rethinking of conventional organizing techniques, classroom processes, campus-community relationships, and research methods. This contrasts with Stall and Stoecker's (1998) model of women-centered organizing versus Alinsky-style organizing. I share Stoecker and Beckman's (2010, p. 11) view of civic engagement as one that "sees university participation as one element in a broad-based effort for the benefit of the entire community. The involvement of faculty and students follows a community-led direction, of which the university community is only one participant. Student and faculty involvement occur[s] in response to the large agenda identified by a diverse coalition, rather than by a faculty member's class or scholarship interests."

In the case of our solidarity work, that larger agenda is transnational and determined in conjunction with multiple community groups in Chiapas.

Moving toward Solidarity

Programs that offer community-based training to students are embedded in and shaped by complex power relationships, a principal one being the nature of the relationship between the university and the community. In contrast to charity or entrepreneurial approaches, which are sometimes used for organizing community and international programs, I utilize the notion of a solidarity relationship that Freire (1989) recognized as involving education for liberation for all parties and praxis-action and reflection upon the world in order to transform oppression and inequality. Fraser (1989; see also Waterman, 1996) refers to a similar stance as solidarity ethics. Both call for taking our cues from the community with our bottom lines addressing structural issues reflecting or associated with the root causes of disparities—poverty, food, sovereignty, political voice, and equity.

This approach also demands engaging ourselves in understanding the roots of the structural inequities that people confront globally and locally, and our own location in that system. Binford (1996, pp. 202–203) describes "practicing the preferential for the poor" as linking investigative human rights documentation work with grassroots organizations,

293

public education that gives voice to witnesses and their resistance to oppression, and scrutiny of the institutions that are at the forefront of the "New World Order" and contribute to attacks on social welfare and growing disparities north and south.

The Solidarity Process

I characterize the solidarity relationship as a process involving alignment, consciousness-raising, and trust building through accompaniment, collective action, practicing oppositional politics, networking, and solidarity. It begins with alignment—identifying one's self with an issue, a person, a movement, or an organization. This might have been preceded by a consciousness-raising process that Freire describes as *conscientization*–the process of becoming aware of oppression in its social, political, cultural, and economic dimensions— and it triggers the process as well.

It is my intention and hope that community-based work in Chiapas and in Oneonta, New York, community spark alignment. For some, working with the little children in Head Start makes them aware of poverty for the first time. Others see the impact of violence on families through work at the local domestic violence shelter and then learn of the same violence in Chiapas. Still others awaken through speakers, course work, and mass mobilizations like the campaign to close the School of Americas. In 2006, after marching in Georgia, students returned to college and built a campus Wick Watch to recruit new members and to raise campus consciousness. Community-based service learning, activism, advocacy, and research create the potential of four years of aligned work at the undergraduate level.

Because this work can be emotionally intense and we all come into it at different stages, I organize students in community action teams (CATs). Minimally, these teams provide shared transportation, course review, and outlets for fieldwork frustration; maximally, they function as support or affinity groups, particularly if students are connecting intense personal experience to community work or feeling alienated in community contexts. In the case of course work in Chiapas, during this process I accompany students through the course and related community-based work, co-op and community members accompany them in field sites, and team members accompany one another.

Accompaniment is supposed to be nonhierarchical. It is based on trust and respect and allows greater trust to potentially develop. Such relationships involve high stakes, sensitive insider knowledge, and emotional attachment and thus can also produce deep hurt and injury (Stacey, 1988).

Consciousness-raising continues throughout accompaniment with increasing awareness of oppression and commitment to challenge it and allows us to conceive of concrete actions in concert with community partners. For many, this involves doing the day-to-day work that organizations require to keep going—from reading stories to kids to babysitting at a shelter. For my work with Jolom, this means doing banking, inventorying, shipping, emailing, grant writing, driving, traveling with members of Jolom, meeting U.S. NGOs (nongovernmental organizations), and seeking out, organizing, and conducting major sales.

Moving to collective organizing and linking with local, regional, national, and international networks is the next stage of the relationship. Attending rallies, marches, meetings, conferences, and speeches and organizing such events in concert with allies give us the bigger picture—one needed to counter the sometimes individualistic, disconnected, and apolitical nature of academia. For those who have chosen to work on transnational economic solidarity, this has meant doing inventorying, making tags, translating, fund-raising, and developing and hosting fair-trade sales events and antisweatshop fashion shows. At Hartwick, students working on fair trade have also become part of the campus antiglobalization and community antiwar movements. I participate in fair trade, transnational global justice conferences, forums, and the antimilitarization movement as well.

Solidarity's primary goal is not to study solidarity but to do it as an activist partner, *compañera* (ally), and friend. I have learned firsthand that our accompaniment creates our solidarity with one another in our struggle north and south, and community-based service learning is a way to introduce students to this process.

Civic Solidarity

Solidarity is praxis. It is a multidimensional personal and political relationship and commitment to doing work together. It is imbued with the complexities of power and privilege and the promise of hope and equity. Accompaniment is a method for enacting and understanding solidarity.

While talking about solidarity is one thing, doing it is another. Mohanty (2003) outlines a feminist solidarity perspective that analyzes common interests, agency, and resistance across borders. Her approach emphasizes a reorientation of feminism toward anticapitalist struggles via a rethinking of pedagogy and scholarship on globalization and through the development of a critique of the anti-globalization movement and its lack of "racialized gender and feminist politics" (2003, p. 13). She adds that such an approach should also teach active citizenship.

For Freire, solidarity is as a radical posture—one where the oppressor stands and fights with the oppressed and sees them not as victims but people "who have been unjustly dealt with, deprived of their voice, and cheated in the sale of their labor" (1989, pp. 34–35). The oppressor must move beyond sentimentality, pity, and individualistic gestures (malefic generosity) and work with the oppressed—through praxis—to transform the concrete situations that spawn inequality. Liberation involves liberation for all parties involved in the oppressor-oppressed relationship. This is coleading through dialogue, relationship, and struggling and working together. The question remains, how is solidarity possible across structural and power fissures?

In arguing against solidarity conceived of as based on sameness or identity, feminist philosopher Jodi Dean (1996), influenced by G. H. Mead's notion of generalized others, posits the notion of reflective solidarity—a solidarity that "offers the possibility of community among those who respect and take accountability for their differences." She asserts that "we are all always insiders and outsiders, not monolithic—a stance, a perspective that allows us to evoke the potential of a community of us all" (1996, p. 34).

Dean argues that "civic solidarity is a commitment to the material needs of fellow citizens as material conditions affect the ability to exercise rights." It involves "standing by and taking responsibility for others who trust each other enough to allow for different perspectives regarding each person's relationship to the group of which we are a part" (1996, p. 41).

Like Dean, Starhawk recognizes contradictions and diversity of perspectives and experience among those involved in movements for change. She describes "solidarity as strengthening our practice of direct democracy, our openness and communication with each other, our willingness to bring everyone to the table and give everyone affected by a decision a voice in making it" (Starhawk, 2002, p. 138).

Solidarity in Action

The solidarity relationship involves praxis, education for liberation, and transformation of oppressive conditions (Freire, 1989). When I was in Chiapas in the summer of 2001, I attended a workshop on Solidarity Economics. Afterward, I asked Jorge Santiago, the presenter, what he saw as the role of people from the North who were in solidarity with the social justice movement in Chiapas, and I knew what he would say: "Go home and create the same movements for social justice in your own country." Working *on* the belly of the beast is part of our sustainability challenge.

In order to understand the solidarity relationship, I examine prominent transnational activists who situate their work within the context of structural violence and foreground grassroots, collective approaches to solidarity and social change. The activists profiled below have influenced my analysis of the work with Jolom Mayaetik.

Paul Farmer and Pragmatic Solidarity

Farmer (1996) calls his approach to programs with genuine sustainability in mind pragmatic solidarity. The bottom-line commitment is to attacking structural violence that produces the health outcomes of AIDS and TB that communities are experiencing in Haiti, for example. He notes:

> Many would now agree . . . that poverty and other forms of social inequality, including gender-based discrimination, are the leading co-factors in the grim advance of the world pandemic of AIDS. . . . Poverty and gender inequality are two reasons why the fastest growing epidemics are among women, who in some regions of the world already constitute the majority of those infected. Large scale social forces—economic, political, and cultural factors—are now placing millions of women at increased risk for HIV infection. At the same time, these same forces render much of the aforementioned scientific advances altogether irrelevant for most women at increased risk. As women living in poverty, they were already denied access to such goods and services before HIV came along to further complicate their lives (Farmer, 1996, pp. xiv–xv).

Farmer discusses the work of Lurie, who in 1995 called for alternative development and, in the meantime, AIDS impact reports, which would require World Bank projects to stipulate the potential impact of loans on HIV transmission throughout Africa, Asia, and Latin America. The World Bank's response to these suggestions was that such proposals were antidevelopment and would mean a return to the Stone Age.

Farmer (1996) raises questions about "empowerment" rhetoric, the muting of the voices of those most affected, accountability, and anthropologists acting as "stenographers of power"—a Chomsky term. With respect to health programs, he criticizes their short-term solutions, shortsighted agendas, and the fact that few work in solidarity with the poor to fight poverty. He also challenges the common educational intervention approach as one that cannot affect rates of transmission if the major forces causing AIDS are economic, including destruction of rural economies and the subsequent migration, dissolution of sexual unions, poverty, child slavery, and forced prostitution.

For those of us doing transnational alliance work, Farmer (1996) profiles community-based organizations that "strive for a comprehensive approach to service delivery which helps HIV positive and at risk women escape the burdens of poverty" (p. 298) and that provide care and support for the HIV positive woman and her family. These include sites across the United States and Mali, Thailand, India, Vietnam, and Haiti, where Farmer works.

Staying Alive: Vandana Shiva's Subsistence Perspective

Vandana Shiva's work with the Chipko movement and others in India also provides us with a community-based model geared toward sustainable, living social justice. Shiva and Mies (1993, p. 303) outline "a vision of non-exploitative, non-colonial, non-patriarchal society," and a subsistence or survival perspective that does not "emanate from research institutes, UN organizations or governments but from grassroots movements, in both the north and south, who fought and fight for survival." They discuss the People's Dam Movement in India as an example of community-based work that produced alternative development, water and food for the people, and alternative agriculture by drawing on people's knowledge, organizing skills, active participation in development, community control of resources, and critique of mainstream science and technology (Shiva & Mies, 1993).

In working with the Chipko community, Shiva took her cues from the women themselves. She asked them what were the three most important things they wanted to conserve and they responded: "Our freedom and forests and food" (Shiva & Mies, 1993, p. 249).

(DESMI) Chiapas, Mexico: Solidarity Economics in Indigenous Communities

At a workshop on solidarity economics, Jorge Santiago (2001) described his 30 years of work in conjunction with communities in Chiapas. He said his emphasis had been on the permanent transformation of poverty through the indigenous people's use of their own perspective, alternative development, solidarity, and accompaniment. Fundamentally, his approach argued that if one person eats, then all others should be able to as well. Economics and politics were interlinked. Jorge argued that without transformation of economic structures, projects had no efficacy. Structural change would be reflected in resource distribution and in the relations of production. He described a process where people work together to create solutions to local conditions shaped by global forces, resulting in constructing alternatives to neoliberalism. In sum, the basic elements include a search for development basic to human needs, development of the person and the community, solidarity and mutual help, construction of democracy, creating social enterprises and development that are local, technology and financing that serve the people, popular education, rights to work, health, rest, and a life with dignity, and changing development to match the values of the pueblo (community).

At the public seminar mentioned above, Jorge discussed his work in Chiapas in conjunction with DESMI and the Catholic Church. He also discussed the work of the grassroots NGO K'inal Antzetik, with its sister organization, Jolom Mayaetik, as an example of solidarity economics.

Weaving Economic Solidarity with Jolom Mayaetik

The work of Jolom Mayaetik has been both global and local with solidarity networks spreading across Mexico, the United States, and Europe linked through shared interest in labor, human rights, fair trade, health, gender equity, and alternative development. Like the authors above, the work of Jolom and K'inal involves grassroots, democratic organizing with a focus on structural conditions—particularly poverty—and a long-term committed economic solidarity relationship. Understanding how race, class, culture, and gender intersect in all social structures, including resistance movements, is a central focus I share with Shiva (Shiva & Mies, 1993) and Kuumba (2001).

As mentioned above, our work takes place across borders, and a specific target is gender inequality, poverty, and the marginalization of indigenous Maya in Chiapas, as well as the international practices, such as "free" trade policies, that cause inequality. We have focused on economic solidarity and popular education with Jolom Mayaetik through the development of the marketing of Jolom textiles across the United States; others have done so in Europe (see Tarrow, 2005; Della Porta & Tarrow, 2005 on scale shift). Health, education, and reproductive rights projects are also part of the ongoing solidarity work. Taken together, the many people, perspectives, and voices involved across time and space produce many "we's" in our solidarity work.

Accompaniment as Participant Activism

Accompaniment is nonhierarchical and collaborative and not directed by me as an analyst (for discussion of collaborative, feminist, and participatory methods see Lassiter, 2005; Stoecker, 2003; Shiva & Mies, 1993; Devault, 1996; Mattingly & Hansen, 2006; Naples, 2002; Starhawk, 2002; Greenwood & Morten, 1998). Accompaniment involves being a participant activist (Nash, 2000) more than a participant observer. Mies (Shiva & Mies,1993) identifies this as a stance of conscious partiality. Respecting the confidences and protecting the safety of fellow solidarity members are bottom-line realities and commitments as well as aspects of solidarity ethics and ethical intellectual practice (Sanford & Angel-Ajani, 2006). Nash (2000) suggests that such activist relations can also produce complicity.

Activities related to facilitating the cooperative's goals take priority. There are moments when the purpose of a meeting, car ride, or conference is to analyze events together. Our discussions are mostly pragmatic. Occasionally, when we co-present at conference workshops—which means we must have someone stay back at the booth and continue selling—we have had the luxury of talking together with others about our transnational solidarity work and issues associated with it. In the United States, the first order of business is business—schlepping textiles, arraying them for sale, discussing them, selling them, and doing the accounting. The Jolom women sell textiles at every opportunity possible. Second is usually eating, and the third is logistics, community talks, and potentially meeting NGOs. Having a little time to walk around whatever town we are in or visit with people and listen to music or see a film is contingent on time, transport, and our solidarity contact's time.

Solidarity's primary goal is not to study solidarity but to do it, and my core position in it is not as an academic observer but as an activist partner, *compañera*, and friend. When working with the cooperative members, we are involved in mutual decision making that builds trust and respect. Our only lengthy transnational analysis together in a decade took place in 2007 and 2010.

As with all decisions, for my research and book, I had to ask permission to write it; I asked to use the speeches of my friends; I asked several to read it, and the text was checked and edited at a number of levels by members of K'inal and Jolom (via translators) as well as others in solidarity. It is activist and collaborative (Lassiter, 2005). In order to tell their personal story, the women of Jolom Mayaetik have written an oral history (2008) of the life course of Mayan women.

At the transnational level, as Manisha Desai (2002, p. 15) suggests, global capital is multisided and multisited. In response, so, too, is women's agency from grassroots movements, to national NGOs, and international feminist networks; the organizing travels south and north (Thayer, 2000). Our shared work is in multiple places, both local, global—glocal (Escobar, 2003)—and imagined in a community where activists from different places commit to economic justice work with Jolom. How connected people feel in our nascent network is varied and emergent. Having met with people in the Jolom-K'inal network from the United States, Canada, Germany, France, and Spain, I can say we share a vision of economic justice, commitment to indigenous and women's rights, commitment to preserve indigenous culture, belief in alternative development, and a critique of militarization and growing economic apartheid. We currently have a wide range of passionate, localized responses to resource mobilization with coordination and communication through K'inal in Chiapas but not fully internationally coordinated. Feminist NGOs and foundations are part of the network through grants and project funding.

There are many moments in the decade-long process where I have had to ask for clarification in order to understand and know how best to proceed, how to present and characterize our work to others for grants or shows, and to decide what next step to take.

There are also occasions like this chapter where I step into the reflective position to frame the solidarity relationship in terms of theory on transnational feminism and antiglobalization and where I draw on the work of others to make sense of convergences, divergences, contradictions, and organizing insights. Theoretically, I am seeking to locate how "the relations of ruling" (Smith, 1992) shape attitudes, interpersonal relations, and organizational priorities across the contexts within which we have worked. Pragmatically, I hope the analysis identifies Achilles' heels and mobilization's next steps. Identifying the macro foundations of micro relations (Burawoy et al., 2000) and the intersection of race, class, gender in globalization—and resistance to it—is a theoretical goal and strategic, organizing necessity.

The Issue of Service in the Intercultural Context

Global service learning can expose students to communities that differ from their own by race, age, class, culture, and life experiences. As Kammer (1988, quoted in Schultz 1990, p. 96) suggests:

> Our experiences also shape our moral feelings and intuitions. Growing up in a white, middle-class neighborhood may make it very difficult for us to empathize with the pain, desolation, difficulties of minorities or the poor. . . . Being immersed in a minority culture, becoming a

minority in another culture may help us to better understand and empathize with the situation of the person whom our society regularly degrades and dehumanizes. Such experiences may awaken new moral feelings in us and so offer us new moral possibilities.

I would add, particularly in the case of transformative, immersion experiences, such work also challenges faculty and students to the core. Programs with community-based service-learning components, especially those that have activist training and expectations of solidarity work, involve levels of risk and commitment at personal and institutional levels that go well beyond traditional courses. I confronted these challenges as my commitments deepened from academic course to solidarity.

My work in Chiapas began in 1996, when Hartwick College faculty members were invited to submit applications for participation in an innovative curriculum development project in global education. The focus was intercultural, international immersion programs for first-year students. The program's goal was to enhance first-year students' effectiveness as learners in an increasingly complicated, interrelated, multicultural world. Ultimately, through dialogue with one another, and through sharing years of intercultural and disciplinary work, the faculty chosen developed shared models for intercultural study programs. Implicit in this approach was the assumption that if first-year students were exposed to challenging, cross-cultural programming early on, as they passed through subsequent courses and majors they would bring a deeper and more personal understanding and knowledge of cross-cultural matters to the entire campus, resulting potentially in a more progressive and informed campus climate.

After meeting for nearly a year and sharing information and views on learning, assessment, course structure, teaching methodology, and group dynamics, my course on Chiapas and my colleagues' course on Germany/France—both taught during January term abroad—became the initial models generated. The next year, programs to Thailand, South Africa, and Jamaica were created. Throughout the 1996–99 years, we debated and analyzed our models from inception to completion.

Of the five first-year models generated, several had service-learning components, including mine in Chiapas. This decision on my part was based on 16 years of community organizing and activism and 10 years of work in service learning and incorporation of this methodology into discipline-based courses including Women and Social Change, Qualitative Methods, Children's Lives, and Introduction to Women's Studies and an interdisciplinary January term that I chaired entitled Vision, Action, and Community. I linked this foray into service in an international context to a first-year seminar that I was teaching at the time, Children's Lives, and to contacts that I had made in San Cristóbal, Chiapas, during two initial preparation visits.

My choice of Chiapas as a site also grew out of 10 years of activist and ethnographic work with the rural poor in the upstate region of New York. I had been working principally with women and children who were the families of dairy farm workers. Chiapas offered me the chance to analyze the gender, class, and ethnic dimensions of structural inequality, social movement organizing, and social change comparatively.

Hartwick College also had an exchange relationship with UNACH—National Mexican University of Social Sciences in San Cristóbal de las Casas. I found a university base promising.

Introducing a service component to my course meant that I had additional concerns to consider. As outlined in the Wingspread Report (Honnet & Poulsen, 1989), effective service learning entails responsible actions for the common good, critical reflection, clear service and learning goals, community definition of need, sustained, genuine commitment, and adequate training, supervision, and evaluation.

Given the challenging situation in Chiapas and an inaugural first-year Hartwick course with students in Mexico during January 1998, I delimited the scope of our community work to action that would be safe, that was requested by local organizations, and that matched my research and activism experience and training and my students' major interests. A focus on poverty with special emphases on women's and children's education and health emerged as service foci. Over time, creating an experience where student learning and projects were not privileged at the expense of organizational members' limited time and huge work obligations meant combining our travel with the cooperative's leaders' need for outreach in the mountain communities and restricting our travel around the state. It also meant that projects emanated from the Chiapas organizations. Finally, it led to foregrounding long-term commitments to people and communities. These changes reflect the impact of solidarity ethics on academic practice—a stance that evolved over time through a relationship still under construction.

Realizing the depth and intensity of such commitments, particularly when it involves challenging our own privilege, can be intimidating and inspiring. The malefic generosity (Turpin, 2008) that often stems from dominance can translate into the desire to "do projects" or "help" rather than listen, learn, and do what is necessary from the perspective of partners. Understanding that work in Chiapas is also training for the ongoing, serious work that needs to take place in the United States is disconcerting to some.

From Seminar to Solidarity

Since I developed the Hartwick College first-year immersion program of 1998 and the Hartwick and SUNY Oneonta program of 1999, both with service-learning components, the nature of the course in Chiapas has shifted to reflect my deepening commitment to solidarity. Such a commitment has entailed learning firsthand from our partners about their processes and philosophies—accompaniment, collectivism, and resistance. Our alignment with the resources and practices of our sister organizations has also meant that in 2002 and again in 2005 we worked with Jolom and K'inal on building projects that they proposed. In 2002, we worked with indigenous people from three villages to build a small weaving center in the mountains. Shortly after its completion, a conflict between Jolom and the local council in the autonomous region resulted in the center's destruction.

In 2005 and 2009, the Hartwick student delegation visited with six communities and in each site spoke with Jolom Mayaetik members and representatives about issues confronting them. Our discussions ranged from women's resistance to patriarchal control as manifested in arranged marriages and domestic violence to family planning, conflict resolution, lack of potable water, washing and toilet facilities, lack of dependable health care, women's extremely long and hard work days, severe economic hardship and poverty, declining price of coffee, rising costs, the need for women's increased weaving work, the benefits of membership in the co-op, and the women's participation in resistance to the privatization of electricity. In each community, we made a financial contribution from course fees for the time and expertise of the members with whom we met. We also met with other civil society groups engaged in organizing against continuing government repression, land conflicts, privatization, and domestic violence. In 2005, part of our time was spent physically working at the new center for training, where we worked with volunteers from New York and California to put in an organic garden with walkways and arbors. We returned to garden work briefly in 2009, but the course's emphasis was on students learning about civil society social justice work from community activists in Chiapas with the goal of bringing this organizing experience back to the United States.

At the same time that delegations were replacing courses, work in the north took on popular education forms and also moved from campus to community. In 2001, I worked with students to create our first Anti-Sweatshop Fashion Show based on Maquila Solidarity Network's model. This proved to be a great way to involve students in a variety of roles from researchers, to models, and DJs—all to make the link between student consumption patterns, clothing produced in sweatshops, and the fair-trade, antisweat alternatives. This type of educational program has continued and has often become an event around March 8, International Women's Day. In 2002, I developed Salsa and Solidarity—Fiesta of Peace, designed to link the work of indigenous women's rights, economic justice, the fair-trade work of Jolom Mayaetik, and the Pastors for Peace Caravan to Chiapas.

Paralleling the local popular education work, the Jolom story became part of national, public tours called "Women Confronting Globalization." These coast-to-coast and Canadian tours link members of Jolom and K'inal with solidarity network people who organize and host meetings with churches, schools, weavers, community centers, citizen groups, and colleges across the United States to discuss the effects of globalization, women's leadership, co-op development, indigenous rights, trade policy, and Mayan weaving. I have toured with Jolom leaders to meet with solidarity members across the United States, and several other members of the solidarity network organize and host tours as well.

Since 2000, in order to meet the economic needs of the cooperative's members and to ensure that members would get paid on a more regular basis and more than every six months, I have developed workshops, presentations, and sales at the Society for Applied Anthropology Annual Conference and at the American Anthropology Conference in 2005, 2006, and 2008. While such conferences offer opportunities to sell textiles to very interested clientele, in the case of the AAA the volume of sales needed to pay the cooperative's members did not materialize, particularly given the high conference fees and travel costs to the United States. Thus, combining tours and conferences became a way to make this more economically advantageous.

In 2005, at a Society for Applied Anthropology meeting in Santa Fe, a colleague told us about the newly created, juried International Folk Art Market that occurred in the summer and urged us to apply. Jolom did so and we participated in UNESCO development and Kellogg-sponsored international marketing training and the folk art market through 2010. The annual event hosts 15,000 to 20,000 individuals and over 100 juried folk artists from around the world. Sales from the Santa Fe Folk Art Market were the largest single source of Jolom income for the year.

It's More Than Academic

From Oneonta to Oxchuc, I have been working with people to address community concerns across the multiple borders of generation, class, culture, and global North and South. I see the central challenge of academics as learning to work cooperatively to construct just, collective responses to the structural problems we all face—using the tools of our trade to facilitate this work. This is the work of public sociology. Making linkages between theory and practice has been the core of my academic work for nearly three decades.

In the 1980s, when I began social justice-centered scholarly work rooted in community organizing as a junior faculty member, I was part of a department that respected individual autonomy, and the tenure committee used a Boyer-based view of scholarship. Administrators often talked of my work as only service or even charity, and initially I did not have the CBSL vocabulary that later emerged to frame it. For most young faculty in many institutions, it remains risky to undertake long-term, social justice collaborations. Later on, serving as chair of Sociology for fifteen years and as coordinator of the Women's Studies program for nine years gave me lots of creative, departmental curricular power. This did not, however, translate into institutional power regarding the construction of a college community partners program.

Substantial challenges in the community-based work that I have undertaken include recognizing how power plays out in various settings. For students and faculty alike, challenges include working collaboratively in groups, collectively organizing and challenging in a systematic rather than haphazard way, using research to inform actions, working with the community members and respecting their knowledge and expertise, learning not to expect immediate results, thinking of work as cumulative, realizing that academic or personal needs do not always come first, learning to negotiate, compromise, challenge, and lobby, and, most importantly, learning not to give up.

For over 20 years I have used a strategy for community-based work and research in the United States—academic courses with activist curricula to structure student involvement—but such courses alone do not cultivate a commitment to "the long haul." The question of cultivating long-term, committed relationships with undergrad students is vexing, but we have to begin the process.

Academic institutions must work to be inclusive and move beyond their often gated culture. The academy can be instrumental in forging new relationships but must honor diverse leaders, history, and structural challenges. Committing to the institutional heavy lifting of building genuine partnerships remains a challenge, although successful models exist (see Mattingly & Hansen, 2006).

With respect to Jolom, the most difficult task remains developing enduring student, institutional, and community commitment. For the academy and community, class interests and power inequities translate into agendas and priorities—thus the transnational solidarity relation is particularly daunting. Potential mechanisms to institutionalize relations include memoranda of mutual understanding, partnerships, centers, institutes, 501(c)(3) nonprofits, coalitions, foundations, social movements, and joint socioeconomic projects.

Weaving Solidarity from Oneonta to Oxchuc

Preparing students for intellectually and emotionally challenging work in the global South has been accomplished through the development of an integrated prep course with a domestic community-based service-learning component and a January intensive program linked with grassroots training by indigenous activists in Chiapas. While such a program addresses the consciousness-raising aspect of the solidarity process and initiates the alignment phase, it does not succeed in assisting students to transit to the next phase of long-term commitment and through their emotional, ideological, and intellectual conflicts. The short time frame of Hartwick College's J term truncates the relationship-deepening affiliation and networking processes, thus exacerbating the chameleon (Kiely, 2004) situation. If genuine solidarity is a goal of our international partnerships, what channels exist to move from "merely taking photos"?

At the academic level, postimmersion classes or workshops and opportunities to continue affiliation work and interpersonal connection with similarly committed people would create a more integrative experience for students. An organization would also give students other opportunities to return to the same questions, concerns, and practice. At Hartwick, I attempted to foster this via campus programming like antisweatshop fashion shows and Salsa and Solidarity events and through allying with the fair-trade campus organization. Despite my strongest efforts to align students with larger policy-oriented networks like United Students for Fair Trade, my efforts failed. Over more than a decade of campus fair-trade organizing, only two students made the transition to connections to social movements. Continuing to connect students to social networks doing social justice work and social movements is essential.

At the institutional level, genuine civic engagement requires that the college build infrastructure to support endeavors that must move beyond the course or professor. Academic institutions could incorporate international solidarity dimensions within their centers for civic engagement or international studies. If motivated by social justice, such a commitment would foreground grassroots concerns and long-term commitments to community-based collaborations on key structural concerns; courses and research would link to those community-determined, structural foci.

While Hartwick has a 50-year history of international programs, its primary manifestation has been short-term immersion classes. Long-term partnerships are largely faculty prerogatives—individually cultivated, organized, supported, and sustained. Whether these faculty-driven programs will be sustained by the college after faculty-initiator retirements is questionable. Because of this structural reality, reaching the goals of social justice and economic solidarity with Jolom Mayaetik remains mostly outside of my academic context, where it has largely existed. If academic institutions cannot meet the solidarity challenge, activists must align themselves with existing nonprofits and networks or establish separate nonprofits and foundations.

Going Public in the United States

During our delegation in 2009, the women of the weaving cooperative reiterated their need for new markets and thanked me for the work I'd done. They also shared with us their continuing struggles around hunger, money, and outmigration of men for jobs in the United States. Since I began this work in 1998, these issues have continued unabated, along with continued low-intensity warfare, crushing economic conditions, a weakened peso, and increasing staple food costs. Income from women's weavings has become a significant and increasing part of family income and is keeping families with food and basic necessities.

After our 2007 *encuentro* in Chiapas revealed our solidarity network's many weaknesses, I asked U.S. solidarity people about forming a U.S.-based nonprofit. I created a modest Internet presence. Not hearing from many in the network, I queried the group again and received mixed responses to organizational development via chapters.

In 2008, I proposed that Hartwick host a Weaving Solidarity Network linked to the Hartwick Center for Interdependence. I thought that this institutional site had the potential to extend the economic solidarity work beyond me and the members of occasional off-campus classes and invite participation from staff, faculty, students, and local Oneonta community members. I did not receive any reply to my proposal. In 2009, after several years of talks with presidents of Jolom, I confirmed with Jolom that creating an independent U.S. solidarity organization was OK.

In 2009, I once again brought the campus proposal forward and received a negative response in 2010. While establishing a Weaving Solidarity Network at my institution was not accepted, a new Center for Professional, Service and Global Engagement has been created.

In light of these developments, I made the decision to go much more public and more formal on the visibility front in order to introduce the U.S. public to the Jolom story in the context of human rights in order to increase sales, volunteers, medical and educational resources, and donors. On the economic front, greater visibility helps to market textiles and develop grants for the network's health and education work and clinic practice. Launching a U.S. foundation or aligning with an existing nonprofit organization with parallel interests is the next necessary step in the solidarity process (see Tarrow 2005 on scaling up).

In conclusion, there are important lessons to be learned at every level by undertaking transnational, civic engagement, and solidarity—lessons that include disciplinary specifics, but which extend far beyond to life, social justice, and the practice of democracy. For me, participatory democracy has meant empowering people and linking campus and community via organizing, programs, curriculum, and local, national, and global projects. We are using our experiences, cross-cultural knowledge, and scholarly frameworks and research to inform our work and analysis and to critically reflect on that same work in the hope of forging community and social justice.

References

Binford, L. (1996). *The El Mozote massacre: A compelling story for everyone concerned with the lives of third world peoples.* Tucson: University of Arizona Press.

Burawoy, M., et al. (2000). *Global ethnography: Forces, connections, and imaginations in a postmodern world*. Berkeley: University of California Press.

Dean, J. (1996). *Solidarity of strangers: Feminism after identity politics*. Berkeley: University of California Press.

Della Porta, D., & Tarrow, S. (2005). *Transnational protest and global activism*. New York: Rowman and Littlefield.

Desai, M. (1995). If peasants build dams, what will the state have left to do? Practices of the new social movements in India. *Research in Social Movements, Conflict, and Change, 19*, 203–218.

Devault, M. (1996). Talking back to sociology: Distinctive contributions of feminist methodology. *Annual Review of Sociology, 22*, 29–50.

Escobar, A. (2003). Place, nature, and culture in discourses of globalization. In A. Basu & F. Weaver (Eds.). *Localizing knowledge in a globalizing world* (pp. 37–59). Syracuse, NY: Syracuse University Press.

Farmer, P., Connors, M., & Simmons, J. (Eds.). (1996) *Women, Poverty, and AIDS: Sex, Drugs, and Structural Violence*. Monroe, ME: Common Courage Press.

Fraser, N. (1989). *Unruly practices: Power, discourse and gender in contemporary social theory*. Minneapolis: University of Minnesota Press.

Freire, P. (1989). *Pedagogy of the oppressed*. New York: Continuum Press.

Greenwood, D., & Morten, L. (1998). *Introduction to action research: Social research for social change*. Thousand Oaks, CA: Sage Press.

Honnet, E., & Poulsen, S. (1989). *Principles of good practice for combining service and learning*. Racine, WI: Wingspread Special Report.

Jolom Mayaetik. (2008). Voces que tejen y bordan historias: Testimonios de las mujeres de Jolom Mayaetik. Chiapas, Mexico: K'inal Antzetik.

Kiely, R. (2004). A chameleon with a complex: Searching for transformation in international service-learning. *Michigan Journal of Community Service Learning, 10*(2), 5–20.

Kuumba, M. B. (2001). *Gender and social movements*. New York: Altamira Press.

Lassiter, E. (2005). Collaborative ethnography and public anthropology. *Current Anthropology, 46*(1), 83–106.

Mattingly, D., & Hansen, E. (2006). *Women and change at the US-Mexico border*. Tucson: University of Arizona Press.

Mohanty, C. T. (2003). *Feminism without borders*. Durham, NC: Duke University Press.

Mohanty, C. T., Russo, A., & Torres, L. (Eds.). (1991). *Third world women and the politics of feminism*. Bloomington: Indiana University Press.

Naples, N. (Ed.). (2002). *Women's activism and globalization: Linking local struggles and transnational politics*. New York: Routledge.

Nash, J. (2000). Postscript. In K. Grimes and B. Milgram (Eds.), *Artisans and cooperatives: Developing alternative trade for the global economy* (pp. 175–179). Tucson: University of Arizona Press.

O'Donnell, K. (2010). *Weaving transnational solidarity: From the Catskills to Chiapas and beyond*. Boston: Brill.

Sanford, V., & Angel-Ajani, A. (Eds.). (2006). *Engaged observer: Anthropology, advocacy, and activism*. New Brunswick, NJ: Rutgers University Press.

Santiago, J. (2001). *Si uno come, que coman todos—economía solidaria*. DESMI, A.C.: San Cristóbal, Mexico.

Schultz, S. (1990). From isolation to commitment: The role of the community in values education. In C. Delve, S. D. Mintz, & G. M. Stewart (Eds.), *Community service as values education* (pp. 91–100). San Francisco: Jossey-Bass.

Schütz, B. (2006). Historias de vida y de organización, nuevas identidades de mujeres indigenas en San Cristóbal de las Casa, Chiapas. MA thesis, Universidad Autonoma Metropolitana.

Shiva, V., & Mies, M. (1993). *Ecofeminism.* London: Zed Press.

Smith, D. (1992). Sociology from women's experience: A reaffirmation. *Sociological Theory, 10*(1), 88–98.

Stacey, J. (1988). Can there be a feminist ethnography? *Women's Studies International Quarterly, 11*(1), 21–27.

Stall, S., & Stoecker, R. (1998). Community Organizing or Organizing Community? Gender and the Crafts of Empowerment. *Gender and Society, 12*, 729–756.

Starhawk. (2002). Webs of power: Notes from the global uprising. Gabriola Island, CA: New Society Publishers.

Stoecker, R. (2003). Community-Based Research: From Theory to Practice and Back Again. *Michigan Journal of Community Service Learning, 9*, 35–46.

Stoecker, R., & Beckman, M. (2010). Making higher education civic engagement matter in the community. Campus Compact. Retrieved online December 29, 2010, from http://www.compact.org/news/making-higher-education-civic-engagement-matter-in-the-community/9748/.

Strand, K., Marullo, S., Cutforth, N., Stoeker, R. & Donohue, P. (2003). *Community-based research and higher education: Principles and practices.* New York: Jossey-Bass.

Thayer, M. (2000). Traveling women: From embodied women to gendered citizenship. In M. Burawoy, J. A. Blum, S. George, Z. Gille, T. Gowan, L. Haney, M. Klawiter, S. H. Lopez, S. Ó Riain, & M. Thayer. *Global ethnography: Forces, connections, and imaginations in a postmodern world* (pp. 203–234). Berkeley: University of California.

Tarrow, S. (2005). *The new transnational activism.* New York: Cambridge University Press.

Turpin, K. (2008). Disrupting the luxury of despair: Justice and peace education in contexts of relative privilege. *Teaching Theology and Religion, 11*, 141–152.

Ward, K., & Moore, T. (2010). Defining the "engagement" in the scholarship of engagement. In H. E. Fitzgerald, C. Burack, & S. D. Seifer (Eds.), *Handbook of engaged scholarship: Contemporary landscapes, future directions*, vol. 1, *Institutional change* (pp. 39–70). East Lansing: Michigan State University Press.

Waterman, P. (1996). *Globalization, social movements and the new internationalisms.* London: Mansell.

When University and Community Partner: Community Engagement and Transformative Systems-Level Change

Judy Primavera and Andrew Martinez

This chapter is the story of a university-community partnership that illustrates the potential that community engagement has to produce systems-level transformational change in the institutional culture of both partners. The partnership is between Fairfield University and Action for Bridgeport Community Development's Early Learning–Head Start Program. Its official name is the Adrienne Kirby Family Literacy Project. From its inception, the Kirby Literacy Project's goals focused on improving low-income preschoolers' school readiness and language skills, increasing low-income parents' effective involvement in their child's education, enhancing university students' academic experience with community-based educational opportunities, and strengthening university students' commitment to future community service. The work on the Kirby Literacy Project began in 1992. Although its size and specific activities have changed and downsized since its peak years of funding and national recognition in the late 1990s to early 2000s, the underlying spirit of work being done today remains the same. Annual evaluations repeatedly confirm that project goals are being met. Over time, however, what also became clear was that slowly but surely the partnership between Fairfield University and Action for Bridgeport Community Development (ABCD) was having a positive effect on the underlying culture of both institutions. What follows is a documentation of the systems-level change that occurred and the authors' musings about the lessons learned along the way of this 20-year journey.

Community Engagement, Community Psychology, and the Kirby Literacy Project

Historically, the academy's attempts at community engagement have taken many forms spawned by an array of varied motivations, some for better and some for worse. At its worst, academy dwellers leave their ivory tower only if there is something to be gained or when propelled by professional arrogance. Indeed, these types of community engagement might best be described as "raping the community" for its data, as a public relations showcase to highlight what the campus is doing "for" the community, or as an academic expert's paternalistic, professionally precious attempt "to help" the less knowledgeable and less fortunate solve some pressing social problem (Heller, Price, Reinharz, Riger, & Wandersman, 1984; Rappaport, 1981; Saltmarsh, Hartley, & Clayton, 2009; Sarason, Levin, Goldenberg, Cherlin, & Bennett, 1966). At its best, community engagement embraces Dewey's (1967; 1997) notion of democratic experienced-based education, Sarason's (1974) vision of a shared psychological sense of community, and Boyer's (1991; 1996) challenge for a new scholarship of engagement.

This thing we call community engagement is truly a horse of many colors with a rich history that can be traced back to many different yet overlapping scholarly traditions, including participatory action research, feminist research, service learning, scholarship of engagement, etc. Truth be told, to a naïve reader it can indeed seem like definitional anarchy (Sandmann, 2004). However, to the authors of this chapter, the vision, the goals, the methods, and the phenomena of interest characteristic of the entity now being called community engagement are all consistent with the processes of research and action known as the field of community psychology. One of the most distinctive values espoused by community psychology is collaboration where the community psychologist and the community citizen are viewed as equals, each having knowledge, resources, and a meaningful role in decision making (Dalton, Elias, & Wandersman, 2007; Kelly, 1971; 1986; 1990, 2002; Prilleltensky, 2001). The Kirby Family Literacy Project was developed and implemented under this conceptual umbrella (Primavera, 2004). It was then and still is today an example of doing *good* community psychology where scholarship and action are integrated; where the relationship between the academy and a community partner is based on reciprocity and mutual respect; and where university and community stakeholders are viewed as competent and equal participants in planning and decision making.

The Partnership: Fairfield University and Action for Bridgeport Community Development

Like any example of community engagement, important to this story is its social-ecological context (Kelly, 1970). Fairfield University is located in an upper-income, somewhat bucolic suburban setting. As a Jesuit university, it has a history of commitment of service to others accomplished through a wide range of local, national, and international outreach programs. Its undergraduate enrollment is approximately 3,500 students, predominantly white and from the mid-to-upper income bracket. Ten miles down the road is the city of Bridgeport, Connecticut, one of our nation's poorest cities for its size. Action for Bridgeport Community Development is a nonprofit urban community action agency founded in the 1960s under the auspices of President Lyndon B. Johnson's Great Society. ABCD provides a broad range of services (preschool Head Start, employment services, energy assistance, weatherization assistance, eviction prevention services, summer youth programs, technology training) to over 26,000 disadvantaged individuals annually. Ninety percent of ABCD's Early Learning–Head Start teaching staff and 95% of the enrolled children are people of color. Most of the children's families can best be described as "working poor," with annual family incomes falling within the $18,000 to $30,000 range.

The Adrienne Kirby Family Literacy Project is a competency-enhancing intervention providing both direct literacy-school readiness for the children in their preschool classrooms and training for parents to help them become more effective first teachers to their children. Fairfield University undergraduates (consisting of a mix of volunteers, students doing service learning, and federal work-study recipients), trained to be literacy coaches, meet weekly with the children in their preschool classrooms. Activities are tailored to the children's identified strengths and weaknesses in language and school readiness skills. Parent training workshops led by trained members of ABCD's teaching staff consists of a series of literacy workshops and parent-child homework activities. In 1992 the project began with 14 parents, 150 preschoolers, and 30 Head Start teachers in 13 classrooms in four different sites with 40 Fairfield University student volunteers. From 1999 to 2002 through grants to Kirby Literacy Project, computers were introduced into the classrooms and a technology-training component for the preschoolers, their parents, and their teachers was added with the goals of both enhancing the work of the existing literacy program and decreasing the digital divide (U.S. Department of Commerce, 1995). At present, the Kirby Literacy Project includes approximately 1,250 preschoolers in 62 classrooms with a teaching staff of 186 in 15 different sites with approximately 160 Fairfield University students participating annually. The parent component reached its peak in the early 2000s, boasting of over 100 parent participants per year; unfortunately today due to the employment pressures of the working poor, parents' ability to commit to attending an eight-session workshop series has dropped significantly. In an attempt to provide some exposure to the Kirby Literacy Project's parent education component, key lessons from the original workshop series are interspersed in the larger parent orientation meetings and monthly site-based parent meetings. Something is certainly better than nothing, but without the shared commitment to a literacy-based group experience the impact is certainly diluted.

The short-term impact of the Kirby Literacy Project is assessed annually and has been reported elsewhere (e.g., Primavera 1999; 2000; Primavera & Cook, 1997; Primavera, DiGiacomo, & Wiederlight, 2001; Primavera, Wiederlight, & DiGiacomo, 2001). However, after over a decade of operation, Fairfield University and ABCD were beginning to look and feel like "different places" as a result of the partnership. It seemed to those of us involved with the project from the beginning that second-order, systems-level change had been set in motion (Eckel, Hill, & Green, 1998; Foster-Fishman, Nowell, & Yang, 2007) and that the relationship between Fairfield University and ABCD had indeed become a mutually transformative partnership (Enos & Morton, 2003).

Transformative System-Level Change

To explore and document the long-term benefits of the project, an external evaluation team from The Consultation Center at Yale University was engaged to conduct the evaluation (Kirby Family Literacy Project Long Term Assessment). Data were collected through focus groups and individual interviews with key informants. Focus group and individual interview protocols were developed collaboratively by The Consultation Center and the Kirby Family Literacy Project research team. Separate focus groups were conducted with classroom teachers at ABCD, administrators/senior coordinators at ABCD, administrators and senior faculty in the Fairfield University Psychology Department, and administrators at Fairfield University. Interviews were conducted with the executive director of ABCD, the ABCD director of early learning, the former dean of the College of Arts and Sciences, the current academic vice president of Fairfield University, a retired Psychology Department faculty member, and the president of Fairfield University. All participants were at their respective institutions before and throughout the length of the project, allowing them to offer particular insights on how the partnership evolved over the years, and how each institution changed as a result of the partnership. Each focus group and interview lasted approximately 45 to 60 minutes. Data analyses were conducted using established iterative techniques for aggregation and synthesis of qualitative data (Shah & Kaufman, 2003).

Overall, the data indicate a significant change had, indeed, occurred in the underlying infrastructure of both institutions. Both Fairfield University and Action for Bridgeport Community Development were, in some very important ways, different places due to the systems-level changes that had taken place. A host of long-term positive outcomes for both the University and for ABCD as institutions as well as for the individual university students, parents, teachers, and children who participated in the project were identified (Shah & Kaufman, 2003).

Changes in Action for Bridgeport Community Development

In a most fundamental way, the partnership altered the landscape of ABCD by introducing and sustaining a "culture of literacy." Prior to the partnership, the ABCD's Early Learning–Head Start program might best be described as "doing the best you can in a resource-poor environment." Through a series of successful grant applications and an endowment fund sponsored by the F.M. Kirby Foundation, teachers were provided with literacy-rich curriculum training, classrooms were supplied with books, computers, and an army of college student volunteers to provide the children with the much-needed one-on-one individualized attention, and the program itself was professionalized with the addition of research-based practices. The classrooms and the teaching practices changed. According to one ABCD teacher, "A lot of things are different now. Things that we didn't know in the beginning we know now; now I feel like it's better . . . And it's all because of what we learned through the training through Fairfield U." In the words of another teacher, "We went from being just babysitters to being real teachers."

At an agency level, ABCD administrators credited a boost in ABCD's reputation to the prestige of its partnership with Fairfield University, the research-based documentation of the Kirby Literacy Project's success, and the local, statewide, and national recognition the Kirby Project had received. Timing was an important issue in that by virtue of the partnership, ABCD found itself "one step ahead of the game" when federal and state early childhood initiatives focused their attention on the issues of emergent literacy, family literacy, and the digital divide. In the words of one ABCD administrator, "We were the first Head Start program in the state to have computers in every classroom. We had a successful family lit-eracy program. We had hundreds of college students volunteering in our classrooms weekly. People were looking to us as the experts. We all felt proud to be a part of it." ABCD admin-istrators believed that it was this increase in status and the documented success associated with the Kirby Project that helped ABCD secure additional funding for its literacy activities as well as other educational initiatives. According to one ABCD administrator, "Because we have this collaboration with Fairfield University, we have all the pieces in place to apply for competitive grants. We can provide them [the funding sources] with good data. It's been a real door opener for us."

Changes in Fairfield University

The partnership between Fairfield University and ABCD provided a different lens through which university administrators and faculty could view research, teaching, and service. Over time, a pronounced change in the university's infrastructure occurred, reflecting a basic shift in the way faculty and student activities in and with the community were conceptual-ized, conducted, and valued. According to many university respondents, the Kirby Literacy Project served as a campus model for community engagement—a model that set in motion a series of interrelated changes in the culture of the university, including an increased inter-est in and support for community-engaged pedagogies and a shift in how community-based research, teaching, and service was viewed in rank and tenure decisions.

Although Fairfield University had a long tradition of volunteer and service-related efforts in the Bridgeport community, the Kirby Literacy Project was one of the first faculty-initiated efforts developed collaboratively with full citizen participation by the community partner. It was the first to include all three of the academic triune, pedagogy, research and service. In many ways, the activities of the Kirby Literacy Project served as evidence that scholarship about *real*-world social issues taking place in *real*-life communities in collaboration with *real* people living in the community was just as valuable as the more traditional scholarly pursuits taking place on campus in its libraries and laboratories. Over time, the concept of a pedagogy blending classroom and community experience was institutionalized. Fairfield University's Office of Service Learning (OSL) opened its doors in 2006. Community-engaged scholarship evolved from a handful of faculty offering optional course-related community service projects to students who were lucky enough to have their own transportation into a pedagogy that the university both endorses and supports financially. At the present time there are over 30 designated service-learning courses being taught by over 20 faculty mem-bers, and there is an active Service Learning Advisory Board consisting of university and community members overseeing OSL activities and courses. Operating funds for the OSL including staff salaries comes entirely from the university's budget. A fleet of university vans are now available to transport students. Courses have special "SL" recognition in the course catalogue. Faculty members are encouraged to develop and refine service-learning courses through faculty development workshops with nationally recognized experts and university-sponsored SL course development stipends.

Faculty involvement in community engagement has a long history of being either ignored or undervalued within the traditional reward system of the academy, and the story of the first author's journey through the tenure and promotion process is no exception. Indeed, many of the university respondents stated that it was the first author's experience with the promotion process that brought to the forefront the question of how scholarship was defined and how community-based scholarship "fits into" the intellectual traditions and culture of Fairfield University. In 2001, the first author was denied promotion to full professor by the faculty Rank and Tenure Committee in spite of her accomplishments within the relevant assessment window: receiving the university's Teacher of the Year Award, receiving honorable mention for both the Ernest A. Lynton Award for Faculty Outreach and for the SBC National Telecommunications University-Community partnership Awards, bringing in over $700,000 in grant money and over $80,000 in endowment funds, coediting one professional book and one special issue of the top-tiered *American Journal of Community Psychology*, authoring five articles in peer-reviewed journals, and doing 19 presentations at international, national, and regional professional conferences. The five outside reviewers who unanimously recommended promotion were all nationally known academics including Edward F. Zigler, one of the founders of Head Start, and Seymour B. Sarason, one of the founders of community psychology. The first author's appeal to the Rank and Tenure Committee included an independent review of her dossier and a recommendation for promotion by the National Review Board for the Scholarship of Engagement. The appeal was denied. The reason given by the Rank and Tenure Committee for promotion denial was that the first author needed to produce more publications in what the committee deemed to be top-tiered professional journals. The university was "talking the talk," but the number of people actually "walking the walk" was in the minority. The culture of the university was still one that held tight to traditional views of scholarship and the myopic belief that scholarship was something that happened on campus and that scholarly activities taking place in the community was either second-rate scholarship or nothing more than service. It was only upon final appeal to the president of the university that the Rank and Tenure Committee's negative decision was overturned and the rank of full professor was granted. In the words of one administrator, "[The first author's promotion denial] really challenged us to examine what Fairfield University stands for and what its mission is . . . it really forced the issue."

Today, scholarly endeavors involving local, national, and international communities are viewed much more favorably, and attitudes about what types of professional activities constitutes *real* scholarship and *good* pedagogy are light years away from the traditional patriarchal constraints faced by the first author a decade ago.

Changes for Both Partners

A common theme of change across the partnership was an increased respect for different racial and ethnic groups as a result of increased opportunity for collaborative interaction. For ABCD's staff and families, who are predominantly people of color, the consistent, positive exposure to university students who are predominantly White middle- to upper-class suburbanites, the partnership helped dispel negative stereotypes that cut across racial and socioeconomic lines. One ABCD teacher observed, "A lot of us teachers and parents are not around a lot of White people. And a lot of the university students aren't used to Blacks and Hispanics. That's just the way it is. Working together every week, it breaks down stereotypes . . .

you come to realize that everybody is just a regular person." This sentiment was echoed by a university administrator, "Our students start to have real relationships with the children and the teachers. Some of the teachers have formed true friendships with our students that have lasted after they have graduated. . . . It has broken down some of the barriers. . . . All of a sudden people are starting to look at each other just as people."

Changes for Individuals within the Institution

The Kirby Family Literacy Project Long Term Assessment documented a host of other positive outcomes for individuals within the larger institution. Fairfield University students, ABCD children, parents, and teachers all experienced both tangible and intangible benefits. Beyond the obvious course enrichment and resume-building perks that typically result from opportunities to participate in these types of supervised internship-like experiences in a real-world setting, Fairfield University administrators believed that undergraduates developed greater insights into social problems and the nature of privilege and a more mature sense of moral citizenship. One university administrator observed, "At the end of the year, the Fairfield University student is completely different person." University administrators also pointed out that these students will be tomorrow's leaders and voters. They viewed the students' experience with the Kirby Literacy Project as a way of promoting a more compassionate citizenship among their alumni.

At ABCD, the children's language and social skills improved and teachers attributed this progress, in large part, to the individualized attention provided by the Fairfield University students. The intergenerational focus of the Kirby Literacy Project was viewed as crucial in providing the parents with the skills needed to be more effective first teachers to their children. Teachers and administrators noted that it was the feelings of competence the parents gained that motivated them to become more active in their child's schooling and pursue more education themselves. Teachers changed their teaching style so that it was more creative, more interactive, and more literacy-rich and that their success resulted in a greater sense of pride and dignity in their work. Teachers also reported that working with college students encouraged them to also pursue college degrees (Shah & Kaufman, 2003).

Lessons Learned about Transformative Systems-Level Change

Important to this story is the fact that 20 years ago, none of the members of the founding group of this partnership gave one thought to the notion of attempting to change the basic fabric of our respective institutions. Our focus was simply on "doing something together" to help the children be better prepared for kindergarten and at the same time enhance the university students' educational experience. At first, it was what Enos and Morton (2003) describe as a transactional partnership in that it was task-oriented and involving a mutually beneficial exchange of goods and services. But it evolved into something more than a relationship based on mutual benefit—it evolved into a transformational partnership characterized by a shifting in intuitional values and mutual growth and change (Enos & Morton, 2003). The question is *how*? Indeed, during the 20 years of the Kirby Literacy Project's evolution there has been an increased effort in a number of academic disciplines to understand systems change and to develop models to describe its key elements and processes (e.g.,

Dunphy, 1966; Eckel, Hill, & Green, 1998; Foster-Fishman, Nowell, & Yang, 2007; Kotter, 1996; Saltmarsh, Hartley, & Clayton, 2009). However, it is our belief that it is because the "systems change" in the case of the Kirby Project was unplanned and occurred naturally that it provides us with a unique opportunity to tease out and identify the key factors involved in the process of transformative systems-level change. In this case, we found the factors of relationship, personality, metaphor, and serendipity to be particularly important.

We describe what we are doing as community *engagement* and scholarship of *engagement*. Although there are other meanings that can be ascribed to the word *engaged*, the one most germane to our work connotes a *meaningful, committed relationship between people*. The first lesson to be learned from the Kirby Project partnership is that, bottom line, before a system can change, the people within that system must change. Fairfield University and ABCD are mere names given to institutional entities. The real relationships and the real partnerships are between the people who populate these institutions—and it is the quality of the relationships between these real-life, flesh-and blood-people that is at the very core of systems-level change. Work in the community and with community citizens *is* personal (Kelly, 1971; Sarason, 1988). In fact, when the participants in the Kirby Literacy Project Long Term Impact Assessment were asked what aspects of the Kirby Project would live on should the project be dissolved, participants most frequently mentioned that it is the relationships between the individuals involved that would remain (Shah & Kaufman, 2003).

That being said, an important concomitant factor to acknowledge is that relationship development, sustainability, and change are greatly affected by the personality and personal values of the key players (Kelly, 1979; Primavera, 2004; Sarason, 1988). In the case of the Kirby Project, the two initiators of the project, the first author and director of ABCD's Early Learning Program, might best be described as "children of the 1960s" committed to social justice and George Miller's (1969) directive to "give psychology away" so that its knowledge might be used to address our nation's most pressing social problems. A first-generation, working-class background and training as a community psychologist made the first author no stranger to the tasks of leaving the professional cocoon and affiliating with diverse types of people. Perhaps most important of all, the participants in the Kirby Literacy Project Long Term Impact Assessment described the first author as being skilled at "creating partnerships of equals" and as being a person "genuinely committed" to the welfare of the children at ABCD and the students at Fairfield University (Shah & Kaufman, 2003).

Another lesson underscored by the Kirby Literacy Project is the importance of the metaphor being used (Dunphy, 1996). We did not set out to "fix" anything that was broken in either Fairfield University or ABCD as institutions. What brought us together was a joint concern for an important social justice issue—the alarmingly deficient school readiness skills of low-income preschoolers (Boyer, 1991). From the very beginning, university faculty and students and ABCD teachers and administrators worked together as participant conceptualizers (Bennett, Anderson, Cooper, Hassol, Klein, & Rosenblum, 1996) to define the problem to be addressed and the methods to be used. We were a collaborative team of coeducators, colearners, and cogenerators of knowledge (Jameson, Clayton, & Jaeger, 2001). The relationship between Fairfield University and ABCD was envisioned as a resource exchange partnership where questions of "What do I have that you need?" and "What do you have that I need?" figured prominently in program development (Sarason & Lorentz, 1979; 1998). The children and parents at ABCD had significant problems related to low literacy, and they were not receiving remedial services due to limited resources. Fairfield University students needed meaningful preprofessional supervised field experiences. Simply put, our mission was to improve the educational experiences of both the children attending Head Start and the students attending Fairfield University. Within the resource exchange metaphor, people and experience, not money or "things," are defined as resources, and as a result Fairfield University and ABCD were able to utilize each other's resources in a mutually satisfying way that, in turn, allowed both institutions to lessen the negative consequences of their own limited resources (see Primavera 2004 for details). The metaphors embraced by the founders of the Kirby Literacy Project represented a paradigm shift from the hierarchical behavioral norms and the power differential found in the more traditional town-gown relationships and thus provided fertile ground for transformational change to occur.

This final insight related to systems change to be discussed might give pause to the weak of heart hoping to either promote systems-level change or to develop a comprehensive model of how transformative change occurs. That is, there is an element of serendipity, of simply being in the right place at the right time with the right constellation of people, which comes into play (Primavera, 2004). Building meaningful relationships and transformative systems change requires time. Unfortunately, sustainability is the nemesis of most university-community partnerships no matter how good the idea is and no matter how successful the short-term outcomes may be. The Kirby Literacy Project had the support of Fairfield University and of ABCD in terms of allocated space, personnel time, etc., to maintain the bare-bones program of placing a small number of university students in a few Head Start classrooms, but that level of operation would result in little more than a barely noticeable ripple in the larger day-to-day operation of either institution. It was an act of fortuitous serendipity that the family of a Fairfield University psychology major alumnus approached the university's Development Office looking for a project involving families for the foundation to endow as a gift for that alum. It was the support and endowment of the F.M. Kirby Foundation that allowed the project to grow and to sustain itself long enough so that the work of the Kirby Literacy Project became a counternormative challenge to Fairfield University's view of scholarship; that it provided the type of repeated and sustained training efforts needed to instill a "culture of literacy" at ABCD; and that it enjoyed a shared history of successful, collaborative, meaningful encounters with persons different from oneself that reduced prejudice and encouraged a respect for diversity.

One final caveat to add is that the potential effect of serendipity depends on the personalities of the people that the serendipitous event happens to. We can only speculate what might have happened if the endowment gift were given to a university project led by a faculty member whose approach to working in the community adhered to the more traditional hierarchical town-gown behavioral norms. Monetary resources certainly "buy time" for ideas to take hold, for relationships to grow, and for transformative change to be set in motion; but without the personal connection and commitment of the individuals involved, is unlikely that any substantive long-term positive change in either the culture of the institution itself or its human constituents would have taken place.

Epilogue and Final Musings

At the present time, the Kirby Family Literacy Project enjoys a legacy of having set in motion important paradigm shifts and changes in infrastructure in both Fairfield University and Action for Bridgeport Community Development. The basic mechanics of training university student volunteers and work-study students to serve as literacy coaches in ABCD's class-rooms remains the same and Developmental Psychology students still engage in an extensive service-learning component in ABCD's classrooms. Gone is the technology-training component and severely minimized is the parent literacy workshop component. The project continues to enjoy the emotional and financial support of Fairfield University and ABCD as well as a generous endowment from the F.M. Kirby Foundation. The positive view expressed by the participants in the Kirby Literacy Project Long Term Impact Assessment (Shah & Kaufman, 2003) that the partnership is a "win-win situation" where each partner benefits in significant ways still exists today. What is missing, however, is a place of prominence in the mind-set of the larger ABCD and Fairfield University communities. Also faded is the wide-spread feeling of a psychological sense of community that we enjoyed in the earlier days of the project when we were synergistically linked by feelings of belongingness, interdepend-ence, and mutual commitment (McMillan & Chavis, 1986; Sarason, 1974). So today we find ourselves in the rather odd situation where the institutions brought together by the Kirby Literacy Project are showing evidence of transformational systems-level change but the Kirby Project itself, although it continues to produce positive annual outcomes, seems to have lost what those of us involved in its inception value most—a shared identity and sense of purpose that comes from a true collaboration of equals.

In the past seven years, both Fairfield University and ABCD experienced significant structural and administrative changes. Fairfield University's administration has undergone a near complete turnover. Not one upper-level administrator shares a history with the proj-ect. There is a new president, a new senior vice president for academic affairs, and a new dean of the College of Arts and Sciences. The administration is supportive, financially and personally, of the Kirby Literacy Project, but the new administration also bought with it its own agenda and its own array of new initiatives that offer faculty and students more choices as to what types of endeavors to devote their energies to. There was a similar turnover in administration at ABCD. Every one of ABCD's key administrators at the Kirby Project's inception has either left the agency or now holds a different administrative position. The size of ABCD's Early Learning Program has doubled in the past 10 years and the combination of staff turnover and new hires has resulted in fewer and fewer ABCD staff members having an appreciation for the history and the purpose of ABCD's relationship with Fairfield Uni-versity. Thus, the Kirby Literacy Project is supported and is showcased by both ABCD and Fairfield University for important visitors and funding sources to see, but the sense of shared history and the sense of pride and of ownership that comes from watching an idea take hold and grow is greatly diminished.

While ABCD's enrollment doubled, the number of participating Fairfield University stu-dents has remained fairly constant at approximately 160 per year. The result is a greatly diluted opportunity for ABCD teachers to be in contact with Fairfield University students on

318

a regular basis. Due to transportation constraints, some sites do not even have Fairfield University students assigned to work there. To make matters worse, ABCD's rapid growth and the problems related to space, transportation, and cost resulted in the disbanding of the project's annual all-day "Literacy Day" training and celebration luncheon held on Fairfield University's campus. It was the one event that brought all ABCD and university project participants together. It was a way to pass on our shared history, to celebrate our collaborative successes, to break down town-gown barriers, and to promote a psychological sense of community (Primavera, 2004). Without it, there is no formal celebratory reminder of the partnership's existence.

Earlier we stressed the important role that personality played in the growth of the Kirby Literacy Project, but the fact that work with the community is personal also renders such endeavors vulnerable. For a three-year period coinciding with the onset of ABCD's rapid growth, the first author and two key project leaders at ABCD experienced life-altering illness and loss in their immediate families. The practical challenges to project operation as well as the less tangible threats to the spirit of collective unity were enormous. Unfortunately the three people who were most invested in the project found themselves with more pressing personal challenges to attend to. While it is unlikely that even the full attention of these three individuals would have been enough to ward off the depersonalization brought on by ABCD's expansion, the question of "What if?" is certainly one worth asking.

Also entering into play is an unfortunate historical twist of fate, something akin to negative serendipity. The George W. Bush administration's imposition of the performance-based National Reporting System (NRS) assessment of children's cognitive progress shifted the focus of Head Start funding recipients from the *process* of literacy promotion to the documentation of observable measurable outcomes. Documentation of everything and anything related to outcome data became a top priority, and ABCD's attention was diverted from the problem of how to address the negative impact that expansion was having on the Kirby Literacy Project.

The shared psychological sense of community no longer serves as the overarching project umbrella. Isolated examples of the "old community" can be seen at certain sites and in certain classrooms where veteran teachers and site managers keep the spirit alive. Although the psychological sense of community in a more global sense is a thing of the past, the development of meaningful, mutually satisfying, and growth enhancing one-to-one relationships at every level of the project is the proverbial glue that holds it all together. Indeed, speaking of a relationship or a partnership between a university and a community agency is a bit of an anthropomorphic folly. The relationship starts and ends with people and successful community engagement is not something to be set to a step-by-step prescription. Every instance of community engagement is unique due to the social-ecological context of the institutions involved and the personalities of the key players (Kelly, 1970; 1971, 1979; Sarason, 1988).

The story of the partnership between Fairfield University and Action for Bridgeport Community Development provides us with some interesting and important insights into the process of transformational systems-level change. Data gathered from key informants at both institutions suggest that as a result of the partnership, Fairfield University is a different place and Action for Bridgeport Community Development is a different place. In very fundamental ways, the Kirby Literacy Project has impacted the landscape of ABCD by introducing and sustaining a "culture of literacy." Fairfield University, as an institution, has come to view the nature of scholarship and service differently. Participants from both institutions developed a lasting appreciation of and respect for people and cultures different from their own. A retrospective analysis of the Kirby Literacy Project's 20-year history suggests that the process of the transformative systems-level change was greatly affected by relationships, personality, metaphor, and serendipity.

Note

The authors wish to thank the F.M. Kirby Foundation for its dedication to and invaluable support of the work of the Adrienne Kirby Family Literacy Project and to the partnership between Fairfield University and Action for Bridgeport Community Development. The authors also wish to thank Dr. Joy Kaufman at The Consultation Center at Yale University, New Haven, Connecticut, and Dr. Seema Shah at the Annenberg Institute for School Reform, Brown University, Providence, Rhode Island, for their work on the Kirby Literacy Project Partnership Assessment. Loving thanks to Seymour Sarason, who is dearly missed and whose spirit inspires all we do.

References

Bennett, C., Anderson, L., Cooper, S., Hassol, L., Klein, D., & Rosenblum, G. (1966). *Community psychology: A report of the Boston Conference on the Education of Psychologists for Community Mental Health*. Boston: Boston University.

Boyer, E. L. (1991). *Scholarship reconsidered: Priorities of the professorate*. Princeton, NJ: Princeton University Press.

Boyer, E. L. (1996). The scholarship of engagement. *Journal of Public Service and Outreach,1*, 11–20.

Dalton, J. H., Elias, M. J., & Wandersman, A. (2007). *Community psychology: Linking Individuals and Communities* (2nd ed.). Belmont, CA: Thomson Wadsworth.

Dewey, J. (1967). *Democracy and education*. New York: Free Press.

Dewey, J. (1997). *Experience and education*. New York: Simon and Schuster.

Dunphy, D. (1996). Organizational change in corporate settings. *Human Relations, 49*, 541–552.

Eckel, P., Hill, B., & Green, M. (1998). *On change: En route to transformation*. Washington, DC: American Council on Education.

Enos, S., & Morton, K. (2003). Developing a theory and practice of campus community partnerships. In B. Jaboby & Associates (Eds.), *Building partnerships for service learning* (pp. 20–24). San Francisco: Jossey-Bass.

Foster-Fishman, P. G., Nowell, B., & Yang, E. (2007). Putting the system back into systems change: A framework for understanding and changing organizational and community systems. *American Journal of Community Psychology, 39*, 197–215.

Heller, K., Price, R. H., Reinharz, S., Riger, S., & Wandersman, A. (1984). *Psychology and community change: Challenges of the future*. Homewood, IL: Dorsey Press; Pacific Grove, CA: Wadsworth.

Jameson, J., Clayton, P., & Jaeger, A. (2010). Community engaged scholarships as mutually-transformative partnerships. In L. M. Harter, J. Hamel-Lambert, & J. Millesen (Eds.), *Participatory partnerships for social action and research*. Dubuque, IA: Kendall Hunt.

Kelly, J. G. (1970). Towards an ecological conception of preventive interventions. In D. Adelson & B. Kalis (Eds.), *Community psychology and mental health* (pp. 126–145). Scranton, PA: Chandler.

Kelly, J. G. (1971). Qualities for the community psychologist. *American Psychologist, 26*, 897–903.

Kelly, J. G. (1979). <ap>Tain't what you do it's the way you do it. *American Journal of Community Psychology, 7*, 244–258.

Kelly, J. G. (1986). Context and process: An ecological view of interdependence and practice and research. *American Journal of Community Psychology, 14*, 581–605.

Kelly, J. G. (1990). Changing contexts and the field of community psychology. *American Journal of Community Psychology, 18*, 769–792.

Kelly, J. G. (2002). The spirit of community psychology. *American Journal of Community Psychology, 30*, 43–63.

Kotter, J. P. (1996). *Leading change*. Boston: Harvard Business School Press.

McMillan, D. W., & Chavis, D. M. (1986). Sense of community: Definitions and theory. *Journal of Community Psychology, 14*, 6–23.

Miller, G. A. (1969). Psychology as a means of promoting human welfare. *American Psychologist, 24*, 1063–1075.

Prilleltensky, I. (2001). Value-based praxis in community psychology: Moving towards social justice and social action. *American Journal of Community Psychology, 29*, 747–778.

Primavera, J. (1999). The unintended consequences of volunteerism: Positive outcomes for those who serve. *Journal of Prevention and Intervention in the Community, 18*, 125–140.

Primavera, J. (2000). Enhancing family competence through literacy activities. *Journal of Prevention and Intervention in the Community, 20*, 85–101.

Primavera, J. (2004). You can't get there from here: Identifying process routes to replication. *American Journal of Community Psychology, 33*, 181–191.

Primavera, J., & Cook, M. J. (1997). *A successful university-community partnership: The Family Literacy Project*. Poster presented at the Sixth Biennial Conference of the Society for Community Research and Action, May, Columbia, SC.

Primavera, J., DiGiacomo, T., & Wiederlight, P. (2001). *Closing the digital divide: Empowering parents and children with computer training*. Poster presented at the Eighth Biennial Conference of the Society for Community Research and Action, June, Atlanta.

Primavera, J., Wiederlight, P., & DiGiacomo, T. (2001). *Technology access for low-income preschoolers: Bridging the digital divide*. Poster presented at the 109th Annual Meeting of American Psychological Association, August, San Francisco.

Rappaport, J. (1981). In praise of paradox: A social policy of empowerment over prevention. *American Journal of Community Psychology, 9*, 1–25.

Saltmarsh, J., Hartley, M., & Clayton, P. H. (2009). *Democratic engagement white paper*. Boston: New England Resource Center for Higher Education.

Sandmann, L. R. (2008). Conceptualization of the scholarship of engagement in higher education: A strategic review, 1996—2006. *Journal of Higher Education Outreach and Engagement, 12*, 91–104.

Sarason, S. B. (1974). *Psychological sense of community: Prospects for a community psychology*. San Francisco: Jossey-Bass.

Sarason, S. B. (1988). *The making of an American psychologist: An autobiography.* San Francisco: Jossey-Bass.

Sarason, S. B., Levin, M., Goldenberg, I., Cherlin, D. L., & Bennett, E. M. (1966). *Psychology in community settings: Clinical, educational, vocational, social aspects.* New York: Wiley.

Sarason, S. B., & Lorentz, E. M. (1979). *The challenge of the resource exchange network.* San Francisco: Jossey-Bass.

Sarason, S. B., & Lorentz, E. M. (1998). *Crossing boundaries: Collaboration, coordination and the redefinition of resources.* San Francisco: Jossey-Bass.

Shah, S., & Kaufman, J. S. (2003). *An evaluation of the long-term impact of the Adrienne Kirby Family Literacy Project: A partnership between Fairfield University and Action for Bridgeport Community Development.* New Haven, CT: Consultation Center, Yale University.

U.S. Department of Commerce. (1995). *Falling through the net: A survey of the "haves" and "have nots" in rural and urban America.* Washington, DC: U.S. Department of Commerce.

Contributors

Jessica V. Barnes, PhD, is the Associate Director for University-Community Partnerships of University Outreach and Engagement at Michigan State University. She is a developmental psychologist, and her work focuses on establishing successful community-university partnerships for research and engaged scholarship as well as identifying supports for establishing community capacity for engaging in research collaborations to support child development.

Mary Beckman is Associate Director of Academic Affairs and Research at the Center for Social Concerns, the University of Notre Dame's center for community-based learning and research. She is also concurrent Associate Professor of Economics and Policy Studies at Notre Dame and co-directs an interdisciplinary program on poverty studies. Prior to her current position, she was a member of the faculty at Lafayette College in Easton, Pennsylvania, after a number of years as an activist. At Lafayette, in addition to her teaching responsibilities in economics, she co-developed a writing-across-the-curriculum program and directed a writing-intensive interdisciplinary first-year seminar program. Her publications can be found in *College Teaching, Journal of Excellence in College Teaching, Journal of Higher Education Outreach and Engagement, Radical Teacher, Review of Radical Political Economics, Women's Studies Quarterly,* and elsewhere.

Ann Belleau (Ojibwe) is the Director of the Inter-Tribal Council of Michigan (ITC Michigan) Head Start and Early Head Start programs. She is responsible for the overall administration of early childhood programming for seven tribal communities. She was co-Principal Investigator of the Wiba Anung research partnership. She serves as the Online Student Advisor for the Bay Mills Community College Early Childhood Education students. She was a member of the American Indian Alaska Native Head Start Research Center Steering

Committee and was President of the National Indian Head Start Directors Association Board of Directors.

Derryl Block is Dean of the College of Health and Human Sciences at Northern Illinois University. With a background in nursing and public health, she focuses on improving the quality of professional education and increasing access to it through the use of distance education. Block was President of the Association of Community Health Nursing Educators and a member of the Quad Council of Public Health Nursing Organizations. She helped develop policy documents regarding essential content for baccalaureate nursing and entry-level community/public health nursing. Her scholarship and publications focus on public health, public health nursing, and public health nursing competencies. Actively involved in promoting civic engagement of communities and students, she was a Robert Wood Johnson Executive Nurse Fellow, and a recipient of both the Association of Community Health Nursing Educators Outstanding Service Award and the American Public Health Association Public Health Nursing Section's Lillian Wald Service Award.

Mary Calcatera (Sault Saint Marie Ojibwe), a member of the Sault Ste. Marie Tribe of Chippewa Indians and a graduate of Michigan State University, is an academic specialist in the Native American Institute, College of Agriculture and Natural Resources at Michigan State University. She is active in American Indian initiatives on MSU's campus and through-out the Michigan tribal community. She was the Interim Director of the Nokomis Learning Center (Okemos, MI) and assisted in the development of Michigan State University's Aanii Program and the Michigan Indian Leadership Program and Youth Retreat. Additional projects have included the development of an American Indian curriculum for the Nokomis Learning Center, the Wiba Anung American Indian Head Start project, and initiatives related to American Indians in higher education and nutrition within Michigan tribal communities.

Karen McKnight Casey is the Director of the Center for Service-Learning and Civic Engagement at Michigan State University. As director, she is responsible for facilitating university initiatives, which provide service-based, experiential learning and civic engagement opportunities for MSU students. Ms. Casey works closely with faculty, university administration and student services, students, and community partners to ensure that active service opportunities are provided for students to meet academic, personal, and professional development goals while meeting the expressed needs of the community. An alumna of the MSU School of Social Work, Ms. Casey's association with the service-learning began as an undergraduate student volunteer in the early years of the center, when it was known as the Office of Volunteer Programs. Prior to becoming an MSU academic specialist in 1991, Ms. Casey's professional experience included work in higher education residence life and teaching, and community agency programming. Her dedication to service and community enhancement is exhibited in work with local community boards and projects.

Katy Luchini Colbry is the Director for Graduate Recruiting and coordinator of the summer undergraduate research program at the College of Engineering at Michigan State University, where she received undergraduate degrees in political theory and computer science. Dr. Colbry earned graduate degrees in computer science and engineering from the University of Michigan, where her research focused on educational technology and the design of software for handheld computers.

David D. Cooper (PhD, American Studies, Brown University), Professor Emeritus of Writing, Rhetoric, and American Cultures at Michigan State University, received the 1999 Thomas Ehrlich Faculty Award for Service-Learning sponsored by Campus Compact. For the past decade he has dedicated himself to the advancement of meaningful education and civic renewal at the local, regional, and national levels. In 1992 Cooper founded the Service-Learning Writing Project at MSU. He developed and implemented a new curriculum for general education writing courses that currently enroll nearly 300 students a year who serve and learn with over 70 community partners. Cooper's interdisciplinary curriculum materials in composition, rhetoric, and civic culture are frequently cited in the professional literature. His innovative teaching practices were recognized by the Phi Kappa Phi Honor Society with its 2000 Excellence Award for Interdisciplinary Teaching. Cooper founded MSU's Public Humanities Collaborative and served as director from 2005–2010.

Pat Crawford, PhD, is Associate Professor of Landscape Architecture in the School of Planning, Design and Construction, and Senior Director of the Bailey Scholars Program at Michigan State University. Her expertise is in landscape design, master planning, and community engagement. Research interests include evaluating participation effectiveness in planning and design as well as curriculum and pedagogical development of professional planning and design education. She is a licensed Landscape Architect and has nine years practice experience. She holds a BS in horticulture from the University of Missouri, a master of landscape architecture from Kansas State University, and a PhD in environmental design and planning from Arizona State University.

Juliette C. Daniels works at the University of Detroit Mercy where she serves as the Director of Student Affairs for the School of Dentistry. Her research interests include opportunities to enhance student health and wellness, graduate and professional student academic enhancement initiatives, collaboration between academic and student affairs, and exploring issues of first-year student transition. Juliette previously worked for Michigan State University with roles in the Counseling Center, the Office of the Associate Provost for Undergraduate Education, the Honors College, and Student-Athlete Support Services. Juliette received her master's degree in student affairs administration from Michigan State University and her bachelor's degree in business management and marketing from DePaul University.

C. Kurt Dewhurst is Director of Arts and Cultural Initiatives and Senior Fellow for University Outreach and Engagement, Michigan State University, and Curator of Folklife and Cultural Heritage, Michigan State University Museum. Kurt coordinates a variety of folklife research, collection development, and outreach and engagement programs. His research interests include cultural change and continuity in folk arts, material culture, ethnicity, and occupational folk culture. Other areas of research include museum studies theory and practice and national and international cultural heritage policy. His research is shaped by a commitment to undertaking research projects in collaboration with representatives of the underserved communities and cultural groups, and responding to social/community needs. He is founding Co-director of the MSU Museum's Great Lakes Folk Festival, past Chair of the Advisory Committee of the Smithsonian Center for Folklife and Cultural Heritage, Chair of the Board of Trustees of the American Folklife Center at the Library of Congress, and Fellow and Past President of the American Folklore Society.

John S. Duley has made significant contributions to the service-learning movement and the greater Lansing communities since the 1960s. While employed at Michigan State University as a professor and campus minister, John was instrumental in the development and implementation of the Student Tutorial Education Project (STEP), a program that utilized MSU students and faculty at summer tutorial programs at Rust College in Holly Springs, Mississippi. In the 1970s he strove to incorporate service learning into MSU's curriculum and helped create the National Society for Experiential Education. As a result of this work, John is known affectionately by colleagues across the United States as the "Grandfather of Service Learning." In the 1980s John founded the Greater-Lansing Housing Coalition (GLHC), a community-wide organization dedicated to supporting quality and affordable housing. In the 1990s, he led an initiative to provide low-income residents with access to computers and the Internet, thus forming Closing the Digital Gap. Recently he initiated the Edgewood Village / GLHC-MSU Service-Learning Tutoring Partnership. In 2007 John organized the fortieth anniversary reunion of the STEP participants and garnered their reflections. At age 91, John Duley continues to exceed community expectations as he aims to encourage voluntary action in all citizens.

Michelle R. Dunlap is a Professor of the Human Development Department at Connecticut College. She has engaged in research with the goal of understanding the cognitive and emotional developmental processes that students experience as they engage in culturally diverse communities. With her student research team she also investigates the social perceptions and misperceptions that service providers and educators have with respect to African-American family communication and child discipline. In her teaching and research with students, she also helps to facilitate service-learning experiences, field trips, and other community engagement opportunities. Professor Dunlap is the 2008 Ernest Lynton Award recipient. She also has written many journal articles and authored and coedited four books, most recently, *African Americans and Community Engagement in Higher Education*, along with Stephanie Y. Evans, Colette M. Taylor, and DeMond S. Miller.

Patricia Farrell (Taos Peublo), PhD, is Assistant Provost, University-Community Partnerships in the Office of University Outreach and Engagement at Michigan State University. Dr. Farrell has extensive community-based experience in school reform, school health, early childhood initiatives, and the promotion of campus-community partnerships. She has served on a number of local and statewide advisory committees related to school health and K-12 education. Most recently, she has worked with community-based projects to improve children's early literacy and school readiness through teacher professional development, parent leadership training, and community mobilization. Dr. Farrell earned a master's degree in social work from the University of Michigan and a PhD in educational administration from Michigan State University.

Hiram E. Fitzgerald is University Distinguished Professor of Psychology and Associate Provost for University Outreach and Engagement at Michigan State University. He is chairperson of the Committee on Institutional Cooperation's Committee on Engagement, is a member of the Association of Public and Land Grant Universities' CEO Task Force on Engagement, is President of the Engagement Scholarship Consortium, and was a member of the Carnegie Foundation Classification Work Team for Community Engagement. He has been actively involved with national efforts to define and measure the scholarship of engagement, create institutional alignment, develop effective models of community-university partnerships, and establish standards of practice for such partnerships. He is a Fellow of the American Psychological Association and of the American Psychological Society, and has received numerous awards, including the Dolley Madison Award for lifetime contributions to the well-being of young children.

Eric Fretz is Assistant Professor of Peace and Justice Studies at Regis University in Denver, Colorado. His writings include articles on civic engagement in higher education and the use of democratic practices in the classroom.

Hope K. Gerde is Assistant Professor in the Department of Human Development and Family Studies at Michigan State University. Dr. Gerde's primary research interests focus on the development and evaluation of approaches to providing early childhood educators professional development via distance-learning processes, particularly for teachers with low education and barriers to accessing traditional educational opportunities. Also, her work focuses on enhancing young children's language and literacy development, including writing skills, particularly for children at risk. She is a co-investigator in the Wiba Anung partnership.

Cynthia Jackson-Elmoore is Dean of the Honors College and Professor of Social Work and Political Science at Michigan State University. She also maintains an affiliation with the Global Urban Studies Program at MSU. Dr. Jackson-Elmoore previously served as Acting Assistant Dean of the Urban Affairs Programs, Director of the Urban Studies Graduate Program in the College of Social Science, and Co-director of the Program in Urban Politics and Policy at Michigan State University. In 2008–9 she was a Fellow in the Executive Leadership Academy Program and a Fellow in the Academic Leadership Program sponsored by the Committee on Institutional Cooperation in 2003–4; and received a Lilly Endowed Teaching Fellowship in 1999 focused on innovation, scholarship, and expertise in teaching. Dr. Jackson-Elmoore previously taught courses in urban politics, public policy processes and analysis, and social welfare policy and services. Her research interests include nonprofits and urban politics, healthy communities, and state and local policy. Dr. Jackson-Elmoore's work has been published in *Urban Affairs Review, Cities, Policy Studies Review, Public Productivity and Management Review, Korean Review of Public Administration, ICMA IQ Reports*, and *National Civic Review*. She coedited *Nonprofits in Urban America* (Quorum Books) with Richard C. Hula. She received her PhD and masters in public administration (public policy emphasis) from the University of Southern California and her bachelors in chemical engineering from the University of Delaware.

Kyung Sook Lee is a research associate at the Community Evaluation and Research Collaborative and the Native American Institute at Michigan State University. Dr. Lee conducts community-based participatory research and program evaluations. Her work focuses on the social-emotional development, family functioning, and academic achievement of children who are at-risk or facing hardship. She holds a PhD in child development and family studies from Michigan State University.

Linda Lindeke is Associate Professor and Director of Graduate Studies in the School of Nursing and the Medical School, Department of Pediatrics, University of Minnesota. She employs civic engagement with her students and was an early adopter of distance education through online modalities. She led a team that received a Technology-Enhanced Learning Award from the University of Minnesota in 1999 and has published and presented nationally regarding teaching distant students with interactive pedagogy. A Fellow in the American Academy of Nursing, Linda oversees graduate nursing educational practices and policies, teaches doctoral students on campus and virtually, and provides continuing education and technical assistance throughout the region and nation. She practices as a pediatric nurse practitioner weekly as part of an interdisciplinary team caring for infants and children who have been born prematurely or have experienced neonatal illnesses. Her research areas include health policy, developmental outcomes following high-risk birth, barriers to advanced practice nursing, and children's perceptions of their health care experiences. Linda is a Past President of the National Association of Pediatric Nurse Practitioners (NAPNAP) and is active on foundations, policy committees, and task forces regionally and nationally.

Joyce F. Long is an Educational Consultant and Executive Director of No Parent Left Behind, a parent involvement program that equips parents to be facilitators of academic learning at home. As a former faculty member at the University of Notre Dame in the Education, Schooling, and Society minor, she taught Educational Psychology, Creativity in the Classroom, and Community-Based Research. Her articles and book chapters appear in a variety of publications related to teaching and learning. Her most recent chapter appears in *Bedtime Stories and Book Reports: Connecting Parent Involvement and Family Literacy.*

Marsha MacDowell is Professor in the Department of Art, Art History, and Design; Curator, Michigan State University Museum; Core Faculty for MSU Museum Studies; and Coordinator, Michigan Traditional Arts Program (an MSU Museum partnership with the Michigan Council for Arts and Cultural Affairs for statewide arts services). As a publicly engaged scholar, her work is grounded in an interdisciplinary approach to material culture and is informed by art historical, folkloristic, and ethnographic theories and methodologies. The overwhelmingly majority of her work has, by design and philosophy, been developed and implemented in collaboration with representatives of the communities and cultural groups whose cultural heritage is focused on. Many of the projects are strategically developed to have a positive impact on identified societal needs. Her work has included many publications for both scholarly and general public audiences, development of curriculum related to community-based knowledge, public policies, exhibitions, festivals, study abroad programs, and the creation of innovative ways, including digital repositories, to increase access to and use of collections of traditional culture. She has been a member of and has led local, state, national, and international research teams and professional organizations.

Patricia Machemer, PhD is Associate Professor of Urban and Regional Planning and Landscape Architecture in the School of Planning, Design and Construction, Michigan State University. Her research focuses on participatory design and planning, with a special interest in children's participation and the Scholarship of Teaching and Learning. As a land use planner at the regional level, she explores the use of geographic information systems in both practice and teaching. She has a PhD in resource management from Michigan State University, and master's degrees in landscape architecture and urban planning from the University of Michigan.

Andrew Martinez is a PhD student in the Community Psychology Program at DePaul University. His research currently focuses on school climate, victimization in schools, student problem behaviors, and exposure to community violence. He received his master's degree in social work at the Graduate School of Social Service at Fordham University, and his BA at Fairfield University in Connecticut. Andrew's previous work has included program evaluation at the Consultation Center at the Yale University School of Medicine, and advocacy work for children's issues at the Bridgeport Child Advocacy Coalition.

Patricia E. O'Connor holds her doctorate in sociolinguistics from Georgetown University. At Georgetown University she is Associate Professor in the Department of English, former Senior Research Fellow of the Center for Social Justice, and former Associate Director of the Georgetown University Writing Program. For over 20 years she directed GU prison outreach programs. She also served as faculty advisor for GU students' Demeter Educational Project for Women in Substance Abuse Recovery from 1995 to 2006. In December 2004 O'Connor was named a Mitsubishi Unsung Heroine for her work in substance abuse treatment centers and prisons. Currently, Dr. O'Connor is researching life stories of those in recovery from drug and alcohol abuse, interviewing those in treatment centers about their experiences of addiction and about their hopes for recovery. O'Connor has been Co-director of the Georgetown University Service Learning Institute and founding member and chair of the national service faculty Educators for Community Engagement (formerly the Invisible College). Her research on narratives of prisoners explores the language of violence and speakers' claims about those acts. This research directly stems from her 20-plus years of teaching and service in the District of Columbia's area prisons and jails. Her publications appear in the *Journal of African American Men*, *Pragmatics*, *Text*, *Discourse & Society*, *Pre/Text*, and several edited volumes. Her book on prison discourse, *Speaking of Crime: Narratives of Prisoners* (2000), is available from the University of Nebraska Press. O'Connor is also coauthor of *Literacy behind Prison Walls* (1992). On Georgetown's campus, O'Connor teaches courses in Theory and Practice of Writing, Prison Literature, Narrative Discourse, Narratives of Violence, Working Class Literature, Appalachian Literature, Persuasive Writing, and first-year English courses in Critical Methods: Narratology. She has also taught for Georgetown at its School of Foreign Service in Qatar (2005–6, 2008, and 2010).

Katherine O'Donnell, a member of the Hartwick College Sociology Department since 1980, is a longtime community activist. She is cofounder and President Emeritus of OCAY-Oneonta Community Alliance for Youth, a nonprofit, youth advocacy organization that created the Oneonta Teen Center. For over a decade, she has worked in economic solidarity with Jolom Mayaetik, a Mayan women's weaving cooperative in Chiapas, to market their hand-woven textiles through Fair Trade and other major commercial venues across the United States. At Hartwick, she established the Women's Center and the Teaching Learning Community, and cofounded the Women's Studies Program and Delaware-Otsego Counties NOW. She was awarded the national NERCHE Lynton Award for Faculty Professional Service and Academic Outreach in 2006.

Arnie Parish (Ojibwe) is an Ojibwa member of the Bay Milles Indian Community and was on the staff of the Michigan State University Native American Institute at the time the

Wiba Anung partnership was developed. He played a key role in the evaluation of the cultural sensitivity of the Tribal Head Start early childhood programs.

Judy Primavera is Professor of Psychology at Fairfield University and the cofounder and director of the Adrienne Kirby Family Literacy Project. Since the mid-1970s her professional efforts have focused on social justice issues, especially enhancing the educational success of high-risk urban youth. She is an active member of the Society for Community Research and Action (Division 27 of the American Psychological Association) and serves on the Steering Committee of the New England Psychological Association. She also serves on the Editorial Boards for the *Journal of Community Psychology* and the *Journal of Prevention and Intervention in the Community*. She has authored numerous research articles and conference presentations related to her varied research interests, including family literacy, school readiness, service learning and volunteerism, school transitions, childhood bereavement, parental divorce, and young children's perceptions of race. She coedited *Diverse Families, Competent Families: Innovations in Research and Preventive Intervention Practice* (2000) with Dr. Janet F. Gillespie and was the guest coeditor of a special issue of the *American Journal of Community Psychology* "Reflections on the Process of Community Research and Action" (2004) with Dr. Anne E. Brodsky. She received Fairfield University's Teacher of the Year Award in 1996, Honorable Mention for the Ernest A. Lynton Award for Faculty Professional Service and Academic Outreach in 2000; the State of Connecticut Department of Higher Education's Leadership in Community Service Award in 2002; the Fairfield University Martin Luther King, Jr. Visions Award in 2004; the Fairfield University Alumni Association's Distinguished Faculty Award in 2006; and the Bridgeport, Connecticut, Community Service Award in 2011. She is also the cofounder and president of the Jamie A. Hulley Arts Foundation.

Warren Rauhe is an Associate Professor of Landscape Architecture in the School of Planning, Design, and Construction at Michigan State University. He is also the Director of MSU's Small Town, Community and Safe Routes 2 School Design Initiatives. Warren's 35–year-plus career has included positions in both academia and the private consulting field. Work with over 70 Michigan communities and schools to develop visions for future physical improvements has combined his interests in planning, design, and community participation. Projects have included award-winning in-service student learning, physical planning and design visions for communities, and published research findings.

Brian E. Rood is Director of Environmental Studies and Policy and Professor of Interdisciplinary Studies at Mercer University in Macon, Georgia. He served as Department Chair of Environmental Science from 1995 to 1999 and as Coordinator of Undergraduate Research for the University from 1998 to 2003. Rood's personal research interest focuses on limnological investigation and paleoecological reconstruction of large and small river, lake, and wetland systems, including the Florida Everglades, Okefenokee Swamp, and the Pantanal wetlands of Paraguay, and watersheds of the state of Georgia. His primary research interest couples technical study and community outreach through the activities of the Ocmulgee River Initiative, a 501(c)3 nonprofit organization. ORI is committed to field study and educational outreach related to water issues in the Ocmulgee River watershed. Rood believes that engaging students and community volunteers in water quality monitoring programs, river cleanups, environmental impact assessments, and educational outreach activities empowers these individuals, who realize that science and technology are valuable tools that should be embraced rather than feared, and that lifelong learning can bear distinct and definable rewards for the self, the community, and the environment.

Nicole C. Springer is the associate director of the Center for Service-Learning and Civic Engagement (CSLCE). She began work with the CSLCE as a graduate assistant during her master's program in bioethics, humanities, and society. Before doing graduate work at MSU, Springer attended Concordia College, where she worked closely with the Office of Student Leadership and Service and later served with AmeriCorps VISTA in Moorhead, Minnesota. At the CSLCE Springer is involved in research, outcome evaluation, curriculum development, and other activities related to the scholarship of engagement. She also advises students and assists with faculty consultations related to service and engagement opportunities.

Cyrus Stewart is Professor of Criminal Justice at Michigan State University, teaching in the Center for Integrative Studies in the College of Social Science. His course offerings focus on persuasion in cults and diversity in American society with specific attention to First Nation Peoples. In these courses, service-learning options have been a consistent opportunity to enrich the student experience. Service-learning experiences were also a significant part of the student experience in the overseas summer program that he designed and directed in collaboration with the Department of Ethnic Studies at the University of Hawaii (Manoa). He has also been a practicing social worker specializing in marriage and family relations. His research interests are adolescent deviance and the clinical treatment of adolescent defiance.

Nicole L. Thompson (Menominee/Mohican) is an Assistant Professor of Elementary Education at the University of Memphis. Dr. Thompson's research focuses on empowerment. Her research with people in education whose voices are typically less heard or unheard allows Thompson to gather deeper, underlying meanings in particular situations. Thompson has three primary interests: American Indian education focusing on professional preparation of young children's caregivers/teachers, middle level teacher preparation, and diversity in educational settings.

Korine Steinke Wawrzynski is the Director for Undergraduate Research in the Provost's Office at Michigan State University and an adjunct faculty member in the Student Affairs Administration master's degree program at MSU. Her research interests include innovative learning opportunities for undergraduate students, the experiences of women leaders in higher education, and collaborative partnerships between academic and student affairs. She has worked in academic affairs administration, and brings 14 years of student affairs administrative experience in the areas of residence life, judicial affairs, peer education, leadership development, and academic advising. Dr. Wawrzynski has earned a master's degree in college student personnel and a doctorate in higher education administration, both from Bowling Green State University.